BIBLE TROUBLE

Society of Biblical Literature

Semeia Studies

Gerald O. West, General Editor

Number 67

BIBLE TROUBLE

Queer Reading at the Boundaries
of Biblical Scholarship

BIBLE TROUBLE

QUEER READING AT THE BOUNDARIES
OF BIBLICAL SCHOLARSHIP

Edited by

Teresa J. Hornsby and Ken Stone

Society of Biblical Literature
Atlanta

BIBLE TROUBLE
Queer Reading at the Boundaries
of Biblical Scholarship

Copyright © 2011 by the Society of Biblical Literature

Erin Runions's "From Disgust to Humor: Rahab's Queer Affect" was originally published
in *Postscripts* 4.1 (2008): 41–69, © Equinox Publishing Ltd (2008).

An earlier version of Gillian Townsley's article was published as "Wittig's Lesbian and the
Corinthian Men: Problematising Categories of Sex in 1 Cor 11.2-16," *Hecate: An Interdisciplinary Journal of Women's Liberation* 33 (November 2007). Hecate Press.

Library of Congress Cataloging-in-Publication Data

Bible trouble : queer reading at the boundaries of biblical scholarship / edited by Teresa
Hornsby and Ken Stone.
     p. cm. — (Society of Biblical Literature. Semeia studies ; no. 67)
    Includes bibliographical references.
    ISBN 978-1-58983-552-8 (paper binding : alk. paper) — ISBN 978-1-58983-553-5
(electronic format)
    Bible—Criticism, interpretation, etc.—History—21st century. 2. Bible—Gay inter-
pretations. I. Hornsby, Teresa J., 1959–. II. Stone, Ken (Kenneth A.), 1962–.
    BS511.3.B52843 2011
    220.6086'64—dc23   2011024013

Printed on acid-free, recycled paper conforming to
ANSI/NISO Z39.48-1992 (R1997) and ISO 9706:1994
standards for paper permanence.

CONTENTS

Abbreviations

AB	Anchor Bible
BerOl	Berit Olam
BA	*Biblical Archaeologist*
BBC	Blackwell Bible Commentaries
BibInt	*Biblical Interpretation*
BL	Bible and Literature
BRev	*Bible Review*
BSac	*Bibliotheca Sacra*
BTB	*Biblical Theology Bulletin*
CBQ	*Catholic Biblical Quarterly*
CH	*Church History*
ChrCent	*Christian Century*
CTJ	*Calvin Theological Journal*
EKKNT	Evangelisch-katholischer Kommentar zum Neuen Testament
FCB	Feminist Companion to the Bible
GCT	Gender, Culture, Theory
HAR	*Hebrew Annual Review*
HTR	*Harvard Theological Review*
Int	*Interpretation*
JAAR	*Journal of the American Academy of Religion*
JBL	*Journal of Biblical Literature*
JECS	*Journal of Early Christian Studies*
JETS	*Journal of the Evangelical Theological Society*
JFSR	*Journal of Feminist Studies in Religion*
JQR	*Jewish Quarterly Review*
JRMA	*Journal of the Royal Musical Association*
JSNT	*Journal for the Study of the New Testament*
JSOT	*Journal for the Study of the Old Testament*
JSOTSup	Journal for the Study of the Old Testament: Supplement Series
JSS	*Journal of Semitic Studies*

JTS	*Journal of Theological Studies*
NAC	New American Commentary
NCB	New Century Bible
Neot	*Neotestamentica*
NovT	*Novum Testamentum*
NovTSup	Novum Testamentum, Supplement Series
NPNF[1]	*Nicene and Post-Nicene Fathers*, Series 1
NPNF[2]	*Nicene and Post-Nicene Fathers*, Series 2
OTL	Old Testament Library
PMLA	*Publications of the Modern Language Association*
RelSRev	*Religious Studies Review*
SBLEJL	Society of Biblical Literature Early Judaism and Its Literature
SBLSP	Society of Biblical Literature Seminar Papers
SemeiaSt	Semeia Studies
SJOT	*Scandinavian Journal of the Old Testament*
SP	Sacra Pagina
TDNT	*Theological Dictionary of the New Testament*. Edited by G. Kittel and G. Friedrich. Translated by G. W. Bromiley. 10 vols. Grand Rapids, Mich.: Eerdmans, 1964–1976.
TJ	*Trinity Journal*
TynBul	*Tyndale Bulletin*
USQR	*Union Seminary Quarterly Review*
VTSup	Vetus Testamentum Supplement Series
WBC	Word Biblical Commentary
WTJ	*Westminster Theological Journal*
ZNW	*Zeitschrift für die neutestamentliche Wissenschaft und die Kunde der älteren Kirche*

Already Queer: A Preface

Teresa J. Hornsby and Ken Stone

Nearly twenty years after feminist film theorist Teresa de Lauretis (1991) first coined the term, "queer theory" continues to develop in dynamic and unpredictable ways.[1] While queer studies have become well-known for interrogating the boundaries and categories that structure discourses of sexuality and gender (e.g., the binary distinctions between "heterosexual" and "homosexual," "straight" and "gay," "male" and "female," etc.), queer analysis today increasingly brings a critical lens to bear on the intersection of sexual dynamics with other dynamics such as race, class, nation, and culture. Rather than forming a separate academic discipline or subdiscipline, queer theories thrive best in the interdisciplinary or cross-disciplinary modes of scholarship that first generated them. Refusing academic as well as sexual normalization, queer analyses remain, in the words of Judith Butler, "against proper objects" (1994, title), methodologically as well as sexually.

A number of attempts have now been made by biblical scholars to bring queer theory to bear on biblical texts and biblical studies.[2] Nevertheless, queer readings of biblical texts not only remain, to use a term long associated with Semeia Studies, "experimental." They also remain remarkably rare.

Bible Trouble: Queer Reading at the Boundaries of Biblical Scholarship hopes to help close that gap by bringing together a series of essays that engage queer theories and styles of reading for purposes of biblical interpretation. The title phrase "Bible Trouble" is, of course, a play

---

1. We would like to thank Brock Perry and Adam Yates for their assistance with this volume.

2. See, e.g., Moore 1998, 2001; Stone 2001b; Runions 2003; Martin 2006; Guest et al. 2006; Hornsby 2006; Stone 2005, 2006, 2008.

on Judith Butler's now-classic volume *Gender Trouble* (1990); and so it
gestures toward one of the primary texts for contemporary queer theory.
By including "boundaries" in the subtitle, however, we hope to indicate
the desirability not only of "troubling" the boundaries between biblical
scholarship and queer theory but also of "troubling" boundaries between
different rubrics used currently in the analysis of biblical literature: sexuality, gender, class, race, nation and border, history, culture, literature,
film, music, etc. As it emerges in these essays, then, queer reading does
not simply spell "trouble" for gender and sexuality. It also "troubles" the
norms of biblical scholarship and widespread assumptions about the ways
in which biblical scholars ought to turn biblical texts into proper objects to
be penetrated with proper tools. Queer reading is characterized not simply
by attention to diverse genders and sexualities but also by diversities of
style, form, critical approach, and so forth (cf. Stone 2001a).

Many biblical scholars will no doubt conclude that any queer "trouble"
found in these essays is simply imposed on the Bible by perverse readers. Against such a conclusion, one might argue instead, in dialogue with
queer theories and the sources that inform them, that our very notion of
"Bible," our very sense of "Bible" as a material product with a fixed form
and meaning, is itself a performative effect of our engagement with particular texts and our engagement in particular interpretive practices (including but not limited to those practices most widely accepted in biblical
scholarship) in very specific contexts (cf. Stone 2008; Martin 2006). Such
an argument raises critical questions about the extent to which a single,
stable "Bible" preexists our interactions with diverse manuscripts, texts,
translations, hermeneutical assumptions, scholarly and other collective
traditions, strategies (implicit or explicit) for reading, contexts for teaching, or institutions of publishing. "Bible" may not be a foundation upon
which interpretation takes place but rather a product of the very practices
that are assumed to rest upon that foundation.

This sort of argument may appear to be a recipe for chaos. But is chaos
entirely negative? More importantly, can it be avoided entirely? Should we
even attempt to avoid it entirely?

As we were ruminating on the essays found in this volume, one of us
(Hornsby) generated the following reflection:

> There are a few phrases I pull out when someone I care about deeply
> comes to me for advice, particularly when she or he seems to be in that
> "dark night of the soul." As we all know, there are no quick fixes; and

no matter what one may have experienced personally, or how wise we may think we are because of those experiences, there is really nothing I can say or do that will help. Still, I fall back on one thing that I believe with all my heart, because I know it, perhaps the only thing I know, to be "true," true in a way that I, as a 50-year-old, former Southern Baptist "lesbian" from East Tennessee, after twenty years as a Bible scholar, can know. It is this: creation only comes from chaos. But what I do not say is also something I know to be true: that all creation remains as chaos—and despite what Western mythology claims as its ground, chaos is indeed a good thing. As queer scholars, we know that *creation*, the tidiness that G-d arranges, the imposed order, is disparate, messy, blurry, unstable, and dynamic. I am reminded of this saying, that creation comes from chaos, as I read the essays in this volume; and this is why: queerness is chaos.

As this reflection recognizes, the association with chaos may be understood as a positive feature of queer movement rather than a criticism of it. Of course, if you think like a Westerner (and we suspect that, if you are reading this, you do to some extent at least), you have been culturally trained (indoctrinated) to be something of a structuralist: everything is (should be) in its proper place; everything can be divided into two parts, with one being better than the other; and those things that do not fit neatly are not kosher, they are not holy, they are not aligned with *good*; they are liminal, they are other, they are queer. When we read in Genesis that out of the deep (the undefined, the chaos) G-d makes order, or in *Enuma Elish* that Marduk defeats Tiamat as the symbol of the deep and of disarray, and from her eviscerated, divided body come the earth and sky, we know that it is from *queerness* that all creation comes. Creation out of chaos is often perceived in terms of a neat categorization into which all things fit. In sexual terms, heterosexuality (allegedly the normative and the naturalized) is aligned in this hegemonic binary with *creation* and queerness with *chaos*. It is not accidental that theologian Catherine Keller, grasping for language to speak about fears of chaos in relation to the biblical account of God's interaction with *tehom*, "Deep," at the time of creation (Gen 1:2), coins the term "tehomophobia" (Keller 2003). For our fears of the forces of chaos (*tehom*) and our fears of gender and sexual heterogeneity (homophobia) have much in common. Yet, pardon our repetition, all creation comes from chaos. And if creation (cosmos) continues to resist easy categorization and is, as we know it, blurry, messy, unstable, and dynamic, what distinguishes creation (and heteronormativity) from the chaos, from the queer? As Edwin Starr said, absolutely nothing. The origin and the evolution of the normative are enveloped within the queer.

As Judith Butler notes in *Gender Trouble*, queerness stands to heterosexuality not as copy to original but as copy to copy (1990, 128). Or perhaps, to draw out this relationship in a slightly different direction, a direction informed by the chaotic water imagery that informs biblical and many other ancient texts, queerness is to heterosexuality as the ocean is to a wave. The production of heterosexuality is from the deep, appears briefly as a precisely formed entity, but moves, shifts, takes on new forms, and dissipates, dissolving back into queerness. Heterosexuality, as a constructed category of modernity, is fleeting, and its permanence is illusory (see, e.g., Katz 1995). It is but one of an infinite number of "sexualities." Across time and space the waves appear again and again, both simultaneously and consecutively, all seemingly identical in appearance, but all different from the other.

One implication of the "ocean to wave" model of the production of heterosexuality for this present volume is that we do not see our work simply as a matter of "queering" the biblical narratives. The stories are in certain respects already queer. Centuries of interpreters have sought to put these texts in a box—to concretize and canonize meaning—a snapshot of an ocean's wave. The stories, the characters, the meanings, and the truths of these passages cannot be organized—or, we should say, cannot be organized for any extended amount of time. The *time* of meaning is what distinguishes queer scholarship from what we would call "mainstream" scholarship. Queer scholars understand that meaning is fleeting; what is true is only true right here, right now, then gone. When time moves (as it always does unless we're dead), I change, you change, meaning changes. And in this volume, Jione Havea's rendering of the Lazarus story, Sean Burke's and Manuel Villalobos's elaborative work with the Ethiopian eunuch, Teresa Hornsby's questions about a New Testament call to submit, Lynn Huber's whoring of assimilation, Joseph Marchal's and Gillian Townsley's analyses of the Corinthian correspondence, Deryn Guest's highlighting of "gender trouble" in Judg 4 and 5, Jay Twomey's account of the Pastoral Epistles, Erin Runions's reading of the figure of Rahab, Heidi Epstein's musical journey alongside the Song of Songs, Jeremy Punt's mixing of queer and postcolonial questions, Ken Stone's unorthodox coupling of the books of Samuel and the film *Paris Is Burning*—all of these mean what they mean *when* they mean. As Ellen Armour notes in her opening "response" to these essays (which, in an appropriately "queer" fashion, serves in this volume as a kind of second introduction), "[r]ather than a two dimensional window, 'the Bible' produced by these essays is multidimensional in time and space" (4). This Bible is chaotic. This Bible is queer.

Like the waves a moment before they dissolve back into the deep, biblical texts have been delivered to readers and believers as stable, coherent narratives at work in the service of "the norm." Yet, the *essence* of the wave is the ocean; from the chaos comes [the appearance of] creation, then it folds [or crashes] once again into the chaos. We are not dealing here simply with "queer" interpretation of the Bible; the Bible is always already queer.

WORKS CONSULTED

Armour, Ellen T., and Susan M. St. Ville, eds. 2006. *Bodily Citations: Religion and Judith Butler*. New York: Columbia University Press.

Butler, Judith. 1990. *Gender Trouble: Feminism and the Subversion of Identity*. New York: Routledge.

———. 1994. Against Proper Objects. *Differences* 6.2–3:1–26.

Guest, Deryn, et al., eds. 2006. *The Queer Bible Commentary*. London: SCM.

Hornsby, Teresa J. 2006. The Annoying Woman: Biblical Scholarship after Judith Butler. Pages 71–89 in Armour and St. Ville 2006.

Katz, Jonathan Ned. 1995. *The Invention of Heterosexuality*. Chicago: University of Chicago Press.

Keller, Catherine. 2003. *Face of the Deep: A Theology of Becoming*. New York: Routledge.

Lauretis, Teresa de. 1991. Queer Theory: Lesbian and Gay Sexualities. *Differences* 3.2:iii–xviii.

Martin, Dale B. 2006. *Sex and the Single Savior: Gender and Sexuality in Biblical Interpretation*. Louisville: Westminster John Knox.

Moore, Stephen D. 1998. Que(e)rying Paul: Preliminary Questions. Pages 250–74 in *Auguries: The Jubilee Volume of the Sheffield Department of Biblical Studies*. Edited by David J. A. Clines and Stephen Moore. Sheffield: Sheffield Academic Press.

———. 2001. *God's Beauty Parlor: And Other Queer Spaces in and around the Bible*. Stanford: Stanford University Press.

Runions, Erin. 2003. *How Hysterical: Identification and Resistance in the Bible and Film*. New York: Palgrave Macmillan.

Stone, Ken. 2001a. Queer Commentary and Biblical Interpretation: An Introduction. Pages 11–34 in Stone 2001b.

———, ed. 2001b. *Queer Commentary and the Hebrew Bible.* Sheffield: Sheffield Academic Press; Cleveland: Pilgrim.

———. 2005. *Practicing Safer Texts: Food, Sex and Bible in Queer Perspective.* London: T&T Clark.

———. 2006. The Garden of Eden and the Heterosexual Contract. Pages 48–70 in Armour and St. Ville 2006.

———. 2008. Bibles That Matter: Biblical Theology and Queer Performativity. *BTB* 38:14–25.

Queer Bibles, Queer Scriptures? An Introductory Response

Ellen T. Armour

I come to this rich set of essays wearing two hats: the first that of a queer feminist philosophical theologian and the second that of a professor, first at a liberal-arts college and now at a divinity school—both in the so-called Bible Belt. In my own scholarship, I draw on many (but not all) of the theoretical resources invoked by the authors of these essays. Reading these essays, then, provided for me a certain *frisson* of the purely academic pleasure that comes from encountering familiar and new figures and ideas in scholarly territories in which I am but an academic tourist. Judith Butler, psychoanalysis, Michel Foucault, postcolonial theory, deconstruction, film theory, New Musicology—all of these and more provide herein theoretical scaffolding enabling insightful and creative work with biblical traditions. The pleasure I find in reading these essays is tinged with poignancy because of my other hat. Teaching keeps me acutely aware of the damage that continues to be done to LGBTQ people in the name of biblical authority—damage carried in the bodies and minds of many of my queer students. This is a reality many of these authors know all too well. Even in their most playful and irreverent moments, these essays evince ethical seriousness. One cannot engage questions of sexuality, race/ethnicity, and gender these days and not be aware of—and to some degree feel responsible to—the fraught status of "the Bible" in ongoing debates over the status of sexual minorities within communities around the globe that take this peculiar collection of texts as "Scripture." In what follows, then, I respond to these essays by sharing some reflections on what reading through them together provoked in me. I do so as a way of taking up alongside these authors my own sense of obligation to respond to the ongoing hostility toward LGBTQ folk, particularly in Christian circles. I seek, in crafting this response, to highlight places of convergence and coalescence in these essays that offer particularly fruitful strategies of intervention in our contemporary context.

First, for all of these authors, to "queer" is to complicate, to disrupt, to disturb all kinds of orthodoxies, including, at least, these two (often intertwined in current debate): those that take our current sex/gender regime as natural and God-given and those that posit "the Bible" as a flat, transparent window into the divine mind. While readers may immediately connect such orthodoxies only to certain anti-LGBTQ positions, these essays occasionally suggest that there are pro-LG (if not BTQ) versions of them as well, if by implication more than by explicit claim. I adopt this highly loaded theological term "orthodoxy" for these positions for a number of reasons. First, these positions are literally *ortho-doxies*—that is, claims to right opinion or belief. As was the case with formative conflicts in early Christianity over what would count as right belief, these orthodoxies often want to claim not only the moral and textual high ground but historical and temporal priority. As was the case with the enemies of Gnosticism and Arianism, for example, contemporary claimants to (sexual) orthodoxy often accuse those they oppose of novelty, of distorting long-established tradition, of incoherence; in the case of anti-LGBTQ positions, of something very close to heresy.

The essays contained herein undo these orthodoxies in various ways. All start from the awareness that no regime of bodies and pleasures, of familial or social structure, is "natural." This applies not only to the content (male/female, feminine/masculine, hetero/homo) but, I would suggest, even to the categories foundational to ours (sex, gender, and sexuality), though these remain (productively) in play here. Scripts for incorporating bodies and pleasures into viable schemes for communal life vary with time and place. As new forms of self-identification emerge (and with them, more forms of nonnuclear family), our regime of binaries proves increasingly untenable. The essays herein suggest that our regime does not map neatly onto ancient contexts or texts either.

To queer, however, is not simply to acknowledge historical distance and textual complexity, though it is that, in part. Despite the distance— and difference—between then and now, the interpellative power of "the Bible" registers forcefully in each of these essays thanks in considerable measure to the current religiopolitical landscape. Several of these writers acknowledge the call and not only reflect on its effects but refract it by turning the text back on itself, in a sense. Indeed, each of these essays could be described as what Jacques Berlinerblau calls counterexegesis (see Twomey). That is, many of these essays effectively (if not always with explicit intention) "destabilize dominant conceptions of 'what the Bible says.'"[1] As Twomey advocates, many of them follow George Aichele's call to "reverse the hermeneutical flow."[2] Rather than reading out of the biblical text (exegesis), they read against it. I do not mean in opposition to it; here, a sailing metaphor may be helpful. One can move across the water by sailing either with or against the wind. Sailing with the wind behind you is deceptively quiet and easy; one flies across the surface of the water with little effort—until it's time to head for home! Sailing with the wind against you requires more skill, effort, and expertise in order to discern, marshal, and direct the resources of energy available in the wind. One must work on a number of levels at once: surface and depth, context (water/air) and container (boat/sail), using hand and eye to manage tiller and sail angle. At the right point of sail, the boat literally leans into the wind, finding not only energy for movement but support for staying upright.

We are in the company of some accomplished sailors. The scholars represented here ably discern from surface signs the deeper currents of historical and social context that produce them. They marshal the energies in and around these texts to move their projects forward. The tools they use to navigate these difficult seas are textual (e.g., Butler, Foucault, Gloria Anzaldúa), musical (Penderecki, New Musicology[3]), and filmic (*Paris Is Burning*, Teresa de Lauretis). They practice the many fine arts required for navigation, attending not only to the fine nuances of ancient language and cultures formative of biblical origins but to interpretive context writ large (religion and science) and small (a prison, a small town in Mexico). They seek to cultivate our intellectual acumen, to be sure, but also urge us to attend to affective import and potential bodily response.

---

1. Berlinerblau 2005, 106; cited by Twomey, 287.

2. Aichele 2006, 198; cited by Twomey, 287.

3. In a very rich and wonderful essay, Heidi Epstein draws on New Musicology to read Krzysztof Penderecki's *Canticum canticorum Salomonis*, a late twentieth-century musical rendering of the Song of Songs. The *Canticum* shakes the Song loose from its traditional heteronormative moorings (construed spatially as the filling of a lack and temporally as the linear movement from foreplay to climax). It invites a reconsideration of sexuality as "the 'circulation' of power, pleasure, and intimacy between bodies" (121)—analogous, then, to music making and to listening.

Rather than a two-dimensional window, "the Bible" produced by these essays is multidimensional in time and space. It occurs/resides at the nexus of past and present insofar as these essays render visible traces of ancient origins, track biblical and postbiblical history of interpretation, and bring to bear contemporary issues and approaches. Of particular interest are the characters that populate this Bible, the gender-bending women and men of diverse ethnicities (Israelite, Canaanite, Ethiopian). These are not necessarily, however, characters with whom contemporary queers can easily identify. Time and time again, these essays remind us of the stubborn refusal of ancient texts to live up to our ideals—and thus our orthodoxies—anti- or pro-GLBTQ.

Open-eyed engagement with queer characters undercuts our search for/desire for queer heroes, as Runions puts it. [4] The queerness of Jael and Rahab, of Jonathan and David, is inseparable from a violence that is troubling in its own right and in its association with ethnic bias. For example, the killing of Jonathan, whose love for him David famously describes as "passing the love of women" (1 Sam 1:26, NRSV), is the all-but-inevitable conclusion of the triumph of David's house over Saul's. It reads differently, however, against the backdrop of the murder of Venus Xtravaganza, a Latina transsexual in Jennie Livingston's film *Paris Is Burning* (Stone). Jael and Rahab are non-Israelite women whose heroism on behalf of Israel arguably queers normative gender and sexual roles. But their disruptive effects appear in a more sobering light when positioned in relationship to the persistent anti-Canaanite polemic that runs throughout the Deuteronomistic history. This polemic figures the Canaanites as sexually deviant and thus subject to divinely sanctioned violence at Israelite hands. Lest we think this is all in the past, Runions attributes contemporary visceral disgust at nonheteronormative sexual practices in part to its influence. That figuration shows up in contemporary antigay polemic (as illustrative of the divine will with regard to sexual deviance) *and* in the distinction gay advocates often draw between contemporary, loving homosex and pagan ritual

---

4. Even Jesus comes out as less than heroic in Havea's essay about reading the story of Lazarus with prisoners in New South Wales. In John 11:13, Jesus says, "greater love has no one than this, that he should lay down his life for his friends" (NIV). This standard takes on flesh and blood in the rough-and-tumble context of prison life. By that standard, Jesus' treatment of Lazarus comes up short. If anything, as these prisoners read it, raising Lazarus from the dead serves Jesus' self-interest, not that of Lazarus himself.

homosex.[5] It is disturbing that both sides end up trading on the encoding of ethnic and religious difference as sexual deviance. It further reminds us that we are hardly immune from such encodings ourselves. The photos from Abu Ghraib, for example, document the vicious use of such encodings by the U.S. military on Arab Muslims.[6]

Similarly, recent shifts toward greater acceptance of LGBTQ people may entangle us in other kinds of complicities. Hornsby and Huber, especially, warn us to beware of the usefulness of contemporary queer identities to economic and imperial machinations. Hornsby, for example, suggests a materialist explanation for the greater acceptance of non-reproductive sexual identities. In a post-industrial age, the U.S. economy needs consumers more than producers. Acceptance of nonreproductive sexual subjects—signaled, for example, by allowing gay marriage—renders us docile targets of conspicuous consumption. Marchal uncovers common ground between Paul's identity discourse in 1 Corinthians and contemporary medical discourse on transsexuality. Insofar as both discourses authorize one's access to a new subject status, both serve as disciplinary regimes that may run counter to the interests of those seeking the goods that come with the change in status.

Still, tracking queer biblical characters provides leverage to crack open normative readings of the Bible that reinforce contemporary orthodoxies. For example, Burke argues that the ambiguity of the figure of the Ethiopian eunuch bespeaks the early followers of Jesus' expansion of their communal boundaries to the very ends of identity markers/systems. Contemporary attempts to limit Christian identity to those who fit within normative—and sanctioned—identity categories come up short by such a standard. The story of the Ethiopian eunuch's border crossing read through Gloria Anzaldúa's evocative work provides concrete hope for Villalobos, who recounts the role of his own border crossings that enable his move into a queer identity.

Taken together, then, what do these examples of counterexegesis offer as addresses to the various forms of attack on sexual minorities that claim biblical warrant? Allow me, if you will, to invoke yet another theological category: that of "Scripture." After all, the Bible matters in our contemporary context because of its status within certain communities as holy

---

5. See also Townsley's essay herein. Homosexuality is the sacrificial lamb in both feminist and antifeminist evangelical readings of 1 Cor 11:2–16.

6. On this, see Armour 2010.

writ. Indeed, awareness of this status arguably runs below the surface of many of these essays. The way the essays move back and forth between the past and present, between text and contexts (ancient and contemporary) is arguably a tacit acknowledgment of the Bible's status as Scripture, of its ongoing power to (over)write us (ideally, for some, to write LGBTQ folk out of the picture), a power that resides in "the Bible" as sedimented and continuously reexcavated past.

Read against that backdrop, none of these authors play it safe. For some, the risk taken involves violating certain proprieties that seek to protect Scripture from the very earthy business of bodies and pleasures (I think here of Guest and Epstein, in particular). For others, the risk lies in responding to the "Hey, you!" of the Bible's call that renders them always already guilty (*pace* Althusser) by the light of its supposed sexual normativities (I think here of Villalobos and Huber, in particular). For yet others, the risk lies in bringing the Bible into close proximity with those deemed deviant in our own day: prisoners in New South Wales (Havea), the "houses" of the New York City drag-ball scene (Stone). Elsewhere, Ken Stone extends Judith Butler's performative theory of gender to the Bible as a way of opening a door for a queer biblical theology (Stone 2008). Specifically, he argues that "the Bible" is a doing, not a being; Bibles are produced through various institutional and individual practices (including but not limited to reading and interpreting). In that spirit, let me suggest that we read these essays not only as counterexegeses but as counter-Scriptures. Their authors find in the cracks and crevices of "the Bible" and its contexts resources for the production of other script/ures, Bibles that authorize doing and thus being otherwise. There is, of course, no way of ensuring that these performative Bibles will displace those that continue to do harm to LGBTQ folk. However, we can surely welcome the disruptive and reinscriptive possibilities that they open up for us.

WORKS CONSULTED

Aichele, George. 2006. Recycling the Bible: A Response. Pages 195–201 in *The Recycled Bible: Autobiography, Culture and the Space Between.* Edited by Fiona Black. SemeiaSt 51. Atlanta: Society of Biblical Literature.

Armour, Ellen T. 2010. Visual Theology: Diagnosing Postmodernity. Pages 175–92 in *Between Philosophy and Theology: Contemporary Interpreta-*

tions of Christianity. Edited by Lieven Boeve and Christophe Brabante. London: Ashgate.

Berlinerblau, Jacques. 2005. *The Secular Bible: Why Nonbelievers Must Take Religion Seriously*. New York: Cambridge University Press.

Stone, Ken. 2008. Bibles That Matter: Biblical Theology and Queer Performativity. *BTB* 38:14–25.

FROM GENDER REVERSAL TO GENDERFUCK:
READING JAEL THROUGH A LESBIAN LENS

Deryn Guest

Genderfuck: a stark, startling word with which to commence a paper.[1] It's an edgy word, capable of offense, especially with that harsh third syllable sitting so indecently within the respectable—decent—domain of biblical studies. Gender reversals are what we are more at ease with; gender reversal has been part of the accepted—acceptable?—commentarial language for Judg 4–5 and the figure of Jael for years; and it is Jael's story that is the subject of this paper. But from a queer perspective, this will not suffice. The terminology of gender reversal reinforces the two-sex, two-gender binary of male/female and masculine/feminine. It simply shifts the ground from one to the other: Jael, the woman, takes on the mantle of military assassin to become, temporarily, male rapist, before being praised and recuperated as "most blessed of women." Genderfuck, however, is the language and business of queer theory. Consistent with its arm of political activism, the confrontational, uncompromising stance of queer theory is one of resistance to such binaries: subverting, undoing, deconstructing the normalcy of sex/gender regimes, cracking them open, focusing on the fissures that expose their constructedness. If the word itself puts one on edge, then it accomplishes its purpose. The narrator of Judg 4 and 5 wrote in a context

---

1. According to Bergman (1993, 7), the term made an early appearance in a 1974 article for *Gay Sunshine* by Christopher Lonc, entitled "Genderfuck and Its Delights," and prior to that, it was associated with the Cockettes, a 1970s drag troupe. Reich's paper, originally published in 1992, defines genderfuck as structuring "meaning in a symbol-performance matrix that crosses through sex and gender and destabilizes the boundaries of our recognition of sex, gender, and sexual practice" (1999, 255). Within biblical studies the term was taken up by Runions in her innovative paper (1998) on the transgression of gender codes in Micah.

that is miles and centuries away from contemporary queer theory and its neologism, genderfuck, but in conjuring a seductive, alluring "woman" who unexpectedly morphs into phallic murderer, the narrator creates more than he bargained for.

When soliciting contributions for this volume of Semeia Studies, the editors encouraged writers to think not only about troubling texts with queer theory but about how disciplinary boundaries between biblical scholarship and other types of scholarship such as queer theory, feminist theory, and studies in masculinity are also troubled in the process. The story of Jael will serve as a good illustration for discussion of such boundary issues. The lesbian perspective that follows brings with it the influences of feminist theory, lesbian and gay studies, queer theory, transgender studies, and queer film criticism, breaking upon the traditional and cherished norms of historical-critical exegesis with all the force of several gate-crashers at a party from which they had long been excluded. Its relationship to traditional biblical studies is similar to that of black, womanist and feminist, postcolonial, and all those approaches that demand ethical responsibility of the interpreter: that is, strained. The theoretical strategies it employs are as far away from the social context of the biblical storyteller as one can imagine. It consciously and deliberately interrogates the text with its own agenda. It reads against the grain, is disobedient in its employment of a hermeneutic of (hetero)suspicion. But, although this runs completely counter to the programmatic agenda of the historical-critical approach as outlined, for example, by Gabler in 1787, it is in keeping with the growing insistence that biblical interpretation has to be ethically responsible and that scholarly objectivity or neutrality is an unworkable and undesirable myth. However, since the impact of the above has already been widely addressed,[2] this paper notes different boundary contestations. First, it poses questions about the borders between feminist and lesbian biblical studies. I have already narrated the uncomfortable experience of owning a strong allegiance to feminism and to feminist biblical interpretation, while having significant reservations about whether this can provide the theoretical home for the questions and issues lesbian perspectives raise (Guest 2008). This essay usefully permits another comparison of the questions,

---

2. See, e.g., Patte 1995, 1999; Schüssler Fiorenza 1988; Segovia and Tolbert 1995a, b; Segovia 2000a, b.

interpretative results, and concerns of a lesbian lens with those of existing feminist interpretations of Jael's story.

Second, in the process of writing this paper, the overlapping yet simultaneous distinctions between butch-lesbian, transgender, and transsexual communities came to the fore in unexpected and complex ways. Halberstam (1998, 141–73) explains how the fault lines of the transsexual and butch-lesbian communities can be set against each other antagonistically. For example, a transsexual perspective might be that butch lesbians remain with their born gender identity and, if they are feminist lesbians, may put a high value on that gendered identity, while FTMs (female-to-male transsexuals) might experience lesbian feminist discourse as one that demonizes and alienates them. Butch-identified people can "become associated with a playful desire for masculinity and a casual form of gender deviance" (143) or be seen as people "who are too afraid to make the 'transition' from female to male" (144), while FTMs can be figured as the ones who are thoroughgoing, having the conviction and commitment to seeing their gender struggles through to the full extent. In contrast, a lesbian perspective on FTMs might be that they reinforce the two-sex model rather than being content to live in some interstitial space between male and female. Some might "see FTMs as traitors to a 'woman's' movement who cross over and become the enemy" (144). The debate is influenced by the place from which one theorizes:

> When theorized from the perspective of the FTM, the stone butch becomes pre-FTM, a penultimate stage along the way to the comfort of transsexual transformation; however, when theorized from the perspective of the butch, the stone butch becomes a nonsurgical and nonhormonal version of transgender identification and does away with the necessity of sex reassignment surgery for some people. (Halberstam 1998, 148)

Such discussion indicates how the popular shorthand "LGBT" is a very loose grouping that can never do justice to the separate concerns of each community. It does little to acknowledge the antagonisms within and between them or the insensitive expulsions that occur as a form of border policing. The contested border between lesbian and transsexual is not exactly troubled in this paper so much as recognized as an issue to be negotiated and acknowledged.

Finally, although not the specific subject of discussion, this paper reasserts a distinct lesbian approach that uses queer theory as a tool, rather

than providing a—more generic—queer reading of biblical texts. If les-
bian-feminist discourse is shunted into the domain of queer theory, it runs
the risk of being assimilated all too soon, especially within the domain
of biblical interpretation, where it is hardly established at all. So I do not
write as a queer critic but from a white, English, lesbian perspective that
might be recognized as "butch" as opposed to "femme"—though these
labels themselves are fluid and, for some, camp performances (see Gibson
and Meem 2005, 121). Signaling this site-specific perspective is important,
for while queer theory might be a useful tool for lesbian hermeneutics, the
distinctive voices beneath that umbrella usage of "queer" need to be heard.

When the Best Men Are Women: The Language of Gender Reversals in Commentary on Judges 4–5

In terms of Clines's indicators of success, the majority of the judges "play
the man" pretty poorly, with a notable decline from the ideal Othniel to the
substantially flawed Samson.[3] Evaluation mechanisms, however, have not

---

3. David Clines's 1995 study of 1 Sam 16–1 Kgs 2 identifies these key indicators
of successful masculinity: courageous warriorhood, intelligence and skills of persua-
sion, beauty, strong bonds with other men at the expense of committed relationships
with women, and musical prowess. The terminology "play the man" comes also from
Clines, who says that he is considering "Play the Man! The Masculine Imperative in
the Bible" as a title for a future publication. He explains: "The 'play' signifies that masculinity is a role, and the imperative verb with its exclamation mark denotes the force
of the social constraint upon biological males to exhibit prescribed male behavior"
(Clines 1998, 354). Such an approach, however, does not question fully assumptions
of the ontological status of "manhood," a stable, sexed core to which attributes or gendered practices are affixed. Yes, it is helpful to unmask the ways in which masculinity
is constructed in the Hebrew Bible, to compare this with what it means to "do" man
in today's culture and to explore how "our images of biblical men have been shaped
by our cultural norms" (Clines 1995, 212). This has the advantage of demonstrating
how hegemonic masculinities get established, yet how they are also contingent upon
social context. In turn, this can be used to expose uncritical discourses that attempt
to impose supposed biblical norms on Christian and Jewish men and women today.
However, Butler's work causes us to ask further questions. Butler writes: "once we dis-
pense with the priority of 'man' and 'woman' as abiding substances, then it is no longer
possible to subordinate dissonant gendered features as so many secondary or accidental characteristics of gender ontology that is fundamentally intact. If the notion of an
abiding substance is a fictive construction produced through the compulsory ordering
of attributes into coherent gender sequences, then it seems that gender as substance,

been informed specifically by their performances of masculinity. Rather, individuals have been thought to have succeeded or failed in accordance with their personification/embodiment of Deuteronomistic norms or their furtherance of the narrator's pedagogical concerns. And yet gender performances contribute significantly to the characterization of the judges, since the narrator appears to negotiate playfully with sex/gender/sexuality categories in the interests of those wider concerns.

In the narratives concerning Jael, Sisera, Barak, and Deborah, two women appear to "do man" better than the men themselves. While Barak is reluctant, arguably cowardly, and is accordingly deprived of expected honor/glory, Deborah is all initiative and boldness. While Jael embarks on a flurry of activity that results in the death of Sisera, he himself is largely passive: he "makes no direct reply ... but simply follows her—silently—into the tent" (Alter 1983, 635), accepting the drink of milk and allowing himself to be covered. In the scenes that follow (4:20–22 and 5:26–27),[4] Jael's active role reaches its peak: hammering a tent peg into Sisera's head, or jaw.[5] Contemporary commentary, in noting these things, has often utilized a language of reversal, so that women take on male traits in unexpected gender twists, or has broadened the category of "woman" so that

---

the viability of man and woman as nouns, is called into question by the dissonant play of attributes that fail to conform to sequential or casual modes of intelligibility" (1990, 24). Anticipating suggestions that resisting attributes might call into question the edges of gender or expand those edges to incorporate anomalies, she writes, "But if these substances are nothing other than coherences contingently created through the regulation of attributes, it would seem that the ontology of substances itself is not only an artificial effect, but essentially superfluous" (24). The indicators of masculinity that Clines identifies are not performances of a subject who preexists as an already-sexed "man." They constitute the doer: "There is no gender identity behind the expressions of gender ... identity is performatively constituted by the very 'expressions' that are said to be its results" (Butler 1990, 25).

4. In this paper I do not make source-critical judgments concerning the priority of one account over the other. I am more sympathetic with Alter's view that trying to ascertain the earliest version is beside the point. He prefers to see these differences as a "matter of the writers' interpretative rendering of the same event," since the poet and the prose writer appear to have "possessed the same basic narrative data, though not necessarily in any written version" (Alter 1985, 48). I will draw on features from both these narratives as required.

5. Fewell and Gunn make a case for seeing the peg being thrust into Sisera's open mouth, in an act that is a "powerful image of reversed rape" (1990, 394). See also van Wolde 1996, 293.

she can incorporate unconventional attributes such as militancy, violence, and, curiously, rape. Papers by Bos, Fewell and Gunn, Niditch, and Yee provide illustration.

Bos's paper is based on a thesis of reversal. In her view, the stories of Tamar (of Gen 38), Jael, and Ruth offer "counter-type-scenes" to the betrothal type-scene. The reversal that takes place is found in the "turn of events, as well as in the arrangement of the central characters" (Bos 1988, 39). When it comes to the discussion of Jael, Bos notes how Jael takes the "man's task" (49). Jael is the initiator of a string of active verbs, particularly when it comes to the assassination. I concur: it is when Jael is being simultaneously imaged as assassin/rapist that Jael's gender appears to be most notably reversed. In this, Jael breaks patriarchal structures: "the story of Yael shows a cracking of the patriarchal structures themselves. ... [Her actions] are not based on derived identity, on her connection with men, nor on the restrictions of certain activities as belonging to one gender, with the public sphere and its activities reserved for the male" (55–56). Bos believes that the gender reversals going on in this story relate to the underdog position of Israel vis-à-vis oppressing foes. Thus, the reversal in Judg 4 is one where

> the powerful (males) show weakness and the weak (females) show strength. This picture makes an apt paradigm for weak Israel, which in the Book of Judges time and again defeats a more powerful enemy. ... The extraordinary feature of Judg 4 and 5 is that women become the "helpers" through whom God accomplishes victory and that one of them is not a member of the Israelite tribes. (Bos 1988, 58)

However, in a trend that is evident throughout a range of papers, Bos puts an emphasis on the womanliness of Jael: "The tools are hers; the actions are a startling reversal of expectations of a female with her family alliances" (1998, 55), and the language of gender reversal removes any possibility of queering the characterization of Jael.

Fewell and Gunn's insightful paper suggests that the narrator has skillfully combined sexual/maternal with masculine language and imagery to present us with Jael as seducer, mother, and male rapist. Notice again the language of gender reversal: chapter 4 begins "with a reversal ... a woman, rather than a man, is judging Israel" (Fewell and Gunn 1990, 391). We meet Jael, whose act with the tent peg is said to be a "powerful image of reversed rape. ... Patriarchal expectation is turned upside down as the warrior's mouth is penetrated by an unmistakably phallic tent peg" (394). Fewell and Gunn note the role reversal between a mothering Jael, trusted by Sisera, and the raping Jael who is his undoing. Then there is the gender reversal made more apparent in the Song of Deborah, which "'masculinizes' (i.e., in patriarchal terms) the event by curtailing the deception and implying sudden confrontation. *Like a man* against his foe in single combat, Jael battles a standing Sisera" (405, emphasis added). Readers, they claim, are

> forced to reconsider stereotypical expectations of women's behavior and power. Women do not, as a rule, seduce their lovers in order to kill them; mothers do not, as a rule, nurture little boys in order to murder them. ... Sisera and [the] patriarchal reader ... do not want to imagine that, under duress, she might herself invade the male monopoly of power, claim the authority of violence. (Fewell and Gunn 1990, 405–6)

The language of this paper is that of reversals: of expectations, of roles, and of sex and gender.

Just one year prior to Fewell and Gunn's publication, Susan Niditch published a paper informed by psychological studies, making connections between death and eroticism. She notes also the connections that have been made between Jael and the goddess Anat, who possesses conventional attributes but also active, militaristic, killing characteristics.[6] In this paper, the language is not focused on gender reversal so much as on broadening the category of woman to incorporate attributes not conventionally expected: "Jael, the beautiful woman who lures the enemy ... is the warrior who fells the unsuspecting Sisera with a massive blow to the head" (Niditch [1989] 1999, 309). Jael's female status remains uppermost in Niditch's discussion, as seen additionally in the statement "Here ... the duelers are not two men, but a male warrior and a woman assassin disguised as a protector and ally" (311). As will be discussed further below, such statements recuperate the femaleness of Jael.

---

6. On possible connections between Jael and Anat, see Hanselman 1989 and Ackerman 1998, 52–68. Ackerman suggests that "in Israelite thinking, especially in texts closely informed by Canaan's Anat mythology, attributes such as compassion more typically associated with the female sphere could go hand-in-hand with the sorts of bellicose violence more usually ascribed to men" (91). Accordingly, the juxtaposition of Jael's nurturing qualities with the murderous act that follows is not a problem and does not undo the basic female gender Jael clearly is thought to occupy. However, this paper wishes to do precisely that, i.e., undo the basic stable gender identity of Jael.

More closely resembling the lesbian questions and concerns to follow is Yee's paper on Jael as liminal "woman warrior." Arguably, the use of "liminal" is problematic, since it could be read as stabilizing the two-sex paradigm. Liminality, insofar as it is suggestive of a "third term," does not sufficiently do the work of disrupting or subverting, creating rather a space "between," one that contains elements of both—stable—sex/gender categories. However, Yee's paper promises much for a lesbian approach to Judg 4 and 5, even as she seems unable to sustain the focus on liminality and the challenge to sex and gender categories.

Yee's opening pages draw on a range of anthropological studies relating to the woman warrior, noting how the very term "woman warrior" provokes dissonance. Its incongruity lies in the "historically substantiated fact that warriorhood is consistently defined by both men and women as a male activity in most cultures" (Yee 1993, 104). Some of the binary oppositions that accrue from this include the association of the male with warrior, protector, conqueror, destroyer and with violence, independence, aggression, and dominance. Woman occupies the counterside of those terms: noncombatant, protected, defeated, nurturer, nonviolent, dependent, meek, and submissive. Breaking these norms, the woman warrior is a liminal figure, "neither female nor male as these are customarily defined, although she shares qualities of each" (105). As such, the liminal figure occupies the ground "apart from the center at the margins of society. It is from the periphery that she exerts her creative power over our thoughts and over our feelings" (99). Note the two female pronouns in this sentence. I shall return to this in a moment.

Given this recognition, it was surprising to find that Yee later discards one of the "syndrome" categories she draws from Antonia Fraser, whose book *The Warrior Queen* identifies certain "syndromes" that have afflicted the representation of queens both during and after their reigns. Yee suggests it is the shame syndrome—the primary function of which is "to shame the weaker males who surround her" (1993, 115)—combined with the voracity syndrome, in which the "warrior queen embodies the sexual license and the unbridled lust that characterize anomalous women" (116), that best apply to Jael. However, one of the other syndromes suggested by Fraser is the tomboy syndrome. This is "where the warrior queen as a girl prefers soldiers over dolls, hunting over domestic activities," which, when applied to certain queens, has the effect of setting "the warrior queen apart from 'normal' females" (114 n. 11). Relegated to a footnote, this syndrome catches the eye of a lesbian reader who can resonate with such preferences and the subsequent stigma. It is not at all clear why the voracity syndrome should be preferred. Although there are evidently sexual *entendres* written into Jael's dispatching of Sisera, are there actually any clear indications of "license" or "unbridled lust"? Given the emphasis Yee has put on liminality, it might have been more fruitful to explore the applicability of the tomboy syndrome—particularly its focus on how such figures trouble the notion of "female." The apparent nonrecognition of how the tomboy syndrome might apply could be an early indicator of how feminist and lesbian feminist interests and resonances differ.

Yee goes on to suggest that this liminal not-man not-woman figure provokes anxiety. Jael is a "dangerous" and "disruptive" figure: "she occupies a structurally anomalous position within the human domain and is thus potentially and actually disruptive. She takes on the attributes, roles and accompanying prestige that are usually reserved for the male, but still remains female" (Yee 1993, 105). In this quotation, and the one above, our limited English pronouns get in the way. The repeated reference to "she," "her," and the phrase "still remains female" threaten to undermine the liminal figure Yee has been at pains to identify. How can gender liminality be preserved when Jael is constantly referred to as "she" or "woman"? The commentarial discourse surrounding Jael produces and stabilizes a female gender category even while speaking of reversals, liminality, or in broadening the category of woman. These papers are not alone in this— there is a long-standing reception history that has repeatedly reinforced a primary—essential—female identity for Jael as if this is the "natural" state or the "ground" from which Jael's performance deviates. The question of whether Jael exits the category of woman altogether is hardly mooted. The questioning of whether there is a stable preexisting category that we name "woman" barely occurs. More on this in the next section. For now, continuing with Yee, it is fruitful to see how she accounts for the anxiety-producing aspect of Jael's liminality.

Yee says that a liminal figure's "rejection of gender roles elicits strong reactions from the rest of society" (1993, 107). If the liminality could be retained and Jael's genderqueer presentation kept uppermost, then there might be more to say about why such figures are "dangerous."[7] But first, Yee's explanation.

---

7. Often used in conjunction with or as a synonym of genderfuck, the term "genderqueer" is explored in Nestle, Howell, and Wilchins 2002. It is deliberately resistant

Following the work of Gottwald (1979) and Meyers (1988), Yee takes on a certain model of Israelite origins that identifies a loose connection of clans in the highlands of Canaan as "Israelite," whose prestate structure meant that the division between the domestic and public was not rigidly maintained. Thus if crisis demanded, women could play their part in battle, though even in this prestate society she thinks the military norm would be one of male leadership and warriorhood. She implies that the story contained in Judg 4–5 has its origins in this premonarchic society and, on this hypothetical basis, suggests that the stories of Deborah and Jael are

> attempts to cope with the tension between the normative maleness of the military and the apparent involvement of women in war in pre-state Israel. They seek to deal with the fluid notions of gender and the public/domestic domains of influence, before they became fixed during the rise of the monarchy with its standing army. (Yee 1993, 114)

Accordingly, Jael is an anxiety-provoking figure because her active, effective, military success threatens to deprivilege biological maleness. Jael can do man better than a man himself.

But other models of Israelite origins are critical of Gottwald and particularly his location of some biblical traditions—including the song in Judg 5—emerging within this prestate period. Although it has long been assumed that any archaeological data relating to Canaan in the early Iron Age has some kind of bearing on the "period of the judges," some argue that no such assumption can be made. Certainly, there is an identifiable population in the Iron Age highlands of Canaan, but any presupposition that this population relates to an "ancient Israel" and, specifically, to the characters that populate the book of Judges, is open to justified challenge.[8]

---

to male/female, masculine/feminine binaries and signifies here a mode of expression that exceeds those limiting and all-too-rigid categories.

8. On the archaeological data, see, e.g., Thompson 1992; Finkelstein 1996; Finkelstein and Silberman 2001. Even if one assumes that source material lies behind the form of Judg we now possess, it is difficult to allocate dates to such material. As Lemche says in regard to the Ehud story, "It might just as easily be pre-Israelite, but assimilated into Israelite tradition. It might just as easily derive from the period of the monarchy, although the oral tradition has assigned it to the Judges. In short, we have no way whatsoever to determine whether any historical tradition at all underlies the narrative ... as long as we lack other sources. Precisely the same judgment applies

The idea that Judg 5, if not Judg 4, has its early origins among such a community is thus open to debate. Accordingly, I have to find an alternative reason for the—much later, in my view—creation of Jael as a genderqueer character, despite the apparent anxiety or dangers such a portrayal is said to provoke; and this will be discussed in the next section.

Prior to that, a summary: I am suggesting that feminist readings, with the understandable focus on Jael *as woman* and the terminology of gender reversal, undermine the potential for genderfuck at various turns. Yee's paper, despite the clear acknowledgment of gender liminality, nonetheless retains a spotlight on the *femaleness* of Jael. Niditch is clear about the masculinization of Jael and the feminizing of Sisera: "The woman Jael becomes not the object of sexual advances … and not the complacent responder to requests for mercy, but herself is the aggressor, the despoiler" ([1989] 1999, 311). She continues, "here the defeated soldier is the woman, the one subdued, raped, and made love to" (311). Jael clearly plays the man, but Niditch immediately returns the focus to the femaleness of Jael: "A man is not rendered womanish by another man, but is despoiled *by a woman*" (311, emphasis added). In order to make this statement Niditch has to keep a female gender uppermost, which enables her to argue that the marginal Jael and her unorthodox activity are in some way "woman Israel": "an archetype or symbol for the marginal's victory over the establishment" (312). The strong case Niditch makes for the image of rape with Jael the active "masculine" penetrator and Sisera the passive victim is, in my view, recuperated all too quickly. In her recent commentary on Judges, Niditch clearly stresses gender reversal when it comes to Sisera but is more reticent about Jael, reinscribing her, in fact, as woman. Thus, commenting on 5:24–31, she notes how Sisera "becomes the woman who is raped, the victor her rapist. Here, ironically, it is a woman who is in the position of rapist, the enemy male general her victim" (Niditch 2008, 81). Yee's insistence on the liminality of Jael gives greater attention to the gender destabilization present in the text but falls foul of the same tendency.[9]

---

to most of the other traditions in the Book of Judges" (1985, 383). It is feasible to question how far the stories of Judg 4 and 5 are the creative work of a storyteller who deliberately composed these narratives, *de novo.*

9. This is not so pronounced, however, as the reification of Jael's female gender found in this comment: "The crowning aspect of her unorthodoxy as a hero is her sex. Yahweh sells Sisera into the hand of a woman" (Webb 1987, 137).

Is it simply the case that our limited language fails as we strain between the clear presentation of Jael as woman on the one hand and the figuration of male rapist on the other? Or have commentators, including feminist commentators, been reluctant—for whatever reasons—to lose sight of Jael as, essentially, a woman? Of course, the papers that have been discussed were all published either just before or just following Butler's influential works *Gender Trouble* (1990) and *Bodies That Matter* (1993). Butler's views on the iterative acts that produce rather than reflect gender, on how intelligible genders paradoxically produce the specter of unintelligible genders that are immediately expelled or cast as "developmental failures or logical impossibilities" (1990, 17), were not yet widely known. Butler's work, however, encourages a move away from the language of gender reversal to the language of genderfuck and from preexisting sexed categories to their production through discourse and institutional policing.

Reading these papers in the light of Butler's work throws into focus how commentators generally, not just in these papers, appear to read from a relentless two-sex paradigm that does not recognize *all gender* as performative. Thus Jael, as rapist, is quite easily "seen"/"read" as a momentary transfiguration, an artificial "reversal" performed in a scene, after which "she" returns to her "real" gender as woman. There is little recognition that her valorized portrayal, "most blessed of women," is *equally a performance of gender* that requires inspection. However, Robyn Fleming, in a discerning term paper written in 2005, rightly asks: "If Jael is in possession of a penetrating phallus, however symbolic, the question now becomes: Is she still a woman? And it is through that question that we begin to finally uncover the root of the phallocentric discomfort occasioned by Judges 4 and 5" (7). In Fleming's view it is not reversal but the "gender confusion," the "complete re-ordering" (7), that makes Jael's such a powerful portrait. To this intriguing possibility we now turn.

From Gender Reversals/Broadening Gender to Genderfuck

Tim Koch (2001) has spoken of scoring "hits" with Scripture. His "cruising" method is one of encounter, in which a text is brought alive to the reader due to some correlation between it and one's own experience. The reader's gaydar bleeps obligingly when a likely text is located. Jael may well set off the gaydar of readers who occupy a genderqueer terrain. For this to work, a slow-motion replay is necessary, one that allows the reader/ viewer to pause on the key verses, refusing to gloss quickly over the scenic

moment of Otherness. Pausing enables us to stop the camera on the genderqueer scene and let it sink in, let its confusion of categories occupy
center stage for more than a second or two.[10]

PAUSING ON GAZE

The slow-motion tracking picks up on earlier threads that offer hints for
what is to come. It enables the reader, first, to take account of an unexpected use of grammar by the narrator. Jael's name is the initial minor
curiosity. The name "mountain-goat" is a masculine proper noun. Lindars
notes that there is a feminine form for "mountain goat" available (Prov
5:19), but "here it is masculine, unlike all other animal names for women"
(1995, 196). Ellen van Wolde also notes how Jael "bears a name which is
marked as masculine" (1996, 292). "Her name is a yiqtol third person *masculine* singular. She is not called *tā'ēl* (third person feminine singular), but
yā'ēl" (292). Neither commentator offers any further thought, other than to
remark upon the oddity of this occurrence. However, such an odd choice of
masculine forms occurs again in 4:20. When Sisera instructs Jael to stand
at the entrance to the tent, the narrator has him issuing a second-person
masculine imperative. Moore acknowledges the "difficulty" in his 1895
commentary, noting the "anomalous" usage. He deals with it by bluntly
stating, "We require the fem., עמדי" (1895, 125). Later commentators recommend emendation. Boling states: "The incongruity of addressing her
with a masculine imperative (MT *'ᵃmōd*) is best resolved by repointing
to read infinitive absolute (*'āmōd*)" (1975, 98). Soggin acknowledges the
oddity of the masculine imperative but immediately notes that scholars,
reading with Targum and Syriac, prefer a correction to *imedī* (1981, 67).

When readers are not proposing emendation of the text, then the masculine imperative has been explained in other ways. Schneider, for example, encourages the reader to imagine a weary army general who "was falling asleep and not concentrating," used, as he was, "to issuing commands,
particularly in the masculine imperative" (2000, 82). The masculine
imperative thus becomes merely a deliberate literary ploy by the narrator

---

10. This is actually consistent with the slowed pace of the narrator. O'Connell
notes that 4:21 "offers the slowest paced description of the narrative. Note the deliber-
ation over detail in the portrayal of the action in 4:21a, which leads up to the moment
of resolution" (1996, 120). Similarly, in the Song of Deborah, "the description leading
up to the cathartic resolution is slow-paced and laden with detail" (122).

meant to make us envision a tired, unthinking man, that is, not a ploy to unhinge our thoughts about gender. True, the narrator then immediately refers to Jael as woman, but this jars the gender contradiction even further.

These moves are, I believe, indicative of recuperative strategies. Writing in a different context, Hanson suggests that the recuperative drive is one that returns to the "real" body that lies "beneath" the performance; the concept of a concrete self; one that assimilates the liminality into the two traditional genders (1999). Hanson is writing as a film critic, specifically concerned with the transgender character in the movie *The Crying Game* (1992), but the case being made has relevance for this paper. Drawing on Marjorie Garber's work, Hanson notes how the recuperative drive can be seen effectively at work in cross-dressing scenarios:

> The appeal of cross-dressing is clearly related to its status as a sign of the constructedness of gender categories. But the tendency on the part of many critics has been to look *through* rather than *at* the cross-dresser, to turn away from a close encounter with the transvestite, and to want instead to subsume that figure within one of the two traditional genders. To elide and erase—or to *appropriate* the transvestite for particular political and critical aims. (Garber 1992, 9)

But when it comes to the transgender (as opposed to cross-dressing) character of Dil in *The Crying Game*, a category crisis occurs.[11] Dil, argues Hanson, is one *posing* questions as opposed to being *questionable*, and accordingly calls the other characters' identities into question, provoking this crisis of categories.

Although the two writers come from different disciplinary contexts, Hanson's comments resonate strongly with Ken Stone's recent paper on gender criticism. Informed by Butler, Stone notes how repeated, compelled acts of gender get "(re)installed as norms; and they come to seem quite solid and substantial. Yet there are differences, gaps, moments of confusion, and multiple possibilities for meaning among these citations" (Stone 2007, 192). The relevance of this for biblical studies is demonstrated in his reading of Judg 9 and the story of Abimelech. He finds that the nar-

---

11. Unlike cross-dressing films—such as *Mrs. Doubtfire* (1993) or *Tootsie* (1982)—where the cross-dressing is made clear from the start and where gender transgressions are recuperated, *The Crying Game* presents us with "dangerous desires" (Hanson 1999, 49) that resist recuperation.

rator casts aspersions on certain men/groups of men: not only Abimelech, for the fallout hits Saul, Jonathan, Benjamin, and the Levites. However, in so doing, the narrator employs a risky strategy, for it has the potential to run out of control. Thus:

> When the manhood of its [Israel's] kings and aspiring kings is represented so often at risk, the manhood of Israel itself would seem to be uncertain. Biblical iterations of gender begin to appear much more often as failed approximations to an ideal, to use Butler's language; and the Bible's contributions to stable norms of sex and gender seem much less clear. (Stone 2007, 199)

When it comes to the story of Jael, there is a similar potential for fallout. It is already apparent that one knock-on effect of positing a strong, active female character—I use female here because the narrator does signal that Jael is a woman even while he disrupts this with the rape imagery—is that the gender iterations of the men in the narrative are compromised. Strong, active Deborah and reluctant, ineffective Barak, strong, active Jael and passive, compliant, deflowered Sisera. It also happens in the Jezebel story, which produces an unmanly Ahab. The two-sex paradigm is not so much upset by this as it is sustained by the balancing act, but there is a glimpse of a more destabilizing effect if one is caused to think about how masculinity is therefore not a given, resulting from biological maleness, but an achievement, a continual assignment.[12] The image of Jael as penetrating rapist presents the reader with the visual anomaly of Jael-with-a-penis. Pressing the pause button at this juncture means that this moment is not quickly recuperated. Rather, it maintains the focus upon genderfuck.

There are so few instances where such genderqueerness comes clearly to the surface that it is important not to relapse readily into the simultaneous imaging of Jael as seductive tent-dwelling woman, *especially* when that female gender status is allowed to overcome something that is thereby reduced to a momentary "figuration." Yet, for what seems like a flickering moment, Jael becomes a recognizable figure for those lesbians who orga-

---

12. Butler speaks of gender as an ongoing achievement, compelled by discursive and institutional constraints. It is therefore "a forcible production" but importantly one that cannot be fully determining: "To the extent that gender is an assignment, it is an assignment which is never quite carried out according to expectation, whose addressee never quite inhabits the ideal s/he is compelled to approximate" (Butler 1993, 231).

nize their gender presentation in butch-ish terms but who are not "men" or "wannabe-men," yet are not comfortable with the category of "woman" either—pausing here is important.

THE MOMENT OF GENDERFUCK

The story of Jael is preceded by that of Ehud, and there are clear short-range connections between the two stories.[13] Ehud is a *left*-handed son-of-the-right-hand who, with a phallic thrust—the dagger into the belly—dispatches the fat Eglon. Jael follows precisely in his footsteps, taking an active, sexual role, transformed, through the narrator's careful word choices and imagery, into another figurative rapist, whose thrust (same verb, *tāqaʿ*) of a piercing object into the flesh of the victim has clear phallic connotations. Just as Eglon had been portrayed as gullible, passive, feminized victim, Sisera likewise is subjected to a characterization that portrays him as seduced, sleeping, penetrated victim who, arguably by his own ironic words, is not a man (4:20).[14] In his attention to *double entendre*, Alter argues that the sexual connotations of Jael's "coming" to Sisera and the driving of the tent peg into him constitute "what our own age would call a phallic aggressive act" (1983, 635). The power of the phallic Jael is more fully realized in the poem of Judg 5, in which the apparent maternal associations are absent and Jael is imaged as triumphal assassin.[15] Alter

---

13. On the terminology of short-range, and long-range, connections between the narratives in the book of Judg, see Webb 1987.

14. Sisera's instruction to Jael that, if anyone should ask if there is man here, she should say no (ʿayin) ironically acknowledges both his imminent death and his unmanning. English Bibles routinely miss the ironic, comic point.

15. Several commentators speak of maternal imagery. Fewell and Gunn suggest that "the powerful warrior becomes an aborted fetus. … Destroyed by a woman whom he could have easily overpowered, he falls between her legs, stillborn" (1990, 404; see also 392–93). Pressler suggests that it is Jael's upsetting of "our own deeply rooted expectations about the behavior of maternal women" (2002, 157) that accounts for commentarial unease: "The violation of motherly norms, therefore, is likely the act that most distresses biblical interpreters" (158). See also Ackerman 2000, 39, and Niditch 2008. However, I refer to Jael's "apparent" maternal role because commentators may have overstated some of this maternal imagery too quickly and too unambiguously. O'Connell notes the semantic ambiguity of verbs of "covering," which can also carry the sense of "overpowering." He thus states: "while the description of 4:21 does not use the verb ותבסהו in the sense 'and she overwhelmed him,' the final position of 4:21 in sequence with the preceding portrayals of Jael voluntarily covering Sisera sug-

writes: "the sharp focus of the poem is simply on the powerful figure of Jael the hammerer, standing over the body of Sisera, whose death throes between her legs—he is kneeling, then prostrate—may be, perhaps, an ironic glance at the time-honored martial custom of rape" (635).

However, the use of the left hand is worth unpacking further. Previously I suggested that the realm of the "left" is historically associated with the untoward, with deviance (2006, 174–76); so, by coupling the left with the euphemism of "hand"—i.e., penis[16]—the narrator is able to imply a deviant sexual act accomplished by Ehud as he plunges his weapon into the fleshy Eglon via his *left* "hand." This queer specter, I have suggested, accounts for readerly unease with his exploits. A comparison with Jael warrants similar questions, for the narrator of the Song of Deborah carefully notes that Jael takes the hammer in the right hand (5:26) so that the tent peg, itself having phallic connotations,[17] is an extension of the left "hand" when delivering the phallic thrust into another enemy's soft tissue. Deviancy is to the fore here, both in terms of genderqueer-ness and in terms of sexual activity.

Eric Christianson (2007) has written a paper suggesting that an examination of *film noir* might offer new questions and insights when reading the Jael narrative. In particular, he suggests that it might be fruitful to read the characterization of Jael alongside *film noir*'s figure of the *femme fatale*. His paper makes intriguing connections. However, drawing on the movie connections already mentioned, I make links with a different kind of late twentieth-century movie figure: that of the transgendered killer. If one is willing to straddle the huge cultural gap between such films and the world of Judg 4, one can glimpse an uncanny resemblance with a characteristic scene where viewers have to watch a hapless victim suddenly realize that he has fallen—all too late—not for a "real" woman but for an aggressive FTM

---

gests this imagery" (O'Connell 1996, 112). O'Connell's exegesis finds warrior imagery and indications of active independence running through the entire characterization of Jael, which seems somewhat inconsistent with a commentarial emphasis on images of maternal care or, interestingly, makes for a very ambiguous and anomalous character. On Jael playing "bad mother" to Deborah's "good mother," see Exum 2007.

16. Certainly *yad* can simply mean "hand," but it can also bear the meaning of penis/phallus—a homographic situation that permits wordplay—as noted by Décor 1967 and Ackroyd 1986, 398–426. References where *yad* seems to indicate the penis include Isa 57:8; Song 5:4; and more questionably Jer 5:31; 50:15.

17. Fewell and Gunn note that "'peg' occurs as a phallic euphemism in Aristophanes and the Anthologia Graeca" (1990, 394 n.13).

who will be his undoing. The audience gasps at the abrupt, totally unexpected exposure of the "woman's" penis, captivated/titillated, horrified, or delighted by this dramatic and unforeseen shift in the plot—depending upon where one's allegiances lie. It is a moment of genderfuck; for here is an unintelligible gender—a "female-with-a-penis." Only by assigning the penis a "real" status can one recuperate the two-sex paradigm and declare: Oh, it was a man all the time. However, penis possession is not necessarily an indicator of maleness. Attention to the emerging stories, desires, and experiences of intersex people shows that a penis may be constructed to create a "man" or excised to construct a "woman."[18] Transsexual journeys, with the various configurations of preoperative, part-operative, and postoperative statuses can create gender-indeterminate figurations.

Speaking of Jael as a woman warrior is thus insufficient. Jael is not a *woman* warrior and equally Jael is not a *male* rapist. The narrator has conjured a figure who carries a resonance he could probably never have anticipated for readers in the early twenty-first century. Jael is a figure who unsettles and destabilizes, whose performativity provides one of those unintelligible genders that give the lie to ideas of sex as abiding substance.

THE APPLAUSE

Historically, films featuring the transgender killer have presented the revelation moment as one of dismay or revulsion, according to Sullivan (2000). The gender and/or sexually deviant character is a monstrously marked figure who engenders precious little spectatorial sympathy.[19] Our biblical narrator, however, seems to relish inflicting a similar scene upon the gullible victim—Sisera—and expects it to entertain his readers. I find myself at odds with those who suggest that the narrator intentionally casts Jael in a negative light.[20] The unexpected revelations that feature in the stories of

---

18. Cheryl Chase, founder of the Intersex Society of North America, estimates that "one in 2000 infants is born with an anatomy that refuses to conform to our preconceptions of male and female ... hundreds and thousands of people in this country alone share my experience" (2002, 207).

19. The films mentioned by Sullivan include *The Silence of the Lambs* (1991), *Psycho* (1960), *The Crying Game* (1992), *Deadly Blessing* (1984), *No Way to Treat a Lady* (1968), *Deranged* (1974), *Homicidal* (1962), *Three on a Meathook* (1973), *Relentless* (1993).

20. Klein (1989, 43–46), for example, describes Jael's acts as deviously carried out during the ominous silence of YHWH. So, although Jael is hailed as "most blessed,"

Ehud and Jael, in order to work, must expect a readerly reaction of astonished glee.[21] The Israelite reader, siding with the narrator—if not with Jael—can applaud and enjoy a turn of events, in which such an unexpected figure unmans a cruel villain. The specter of the gender-indeterminate "it"—the term "phallic woman" is smoother but places too much focus on a two-sex binary—is neutralized—neutered?—because "it" does not belong fully within the Israelite community.[22] The storyteller has already carefully established that this figure is a member of the Kenite clan, carefully acknowledged to be at peace with Jabin of Canaan.[23] David Chalcraft

---

Klein does not believe that Jael acts on her own initiative without YHWH's sanction (46). Yee argues that the narrator portrays Jael in a deliberately negative way as "temptress, deceiver, and ultimately a castrator," because he does not want to endorse this image of a woman warrior (1993, 117).

21. As Webb comments, "the killing of Sisera is dwelt upon with savage delight" (1987, 143). Pressler writes: "The biblical authors have no ... qualms about Jael's action. She fulfills God's word" (2002, 158), later adding, "The song extols Jael. ... With unabashed delight, the singers declare, 'Most blessed of women be Jael' (v. 24). ... Both story-teller and singer are concerned with Israel's deliverance, not with abstract compliance to the laws of hospitality" (165). Schneider similarly notes how Jael is twice said to be blessed of women, which is "important because it indicates that the actions Jael is about to take ... are condoned. Despite some modern scholars' trouble with Jael's actions ... the biblical text is clear about then; Jael is 'blessed'" (2000, 92). Indeed, it is worth noting that the writer of the Song of Deborah pointedly redirects against any repugnance the reader might have experienced in respect to Jael's actions toward Sisera's mother and her court.

22. I strongly dislike using "it" to refer to this character. Experiences of being thought of as a "freak" and referred to abusively as an "it" are all too real for those who are working through transsexual journeys, as they are for those who habitually reside in transgender and intersex spaces. Commenting on Butler's 1993 work, Esposito puts it well: "We are not completely free agents in this process of interpellation. What happens when the 'it' is 'girled' but resists, refuses, negotiates this 'girling'? What happens when the 'it' who is hailed by the category 'girl' runs full speed to the category 'boy'? Genderfuck. Hybridity. Border crossing. The 'it' becomes neither 'boy' nor 'girl' but remains 'it' or 'freak' or 'monster'" (2003, 233–34). But I wish to avoid terms that inevitably reinforce Jael's womanliness rather than the liminality. There are gender-neutral alternatives—see the work of Leslie Feinberg (1993, 1998, 2006), for example—but I have not been able to locate something that can adequately stand for not-woman-not-man. The decision to remain with "it" is driven by the desire to make the genderqueerness stand out in this paper and also by its ready demonstration that referring to people as "it" carries notions of stigma and/or anxiety.

23. Commentators have differing views on Jael's ethnicity and/or her political allegiances, but only a few claim an unambiguous Israelite ethnicity. See Klein 1989,

rightly notes that Jael can therefore be praised and exonerated because of her outside status: "Jael's deviance is legitimate, and therefore not deviant, because it is performed within the out-group against the out-group" (1990, 183). Jael is thus not "inside" their self-definition but nonetheless wins a victory on their behalf by destroying a hated enemy. Win-win![24]

The "win," however, can accrue only to those who subscribe to the narratorial pro-Israelite ideology. The message is that these marginals—*they*—can do all the dirty work, for it won't rub off on *us*. A lesbian perspective, however, can question that assumption and suggest, contrarily, that it *does* rub off on the writer and his community. If Jael is a question*ing* rather than a question*able* figure, then some Israelites of this story are shamed and called to account. This much, of course, the narrator is happy to concede, willing to let Jael's actions throw into relief the way some tribes failed to fulfill their social obligations. As Schneider indicates, when the best men are women, Judg 4 and 5 highlights

> what women should *not* be doing in the story where they did it. Women should *not* be capturing the opponent's military commander. When women fight in battles men lose glory. The implication is that men, or maybe especially Israelite men, fought for glory or renown, not, as Deborah stated, because the deity commanded it. (Schneider 2000, 70)

Yes, the tribes are shown up and Barak's cowardice or reluctance is highlighted as an example of the way an Israelite *geber* should *not* act. But is the questioning, once opened, entirely contained? Is there not a danger of excess that the specter of Jael will continue to haunt the imagination in unforeseen ways or depths and compel an uncomfortable worry about whether *any* Israelite *geber* is actually up to the job, whether gender norms

---

43, for an example. The majority suggest foreign status but with ambiguous political loyalties. Lindars, for example, says Jael "was not an Israelite, but a member of a well known nomadic clan who might be willing to help Sisera, a clan that was politically neutral" (1995, 191). As for the connection of Jael with "Heber," this may refer to an allied clan or coalition of villages, rather than a name. See Ackerman 1998, 99; Schneider 2000, 77–78.

24. This is therefore different from the story of Ehud. His deviance—the figurative male-male sexual encounter with Eglon—comes from within a tribe of Israel. However, Ehud is a Benjamite and given the bias that exists in the Dtr history against the Saulide dynasty, the narrator arguably risks this in order to denigrate them. See further Guest 2006, 171–72; Stone 2007, 197.

are really fixable and recoverable once the cat is out of the bag, and how far one's definition of the "inside" is only held in place by the "outside"—an uncomfortable concession. Insofar as Jael is applauded, it remains an uneasy applause.

AN UNEASY APPLAUSE

Jael has long been a person who elicits concerns (see Gunn 2005). At times, it is just the anxiety that is noted, without much recourse to explanation. Soggin, for example, expresses his belief that "the scene remains sinister; even if one could interpret the glorification of the woman as a glorification not so much of her act as of her choice, it cannot but raise negative reactions in us, in the same way as the classical parallels ... caused their audience to shudder" (1981, 78). Trying to offer more by way of explanation, Yee puts it down to the deprivileging of biological maleness. If Deborah and Jael can perform so well as agents of warfare, what is so significant about being born male (1993, 114–17)? A different explanation comes from Niditch, who describes the characterization of Jael as "dripping with phantoms of male fears and insecurities" ([1989] 1999, 312). Niditch appeals to Freudian and Jungian ideas concerning Eros and Thanatos and to David McClelland's work on death as the harlequin seducer/lover. In her view Jael's characterization "manifests a man's fear of both death and his own sexuality, his insecurities, a male fantasy of Eros become Thanatos" (Niditch [1989] 1999, 311–12). But, because the writer turns Jael against the enemy, he and his Israelite readers are shielded somewhat from this anxiety-provoking power. Jael "is turned against the enemy, thereby doubly strengthening the self-image and confidence of the writer himself. What the author fears most he turns outwards against his enemy" (312).

I concur with Niditch and Yee that there is anxiety-provoking power in the story of Jael but suggest that there is more to be said on this topic. Fleming, again, contributes significant insight when she argues that it is the "profoundly disturbing" gender mutability that is the primary reason for readerly unease:

> By making Jael a woman warrior, a character with a liminal and fluid gender identity ... Jael begins to destabilize the genders of those around her—the author has accomplished much more than the humiliation of Sisera and Barak. Jael has been created as the specter of the phallic mother, of the masculine woman, of the castrating vagina dentata. She is

> threatening to the very desire for patriarchal reinforcement that, accord-
> ing to Yee, created her. Jael is almost the personification of gender blur,
> that force most threatening to the hierarchical structure of patriarchy. If
> you can't tell for sure which people are men, and which are women, how
> can power structures based on gender inequality be maintained? This,
> then, is the source of the phallocentric reader's unease about the charac-
> ter of Jael. The problem is not that she breaks with laws of hospitality, or
> even that she is a rapist, quite. The problem is that in doing those things,
> and in order to do those things, she destabilizes both her own gender
> construction and the gender identities of others. (Fleming 2005, 11)

I am uncomfortable with all the female pronouns in the above quotation, but Fleming's ideas take us in the right direction. If we return to film
theory again, Hanson's analysis of *The Crying Game* notes the moment
of sudden revelation when the male protagonist, Fergus, discovers that
the body of someone he has hitherto considered female has a penis. This
prompts a category crisis wherein "the *presence* of the penis has the potential to institute crisis rather than to stand for the socio-symbolic order. The
presence of the penis thus brings into question the concept of 'a defining
term' between the sexes, and brings into question the relative gender positions of masculine or feminine within the symbolic" (Hanson 1999, 64).
Reading Jael against the genre of transgender film, and against this comment in particular, causes us to look around at the characters that populate
Judg 4 and 5 and wonder whether *geber* can ever be fixed so unthinkingly
to "men" ever again and, simultaneously, whether our certainties about
"women" can ever be the same. This much, a lesbian perspective relishes;
the genderqueer moment offers far more than the original storyteller ever
expected, resonating with centuries-later readers who can applaud longer
and louder than his original—probable—male audience ever could, undoing both them and the narrator himself who is hoist with his own petard.

A Lesbian Celebration of Jael

One might be forgiven for imagining that we must have reached a point
in history where some of those who are thought to belong to the category of "women" are free enough to inhabit alternative genders without
serious repercussion. In the U.K., despite the unrelenting existence of
"women's" and "menswear" sections of department stores, "women" are
free to inhabit clothing predominantly sold to "men" (I object strongly to

the label "menswear"); find jobs in locations that were traditionally not theirs; live in committed relationships with other "women," which was, until very recently the legal preserve of "men"; and partake generally in what society has on offer. But this belies the reality of a world where butch-lesbian and transgender living continues not to be readily catered for—at best—and stigmatized—at worst; where tomboyism, tolerated while the child is young, is punished "when it appears to be the sign of extreme male identification ... and when it threatens to extend beyond childhood and into adolescence" (Halberstam 1998, 6). It is thus not just the difficult practicalities of trying to find clothing that feels appropriate and actually fits, though this is sometimes hard enough, but the deeper issues of shame and dysphoria that can accompany one's transgression of expected norms.[25]

Genderqueer readers, especially perhaps those for whom the Bible remains a significant and/or sacred text, might find Jael's occupation of a not-man-not-woman ground not only of interest but a joyous and unexpected treasure within a canon of texts that are often used to provide ammunition against their choices. Given that Jael's liminality is celebrated, and that this is a powerful performance, Jael seems to provide an unforeseen biblical character for those butch lesbians who desire to wear their genderqueerness with pride. For this to occur, the genderqueerness of Jael needs to remain uppermost in this interpretation. It is not a monolithic, unified "woman" that we are celebrating here but one who breaks the borders between male and female and reveals that all gendered acts are performative (though there has not been space in this paper to develop this latter aspect).

But before Jael is "lesbianized," Jael's resonance for transgender and/or queer rebels who may be inhabiting indeterminate spaces, for those on a journey of transitioning between genders, and for transsexuals who have completed reassignment should be noted. Given how we/they have to swim against the strong current of heteronormativity and its waves of overt hostility, we can share an interest in the text, but I do not wish to assume uncritically that I can assimilate all into an "us," a fictional reading community with shared interests. So I acknowledge my own butch lesbian stake in the text while acknowledging that there may also be a

---

25. I acknowledge the need to balance the depictions of the pain, shame, and dysphoria with more positive narrations of lesbian, transgender, and transsexual experiences as noted in Detloff 2006.

differently negotiated stake for those who inhabit, in diverse ways, transgender spaces.

Here then is the issue of borders. Having been critical of feminist biblical studies for suppressing, unconsciously or otherwise, the voices of lesbian feminists, lesbian interpretation should not render invisible the specifics of transgender and transsexual histories, communities, and acts of interpretation. Jael cannot be claimed as a "lesbian" hero without acknowledging the potential appeal to those communities also. This is particularly the case if biblical studies is going to avoid the hotly contested territory wars, the hurt and the antagonisms, that have been evident in other disciplines.

Speaking from my context as one of Calhoun's lesbians who have little option but to "exit the category 'woman' altogether" (2000, 32), I find something appealing in the story of Jael: a resonant, celebratory figure that feminist readings to date have not quite been able to imagine. I appreciate Niditch's recognition that Jael's "tale is rich in images of directed action, self-assertion, and consciousness on the part of the underdog" and that Jael can offer "a powerfully charged model for all marginals, in particular, women" ([1989] 1999, 313). But when I read that claim, I wondered to which group I belonged.[26] Are butch lesbians already part of the "women" group, or are they part of a different "marginal" community? And who decides? I would argue that any attempts to incorporate lesbians into the feminist home by expanding/reshaping what "woman" might mean/include may be wrong-headed. Such attempts, while well-meaning, would not recognize that some lesbians have already announced their defection from that category.

One would also have to query how far feminists would be willing to broaden the category anyway. Calhoun argues that in order to include the lesbian specifically, feminism would have to open up that binary between woman and man so that all those who occupy the not-woman-not-man space are embraced. For Calhoun, this would mean the inclusion of *all* those who inhabit the space of female masculinity, whether they be or male-to-female transsexuals (MTFs), transvestites—gay and straight; and that these subjects would be seen "*not* as men or imitation women, but as the third term between gender binaries. In an opened frame, these male bodies could no longer be constructed as Other to women. They would

---

26. There is a play here on a significant paper by Vicinus entitled " 'They Wonder to Which Sex I Belong?' The Historical Roots of the Modern Lesbian Identity" (1992).

be fully feminist subjects" (2000, 73). She suspects that the cost would be too high for most feminists. This is a suspicion that Wilchins extends to lesbian feminists. Lesbian communities, writes Wilchins, "have remained deeply unreceptive to the new barbarians at the gate—F-to-Ms, M-to-Fs, passing women, cross-dressers, drag kings and queens, and tranz youth— who seem to threaten the very foundation of Woman" (2002, 58). But, in my view, there is also the counterquery of whether that cost of opening the borders might actually be too high also for transsexuals who might not wish to become "fully feminist subjects."

But at What Cost …

Before finalizing any views on Jael as a celebratory, resonant figure for lesbian readers, one has to consider some other significant factors. A positive evaluation of Jael's performance comes at a cost, and this concerns further boundaries that the editors encouraged writers to trouble: the different rubrics, such as race, religion, nation, and class, that are often kept separate inside biblical scholarship from the hermeneutics of sexuality. What does one do with the racial and class ideologies that allow Jael to be praised?

It has already been noted that it is as ethnic outsider, marginal, and "other" that Jael's presentation is celebrated. The narrator can shame Barak and some of the tribes simultaneously by the creation of a character whose deviant act is placed *outside* Israelite ethnic borders. Randall Bailey (1995) reminds us that it is often the case that the one who is "out" is distinguished on the basis of their practices of a taboo sexual act. Jael appears to fall into this category. Lesbian, transgender, and transsexual readers might not find much in the way of liberation when Jael is redeemed by virtue of being placed outside the privileged insider group. Rather, they might ask: What's new? Here we are again, operating as the disruptive category, the marginal brought for a moment to the center, only to be returned again to the margins when the desired job is done. While a range of readers might experience enjoyment of Jael's disruptive performance, the queer reader— be they lesbian, transgender, or transsexual—cannot easily return to the safety of the "normal" world after the scenic entertainment. Again, a film critic's observations are helpful. Harry Benshoff's paper on "The Monster and the Homosexual" notes how

> some depictions of queer monsters undoubtedly conflate and reinforce certain sexist or homophobic fears within the public sphere. For specta-

tors of all types, the experience of watching a horror film or monster
movie might be understood as similar to that of the Carnival as it has
been theorized by Bakhtin, wherein the conventions of normality are
ritualistically overturned within a prescribed period of time in order
to celebrate the lure of the deviant. ... However, while straight participants in such experiences usually return to their daylight worlds, both
the monster and the homosexual are permanent residents of shadowy
spaces: at worst caves, castles and closets, and at best a marginalized and
oppressed position within the cultural hegemony. Queer viewers are
thus more likely than straight ones to experience the monster's plight in
more personal, individualized terms. (Benshoff 2004, 66)

There is, accordingly, a price to be paid for the enjoyment of being represented as the subversive figure. For all the claims I have made for excess,
whereby Jael's actions do rub off on the privileged group, one has to weigh
whether the possibility of this is enough to merit a positive reclamation of
Jael's story.

Then there is the fact that Jael's otherness is celebrated at the expense
of siding against the more archetypal racial, symbolic Other: the Canaanites.[27] Judges 5 deliberately contrasts Sisera's fate with the expectations of
the Canaanite women waiting at the window for their men to return. In
5:20 Sisera's mother asks her female advisors[28] why the men have been
delayed. The ironic answer is that each man must be enjoying a *raḥam
raḥămātayim* and collecting booty of embroidered and dyed cloths. As
Schneider comments, *raḥam raḥămātayim* is a "graphic" term "from
the root *r-ḥ-m* whose primary meaning is, 'to be soft, wide,' leading to,

---

27. Lemche states that the writers of the Hebrew Bible were "far removed from
historical reality," so much so that "it must be stressed that ... [they] never tried to
write or to publish historical information about these peoples: instead of this they
actually 'played' with strange and foreign ethnic names ... in order to populate the
land of Canaan" (1991, 100). He speaks of the Canaanites as the "bad guys" of the
Hebrew Bible, foils who "owe their existence to a construction made by the biblical
historians" (168).

28. Schneider objects to translations that dilute the word *śārôt* to "ladies," for
"the term carries the connotation of someone in a high office with a fair amount of
power, exactly like Sisera" (2000, 62). In the masculine, the implication is of "some
governmental capacity, usually as advisors to political officers. The one time the term
appears in the feminine plural it suddenly refers to a group of women sitting around
whining" (95). Schneider thus justifiably translates *śārôt* as "advisors." Others have
"princesses"—see Moore 1895; Gray 1967.

'female cavities,' often translated as, 'womb'" (2000, 96). In English this has been gallantly translated: "a damsel or two" (KJV), "a maiden or two" (RSV), "a woman or two" (GNB), a "girl or two" (NIV). This is simply misleading. The narrator had words for "woman" or "maiden" at his disposal but opts for "womb or two." The crudeness of the language has long been noticed. Moore's commentary notes its intentional use and he suggests this translation: "A wench or a couple of them for each man" (1895, 168). Maybe "wench" had connotations not so apparent today—though Niditch seems to see some value in it since it is noted in her 2008 commentary. One commentator who tries to do a modern job of grasping the rawness of the language suggests the translation of "one or two broads/bikes" (Younger 2002, 156). This does reflect the coarseness of the language, but it unnecessarily casts aspersions on the women—to be labeled a "bike" implies that the woman is always up for intercourse by any man. So, although it is unpalatable, I wonder if a more realistic translation would be "a cunt or two for every dick." This catches the fleshy reference to women's bodily parts and also the euphemistic connotations of "for each *head* of a *geber*" (5:30). Such an understanding of "head" is implied in the scare quotations supplied by Fewell and Gunn: "Sisera found a 'womb' for his 'head' alright, but not one that would take his abuse. Instead of capturing a womb, a womb captured him. And thus the singers celebrate poetic justice" (1990, 408). An advantage of such a vulgar translation is that it jars strongly with the fact that it is being put into the mouth of a woman of pedigree. One does not expect members of the ruling class to use such crudities and such a translation readily exposes the hard, scathing dislike the narrator encourages for these Canaanite Others.

The salient point of this discussion is that the narrator is encouraging the reader to have no sympathy for women who can muse about the activities of their menfolk with such little concern for those who are the victims of their rape. Accordingly this text enables a positive evaluation of Jael, an outsider tent-dweller who nonetheless acts on behalf of Israel, by encouraging us to read against the higher class Canaanite women.

O'Connell expresses this clearly:

Whereas the sympathy evoked for Sisera through Jael's betrayal of his trust ... may have invited repugnance at Jael's methods, in 5:28–30 the callousness of the foreign nobility is exposed for the first time through a "woman and the window" type-scene. The satire is pointedly anti-

Canaanite ... and all the more so because such callousness is depicted
even among the noble ladies. (O'Connell 1996, 131–32)

Here a shared feature between feminist and lesbian strategies comes to
the fore. As with feminist approaches, a lesbian perspective is alert to the
way women are set against each other within biblical texts and the ways
in which readers are routinely expected to read against their own interests. While some lesbians may not be "women," they can be fiercely pro-
women, emotionally, physically, politically, and intellectually. The narratorial encouragement to side against Othered women is thus resisted.

A transsexual perspective arguably has more to resist. Janice Raymond
(1979) infamously privileged the "woman-born-woman" over the MTF and
questioned the allegiances of transsexuals, suggesting that the latter will do
the bidding of the "rulers of patriarchy" if and when the rulers decide to
control and contain the lesbian feminists. If Jael is redeemed via an expression of revulsion for Canaanite women, it puts such readers in precisely the
dilemma Raymond imposes: a transsexual hero at the cost of other—natural?—women. There is thus an added edge that has to be negotiated.[29]

It is a difficult equation. The costs of appreciating Jael's genderqueer
performance may well outweigh the benefits. Feminist readings have had
to face the same quandary. Ultimately, for all the entertainment value that
Fewell and Gunn find in Deborah and Jael's characterization, they close
with the dismal acknowledgment that Deborah's verdict—"So may they
perish ..."—leaves us with "a woman in a man's world, her voice harden-
ing, merging with a man's voice" (1990, 409). Accordingly, it is not just the
racial othering that requires thought but the feminist insight that Jael, like
Deborah, remains trapped in a patriarchal framework that honors the use
of violence against the other. In their view, Jael does not break the mold
but simply reinforces it.

Niditch, as we have seen, is a little more positive. In her view the story
also "has important resonances both for feminist appropriators and all
marginals" ([1989] 1999, 312). The writer, she goes on to suggest, uses "the
permanent marginal in Israelite patriarchal culture" as a "lens through
which to appreciate and sympathize with poorly armed Israelite peasant
revolters who face well-armed Canaanite soldiers of the establishment"
(312). This leaves open the opportunity for Jael to become a "powerfully

---

29. For an interesting take on this in relation to another biblical story—that of
Jezebel—see Kolakowski 2000.

charged model" for marginals, including lesbian, transgender, and trans-sexual readers, but only by a) celebrating one's marginality and the disturbing ripples this can create without being concerned about being left in the margins; and b) not worrying about how the Canaanite women are portrayed. When postcolonial critics, such as Kim (2007) rightly call us to account for the imaging of the Other in biblical texts, we cannot afford to let the representation of the Canaanites be a casualty of an approach that liberates some "marginals" at the expense of others.

CONCLUSION

In this paper I have tried to carve out a lesbian-specific engagement with the story of Jael. I have suggested, first, that existing commentary, while clearly recognizing the gender play at work in Judg 4 and 5, recuperates the femaleness of Jael far too readily. Second, the existing commentary has not adequately dealt with the fact that Jael's acts of seduction or maternal womanly attributes are equally performative of a sex that has no abiding substance. Third, the anxiety Jael provokes, the disturbing ripples that are produced, are not to do with gender reversal but gender confusion: a category crisis is prompted. Finally, I have suggested that the story of Jael might have a resonance for lesbian readers that they would not have expected to find in the Bible—which can be a joyous moment of discovery. However, this is quickly undercut when one considers the costs involved in reclaiming Jael as some kind of lesbian hero.

In making these suggestions, I have drawn on the conventional tools of biblical studies and been informed by a range of commentaries and articles on this text; but a lesbian approach is not one that tries to get at the authorial meaning of the text or grapple with historical contexts and assumed motivations for Jael's actions. Like feminism, it has a different focus. It is about exposing, critiquing, being resistant, imagining differently; it is about politics and transformation. However, though it shares many interests with feminism, it is not at ease within feminist biblical scholarship because of its site-specific interests, concerns, and dialogue partners. It can have a feminist edge and owe much of its theoretical development to feminist theory and the results of feminist biblical scholarship, but it asserts its own voice that can, sometimes, be at odds with existing feminist interpretation.

Accordingly, it requires new dialogue partners: those in lesbian studies such as Calhoun, queer theorists such as Butler, and critics within the domain of queer cinema such as Hanson. Disciplinary boundaries between conventional biblical studies and other types of scholarship are thus rendered permeable. Trying to figure out where "home" is for the lesbian feminist reader of biblical texts may be looking for something elusive. The interdisciplinary nature of lesbian and queer engagement with biblical texts might have more in common with a nomadic existence.

When Rosi Braidotti speaks of the nomad, she speaks of one who drifts in and out, who makes live connections, who does not stay long enough to become immovable, but who, in coming back again and again, can form connections rather than identifications. In fact, it is only through journeying that one can see where one has forged identities because identity, she suggests, is retrospective: "we can draw accurate maps, indeed, but only of where we have already been and consequently no longer are" (Braidotti 1994, 35).

Braidotti's concept of the nomadic subject is attractive for one who is sometimes in and sometimes outside the category "woman," sometimes a staunch feminist and sometimes critical of feminism's blind spots, sometimes queer and sometimes frustrated with the white male dominance within queer theory. The nomad does respect boundaries, in fact the nomad is acutely aware of them and the way they impinge, but the nomad's simultaneous awareness of the "nonfixity of boundaries" lends an "intense desire to go on trespassing, transgressing" (Braidotti 1994, 36).

Compared with my training in biblical studies with its emphasis on *ex-* rather than *eis*egesis, with its emphasis on objectivity, this lesbian reader has certainly gone trespassing on other people's territory, coming back to biblical studies with new, unexpected friends to ride roughshod over some treasured notions. To be honest, it doesn't always feel comfortable, but then, perhaps one can only be expected to feel somewhat *queer* about the whole enterprise.

WORKS CONSULTED

Ackerman, Susan. 1998. *Warrior, Dancer, Seductress, Queen: Women in Judges and Biblical Israel.* New York: Doubleday.

———. 2000. What If Judges Had Been Written by a Philistine? *BibInt* 8:33–41.

Ackroyd, Peter R. 1986. יד. Pages 397–426 in vol. 5 of *Theological Dictionary of the Old Testament.* Edited by G. Johannes Botterweck and

Helmer Ringgren. Translated by David E. Green. Grand Rapids: Eerdmans.

Alter, Robert. 1983. From Line to Story: Biblical Verse. *Poetics Today* 4:615–37.

———. 1985. *The Art of Biblical Poetry*. New York: Basic Books.

Bailey, Randall C. 1995. They're Nothing but Incestuous Bastards: The Polemical Use of Sex and Sexuality in Hebrew Canon Narratives. Pages 121–38 in Segovia and Tolbert 1995a.

Benshoff, Harry. 2004. The Monster and the Homosexual. Pages 63–74 in *Queer Cinema: The Film Reader*. Edited by H. Benshoff and S. Griffin. New York: Routledge.

Bergman, David, ed. 1993. *Camp Grounds: Style and Homosexuality*. Amherst: University of Massachusetts Press.

Boling, Robert G. 1975. *Judges: A New Translation with Introduction and Commentary*. AB 6A. New York: Doubleday.

Bos, Johanna W. H. 1988. Out of the Shadows: Genesis 38; Judges 4:17–22; Ruth 3. *Semeia* 42:37–67.

Braidotti, Rosi. 1994. *Nomadic Subjects: Embodiment and Sexual Difference in Contemporary Feminist Theory*. New York: Columbia University Press.

Butler, Judith. 1990. *Gender Trouble: Feminism and the Subversion of Identity*. New York: Routledge.

———. 1993. *Bodies that Matter: On the Discursive Limits of "Sex."* New York: Routledge.

Calhoun, Cheshire. 2000. *Feminism, the Family, and the Politics of the Closet*. Oxford: Oxford University Press.

Chalcraft, David. 1990. Deviance and Legitimate Action in the Book of Judges. Pages 177–201 in *The Bible in Three Dimensions: Essays in Celebration of Forty Years of Biblical Studies in the University of Sheffield*. Edited by D. J. A. Clines, S. E. Fowl, and S. E. Porter. JSOTSup 87. Sheffield: Sheffield Academic Press.

Chase, Cheryl. 2002. Affronting Reason. Pages 204–19 in Nestle, Howell, and Wilchins 2002.

Christianson, Eric S. 2005. The Big Sleep: Strategic Ambiguity in Judges 4–5 and in Classic "Film Noir." *SBL Forum* 3.4. Online: http://www .sbl-site.org/publications/article.aspx?articleId=393.

Clines, David J. A. 1995. David the Man: The Construction of Masculinity in the Hebrew Bible. Pages 212–43 in idem, *Interested Parties: The Ide-*

ology of Writers and Readers of the Hebrew Bible. JSOTSup 205. GCT 1. Sheffield: Sheffield Academic Press.

———. 1998. *Ecce Vir*, or, Gendering the Son of Man. Pages 352–75 in *Biblical Studies/Cultural Studies: The Third Sheffield Colloquium*. Edited by J. C. Exum and S. D. Moore. JSOTSup 266. Sheffield: Sheffield Academic Press.

Décor, Fitzgerald. 1967. Two Special Meanings of the Word in Biblical Hebrew. *JSS* 12:230–40.

Detloff, Madelyn. 2006. Gender Please, without the Gender Police: Rethinking Pain in Archetypal Narratives of Butch, Transgender, and FTM Masculinity. Pages 87–105 in *Challenging Lesbian Norms: Intersex, Transgender, Intersectional, and Queer Perspectives*. Edited by A. P. Aragón. Binghamton: Harrington Park Press.

Esposito, Jennifer. 2003. The Performance of White Masculinity in "Boys Don't Cry": Identity, Desire, (Mis)Recognition. *Cultural Studies: Critical Methodologies* 3:229–41.

Exum, J. Cheryl. 2007. Feminist Criticism: Whose Interests Are Being Served? Pages 65–89 in Yee 2007.

Feinberg, Leslie. 1993. *Stone Butch Blues*. Firebrand Books.

———. 1998. *Trans Liberation: Beyond Pink and Blue*. Boston: Beacon.

———. 2006. *Drag King Dreams*. New York: Carroll & Graf.

Fewell, Danna Nolan, and David M. Gunn. 1990. Controlling Perspectives: Women, Men and the Authority of Violence in Judges 4 and 5. *JAAR* 58:389–411.

Finkelstein, Israel. 1996. Ethnicity and Origin of the Iron I Settlers in the Highlands of Canaan: Can the Real Israel Stand Up? *BA* 59:198–212.

Finkelstein, I., and Silberman, N. 2001. *The Bible Unearthed: Archaeology's New Vision of Ancient Israel*. London: Simon & Schuster.

Fleming, Robyn C. 2005. Jael's Gender: A Story of Appropriation. Online: http://revena.dreamwidth.org/128023.html?#cutid1.

Fraser, Antonia. 1990. *The Warrior Queens: The Legends and the Lives of Women Who Have Led Their Nations in War*. New York: Vantage.

Gabler, J. P. (1787) 1980. An Oration: On the Proper Distinction between Biblical and Dogmatic Theology and the Specific Objectives of Each. *SJT* 33:133–58.

Garber, Marjorie. 1992. *Vested Interests: Cross-Dressing and Cultural Anxiety*. New York: Routledge.

Gibson, Michelle, and Deborah T. Meem. 2005. Reforming Transformation: Reflections of a Lesbian Academic Couple." *Journal of Lesbian Studies* 9 (4):107–28.

Gottwald, Norman K. 1979. *The Tribes of Yahweh*. Maryknoll, N.Y.: Orbis.

Gray, John. 1967. *Joshua, Judges and Ruth*. NCB. London: Nelson.

Guest, Deryn. 2006. Judges. Pages 167–89 in *The Queer Bible Commentary*. Edited by Deryn Guest et al. London: SCM.

———. 2008. Looking Lesbian at the Bathing Bathsheba. *BibInt* 16:227–63.

Gunn, David M. 2005. *Judges*. BBC. Malden, Mass.: Blackwell.

Halberstam, Judith. 1998. *Female Masculinity*. Durham, N.C.: Duke University Press.

Hanselman, Stephen W. 1989. Narrative Theory, Ideology and Transformation in Judges 4. Pages 95–112 in *Anti-Covenant: Counter-Reading Women's Lives in the Hebrew Bible*. Edited by M. Bal. JSOTSup 81. BL 22. Sheffield: Almond Press.

Hanson, Helen. 1999. The Figure in Question: The Transvestite Character as a Narrative Strategy in "The Crying Game." Pages 49–66 in *The Body's Perilous Pleasures: Dangerous Desires and Contemporary Culture*. Edited by M. Aaron. Edinburgh: Edinburgh University Press.

Kim, Uriah Y. 2007. Who Is the Other in the Book of Judges? Pages 161–82 in Yee 2007.

Klein, Lillian. 1989. *The Triumph of Irony*. JSOTSup 68. BL 14. Sheffield: Almond Press.

Koch, Tim. 2001. Cruising as Methodology: Homoeroticism and the Scriptures. Pages 169–80 in *Queer Commentary on the Hebrew Bible*. Edited by K. Stone. JSOTSup 334. London: Sheffield Academic Press.

Kolakowski, Victoria S. 2000. Throwing a Party: Patriarchy, Gender, and the Death of Jezebel. Pages 103–14 in *Take Back the Word: A Queer Reading of the Bible*. Edited by R. E. Goss and M. West. Cleveland, Ohio: Pilgrim.

Lemche, Niels Peter. 1985. *Early Israel: Anthropological and Historical Studies on the Israelite Society before the Monarchy*. VTSup 37. Leiden: Brill.

———. 1991. *The Canaanites and Their Land: The Tradition of the Canaanites*. JSOTSup 110. Sheffield: Sheffield Academic Press.

———. 1994. Is It Still Possible to Write a History of Ancient Israel? *SJOT* 8:165–90.

Lindars, Barnabas. 1995. *Judges 1–5: A New Translation and Commentary*. Edited by A. D. H. Mayes. Edinburgh: T&T Clark.

Meyers, Carol. 1988. *Discovering Eve: Ancient Israelite Women in Context.* New York: Oxford University Press.

Moore, George F. 1895. *A Critical and Exegetical Commentary on Judges.* Edinburgh: T&T Clark.

Nestle, Joan, Clare Howell, and Riki Wilchins, eds. 2002. *Genderqueer: Voices from beyond the Sexual Binary.* Los Angeles and New York: Alyson Books.

Niditch, Susan. (1989) 1999. Eroticism and Death in the Tale of Jael. Pages 43–57 in *Gender and Difference in Ancient Israel.* Edited by Peggy Day. Minneapolis: Fortress. Repr. as pages 305–16 in *Women in the Hebrew Bible: A Reader.* Edited by Alice Bach. London: Routledge.

———. 2008. *Judges: A Commentary.* OTL. Louisville: Westminster John Knox.

O'Connell, Robert H. 1996. *The Rhetoric of the Book of Judges.* Leiden: Brill.

Patte, Daniel. 1995. *Ethics of Biblical Interpretation: A Re-evaluation.* London: Westminster.

———. 1999. The Guarded Personal Voice of a Male European-American Biblical Scholar. Pages 12–24 in *The Personal Voice in Biblical Interpretation.* Edited by I. R. Kitzberger. London: Routledge.

Pressler, Carolyn. 2002. *Joshua, Judges and Ruth.* Westminster Bible Companion. Louisville: Westminster John Knox.

Raymond, Janice. 1979. *The Transsexual Empire: The Making of the She-Male.* Boston: Beacon Press.

Reich, June. 1999. Genderfuck: The Law of the Dildo. Pages 254–65 in *Camp: Queer Aesthetics and the Performing Subject; A Reader.* Edited by F. Cleto. Ann Arbor: University of Michigan Press.

Runions, Erin. 1998. Zion is Burning: "Gender Fuck" in Micah. *Semeia* 82:225–46.

Schneider, Tammi J. 2000. *Judges: Studies in Hebrew Narrative and Poetry.* BerOl. Collegeville, Minn.: Liturgical Press.

Schüssler Fiorenza, Elisabeth. 1988. The Ethics of Interpretation: De-centering Biblical Scholarship. *JBL* 107:3–17.

Segovia, Fernando F. 2000a. *Decolonizing Biblical Studies: A View From The Margins.* New York: Orbis.

———. 2000b. *Interpreting Beyond Borders.* Sheffield: Sheffield Academic Press.

Segovia, Fernando F., and Mary Tolbert, eds. 1995a. *Reading from This Place, Volume 1: Social Location and Biblical Interpretation in the United States.* Minneapolis: Fortress.

———. 1995b. *Reading from This Place, Volume 2: Social Location and Biblical Interpretation in Global Perspective.* Minneapolis: Fortress.

Soggin, J. Alberto. 1981. *Judges.* London: SCM Press.

Stone, Ken. 2007. Gender Criticism: The Un-Manning of Abimelech. Pages 183–201 in Yee 2007.

Sullivan, K. E. 2000. Ed Gein and the Figure of the Transgendered Serial Killer. Pages 38–47 in *JumpCut: A Review of Contemporary Media* 43. Online: http://www.ejumpcut.org/archive/onlinessays/JC43folder/EdGein.html.

Thompson, Thomas L. 1992. *Early History of the Israelite People from the Written and Archaeological Sources.* Leiden: Brill.

Vicinus, Martha. 1992. "They Wonder to Which Sex I Belong?" The Historical Roots of the Modern Lesbian Identity. *Feminist Studies* 18:467–97.

Webb, Barry G. 1987. *The Book of Judges: An Integrated Reading.* JSOTSup 46. Sheffield: Sheffield Academic Press.

Wilchins, Riki. 2002. Deconstructing Trans. Pages 55–63 in Nestle, Howell, and Wilchins 2002.

Wolde, Ellen van. 1996. Deborah and Ya'el in Judges 4. Pages 283–95 in *On Reading Prophetic Texts: Gender-Specific and Related Studies in Memory of Fokkelien van Dijk-Hemmes.* Edited by B. Becking and M. Dijkstra. Leiden: Brill.

Yee, Gale A. 1993. By the Hand of a Woman: The Metaphor of the Woman Warrior in Judges 4. *Semeia* 61:99–132.

———, ed. 2007. *Judges and Method: New Approaches in Biblical Studies.* 2nd ed. Minneapolis: Fortress.

Younger, K. Lawson. 2002. *Judges/Ruth.* NIV Application Commentary. Grand Rapids: Zondervan

From Disgust to Humor: Rahab's Queer Affect[*]

Erin Runions

Disgust, abhorrence, abomination. How do these strong feelings get
attached to nonheteronormative sex? Why is "That's disgusting!" such a
knee-jerk response to unfamiliar sexual practices? It might be obvious to
point to the Bible as having cultivated readers' disgust for certain forms
of sexuality, but it might also be worth dissecting precisely how disgust is
biblically generated. A central premise of this paper is that contemporary
disgust toward nonheteronormative sexuality in the United States is conditioned by the racialization of certain representations of sexuality in the
Bible, even where the biblical heritage and/or racialization is no longer
obvious. Such an approach is centrally informed by feminist, queer, and
postcolonial critique, which have analyzed the persistence of racialization
through sexualization and nonheteronormativity (for a small sampling
see J. Butler 1993; Carby 1987; Ferguson 2004; Gilman 1985; Hammonds
1997; Muñoz 1999; Puar 2007; Yeğenoğlu 1998). It is worth highlighting
that biblical descriptions of disgusting sexuality cannot be separated from
racialization and that texts about Canaanites are key in the ongoing production of disgust over nonnormative sexuality. Following from Randall
Bailey's trenchant assessment of the biblical "sexualization of the indigene"
(2005, 20), I might borrow one of queer theorist Roderick Ferguson's concept phrases to say that in the Tanak, Canaanites are *racialized as nonheteronormative* (2004, 27). The task I set for myself is to consider how the
biblical text itself participates in generating disgust through the racialization of nonheteronormativity and at the same time might be deployed to

* I am grateful to Robert Culley, Chris Guzaitis, Francis Landy, Katrina Van Heest,
and the Feminist Theories and the Study of Religion group at the Chicago Divinity
School (Larisa Reznik, Marsaura Shukla, Sarah Imhoff, James Hoke, and Kristel Clay-
ville) for their most helpful engagements with versions of this paper.

disrupt that affect. My purpose is to consider how another biblically produced affect—laughter—can be put to work against the Bible's generation of disgust over racialized sexuality.

To this end, I will reread the story of Rahab, the Canaanite prostitute in Jericho, as a sort of wedge or crossover text that might shift disgust with racialized nonheteronormativity to an appreciation of it through humor. In Josh 2, Rahab hides from her king two Israelite spies who have come to her house at the beginning of their mission. Presciently recognizing Yahweh's power and victory over Jericho, she negotiates with the spies for the safety of herself and her family in the coming conquest, before letting them down out the window and sending them back to Joshua. As others have noticed before me, the details of the story are amusing, and Rahab is valorized by the text. Rahab is racialized as nonheteronormative in the story, to be sure, but the usual disgust with "whoring" Canaanite sexual behavior is not present, either for the story's narrator or its interpreters. Given that the affective response to Rahab is not the usual, it might be used to disrupt the disgust that is so prevalent elsewhere in the biblical text.

As I will argue, the story of Rahab revalues the usual affect that buttresses depictions of the Canaanites in the Tanak: it uses humor to represent the racialized nonheteronormative subject positively, and it undercuts the positive aura surrounding the Israelites' conquest. In particular I want to pick up on the suggestion made by Yair Zakovitch that Rahab's story is a humorous one built from various traditional folktales, though I find the punch line in different places than does Zakovitch. Yet this work cannot be done without examining the troubling way in which Rahab collaborates with the conquest of her city, as articulated by postcolonial scholars such as Randall Bailey (2005), Musa Dube (2006), Laura Donaldson (2006), Judith McKinlay (1999), and Kwok Pui-lan (2006). Disrupting disgust with the Canaanites requires the interrogation of the commitments to conquest that allow for this response. So, picking up on the scholarly consensus that there are many redactional layers in this text, I will posit an entertaining earlier indigenous tale that undercuts the story's impulse to subjugation and genocide. By "earlier indigenous tale," I mean one that may have existed in oral and written form before Israelite identity came to be textually and/or physically carved out from Canaanite identity. In other words, one plausible redactional layer of Josh 2 comically works against the later conquest narrative and the Israelite identity construct it supports, right at the very start of its narration. This earlier story disrupts the affective values of the story's final form, with attendant emotions circulating around conquest of the Canaanites, holy war (חרם), the divine warrior, and even Rahab's own heroism.[1]

My reading responds to Ken Stone's call to queer the Canaanite (2004) and Marcella Althaus-Reid's reading of Rahab as queer woman of wisdom (2007). In accord with queer theory's efforts to question identity categories, Stone helpfully shows how the term "Canaanite" is similar in many ways to the term "homosexual," in that it acts as a discursive outside to a normative identity position (Israelite, heterosexual). On closer examination, however, the line between inside and outside is not as clear as asserted; it is not always so easy to tell Canaanite from Israelite or make straightforward divisions on sexual identity. "Canaanites" and "homosexuals" are queer in that they blur lines of identity and power relations between self and other (129–31). Along these lines, Rahab is a queer figure in the way that she troubles sexual- and ethnic-identity divides (Althaus-Reid 2007). Most obviously, she does not conform to biblically sanctioned demands of heteronormativity (associated as those demands are with monogamous and reproductive heterosexual relations). She perhaps engages in heterosexual sex acts (though the text is ambiguous on this point), but she is not *heteronormative*. Further, as Michael Carden has observed and as I will elaborate below, the queer functioning of Rahab's marginal sexual status also critiques a clear-cut Israelite identity (2006, 157–58). I will suggest that in her borderline position (sexually, ethnically, textually, decorously), Rahab queerly challenges the genocidal ideology of the set of texts scholars call the Deuteronomistic History (Joshua–Kings). Such a reading does not "rescue" Rahab from her disturbing collaborator status for queer purposes as much as it unsettles any bid for finding heroes, including queer heroes.

This approach to Josh 2 is partly informed by Ferguson's treatment of canonical sociological discourse about African Americans in the United States in his book *Aberrations in Black: Toward a Queer of Color Critique* (2004). Ferguson's work suggests a way to think about critically interacting with the much older canonical discourse of the Bible. Ferguson reads African American cultural forms, in particular novels, "as both within and outside canonical genealogies, pointing to the ruptural possibilities of those forms" (26). He argues that canonical sociological discourse in

---

1. Here I am informed by Culley's contention, with respect to discerning the stages of textual development, that one can speak more readily about degrees of plausibility than probabilities (1984, 32).

the United States has done much to racialize African Americans through nonheteronormativity. In his words, sociological "canonical formations ... produce racial, gender, and sexual difference to articulate our relationship to the normative" (63). In order to critique and rupture canonical "claims to universality ... [and] the regulatory and exclusionary imperatives of those claims" (22), he turns to literature that is both within and outside the disciplinary regimes around sexuality that also produce canonical scholarship. Not so different from canonical sociology, the Bible inscribes difference at the same time as it prescribes norms, and it makes promises for inclusion into the norm with proper behavior. Thus, the Deuteronomistic History, as a composite, redacted text, is a good place to look for alternate cultural forms, perhaps even indigenous cultural forms, which may be disciplined and tamed by their final redaction. The Rahab story—conforming to the canon that it also resists—offers humorous potential to "exploit its alienation from canonical presumptions of universality and normativity" so as to intervene in the affective results of the way that Canaanites "have been racialized as pathologically nonheteronormative" (24).

In what follows, I begin with biblical and subsequent cultural circuits of disgust around nonheteronormative racialized bodies. In order to do this work, I draw on recent cultural-studies analyses of emotion and affect, which, to simplify more than a little, broadly understand affect to be unconscious or nonconscious structures of feeling that are grounded in the body.[2] Specifically, the works of Brian Massumi (2002) on affect and Sarah Ahmed (2004) and Jasbir Puar (2007) on racialization and affect are extremely helpful in theorizing biblically produced affect. I then turn to the dynamics of the Rahab story to see how the emotions that circulate in that story might be used to disrupt the more usual attitudes to racialized nonheteronormativity. With respect to my own political commitments and social location, I write as one (caucasian Canadian, living and teaching in the U.S.) who has occasionally experienced others' disgust for various choices around gender and sexuality and who has also watched it devastate people close to me. I am aware that my analysis, like any, is conditioned by my social location and may therefore suffer from some uninterrogated forms of misrecognition about which I welcome dialogue. Nonetheless, I offer this analysis, drawing on important queer-of-color

---

2. For a helpful genealogy of the "affective turn" in cultural studies, see Clough 2007, 1–33.

and cultural-studies critiques, because I agree with feminists and antira-cism activists that the burden of change should not be relegated to particu-lar identity groups.

The Bible and the Circulation of Affect

If affect is central to cultural and political reasoning, as cultural and queer theorists have recently been suggesting (e.g., Massumi 2002; Ahmed 2004; Clough 2007; Puar 2007), then it is important to consider how important cultural texts like the Bible are purveyors of feelings and bodily responses to queer desires and practices. In her book *The Cultural Politics of Emotions* (2004), Sara Ahmed suggests that affect does not reside in any one place but "is the effect of the circulation between objects and signs. ... [T]he more signs circulate, the more affective they become" (45). Ahmed is interested in the way that affect circulates through the movement of objects and bodies (11). She suggests that affect, including hatred and disgust toward racialized bodies, "sticks" to particular objects through the circulation of signs. Given the centrality of the circulation of biblical signs in U.S. culture and its wars, the Bible must then be considered a key text around and through which affect circulates, and disgust over sexual-ity in particular.

Let me offer a few examples of this kind of circulation of disgust through biblical signs. Psychoanalysts Robert M. Galatzer-Levy and Mayer Gruber consider Hebrew Scripture an excellent means through which to study disgust. Though explicitly concerned with explicating affect (in this case, disgust) as it relates to bodily impulses, their study is instructive in showing how the Bible becomes a prototype for sticking disgust to racial-ized sexuality. Based on the terminology for disgust in the Tanak, which they detail, Galatzer-Levy and Gruber conclude that disgust is a bodily reaction conditioned by early childhood experiences with bad-tasting food and triggered by forbidden things unconsciously associated with those early experiences (1992, 89). (Here they disagree with Freud and others that disgust is the transformation of an early childhood fascina-tion with feces.) Much of their discussion strangely focuses around for-bidden sexuality, presumably because disgust with forbidden sexuality is sometimes described in the Tanak with terms that could also be applied to food. For instance, they call attention to the fact that in texts such as Lev 18 and 20, "the Israelites are warned that should they, like the Canaanites, engage in ... forbidden forms of sexuality, they too will be vomited out of the land" (83). Forbidden sexuality is expelled from the land like bad-tasting food from the body. The example of the Canaanites' emetic qualities is a clear indicator of the way that the Tanak uses sexualization as a general strategy in characterizing and destabilizing threatening neighbors (Canaanites, Egyptians, Hittites, etc.).[3] But by using the biblical text as a kind of scientific data set on disgust, Galatzer-Levy and Gruber unwittingly point to, and continue, the relation between sexualization, racialization, and the production of disgust.

Cynthia Burack's recent analysis of antigay rhetoric on the Christian right provides another example of the way that disgust with nonheteronormativity is stuck, through the circulation of biblical signs, to racialized Canaanite bodies. Burack mentions, in passing, a scene that depicts disgust with Canaanite sexual practices in "The Gay Blade," one of Jack Chick's widely circulated Christian cartoon tracts expressing God's wish to eradicate homosexuality (2008, 63). In the comic frame that Burack mentions, several archaeologists display disgust over a find in Canaan: "Good Lord, I can't believe my eyes. We can't publish this, it's filthy!" says one, covering his eyes, while another retches, "I'm going to vomit!" The image is framed by the following textbox:

> In 1904–1909 archaeologists uncovered Canaanite ruins depicting their religious worship of about 1500 B.C. … The evidence clearly shows why God told Israel, "Thou shalt smite them and utterly destroy them. Thou shalt make no covenant with them, nor show mercy unto them." It was the only way to keep the filth and brutality from spreading. (Chick 1984, n.p.)

Given the overall message of the tract, the reader is left to surmise that these religious practices include nonheteronormative sex.[4] Not only does the image suggest a visceral (and therefore, presumably natural) response to nonheteronormativity, but it also implies violence is the appropriate response to objects of disgust.

Although such attitudes have been challenged in biblical scholarship, they still persist in popular culture. Scholars have argued that the biblical descriptions of Canaanite practice and the once-accepted scholarly

---

3. For an excellent discussion of this textual strategy, see Bailey 2005, 20–22.

4. Burack uses this example to show how so-called scientific discourse (here archaeology) is used to lend authority to an antigay rhetoric.

description of the Canaanite fertility cult are not attested in the ancient Near Eastern material and textual record, nor is a strong division in material culture between Israelite and Canaanite apparent (e.g., Hillers 1985; Smith 2002, 5–9; Knoll 2001, 259–61; Stone 2004, 115–27). Nonetheless, assertions of disgust around Canaanite religious practices contribute significantly to the continued circulation of disgust around nonheteronormative, racialized bodies. For instance, even the writers for the presumably progressive website GayChristian101.com exhibit this kind of disgust. They contextualize the prohibitions on same-sex relations in Lev 18:22 and 20:13 by saying, "Believing Jews and non-Jews living in the land of Israel were prohibited from pagan sexual worship of the Canaanite fertility goddess because God viewed such pagan worship as an abomination." They are at pains to point out that their own sexual practices do not resemble these pagan rituals and therefore are acceptable within Christian life. Such attitudes leave notions of racialized nonheteronormativity intact.

It should be noted that these examples show anxiety and disgust not only with supposed Canaanite same-sex desires but also with other kinds of nonheteronormative, nonmonogamous practices. Many scholars have associated so-called Canaanite fertility rites with the biblical phrase "whoring after other gods" and so with literal prostitution. Disgust with nonmonogamous sex becomes most clear in scholarly and lay commentary on prophetic metaphors for Israelite "whoring" (e.g., Hos 1–3; Ezek 16), wherein exegetes become vitriolic in their condemnation of the prophets' metaphorically libidinous women.[5] In this view, same-sex desires and nonmonogamy (especially for women) are the disgusting heritage of Canaan. This point will become significant in thinking about how Rahab the prostitute is treated a little differently by the text and can therefore help to disrupt disgust with nonheteronormative sexuality.

Responses to Canaanite sexuality illustrate Ahmed's point about the way in which affect "sticks" to some bodies. She suggests that stickiness is created, in part, through the repetition of signs. In her discussion of disgust, she argues that signs have the real effect of drawing objects into proximity, so that disgust can be felt, and at the same time, of repelling them (Ahmed 2004, 85). Ahmed suggests that insulting words become sticky through repetition, attaching themselves to particular objects or

---

5. For a small sampling of feminist analysis of the kind of commentary that is not able to deal with the nonmonogamous woman, see Day 2000; Y. Sherwood 1995; Runions 2005.

bodies. These signs, she argues, further accumulate negative value through association with other negative terms. She takes as an example the term "Paki," which is repeatedly used as an insult and "might then stick to other words that are not spoken: immigrant, outsider, dirty, and so on" (92). Use of an affective term like "disgusting" operates in a similar way, as a performative speech act. It gathers value through repetition and association; it cites "previous norms and conventions of speech, and it generates the object that it names" (93). Ahmed writes, "To name something as disgusting is to transfer the stickiness of the word 'disgust' to an object, which henceforth becomes generated as the very thing that is spoken" (94). Thus, the declaration "That's filthy, I'm going to vomit" acts as a performative, sticking disgust to the Canaanite and the Canaanite to other associated concepts: outsider, nonheteronormative, pagan, and (putative) child sacrificer. Moreover, as Ahmed points out, this kind of performative process requires "shared witnessing of the disgusting thing ... for the affect to have effect" (94). Biblical interpretation is of course an important site of shared witnessing.

The corollary to this particular constellation of associations and affect around the Canaanites is, of course, another set that accrues to the Israelites (and those who identify with them) and is universalized as truth. As Ahmed suggests, the process of sticking the affect of disgust to an object has a dual effect: not only does it create repulsion toward the object, it creates or reinforce the subject from whom the object is repelled. "By naming the event [or object] as disgusting, the subject 'stands out' in the 'standing apart' or 'pulling away' of the event" (2004, 96). The Israelite subject of the biblical text is attached to the disgusting Canaanite and yet tries to pull away. As the chosen recipients of promise, the Israelites are affiliated with hope, inclusion, and safety—in effect, the opposite of the bodily rejection of disgust. A condition of "sticking" to promise is the association of the Israelites with "proper" forms of sexuality, ritual cleanness, and worship. According to the covenantal terms in which most of the biblical texts about Canaanites are framed, straying from the prescriptions of the text means being ejected from the promise. Moreover, the promise is made and guaranteed by "truth," which is represented by the one true God, Yahweh. As a symbol of truth and monotheism, Yahweh and associated affects are allied in much biblical interpretation with universal norms. So the fear of becoming like the Canaanites is also a fear of exclusion from universal truths. It is a fear of being vomited from the land, like the Canaanites, as well as from the promise and the hope and inclusion associated with it.

This "vomiting" is not passive either, as John J. Collins (2003) and Bailey (2005) have shown in their discussions of the violence legitimated, by the text and by later interpreters, toward Canaanites and any groups meta-phorically associated with them.

These are powerful emotions that circulate in and around the bibli-cal text, and one can readily see how they map on to understandings of race in the United States, where a large portion of the population identi-fies with ancient Israel over and against whatever given racialized, threat-ening Other. As Ferguson has importantly emphasized, racialization in the United States cannot be separated from sexualization. He shows how heteronormativity and heteropatriarchy become a property of whiteness and ideal citizenship, while anything that deviates from heteropatriarchy signifies "race." He writes, "As a technology of race, U.S. citizenship has historically ascribed heteronormativity (universality) to certain subjects and nonheteronormativity (particularity) to others" (Ferguson 2004, 14). Clearly this sexualization of race is deeply rooted in the nation's bibli-cal self-understanding and nourished by the affects generated by the text and attached to particular bodies. The universality of white heteropatri-archy is associated with monotheism and promise, while the particular-ity of nonheteronormative racialization is associated with fear of being excluded from the promise and loathing for those who are associated with exclusion.

This mapping of biblical identity onto national identity exhibits what Ahmed describes as the process whereby disgust creates both an object (the Canaanites, and associated forms of sexuality) and a subject (the Isra-elites, and those so identifying) at the same time (2004, 96). It is not sur-prising to see this dynamic emerge in biblical interpretation, given that, as Stone has persuasively argued, biblical texts about the Canaanites them-selves exhibit border anxieties. Drawing on the scholarly consensus that there is likely no real ethnic, cultural, or geographic distance between the Canaanites and the Israelites, Stone suggests that such an anxiety "arises as part of an attempt to establish those boundaries more firmly and to avoid the 'fear, nervousness and aversion' that result from any fluidity in those boundaries [quoting from Kristeva on the abject]" (2004, 123). Ahmed helpfully highlights the way that the boundary created and marked by disgust is liminal, attached to the object and detaching at the same time. The disgusting object, the Canaanite, is both inside and outside of Israel-ite identity (123). Yet as I will discuss presently, it is precisely this liminal status that may allow for usual responses to be disrupted and shifted.

Disrupting Disgust

The problem, then, is in how to disrupt this circulation and accumulation of affect. Ahmed suggests that not only does affect stick to particular objects and signs but also, in so doing, the signs become "blocked"; they themselves seem not to be able to accrue new value or meaning, except in the way that they stick to other associated negative signs. But it seems to me that signs are never quite so static as they might appear. With some pushing and pulling, objects and affect can perhaps be unstuck and reconfigured. Here the insight of queer theorist Jasbir Puar might be helpful. In *Terrorist Assemblages: Homonationalism in Queer Times* (2007), Puar critically draws on the work of Ahmed in an analysis of the association of sexuality with racialized bodies and terrorism. Puar finds Ahmed's work important and yet wants to take analysis of affect beyond an understanding of "signification, narrative and epistemological coherence ... [as] what subtends and mediates the stickiness" of affect (Puar 2007, 188). For Puar, such an approach leaves affect in the realm of representation; it does not attend to extra- or prerepresentational affective energies produced in the body. She prefers to take a Deleuzian approach—via the work of Brian Massumi—that understands "affect [as] ... a physiological and biological phenomenon ... what escapes or remains outside of the discursively structured and thus commodity forms of emotion, of feeling ... as what escapes our attention, as what haunts the representational realm" (207). For Massumi, nonconscious bodily movement provides a set of *indeterminate potentials* that might be harnessed for change, though these potentials often "contract" into identifiable emotions that conform to dominant ideological discourses (Massumi 2002, 28–39). Like Massumi, Puar wants to tap into nonrepresentational affective energy.

Puar raises the important issue of how to theorize the movement between nonconscious bodily energy and representation in analyses of affect, while admitting the difficulty in trying to theorize, or represent, that which is outside of representation. Clearly, a project of biblical interpretation is very much bound to the realm of signification and resignification. If, as I have indicated, biblical signs become the bodily response that is disgust, then evidently signification can trigger bodily energies that go beyond what can be captured in words. There is still a connection between words and affect, at least when it comes to a text like the Bible. The trick is to find places where signification can produce bodily energies able to intervene in the usual affective circuits. Humor may be one such place.

Words may be funny, in varying degrees, but humor also has physical effects that cannot be simply reduced to signification. If affect circulates through attachment and repulsion from particular objects, as Ahmed suggests, perhaps humor works similarly, drawing affective energy close to some objects and pulling it away from others.

The question is whether humor can intervene in the negative attachments produced by disgust. Certainly humor is used in serious resistance of racialization on the level of signification (see Gates 1988, 44–88; Wimbush 2008, 4; Pellegrini 2001, 185–90; Muñoz 1999, 93–115).[6] One of the reasons humor can be disruptive in reinterpreting texts is precisely *because it relies on signification but produces bodily energy that cannot be reduced to or captured by that signification.* Good-natured laughs and chuckles, as well as cynical snickers, all have movement in the body of the kind that Massumi and Puar argue escapes containment. This bodily agitation has potential to arrive at an unforeseen destination. Laughter starts movement in the body that might work ahead of any agency or will (cf. Massumi 2002, 23–38). The movement that it provokes has potentiality to revalue the emotions into which affective energies might more habitually congeal, like disgust. It is movement that has the potential to be pleasurable rather than punishing, freeing rather than constraining, inclusive rather than exclusionary.

Another reason that humor works is that it plays with what is known, what is familiar, but gives it a twist. In order to be funny it has to come from the inside. Something like disgust, humor is both inside and outside. Humor starts with received emotional "capture" of affect (Massumi 2002, 35) and juxtaposes it in odd ways. The result is another eruption of energy that is not so easily pinned down.[7] Try, for instance, to explain exactly why something makes you laugh. Laughter is often beyond signification, an energetic movement in the body, a feeling of release that disrupts habits, norms, and categories. Laughter can be rather queer. Notably it is a kind of

---

6. Wimbush, Gates, Muñoz, and Pellegrini point to phenomena of language and performance that are much more than simply funny, but humor is involved.

7. Massumi argues that some affect always escapes this capture: "Something remains unactualized, inseparable from but unassimilable to any particular, functionally anchored perspective. That is why all emotion is more or less disorienting" (2002, 35). Some excesses seem to be more easily pinned down than others, as in the case of disgust. For instance, it is easier to explain why something is disgusting than why something is funny.

queerness that makes odd connections, that moves toward usually reviled objects rather than pushing them away.

At the same time, humor, like text, is indeterminate. Laughter and disgust can go together. In order to be queer, to help queer, laughter has to move away from the usual "capture" of affective response to gender and sexuality (i.e., disgust) to create affective reverberations that work differently. The trick is to set affective potentiality in motion. I would suggest that one way it can be put into play is through interpretation of an indeterminate text, uncoupling the usual semiotic links between disgust and sexuality and turning more negative tropes of humor on their heads. As queer and critical race theorists have pointed out, this kind of humor is already practiced by performance artists (see n. 6). I am suggesting that literary and biblical critics could emulate these practices (though appropriate skill sets might be an issue) or find texts to do it for them. Though interpretation that queerly makes use of humor cannot escape the realm of signification, in the way that Puar and Massumi advocate, it may be one way of activating affect. Thus, if the project is to disrupt disgust with Canaanites and their contemporary, culturally-ascribed, racialized nonheteronormative heirs, what better way than to start with an indeterminate biblical text, itself humorously exhibiting border anxiety? The story of Rahab the prostitute, situated at the beginning of the imperializing Deuteronomistic History, is such a text. A queer interpretation can make much of the text's multiple voices, odd juxtapositions, "unsaids," and ambivalences.

Rereading Rahab

Ferguson opens his analysis of racialized nonheteronormativity with the specter of the prostitute in Marx. In order to take up the historical-materialist approach, Ferguson first has to uncover historical materialism's own commitments to heteropatriarchy. He reads Marx critically, wanting to distance himself from the assumptions about sexuality and race that he uncovers there. He points out that Marx uses the example of prostitution as an expression of the alienation of capitalism; the prostitute is a particular instance of the kind of transaction to which every laborer is subjected (Ferguson 2004, 7). As Ferguson glosses Marx, "the prostitute proves capital's defilement of man" (8). But from what is the prostitute alienated, exactly? Ferguson astutely points to the assumption of patriarchal heteronormativity as the norm from which Marx sees humans to be alienated in capitalism. Ferguson further shows how Marx's discourse has a surprising affinity—though surely unintended—with other nineteenth-century bourgeois discourses, in which the prostitute becomes the symbol of the potential gender and racial chaos of the working class (8–10). Let me do what Ferguson suggests then, and use the racialized, nonheteronormative prostitute as a starting point for critique, rather than as a symbol of failed heteropatriarchy (10).

Rahab is clearly racialized as not conforming to heteropatriarchal norms, as is typical of the biblical and postbiblical treatment of the Canaanites. She is neither monogamous nor wife and mother. Her conversion to Yahwhism in the story emphasizes her initial narrative position as a departure from the universal norm to which she assimilates. Both text and subsequent interpretation emphasize her assimilation. As Lori Rowlett puts it, "It is hardly surprising ... that Rahab is a converted sex worker. She is a symbol of (among other things) the transformation of the land from sexually lascivious paganism (in Hebrew eyes) to colonized docility" (2000, 68). Though the text does not say that she quits the sex trade after she is spared in the conquest of Jericho, tradition assumes it and in some cases has filled in this detail with specifics. Perhaps the most famous of these is Rahab's inclusion as an ancestress in the genealogy of Christ in Matt 1.[8] The rabbis too were concerned with Rahab's sexuality. As Phyllis Kramer outlines, in the Talmud and midrashim, Rahab laudably left her prostitution and became a woman of faith (Pesiq. Rab. 40.3–4); married Joshua following her conversion (b. Meg. 14b); and bore children from whom Jeremiah descended (Pesiq. Rab Kah. 13.5; Kramer 2000, 159). Early Christian writers also find ways to minimize Rahab's sexuality, either through allegory or repentance, as William Lyons has pointed out (2008). Origen, for instance, read the etymological link between the proper name Rahab and the Hebrew verb "to make oneself wide," not as an indicator of sexual openness but as an allegory for "this Church of Christ which is gathered from sinners as if from prostitution" (Hom. Josh. 3.4).

Though Rahab is assimilated in the story and heteronormativized in the tradition, the narrative requires her initial position as indigenous prostitute in order for the story to be effective (Frymer-Kensky 1997, 130; Gillmayr-Bucher 2007, 146–47). Her difference is needed to make the story

---

8. See Bauckham 1995 for a discussion of a possible earlier tradition, to which Matthew refers, in which Rahab marries Salmon, possibly derived from 1 Chr 2:54–55.

signify on multiple levels: as a proclamation of Yahweh's power and right to the land (Stek 2002); as a model of faith and righteousness (as represented in Heb 11:31 and Jas 2:25); as an etiology and/or polemic for the continued existence of Canaanites and other outsiders among the Israelites (Nelson 1997, 43; Frymer-Kensky 1997, 67); or as a critique of Joshua's methods in beginning the conquest by sending out spies (A. Sherwood 2006, 60). Both her racialization and her assimilation are necessary for these readings. In this sense, Rahab remains in a position of the "almost but not quite" position of hybridity (Bhabha 1994, 122–23): she is almost assimilated into the Deuteronomistic norm, but not quite, as the text also maintains and makes use of her racialized nonheteronormativity.

It is precisely Rahab's hybridity in Josh 2, however, that allows this text to become a starting point for a different kind of affective circulation around racialized nonheteronormativity. Using it as such does not negate its troubling aspects. Without a doubt, it is highly disturbing to read this story of collaboration with the invader, as postcolonial critics like Bailey (2005), Dube (2006), Donaldson (2006), McKinlay (1999), and Kwok (2006) have pointed out. As a whole the story does not offer a heroic point of identification for those wishing to contest conquest and domination. Rahab is, as McKinlay has argued, an Israelite construct (1999, 49–51). But it is precisely because she is so constructed that she is not treated with any sort of disgust, even though still marked as other through racialized nonheteronormativity. The indigenous prostitute is integrated into the promise and its affiliated affects.

The structure of the text itself, as well, allows it to function as a wedge text. Many scholars recognize the text to have gone through some process of redaction and have discerned a variety of layers from oral traditions to Deuteronomistic redactions (Nelson 1997, 41–46; Soggin 1972, 37–38; Tucker 1972; T. Butler 1983, 29–30). A number have suggested that the odd placement of details and repetitions indicates that the text may amalgamate and smooth out earlier oral and textual traditions (Culley 1984, 32; Tucker 1972, 75–76; Zakovitch 1990, 78–79). Though the actual process of redaction can never be fully known, there do seem to be some pieces that can clearly be marked as additions. On the basis of these, I would like to outline two plausible textual layers of the story, though perhaps there were more. The first is a humorous early tale of unknown but possibly indigenous origin, in which Rahab is strong, free, and resistant. This early textual version of the tale contains the narrative lines that are elaborated in the later versions. Robert Culley (1984, 30) and Zakovitch (1990, 78–79) have called these the spy mission and the rescue story, elements that they suggest are likely taken from oral traditions. The second textual layer is a Deuteronomistic redaction of the story, in which Rahab converts to Yahwism and sells out her city.

To be clear, the text of Josh 2 plausibly contains an early textual version of an even earlier oral mode that is later redacted to fit the Deuteronomistic History. These two versions of the story, as we shall see, work in tension with one another. If the earlier tale is accepted as conceivably indigenous, then it might be, as Ferguson suggests of African American novels, a site of rupture, within the canon yet outside of it as well. The positive affect surrounding the final form of the story allows the earlier story to be read more positively, while at the same time the humor of the earlier story can be used to undercut the seriousness with which the affect of the final form ought to be taken. The final form tries to reduce the critique of the earlier tale, but is never quite successful.

Helpful here is the important work of postcolonial biblical critic Althea Spencer Miller on the need to recognize oral modes within biblical literature. Spencer Miller argues that modes of orality, like folktale, can continue to be at work within literary works and that these modes of orality can represent "a cross-cultural conversation in which bartering for cultural primacy is transacted on the plane of folktales" (2007, 214). As she points out, folktales and story telling are often powerful forms by which colonized peoples critique their colonizers. Influenced by Dennis Mac-Donald's concept of transvaluation, in which a mythic hypotext is transformed by a hypertext (for MacDonald, Acts transforms Homer), Spencer Miller suggests that within an oral worldview, the readers/hearers of a literary hypertext might be aware of a set of oral stories upon which the text is based. This awareness is as much an aspect of an oral mindset as it is of literacy (180). Thus, the oral tradition continues to interact with a literary text and "the cultural conversation is continued" (224). Spencer Miller argues persuasively that orality ought not to be relegated to the realm of the preliterate in the usual colonial models of progress, as if somehow less developed than literary output. Recognizing oral modes within the biblical text is also a way of countering the colonial bias toward literary skill in much biblical scholarship (180–81). I am drawing on this idea to suggest that an older indigenous tale still works powerfully and affectively within its literary context to critique the emotional responses normally generated by Deuteronomistic thought. Following Spencer Miller's hypothesis about the functioning of oral modes, the early textual version would also recruit any knowledge of a larger oral tradition, now lost to us. The early textual version of the story still rubs up against its later redaction and erodes its authority.

Moreover, Spencer Miller argues that oral stories can be emotionally, rather than empirically, powerful, and speak their truth differently (2007, 24, 240–45). She tells the story of Nanny, the national hero of her birth country, Jamaica. Nanny was a rebel leader of the "fiercest reputation" around whom epic stories formed. In one attack by British militiamen, Nanny is said to have bared her bottom to distract them from shooting her fleeing soldiers and nonfatally absorbed the bullets "with the giftedness of her r(e)are endowment" (243). The point is not whether or not the story is factual but rather that it is true in its hilarious critique of the British, in proving her worth as a leader, and in exemplifying the Jamaican fighting spirit (242–43). This story is illustrative of the way that I imagine the early Rahab tale to function, in that it represents resistance not only through action but also with the double edge of laughter.[9]

REDACTIONAL LAYERS

The text's multiple voices have long been recognized by scholars and variously explained. The text's two long speeches—Rahab's confession of faith and negotiation with the spies to save her family in conquest (vv. 9–14) and the spies' conditions on Rahab (vv. 17–21)—seem to be later elaborations on a more condensed narrative, as does the spies' report to Joshua (v. 24).

Many commentators have considered Rahab's foreknowledge of the Israelites' victory over Jericho (2:9–11) to be inserted by the redactor of the Deuteronomistic History (Culley 1984, 33; Soggin 1972, 41; Tucker 1972, 70; Campbell and O'Brien 2000, 111; McKinlay 1999, 51; Gillmayr-Bucher 2007, 145). Using stock phrases and images of the Deuteronomistic History, Rahab proclaims Yahweh's right to the land and the surety of the Israelites' success in light of her own people's fear. Danna Fewell and David Gunn suggest "she is tamed by this speech." In their view, Rahab is "set up by the narrator to communicate the Deuteronomistic thesis" as a way

---

9. Space does not permit a full engagement of Spencer Miller's brilliant project on Acts, which examines how Acts uses mythic oral themes to contest both Jewish and Greek histories. Her work draws on contemporary subaltern oral traditions to suggest the ongoing power of oral stories as they continue to work within literary contexts.

of controlling her difference and making her "'safe,' for the Israelite community" (Fewell and Gunn 1993, 119). Along these same lines, the spies'
report to Joshua in 2:24 is probably also a later addition, since they repeat
back, almost word for word, what they have learned from Rahab, namely,
that the people of the land are melting in fear (Tucker 1972, 83). As Richard Nelson puts it, "they give Joshua a report entirely based on Rahab's
words and interpret the situation with a faith statement also derived from
her" (1997, 52).

Likewise, the spies' conditions for saving Rahab and her agreement to
their demands (2:17–21) seem to be tacked onto the story. As many scholars have noticed, it is odd that the spies start setting conditions for the deal
only after Rahab lets them down from the window, yelling up from the
ground when they should be escaping silently (Tucker 1972, 76). Though
this narrative oddity has been explained in various ways,[10] it is probable, as
Zakovitch suggests, that 2:17–21 are a later addition (1990, 92).

Even without her confession of faith and the spies' conditions on her,
an early version of the story might still contain Rahab's bargain for her life
(vv. 12–14), to fulfill the etiological function of explaining why Canaanites
continue to live with the Israelites. Nelson suggests that this etiological tale
may have been the earliest version of the story, one that might have gained
popularity as "landless Israelites, their peasant descendants and the clan of
Rahab stand together in a social sense as marginalized groups over against
Jericho's king, who represents the centralized power of the royal establishment" (1997, 44). Here Nelson imagines the kind of subversive work of an
oral story for which Spencer Miller argues—the story could be heard to
register dissatisfaction with the royalty, as peasants identify with Rahab
and her clan, working to outsmart the king.

The question is whether or not Rahab's bargain for her life and the
men's first response to her (2:12–14) can legitimately be separated from
the Deuteronomistic insertion of Rahab's speech (2:9–11) in the way that
Nelson suggests. Verses 9–14 seem to form a unit. For instance, the proclamation of Yahweh's gift of the land acts as a kind of inclusio. The men's
agreement to make a covenant with Rahab "when Yahweh gives the land
to us" (בתת יהוה לנו את הארץ) in verse 14 mirrors Rahab's opening assertion in verse 9, "I know that Yahweh has given you the land" (ידעתי כי נתן

---

10. See Zakovitch 1990, 92, for a discussion of various solutions to this textual
oddity.

יהוה לכם את הארץ). Moreover, any version of the story that preserves Rahab's bargain presumes a danger from which she must escape. Without her declaration of the conquest as foreordained, there is no motive for her to make a bargain with her visitors. As Susanne Gillmayr-Bucher puts it, her confession of faith "establishes a basis for her following request" (2007, 145). Thus, it appears that her request and the spies' response are logically, narratively, and linguistically connected to her Deuteronomistic confession and can plausibly be understood also to be a later addition.

Rahab Thwarts the Colonizers and the Meddling King

Without these additions, the early version of the story would consist of 2:1–8, 15–16, 22–23, in which Rahab deals with the Israelite spies while at the same time keeping her business safe from the intrusions of the king's men. It could be imagined then as an indigenous tale or joke originally circulating to make fun of any attempted colonizer. It can be read as a kind of bawdy humor, perhaps in the genre of something like *La Cage aux Folles*. The brothel has been disturbed: people are being shoved under bundles of flax, clothes are flying, there is much lying down and getting up, desires are thwarted, and the lady of the house is trying to keep it all under control, with a sense of humor.[11]

Joshua sends two spies to Jericho. One might expect them to be diligent soldiers, working hard to win the land. But they immediately abandon the task at hand and head for more leisurely pursuits. Both Zakovitch (1990, 81–82) and Aaron Sherwood (2006, 49) notice that the spies do not exactly follow Joshua's instructions. There is a disturbance in the common pattern in Hebrew narrative, whereby an imperative is followed by a report of compliance. Joshua's imperative in verse 1, "Go, see the land" (לכו ראו הארץ), is only partially followed: "and they went" (וילכו). The second imperative, "see" (ראו), appears not to be a worthwhile endeavor for the spies. Instead, "they enter the house of a prostitute" (ויבאו בית אשה זונה), further elaborated by the clause "and they laid down there" (וישכבו שמה). As A. Sherwood puts it, "the first instance of command/fulfillment pattern in the book of Joshua … is *prima facie* an instance of command/failed fulfillment" (49).

---

11. For a sex-positive reading of Rahab as the owner of a brothel, see Brenner 2002.

There is humor in the broken expectation. One can almost hear the wink and the nod. Much has been said about whether the spies' "lying down" constitutes sexual activity or not. Many scholars point to the association of the verbs "to enter" and "to lie down" (שכב and בוא) with sexual activity elsewhere in the Hebrew Bible (e.g., Hawk 1991, 62; A. Sherwood 2006, 50–51; Nelson 1997, 43; Zakovitch 1990, 83). Those wishing to preserve the reputations of the spies have followed Josephus to argue that Rahab's house was simply an inn (e.g., *Ant.* 5.1.2; Howard 1998, 98–99; Drucker 1982, 110). The question does not really have to be decidable in a humorous story, as long as the implication is there. In fact, it is funnier if left to speculation.

To Rahab's dismay, the spies bring military business to the brothel. Somehow, the king of Jericho knows the spies have arrived—perhaps indicating the spies' incompetence—so he sends men to apprehend them. But Rahab is practiced in many arts. The spies have to be hidden. One can imagine their surprise—interrupted in their lying down—and relative stages of undress and disorientation as they are hurried up to the roof to hide in hot and scratchy bundles of flax. It may not exactly have been what they had in mind, although, ironically, it is the kind of undercover discomfort hardworking spies might expect. Rahab runs back down the stairs[12] to deal with the king's men. This she does by sending them off on a hopeless quest: "I'm sorry good sirs, the spies left the city already because the gates were closing; you had better hurry to catch up." Rahab's motive in deceiving the king's men is not given, though several could be imagined, including a need to keep her business on the down low, a dislike of being disturbed at work, resistance to military operations, or simply a sense of humor needing an elaborate foil. As Culley points out in his analysis of the narrative structures that give the story coherence in spite of its gaps and tensions, there is much that is not said in these verses, for instance, why exactly the men arrived at Rahab's house or how the king knew about their presence (1984, 32). Yet there is inference, wherein comedy dwells.

---

12. The fact that Rahab seems to hide the spies twice—both before and after she speaks to the king's men (vv. 4, 6)—has been the subject of much discussion and has been taken as a sign of the stitching together of two versions of the same story (Tucker 1972, 75; Soggin 1972, 37). It could also be understood as a narrative technique of creating suspense (Zakovitch 1990, 87–88; Hawk 1991, 63; Nelson 1997, 49; A. Sherwood 2006, 53).

Knowing that the city gates will close behind the search party and keep them out of the way, Rahab goes up to the roof to deal with the spies. One can imagine her sighing with exasperation at having to deal with all this nonsense. For their part, the spies are ready to get down to business. But, "before they lay down," (והמה טרם ישכבון; v. 8)—read: get what they came for—Rahab hustles them out of the window. The spies' one main action in Jericho besides attracting the attention of the king—to lie down—is interrupted, again. The men just cannot obtain. Certainly to an audience on the receiving end of oppressive physical or ideological boundary staking, this interruption of the conquerors' efforts at sexual conquest might be quite funny.

Rahab sends them off in the opposite direction from the king's men for a three-day wander in the wilderness. Calm is restored, while military men run about the countryside in opposite directions, frustrated, and on futile missions. The spies' futility and lack of success on both military and personal fronts is emphasized by the repetition of the phrase from verse 1, וילכו ויבאו ("they went and entered"), at the end of the story (v. 22). The second time, they enter the mountains, far from their two ostensible goals: military intelligence and female comfort. When they finally return to Joshua, they have lost valuable time, they have had their own plans and desires foiled, and they have not gained any real information. The king's men fare no better. Territory-seeking and defending men run around the country, somewhat aimlessly. The spies especially look silly.

The humor of the tale contains the elements that some scholars have identified as critical of the Israelites, even in the final form. For instance, Zakovitch finds the spies to be portrayed as "first-class bunglers" (1990, 85), whose masculinity is put into question by Rahab's competence (76). A. Sherwood suggests that the secrecy of Joshua's mission, and the sexual innuendo of the story, "sets up the reader to expect that disaster will fall upon the spies and Joshua's mission will end in failure" (2006, 52). Hawk reads the story as negatively evaluating the spies through their association with Rahab: "The story of the spies and Rahab is an antithesis of the construct of obedience and faith presented by the introductory speeches in Joshua 1. Having entered the land in preparation for subjugating it, the two Israelite spies have themselves been mastered and ensnared by their Canaanite counterpart" (1991, 68). These scholars read from the perspective of the Deuteronomistic final form of the story and so are favorably disposed to its agenda of God-given conquest and, to varying degrees, sex-negative in their assessment. Others, like Culley (1984, 35) and Athalya

Brenner (2002), understand the story to be both critical of the Israelites and positive toward Rahab, without adopting the Deuteronomist's attitude toward the invasion of Canaan. In my view, the early version of the story presents Rahab in a positive light and the spies in a negative light, in anticolonial fashion.

DISRUPTIVE HUMOR

Let me return to the question of the potential affective disruption of humor. Reading the story this way works to disrupt both sets of affect associated with the Canaanite/Israelite relationship: disgust with racialized nonheteronormative sexuality and hope for inclusion in the universal norms associated with a particular notion of God.

As mentioned, Rahab is not treated with disgust. As feminist scholars have noted in analyzing the story's final version, she is the protagonist of the story, the one who is in control; she is "smart, proactive, tricky, and unafraid to disobey and deceive the king" (Frymer-Kensky 1997, 60), reversing normal expectations for a *zonah* (Bird 1989, 130–31; see also Gillmayr-Bucher 2007, 147). She is the subject of the verbs in the narrative (McKinlay 1999, 46–47). Notably, the spies are more than once the objects of those verbs: Rahab takes the two men (ותקח האשה את שני האנשים) and hides them (ותצפנו; v. 4);[13] she takes them up to the roof and hides them (והיא העלתם הגגה ותטמנם; v.6); she lowers them (ותורדם) from the window (v. 15); and she commands them to go to the mountains (לכו) for three days (v. 16). Her imperative, "go," in verse 16 echoes Joshua's original imperative and is obeyed with greater precision; they do exactly what she tells them (v. 22). Indeed, Rahab's actions disrupt the patriarchal authority assumed by the text for military men, subverting the authority of Joshua and the king of Jericho.

Moreover, her sexual behavior is not a subject of comment, let alone critique or censure, in the tale. Certainly later commentators are concerned with either explaining her profession away or making it an object of her repentance, but the text does not moralize. Nor is she a victim of patriarchal objectification and sexual use. She behaves as one very much in

---

13. The text switches to the 3ms suffix here ("she hid him"), indicating perhaps an older version of the story in which just one man was saved, as in Zakovitch's suggestion of the type-story "Woman Rescues a Man" (1990, 79). For rabbinic explanations, such as Rashi's explanation that she hid each separately, see Drucker 1982, 116.

control of her situation, with no real patience for the (explicit and implicit) demands of the men in the story.[14] Although the tradition marries her off, the text itself nowhere comments on her activities once she has been rescued. As the text reports in Josh 6:25, "Joshua rescued Rahab *the prostitute* ... and she lives among the Israelites to this day." The story could be called sex-trade positive. Perhaps it also served as an etiology for the accepted practice of the sex trade in Israel.

How does humor work affectively then to dissipate disgust? In this case, the usual lines of affective movement are unexpectedly reversed. The tremors of the body in laughter of the reader move in a different way than in disgust. The usual object of disgust (the Canaanite)—normally repelled by the subject (the Israelite, or the reader so identified)—becomes the subject (the Canaanite Rahab) repelling the object (the Israelite spies). Combined with a positive revaluation of the new subject, this reversal is funny. Because the new subject is the protagonist of the joke and the new object the butt of the joke, the positive revaluation of the Canaanite increases. The recipients of the story listen and laugh, drawing near to the Canaanite and away from the colonizers. Even commentators with more traditional conclusions note that Rahab is viewed positively (e.g., Zakovitch 1990; A. Sherwood 2006) and move toward her and away from the Israelites. The signifying operations that stick disgust to the Canaanite are reversed. They lose their stickiness.

But the story's final version works against such an easy revaluation of affect. Both Zakovitch and A. Sherwood, for instance, argue that the point of the story's critique of the Israelites is to bring glory to Yahweh. As Zakovitch puts it, the story, "which is none other than a parody of spy stories, comes, then, to a happy ending. God, whose will in any event is to deliver his people, will indeed deliver them" (1990, 95). Such readings must be influenced by the Deuteronomistic insertion of Rahab's proclamation of

---

14.Here I read Rahab rather differently than Kwok Pui-lan, who, reading as a "critic from Asia, where sex tourism is a flourishing business" (2006, 38), wonders if Rahab might have been something like prostitutes in Asia at the mercy of imperialist forces (38–39). Kwok rightly insists on a contextual economic understanding of the conditions in which prostitution thrives before demonizing either the practice or Rahab for making the choices she made; however, in my view Rahab's strong subject position and control in the text do not support a reading that suggests that she is engaging in survival sex. Like Brenner, I read Rahab's involvement in the sex trade more positively.

Yahweh's victory over the weak and ineffectual Canaanites, since as Culley points out, Yahweh is "remarkably absent from the action" of the story (1984, 33). Clearly, as a taming strategy, this speech is successful: while readers may pull away from the Israelites, they are not encouraged to move too close to the Canaanites, who in Rahab's speech are melting in fear, dissolving before their very eyes. So they move toward Yahweh. Many of the textual details that could be said to add to the humor of the early version are recuperated by the agenda of the final form. For instance, in Hawk's reading, the spies' response to Joshua's order becomes an example of lack of faith and obedience (1991, 68). In a Deuteronomistic framework, lack of obedience is morally problematic, whereas from an earlier perspective it might just be a humorous indicator of incompetence.

Nonetheless, the humor of the early version of the story resonates against the final version and creates a kind of static—to borrow a term from Culley on the effect of tensions in the text (1984, 34) and from Massumi on affective intensity (2002, 26)—that might disrupt a too-easy movement toward Yahweh. To return to Spencer Miller's point about orality, knowledge of earlier traditions can interact with final literary forms as a kind of cultural contestation. In this case, the early version of the story sits uneasily with Rahab's speech, which tells the tale of an effective holy war of the Israelites on their enemies. John H. Stek calls the speech a proclamation of "the *universal sovereignty* of Yahweh" (2002, 31, emphasis added); however, the earlier narrative frame pushes against the later speech and raises questions about the "universal" promises made in it. For instance, many scholars have pointed out that Rahab's speech represents Yahweh in the strongest terms, as divine warrior, using the language of holy war (חרם; Nelson 1997, 45, 52; T. Butler 1983, 35; Boling 1982, 146, 151; McCarthy 1971, 228–30; Frymer-Kensky 1997, 62; Tucker 1972, 79). Yet as mentioned, it is Rahab, not Yahweh, who is the subject of the actions in the story. Rahab's very presence in the text, her inclusion into it, and the need to manage her story indicates that in fact the Deuteronomistic terms of holy war (חרם) —complete extermination, as outlined in Deut 20:17—have not been met (Frymer-Kensky 1997, 63–65). A number of scholars point out Rahab's citation of the Song of Moses (specifically Exod 15:15–16), celebrating Yahweh's conquest over the Red Sea and Canaan in the exodus (Zakovitch 1990, 89; McCarthy 1971, 229; Hawk 1991, 66; Gillmayr-Bucher 2007, 145). But what this story shows, through the spies' easy misdirection, is that despite Yahweh's conquest over the sea, once out of Egypt, the people are not directed very effectively.

Moreover, Rahab's take-charge attitude in the early story suggests that the Canaanites are not actually melting in fear. Certainly she is not. She is feeling good enough to play jokes and/or wreak military havoc. In contrast to her description of the crushed Canaanites—"your terror has *fallen upon* us" (נפלה אימתכם עלינו; v. 9), "the spirit of a man will *not rise* again" (ולא קמה עוד רוח באיש; v. 11)—the verbs used to narrate her actions are telling: she *goes up* to the roof, literally upon them (עלתה עליהם; v. 8),[15] and she lets the Israelites *down* (ותורדם; v. 15)—where it seems they prefer to be given their main (attempted) action in the story, to lie down (שכב; vv. 1, 8).[16] Nor is the king of Jericho falling down in fear, since he tries to apprehend the spies. In fact, the spies are more dissolute than the Canaanites in more ways than one. The irony of the situation is intensified when it is noticed that after entering Rahab's house the spies are not the subject of any other verbs than שכב (to lie down) until they go into the mountains and return to Joshua. As McKinlay notices, after verse 1, the spies and Joshua are no longer in control (1999, 45–46).

So the humor of this story works on multiple levels. It critiques the Israelites, it represents Rahab positively, and it disputes the claims of the Deuteronomist made in Rahab's name. The reader might normally be repelled from the sexualized Canaanite and drawn toward Yahweh the divine warrior, but the humor works in the opposite direction. Disgust at the Canaanite dissipates, while the universal promise, for which Yahweh is a symbol, appears as less full than it asserts itself to be. Rahab's story illustrates what Ferguson has written of the much later context of sociology in the United States: "While canonical formations promise normalcy … the queer of color subject reminds us that such promises are techniques of discipline rather than vehicles toward liberation" (2004, 65).

---

15. Clearly על can also mean "to." Drucker points to some rabbinic readings that suggest that Rahab was positioned above the spies as she spoke to them (1982, 119). One might also wonder about the sexual implications here.

16. Hanson points out that the rabbinic tractate b. Zeb. 116a–b reads this language of fallen spirits with sexual innuendo, to mean that the men of the land had lost their virility—a fact to which Rahab would have had access (1978, 58). Reading the verbs in this way would suggest Rahab as more virile than the Israelites.

QUEER ENDINGS

Rahab the prostitute comically revalues the usual disciplinary responses to Canaanite sexuality. Her sexuality is not condemned. No longer disgusting and repulsive, but instead brilliant, assertive, and funny, the racialized, nonheteronormative woman has the upper hand, which she demonstrates by turning military proceedings into futile silliness. Instead of being vomited from the land, Rahab drolly expulses the putative victors from her business and her city. Even as the story's redaction tries to diminish these effects, the earlier story works against it. The shift in affect challenges the assumed heteropatriarchy through which the story is usually read, as well as the concomitant Deuteronomistic vision of the story's final form and "universal" norms of sexual behavior associated with that promise. The reader's body responds differently too. Dry heaves become mirth; repulsion becomes connection.

But is Rahab a queer hero? As noted, the promise of conquest in the final form—which is what most readers read—makes an easy reclamation of Rahab difficult. As McKinlay suggests, calling Rahab a hero invites an identification that dangerously condones imperialism in all its forms (1999, 56). But if queerness is transgressive, rather than liberative, as many insist, then the very idea of queer hero is problematic. Indeed, heroism produces affective responses much like those associated with the masculinist, salvific divine warrior, who guarantees the universal (through extermination of the other) and casts aspersions on any (who happen to remain) outside. It is precisely these conquestorial emotions that the story of Rahab revalues through laughter, silliness, futility, frustration, parody, and eyebrow raising. She is not a hero.

Nor is she completely transgressive. The final Deuteronomistic form of the story disallows it. Perhaps Rahab's textual situation is a more accurate reflection of the position in which most people find themselves: implicated in power dynamics that are not their choosing but from which they cannot so easily abstract themselves or obviously resist. As Puar puts it, the very notion of transgression assumes "an impossible transcendent subject who is always already conscious of the normativizing forces of power and always ready and able to subvert, resist, or transgress them" (2007, 24). Her point is that the very notion of queer transgression relies on a liberal paradigm of agency (here she is following Saba Mahmood and others). Puar is more interested in the process of "foregrounding power affiliations and disaffiliations … often rife with contradictions … [to] generate greater room for self-reflection, making mistakes, and autocritique." Certainly reading Rahab's story does make us aware of the working of power—in ancient Israel, in the redaction of the text, and in contemporary readings of it. As McKinlay has shown, it does provoke critical self-reflection.

Maybe the best designation for Rahab is trickster (Fewell and Gunn 1993, 121; McKinlay 1999, 49; Frymer-Kensky 1997, 66). Scholars who have called her a trickster are, no doubt, building on the excellent feminist work done in biblical studies on folklore (Niditch 1987; Exum and Bos, 1988). Yet the designation of trickster also links up with reclamations of this figure by critical race and postcolonial theorists as a (notably gender-queer) figure that humorously mimics, shadows, and critiques the dominant and oppressive culture (e.g., Gates 1988; Roberts 1990; Horne 1999; Vizenor 1990, 1993). As First Nations scholar Dee Horne writes, "tricksters ... give us refracted images in which the colonial discourse is re-contextualized" (1999, 130). Rahab, in her almost-but-not-quite hybridity—between the city and the gate, text and redaction, Canaanite and Israelite—is well positioned to make the jokes that upset the status quo, even while perhaps seeming uncomfortably to maintain it. As a textual construct, in an ancient text, she is, as Henry Louis Gates Jr. says of the African trickster Esu, a master of indeterminacy (1988, 23–43). At the same time, "by re-presenting settlers [Israelites] and their rules in a refracted image, they [tricksters/Rahab] enable listeners and readers to recognize not only ourselves as we are but also ourselves as we might be" (Horne 1999, 130).

It is as a trickster that Rahab brings the queer hilarity that can move affect in another direction, away from the disgust that guards the promise of the hope, inclusion, and safety of white heteronormative citizenship. It is as a trickster that she is the indeterminate figure that demands interpretation; she causes the discomfort that both solicits interpretation and conscripts interpreters to laugh. And it is as a trickster that she starts us laughing with others and at ourselves, shifting affective energies so that what we might become is not conscribed by signifiers of scripture sticky with the regurgitations of disgust.

WORKS CONSULTED

Ahmed, Sara. 2004. *The Cultural Politics of Emotions*. New York: Routledge.

Aichele, George, ed. 2000. *Culture, Entertainment, and the Bible.* JSOTSup 309. Sheffield: Sheffield Academic Press.

Althaus-Reid, Marcella. 2007. Searching for a Queer Sophia-Wisdom: The Postcolonial Rahab. Pages 128–40 in *Patriarchs, Prophets and Other Villains.* Edited by Lisa Isherwood. London: Equinox.

Bailey, Randall C. 2005. He Didn't Even Tell Us the Worst of It. *USQR* 59.1–2:15–24.

Bauckham, Richard. 1995. Tamar's Ancestry and Rahab's Marriage: Two Problems in the Matthean Genealogy. *NovT* 37:313–29.

Bhabha, Homi K. 1994. *The Location of Culture.* London: Routledge.

Bird, Phyllis A. 1989. The Harlot as Heroine: Narrative Art and Social Presupposition in Three Old Testament Texts. *Semeia* 46:119–39.

Boling, Robert G. 1982. *Joshua.* AB 6. New York: Doubleday.

Brenner, Athalya. 2002. Wide Gaps, Narrow Escapes: I Am Known as Rahab, the Broad. Pages 47–58 in *First Person: Essays in Biblical Autobiography.* Edited by Philip Davies. London: Sheffield Academic Press.

Brentlinger, Rick. 2007. Who Was Molech or Moloch? Online: http://www.gaychristian101.com/Molech.html.

Butler, Judith. 1993. *Bodies That Matter: On the Discursive Limits of "Sex."* New York: Routledge.

Butler, Trent C. 1983. *Joshua.* WBC 7. Waco, Tex.: Word.

Campbell, Antony F., and Mark A. O'Brien. 2000. *Unfolding the Deuteronomistic History: Origins, Upgrades, Present Text.* Minneapolis: Fortress.

Carby, Hazel V. 1987. *Reconstructing Womanhood: The Emergence of the Afro-American Woman Novelist.* Oxford: Oxford University Press.

Carden, Michael. 2006. Joshua. Pages 144–66 in *The Queer Bible Commentary.* Edited by Deryn Guest et al. London: SCM.

Chick, Jack. 1984. The Gay Blade. Online: http://www.chick.com/reading/tracts/0084/0084_01.asp.

Clough, Patricia. 2007. Introduction. Pages 1–33 in *The Affective Turn: Theorizing the Social.* Edited by Patricia Clough. Durham, N.C.: Duke University Press.

Collins, John J. 2003. The Zeal of Phinehas: The Bible and the Legitimation of Violence. *JBL* 122:3–21.

Culley, Robert C. 1984. Stories of the Conquest: Joshua 2, 6, 7, and 8. *HAR* 8:25–43.

Day, Peggy L. 2000. The Bitch Had It Coming to Her: Rhetoric and Interpretation in Ezekiel 16. *BibInt* 8:231–55.

Donaldson, Laura E. 2006. The Sign of Orpah: Reading Ruth through Native Eyes. Pages 159–70 in Sugirtharajah 2006.

Drucker, Reuven. 1982. *Yehoshua*. Brooklyn: Mesorah.

Dube, Musa W. 2006. Rahab Says Hello to Judith: A Decolonizing Feminist Reading. Pages 142–58 in Sugirtharajah 2006.

Exum, J. Cheryl, and Johanna W. H. Bos, eds. 1988. *Reasoning with the Foxes: Female Wit in a World of Male Power*. Semeia 42. Atlanta: Scholars Press.

Ferguson, Roderick A. 2004. *Aberrations in Black: Toward a Queer of Color Critique*. Minneapolis: University of Minnesota Press.

Fewell, Danna Nolan, and David M. Gunn. 1993. *Gender, Power, and Promise: The Subject of the Bible's First Story*. Nashville: Abingdon.

Frymer-Kensky, Tikva. 1997. Reading Rahab. Pages 57–67 in *Tehillah le-Moshe: Biblical and Judaic Studies in Honor of Moshe Greenberg*. Edited by Mordechai Cogan, Barry L. Eichler, and Jeffrey H. Tigay. Winona Lake, Ind.: Eisenbrauns.

Galatzer-Levy, Robert M., and Mayer Gruber. 1992. What an Affect Means: A Quasi-Experiment about Disgust. *Annual of Psychoanalysis* 20:69–91.

Gates, Henry Louis, Jr. 1988. *The Signifying Monkey: A Theory of African-American Literary Criticism*. Oxford: Oxford University Press.

Gillmayr-Bucher, Susanne. 2007. "She Came to Test Him with Hard Questions": Foreign Women and Their View on Israel. *BibInt* 15:135–50.

Gilman, Sander L. 1985. Black Bodies, White Bodies: Toward an Iconography of Female Sexuality in Late Nineteenth-Century Art, Medicine, and Literature. *Critical Inquiry* 12:204–42.

Hammonds, Evelynn M. 1997. Toward a Genealogy of Black Female Sexuality: The Problematic of Silence. Pages 170–82 in *Feminist Geneaologies, Colonial Legacies, Global Movements*. Edited by M. Jacqui Alexander and Chandra Talpade Mohanty. New York: Routledge.

Hanson, A. T. 1978. Rahab the Harlot in Early Christian Tradition. *JSNT* 1:53–60.

Hawk, L. Daniel. 1991. *Every Promise Fulfilled: Contesting Plots in Joshua*. Louisville: Westminster John Knox.

Hillers, Delbert R. 1985. Analyzing the Abominable: Our Understanding of Canaanite Religion. *JQR* 75:253–69.

Horne, Dee. 1999. *Contemporary American Indian Writing: Unsettling Literature*. New York: Peter Lang.

Howard, David M., Jr. 1998. *Joshua.* NAC 5. Nashville: Broadman & Holman.

Knoll, K. L. 2001. *Canaan and Israel in Antiquity: An Introduction.* Biblical Seminar 83. Sheffield: Sheffield Academic Press.

Kramer, Phyllis Silverman. 2000. Rahab: From Peshat to Pedagogy, or: The Many Faces of a Heroine. Pages 156–72 in Aichele 2000.

Kwok Pui-lan. 2006. Sexual Morality and National Politics: Reading Biblical "Loose Women." Pages 21–46 in *Engaging the Bible: Critical Readings from Contemporary Women.* Edited by Choi Hee An and Katheryn Pfisterer Darr. Minneapolis: Fortress.

Lyons, William L. 2008. Rahab through the Ages: A Study of Christian Interpretation of Rahab. *SBL Forum* 6.7. Online: http://www.sbl-site. org/publications/article.aspx?ArticleId=786.

Massumi, Brian. 2002. *Parables for the Virtual: Movement, Affect, Sensation.* Durham, N.C.: Duke University Press.

McCarthy, Dennis J. 1971. Some Holy War Vocabulary in Joshua 2. *CBQ* 33:228–30.

McKinlay, Judith E. 1999. Rahab: A Hero/ine? *BibInt* 7:44–57.

Muñoz, José Esteban. 1999. *Disidentifications: Queers of Color and the Performance of Politics.* Cultural Studies of the Americas 2. Minneapolis: University of Minnesota Press.

Nelson, Richard D. 1997. *Joshua: A Commentary.* OTL. Louisville: Westminster John Knox.

Niditch, Susan. 1987. *Underdogs and Tricksters: A Prelude to Biblical Folklore.* New York: Harper & Row.

Pellegrini, Ann. 2001. Laughter. Pages 177–90 in *Psychoanalysis and Performance.* Edited by Patrick Campbell and Adrian Kear. New York: Routledge.

Puar, Jasbir K. 2007. *Terrorist Assemblages: Homonationalism in Queer Times.* Next Wave: New Directions in Women's Studies. Durham, N.C.: Duke University Press.

Roberts, John W. 1990. *From Trickster to Badman: The Black Folk Hero in Slavery and Freedom.* Philadelphia: University of Pennsylvania Press.

Rowlett, Lori. 2000. Disney's Pocahontas and Joshua's Rahab in Postcolonial Perspective." Pages 66–75 in Aichele 2000.

Runions, Erin. 2005. Refusal to Mourn: U.S. National Melancholia and Its Prophetic Precursors. *Postscripts* 1:9–45.

Sherwood, Aaron. 2006. A Leader's Misleading and a Prostitute's Profession: A Re-examination of Joshua 2. *JSOT* 31:43–61.

Sherwood, Yvonne. 1995. Boxing Gomer: Controlling the Deviant Woman in Hosea 1–3. Pages 101–24 in *A Feminist Companion to the Prophets*. Edited by Athalya Brenner. Sheffield: Sheffield Academic Press.

Soggin, J. Alberto. 1972. *Joshua: A Commentary*. OTL. Philadelphia: Westminster.

Smith, Mark S. 2002. *The Early History of God: Yahweh and the Other Deities in Ancient Israel*. 2nd ed. Grand Rapids: Eerdmans.

Spencer Miller, Althea. 2007. Orality and the Narrative Techniques of the Acts of the Apostles, the Homeric Epics, Greco-Roman Novels and Greco-Roman Historiography: A Comparative Approach. Ph.D. diss., Claremont Graduate University.

Stek, John H. 2002. Rahab of Canaan and Israel: The Meaning of Joshua 2. *CTJ* 37:28–48.

Stone, Ken. 2004. Queering the Canaanite. Pages 110–34 in *The Sexual Theologian: Essays on Sex, God, and Politics*. Edited by Marcella Althaus-Reid and Lisa Isherwood. Queering Theology. London: T&T Clark.

Sugirtharajah, R. S., ed. 2006. *The Postcolonial Biblical Reader*. Oxford: Blackwell.

Tucker, Gene M. 1972. The Rahab Saga (Joshua 2): Some Form-Critical and Traditio-Historical Observations. Pages 66–86 in *The Use of the Old Testament in the New and Other Essays: Studies in Honor of William Franklin Stinespring*. Edited by James M. Efird. Durham, N.C.: Duke University Press.

Vizenor, Gerald. 1990. Trickster Discourse. *American Indian Quarterly* 14:277–87.

———. 1993. The Ruins of Representation: Shadow Survivance and the Literature of Dominance. *American Indian Quarterly* 17 (1):7–30.

Wimbush, Vincent L. 2008. Introduction: TEXTureS, Gestures, Power: Orientation to Radical Excavation. Pages 1–20 in *Theorizing Scriptures: New Critical Orientations to a Cultural Phenomenon*. Edited by Vincent L. Wimbush. New Brunswick, N.J.: Rutgers University Press.

Yeğenoğlu, Meyda. 1998. *Colonial Fantasies: Towards a Feminist Reading of Orientalism*. Cambridge: Cambridge University Pres.

Zakovitch, Yair. 1990. Humor and Theology or the Successful Failure of Israelite Intelligence: A Literary-Folkloric Approach to Joshua 2. Pages 75–98 in *Text and Tradition: The Hebrew Bible and Folklore*. Edited by Susan Niditch. SemeiaSt. Atlanta: Scholars Press.

Queer Reading between Bible and Film:
Paris Is Burning and the "Legendary Houses" of David and Saul

Ken Stone

Over the course of a decade or more, a number of papers and publications have encouraged the coupling of Bible and film. The pairing of Bible and film remains uncommon in biblical studies, however, and even when Bible and film are brought together, there is no single way of staging the relationship between them. Many biblical scholars who write about Bible and film concentrate on movies that retell the stories of biblical characters: *The Ten Commandments, David and Bathsheba, The Passion of the Christ*, and so forth. In this sort of analysis, the combination of Bible and film can be understood as part of a wider interest in the Bible's reception history. But Bible and film are also brought together in less conventional ways. So, for example, Carol Newsom has attempted to explicate the assumptions about women found in the biblical book of Proverbs by comparing it with the movie *Fatal Attraction* (Lyne 1987). As Newsom notes, both Proverbs and *Fatal Attraction* draw on a polarized distinction between the good wife at home and the dangerous female sexual subject that a man may encounter in public. The goal of Newsom's turn to film is not to sketch the history of the Bible's reception, for *Fatal Attraction* never refers to Proverbs. By reminding her own reader of the dynamics at work in *Fatal Attraction* and Proverbs, Newsom attempts rather to use Bible and film to shed light on one another and on the assumptions about gender and sexuality that, in her view, structure both texts (Newsom 1989; cf. Stone 2005, 134–35).

As this example from Newsom's work indicates, matters of gender and sexual practice have played an important role in discussions of Bible and film. Indeed, feminist biblical scholars have been at the forefront of the writing that does exist on film and biblical interpretation (cf. Bach 1996,

1997; Exum 1996). In spite of this concern about gender and sexuality, however, the study of Bible and film has had relatively little to do, to date, with the emergence of queer readings of the Bible.

Recently, however, in the context of a larger study of Bible and film, Erin Runions has taken some steps in this direction. In the introduction to her book *How Hysterical*, Runions alerts her reader to her intention to read Bible, film, and contemporary theory together, "regardless of whether the Bible appears as direct citation in the film. … In comparing seemingly disparate texts, the similarities and differences can bring to light and critique sites of identification and resistance that might otherwise be obscure" (Runions 2003, 2). The six essays that make up Runions's book do engage a wide range of "seemingly disparate texts," biblical, theoretical, and filmic. More significantly for my purposes here, at least two of these essays make interpretive moves and engage theoretical discourses that we might usefully consider "queer."

As someone who has been engaged for some time in encouraging queer readings (always in the plural) of the Bible, I would like to use one of Runions's essays as a point of departure and a dialogue partner for a reflection of my own on the practices of queer reading between Bible and film. However, I understand my primary goals to be slightly different from those of Runions. Runions' book is focused first of all on reading Bible, film, and theory together. As part of that larger project, Runions selects queer theory as one among several theoretical discourses that allow her to think in different ways about the relations between Bible and film. My own interest lies more specifically in the experimentation with queer readings, particularly in relation to the Bible (see, e.g., Stone 2001a, 2005, 2006, 2007, 2008). The space between Bible and film is thus for me simply one among several sites on which to carry out that experimentation. So, to oversimplify a bit, there is a sense in which what is primary for my focus is secondary for the focus of Runions' book; and what is primary for that text is secondary for my own. Nevertheless, I intend to follow parts of Runions' argument rather closely. In the reflections that follow, I will first try to summarize a few of the moves that I understand Runions to be making in the essay that primarily interests me here. With some inspiration from Runions, however, I would then like to continue lingering over a film that she has selected for discussion while bringing that film into relation with a different body of biblical material than that examined by Runions. My goal will be to experiment with a practice of queer reading between Bible and film that engages biblical scholarship without being restricted by all of its norms.

BIBLE, "GENDERFUCK," AND *PARIS IS BURNING*

So, what is Runions up to in the fourth chapter of her book, which is the chapter that most interests me here? In that essay, titled "Zion Is Burning," Runions reads the biblical book of Micah alongside *Paris Is Burning* (Livingston 1991), a now-famous—and, for some reviewers, infamous—documentary on New York City drag balls that was released in 1991. Although the film was directed by a white lesbian filmmaker (Jennie Livingston), it focuses primarily on a drag culture created by African American and Latino gay men. The film won several awards and was much discussed when it first appeared, and it has since been a recurring object of analysis for queer discussions of film. However, at least so far as I am aware, Runions is the first scholar to publish a reading of the Bible that actively engages both *Paris Is Burning* and the critical debates that followed it. Her suggestion is that "both text and film exhibit what is technically termed 'genderfuck,' that is, the mixing of masculine and feminine gender codes in ways that subvert the present bipolar gender system." And here again we may have a first in the interpretation of the Bible: "genderfuck" is not a term that will be found in many methodological handbooks for biblical studies. As Runions sees it, however, both the biblical book of Micah and *Paris Is Burning* "perform genderfuck by setting up gender norms that are then repeated in ways that call those norms into question" (2003, 93).

In order to make this argument, Runions examines transgressions of gender codes that take place in both texts. Such transgressions are perhaps obvious in *Paris Is Burning*, which after all focuses on drag balls. For my purposes here, it is important to note (for reasons that will eventually become clear) that most of the participants in these balls organize their lives around so-called "houses," social networks of support that are referred to also as "families" by one of the film's speakers. These "houses" arguably function as something like alternative kinship structures, especially for those individuals who, because they are gay or transgendered, can no longer live with families of origin. Within a particular house, one member serves as a symbolic "mother" who, as one of the mothers puts it in the film, "rules" over the house. Kinship language and the language of monarchy are therefore interwoven in the discourse of the speakers in the film. Some of the "houses" have "fathers" as well as "mothers," although the "fathers" seem to be secondary in status to the "mothers." At the drag balls, members of the houses, who refer to one another as "children" and occasionally as "sisters," compete in specific categories to see who can best embody standards used to define the categories. Thus individuals who are or have been biologically male (to use, for convenience, the conventional language) are competing in categories that are in many cases marked as feminine. Moreover, as the film shows, a number of these individuals also attempt to live or pass as female outside of the drag balls. Partly as a consequence, *Paris Is Burning* has become, as Runions notes, something of "an iconic text" for "transsexuals, transvestites, drag queens, and other gender transgressors" (2003, 93).

It is important to note, however, that a few of the categories in which competitors perform at the balls are marked as masculine rather than feminine. Some of the house children perform the roles of male students, for example, and still others dress up and act as male soldiers in uniform or male business executives. Thus masculinity, as exhibited by men, is also a kind of "drag" in *Paris Is Burning*, and it is performed by gay men who consciously act out a role.

Whether they embody "female" or "male" roles, however, participants emphasize the importance of what the film calls "realness," the ability to "pass" as members of the category that, on stage or in life, they attempt to perform. Moreover, individuals or houses that achieve enough victories at the balls or secure their reputations in the eyes of other houses also achieve a status that is described by ball participants as "legend" or "legendary." Thus, Pepper Labeija, one participant in the film who has made a name for himself on the circuit as a consequence of her performances, refers to himself as the "legendary mother of the house of Labeija ... I just rule it now."

Transgressions of gender norms do play a role, then, in *Paris Is Burning*, as Runions suggests. Turning to the biblical prophetic book of Micah after summarizing the film, however, Runions makes a case for finding elements of gender transgression in the biblical text as well. So, for example, she highlights mixtures of gendered linguistic forms in the Hebrew text (involving imperatives, pronominal indicators, and so forth) that are often explained away by commentators or smoothed over in translations. In addition, she shows how personified cities and nations are represented in ways that combine both "masculine" and "feminine" cultural gender signals. Thus gendered conventions of language and culture are utilized by Micah, but not always in consistent or expected ways. To put the matter in language associated with the theories of Judith Butler and Homi Bhaba (the two theorists who serve as major dialogue partners in this chapter of Runions's book), Micah repeats or cites gender norms, but the book's iterations of gender are not simply duplications of those norms. Slippage and difference occur within the repetition of norms.

Yet as Runions points out, gender transgressions in both the biblical text and the film are also met with violence. A case can be made, moreover, that both texts actually reconfirm hegemonic norms, at least to some extent. The norms to which one must attend in order to analyze this possibility are not only gender norms but also norms of nation, economic status, and race or ethnicity. Indeed, several critical responses to the film, including a much-cited discussion by bell hooks (1992), emphasize the fact that the drag players in *Paris Is Burning*, though predominantly African American and Latino, appear often, in their speech and aspirations, to valorize norms derived from white, middle- and upper-class North America. Micah, too, appears to accept dominant norms from his own time (relying for example upon the widespread ancient dichotomy between active masculine and passive feminine) while also articulating gender notions with matters of nation and distinctions among peoples. Thus Runions asks whether these texts, even with their gender transgressions, can be considered subversive. Moreover, if we note that violence and hegemonic notions as well as gender transgression structure the texts, then we must ask about the responsibility of viewers or readers vis-à-vis such texts. By emphasizing or valorizing matters of gender transgression in the texts, do we risk being complicit in the relations of violence and domination that also structure the two texts?

Runions, to her credit, raises such questions but refuses to give them easy answers. Avoiding a dualistic approach, which might lead one either to idealize the texts or reject them out of hand, she recalls instead Butler's suggestion, in a discussion of *Paris Is Burning*, that drag performance in the film "both appropriates and subverts" norms of gender and race. Butler therefore characterizes the film's relation to such norms as one of "ambivalence" (Butler 1993, 128; cf. Runions 2003, 104). The term "ambivalence" becomes key for Runions, who uses it to characterize Micah as well as *Paris Is Burning*; and it offers Runions a route to connect not only with Butler's work but also with the work of Homi Bhaba (Bhaba 1994). Runions acknowledges that the relevance of Bhaba's work for an analysis of gender rather than colonialism might not be easily granted. Nevertheless, picking up a suggestion by performance theorist Peggy Phelan (1993, 187–88) that Bhaba's work could shed some light on *Paris Is Burning*, Runions points out that Bhaba, like Butler, utilizes the term "ambivalence," specifically, while explicating implications of the fact that colonizers desire mimicry

from those they colonize. This demand for mimicry corresponds to a disavowal of threatening difference: the colonizer does not want the colonized
to be *too* radically other. According to Bhaba, however, such mimicry must
not be exact, either, for colonizers do wish to maintain their own identity as authentic, pure and original. The consequence is something hybrid,
something similar to and yet different from the supposed original. This
simultaneous presence of similarity and difference in the relation between
colonizer and colonized generates ambivalence; but so does the fact that
hybridity, by repeating with a difference, threatens to expose the supposed
authenticity of the original as a myth and undermine colonial authority in
the eyes of the colonized. As with Butler's theory of gender performativity,
then, so also with Bhaba's theory of mimicry, hybridity, and ambivalence,
instances of repetition cannot always be classified neatly as simply consoli-
dating or subverting norms. Rather, norms appear to be *both* affirmed *and*
undermined by such repetitions.

Armed with these concepts, Runions uncovers in both film and biblical text evidence of a gender hybridity, which potentially exposes the artificial nature of dominant norms. Significantly, for both viewers of the film
and readers of the biblical text, Runions raises questions about the effects
produced by the possibilities for identification with hybrid subject positions. Her hope, she tells us frankly at the end of her chapter, is that reflection on such possibilities will inspire genderfuck among her own readers.

The Legendary Houses of David and Saul

So, what is one to do with this? How might we take Runions's reading of
Paris Is Burning and Micah and "put it to work," to borrow some language
that Runions uses elsewhere in her book (2003, 115)?

Let me note first that it was nearly impossible to be a graduate stu-
dent during the early 1990s, interested (as I was) in the critical analysis of
gender and sexuality, and *not* be involved in discussions of *Paris Is Burning*. This was true even for those of us who studied Bible. Indeed, I recall
sitting in the Vanderbilt Humanities Center, in a seminar room full of
faculty members and doctoral students, from a range of disciplines but all
interested in what was then the newly emerging field of lesbian and gay
studies, and participating in lively arguments about the film. Our arguments were, to a significant degree, structured around many of the same
questions that both Runions and Butler raise and then complicate: Do
the drag performers in *Paris Is Burning* consolidate or subvert dominant

norms of gender, race, and class? I have probably watched *Paris Is Burning* ten or twelve times, though not for several years until relatively recently. Yet I have to confess that, until I encountered Runions's reading of it, I don't recall having given much thought to ways in which the film might be brought into dialogue with biblical interpretation. I was certainly interested in rereading the Bible in the light of theoretical analyses (such as Butler's) that were written in dialogue with the film, and I had made use of Butler's book *Bodies that Matter* (which is the volume that includes Butler's reading of *Paris Is Burning*). I was even committed to analyzing and complicating, in relation to the Bible, the very sorts of questions that we had debated in relation to *Paris Is Burning*, specifically, how does this text relate to the consolidation or subversion of hegemonic norms? Yet the film itself remained at some distance, consciously at least, from any of my interactions with the biblical text. It never occurred to me to allow such a modern film to frame my readings of biblical texts in the way that I was, for example, as part of a larger trend in biblical scholarship, allowing texts from the twentieth-century anthropology of honor and shame to frame those readings (cf. Stone 1993, 1994, 1995, 1996). Perhaps it would even have seemed improper for a disciplined biblical scholar to read biblical texts in dialogue with *Paris Is Burning*.

But impropriety is the stuff of queer reading. A queer reading of the Bible may find it useful to trouble not only norms of sex and gender but also the norms that constrain biblical interpretation, in both popular and scholarly modes, by directing us to read biblical literature alongside these texts but not those. And so, encouraged by Runions's own example of finding in Bible and film unexpected similarities, I more recently returned to this film about so-called legendary houses and rulers and watched it again. I heard once more the assertion made by several house members that their balls and contests were really "fights" and even "wars." And I recalled immediately the biblical reference in 2 Sam 3:1 to a "long war" between two ancient kinship entities referred to explicitly as the "*house* of Saul" and the "*house* of David." I have long been intrigued by questions about the role of gender and sexual practice in that war (see, e.g., Stone 1993, 1994, 1996). But returning to those questions in the light of both *Paris Is Burning* and Runions's reading of it, I found myself thinking of the biblical war between the house of Saul and the house of David as a sort of contest of "realness," perhaps even "executive realness" (to cite one of the specific categories of manhood identified in *Paris Is Burning*). After all, the question that must be decided in the books of Samuel is: Which of these "legendary houses," the house of Saul or the house of David, will rule over Israel? Which house will produce Israel's "chief executives" (to quote the film again)? In order for the matter to be decided, members of each biblical house must demonstrate their ability to embody features apparently considered desirable in Israelite "rulers" (to use the language also applied to house "mothers" in *Paris Is Burning*). They must show that they can "pass" as "real" kings in the eyes of Israel. And the criteria used to evaluate their competitive performances are inextricably intertwined, in 2 Samuel as in *Paris Is Burning*, with norms of gender.

Let us recall how this happens in 2 Sam 3. Although Saul himself is dead by this point in David's story, the chapter does open with that reference to "the long war between the house of Saul and the house of David" (3:1) and then notes that the house of David was growing stronger while the house of Saul was growing weaker. Immediately after this, four biblical verses list six sons of David borne by six different women. Commentaries sometimes dismiss these four verses as a later "insertion," not on the basis of text-critical evidence but rather on the grounds that they "interrupt … the flow of the narrative from 3:1 to 3:6" (McCarter 1984, 102). In verse 6 we do find another reference to "the war between the house of Saul and the house of David," which reminds us of verse 1. But do the four verses in between really "interrupt" the narrative? Or might they be seen instead as a representation of David's performance of the category of Israelite manhood, which performance helps the audience understand *how* the house of David is growing stronger than the house of Saul? After all, the verses reveal David's ability to secure multiple women and sire multiple sons, in a world where acquiring women and siring sons are signifiers of masculinity. Moreover, one of these women, Abigail, is the wife of one of David's former rivals; another, Ahinoam, carries the same name as a wife of David's other rival, Saul. Thus the listing of women and sons in 2 Sam 3 not only demonstrates David's sexual potency but also serves to remind an audience that he is flourishing while previous military rivals (including Saul, the father of his current rival) have been removed.

David's success at such manly performance is contrasted immediately with a demonstration that the house of Saul simply cannot compete, for in 2 Sam 3:7 we learn how the current representative of the house of Saul, Saul's surviving son Ishbaal (or Ishboshet), tries but fails to demonstrate his authority over other members of his own house. According to the narrator, Abner, Ishbaal's great-uncle and military chief, "was making himself strong in the house of Saul" (3:6b, NRSV). This strengthening is then illustrated in much the same way that the strengthening of the house of David has been illustrated already: by a narrative account of sexual relations. Abner, we learn, has been having sexual relations with Rizpah, a woman who had belonged to Ishbaal's dead father, Saul. This one woman is, of course, many fewer than the six who have just been named for David; and in a world where the accumulation of women corresponds to the accumulation of power and prestige, this cannot have gone unnoticed by those judging between the house of Saul and the house of David. But even Abner's modest performance exceeds that of his nephew Ishbaal. For when Ishbaal attempts to assert his manly rights over the women of the house of his father Saul, Abner rebuffs him with an angry speech indicating that Ishbaal's power, such as it is, depends entirely upon Abner (3:8).

This testy reply is surely an insult. Or perhaps we could refer to it as what the ball children call a "reading." For in *Paris Is Burning*, "reading," as one of the characters puts it, "is the real art form of insult." Within the social discourse of the ball participants, "reading" is not first of all an interaction with a written text. "Reading" is, rather, a kind of dramatic way of putting someone in their place by letting them know through derisive speech that they have been "read," that they have been recognized as inadequate, as lacking in abilities to perform, and as something far short of the legend they so want to be. As Butler rightly notes, someone who can be "read" has failed to embody convincingly the ideals she or he attempts to approximate (1993, 129). The person who carries out a "reading" thus exposes the person who is "read" as having been unsuccessful at "realness." And so, having read Ishbaal's failure to approximate ideals of manly kingship, and having exposed this son of Saul as something less than a "real" man, a "real" king, Abner switches his loyalties from the house of Saul to the house of David, with an explicit acknowledgment that even God intends to make David king (2 Sam 3:9–10). David is thus, in Abner's eyes, now recognized as what the ball children in *Paris Is Burning* call a "future legend," an "up-and-coming legend."

It does at least seem possible, then, to redescribe certain dynamics from the story of the house of David and the house of Saul, as told in 2 Samuel, in terms of certain dynamics from the film *Paris Is Burning*. And I have to confess to experiencing a queer bit of pleasure in being able to reimagine this great biblical epic of manly struggles as something like a drag ball, a contest in the performance of gendered "realness."

But let us think further about the presence of "very ambiguously gendered characters," which Runions finds in the book of Micah as in, more obviously, *Paris Is Burning* (2003, 98). Do we see such characters in the competition between the house of Saul and the house of David?

To the extent that David, Abner, and Ishbaal are represented in 2 Sam 3 in relation to cultural norms for manhood, Ishbaal's failure to embody those norms as successfully as David translates, I would argue, into a kind of diminished masculinity. Ishbaal is shown to be a less manly man and hence, potentially, something less than a real man. That such a point is made in the context of a military struggle between the house of Saul and the house of David is significant. After all, in Israel as elsewhere in the ancient Near East, military success and failure were sometimes symbolized in gendered ways. As Cynthia Chapman has recently reminded us in a study of biblical and Assyrian gendered military imagery (2004), to be defeated militarily in the ancient Near East is, for a man, somewhat akin to being feminized.

However, gender ambiguity and the feminization of men appear in the biblical representation of the struggle between Israel's legendary houses even prior to 2 Sam 3. If we look carefully at earlier stages of the story, we may find something rather closer to Runions's notion of biblical gender "mixing" in the figure of the brother whom Ishbaal apparently replaces, another one of the legendary children of the house of Saul: Jonathan.

A number of biblical scholars have noted how Jonathan's role in 1 Samuel parallels in certain respects the role of his sister Michal, another one of the wives of David. Both siblings are characterized in terms of their "love" for David; both siblings are instrumental in saving David from their father at crucial points in the narrative; and both siblings are called to account by their father for what they have done. In 1 Sam 18—the very chapter in which both Jonathan and Michal are twice said to "love" David—David's covenant with Jonathan toward the beginning of the chapter arguably parallels David's marriage to Michal toward the end of the chapter. Yet as Susan Ackerman points out in an important recent study, the marriage to Michal in chapter 18 is followed by another account of David's relationship to Jonathan at the beginning of chapter 19, so that Jonathan appears actually to supplant Michal in the course of the narrative. Michal does reappear later in the chapter; but then Jonathan reappears in chapter 20, where a longer account of his interactions with David is found. Ackerman notes, moreover, that the Samuel narratives are put together in such a way as to compare David's relationship to Jonathan not only with David's relationship to Michal but also with David's relationship to their other sister, Merab, who at one point in the story might also have become David's wife. Thus, as Ackerman sees it, Jonathan, "although male, is over and over depicted as wife-like in relation to David" (2005, 210).

However, in addition to noting parallels between Jonathan and David's wives (including also Abigail, who is mentioned in the list of David's wives in 2 Sam 3), Ackerman revisits the question of Jonathan's love for David, famously said by David in 2 Sam 1:26 to exceed the love of women. Many biblical scholars interpret the love between Jonathan and David in terms of the vocabulary of ancient Near Eastern political covenant relations. Ackerman, however, while not disputing the relevance of that parallel, nevertheless notes (agreeing, on this point, with a recent article by Saul Olyan [2006]) that 2 Samuel's specific comparison of a political relationship between men to the love of women, which is in turn normally understood as erotic or sexual love, is quite unusual in the ancient Near East. The peculiarity is heightened when we put the statement together with other unexpected textual phenomena. There is, for example, the statement in 1 Sam 18:1 that Jonathan loved David "as his own soul," which may recall the five references by the female speaker in Song of Songs to the one "whom my soul loves" (Song 1:7; 3:1–4). There is the reference to Jonathan's "delight" for David in 19:1, using a word that has connotations of sexual desire in Gen 34 and appears together with "love" in Song of Songs. And there are the sexual connotations of language about "your mother's nakedness" that Saul uses when rebuking Jonathan angrily for his relationship to David in 1 Sam 20:30.

The accumulation of such details is, for Ackerman, finally too great to be handled solely by appeals to ancient conventions of political covenant making. Thus Ackerman concludes that the books of Samuel communicate a complex message about Jonathan and David, in the context of an apologetic attempt to legitimize the house of David and undermine the house of Saul. While in certain passages Jonathan acts like the manly warrior prince that one expects Saul's son to be, other passages represent Jonathan as submitting politically to David, whom Jonathan loves and in whom Jonathan delights. The message of political submission is emphasized by what Ackerman calls a "feminization of Jonathan within a homoeroticized context" (2005, 221). Ackerman is careful to distinguish "homoerotic" here from modern notions of homosexual identity. Her understanding of "homoeroticism" is developed in relation to the ancient network of gendered and sexual conventions according to which eroticism involved an active social superior (properly male) and a passive social subordinate (properly female or feminized). Against the backdrop of such conventions, Jonathan's love for David (which has connotations of both political covenant *and* personal affection) underscores Jonathan's *submission* to David. And it does so in terms of mixed gender. Jonathan is a man, indeed a warrior prince, whose characterization here can nevertheless be described by Ackerman as "wife-like" (223 and passim) and "womanlike" (221 and passim). Jonathan is thus—to bring our discussion back to Runions's language—"a very ambiguously gendered character" (2003, 98). And the ambiguity seems to be recognized by other readers attentive to the literary dynamics of the biblical text. The remarks made by numerous biblical scholars about these characters are revealing. Thus, Adele Berlin speaks of David having "related ... to Jonathan as to a woman" (1983, 25); Danna Nolan Fewell and David Gunn observe that "Jonathan is a woman, more woman than women are" (1993, 151); and David Jobling remarks that Jonathan is represented in the text as "a better woman than David's women" (1998, 162).

To the extent, then, that "genderfuck" involves, for Runions, "the mixing of masculine and feminine gender codes in ways that subvert the present bipolar gender system" (2003, 93), Jonathan's characterization in the Bible appears to be moving in that direction. Certainly the "mixing of masculine and feminine gender codes" seems to be present in Jonathan's story.

But what about the subversion? Here we have to note something about the story of Jonathan that Runions notes about both *Paris Is Burning* and the book of Micah: gender ambiguity is met with violence. One of the ball children in *Paris Is Burning*, Venus Xtravaganza, who uses feminine "realness" not only to walk in the balls but also to turn tricks outside of them, is murdered before the film ends, apparently when her male genitalia are discovered by a client. The dangers inherent in gender ambiguity are recognized by another speaker in the film, Dorian Corey, who observes that "when they're undetectable, when they can walk out of that ball room, into the sunlight and onto the subway and get home and still have all their clothes and no blood running off their bodies, those are the femme realness queens." Those who can pass the test of "realness" may escape violence, while those who are more obviously characterized by gender ambiguity may end up with "blood running off their bodies."

But Jonathan, too, may suffer the violent fate of *Paris Is Burning*'s more ambiguous gender transgressors. He does, after all, die in the story of David. Moreover, his sister Michal, sometimes seen as an "ambiguously gendered character" herself (cf., e.g., Berlin 1983), is silenced in the text as well. Thus one might conclude from the fates of these legendary children that gender transgression will be firmly disavowed and disallowed by the biblical text.

Exactly at this point, however, Runions's appeal to ambivalence and hybridity may be relevant. Within the framework of Bhaba's theory as used and developed by Runions, ambivalence plays a role in at least two dynamics. There is a complex relation of similarity and difference, in which two entities (for Bhaba, the colonizer and colonized) are similar but not too similar, different but not too different. The hybridized entity must be seen as an *imperfect* imitation of the supposedly more pure counterpart. However, there is also a tendency for perceived similarities, which are necessary for imitation, to undermine the authority of the player who claims to be authentic and pure (Bhaba's colonizer). The authenticity of the latter tends to be undermined by the imperfect imitation of the other.

Now, granting that I have just oversimplified the structural dynamics of a very complex theory, it seems to me that both of these dynamics can also be found in the relations of Jonathan and David, especially if we follow Runions's example and consider not only the text but also its reception, which involves complexities of identification. In order to represent the house of David as the embodiment of authentic royal manhood, the books of Samuel represent the house of Saul as an imperfect imitation of such manhood. The imperfection can be seen, among other places, in the manifestations of "womanliness" in the character of Jonathan, who therefore both is and is not a manly warrior prince. The fact that Jonathan does sometimes act as a warrior prince, and does sometimes act as David's superior, can be confusing if one expects to find in the Bible only and always consistent gendered characterization. On the other hand, Jonathan's characterization makes more sense if viewed from the perspective of hybridity and ambivalence. Jonathan is not totally devoid of manly ideals but is rather an imperfect imitation of manly ideals, a hybridized gendered character who is represented in ambivalent ways. It is David, his Judahite house, and the nation that identified with them which aspire to be seen as embodying manly ideals in a more pure, authentic fashion that Jonathan can only mimic.

But are David and his house in fact so seen by readers? Ackerman argues that, in order to accomplish the apologetic intent of the story of David and Jonathan, Jonathan must be shown, by writers who prefer David and his house, to be "in a position of status subordination" to David (2005, 222). The insinuation of homoerotic love and "wifelike" delight on the part of Jonathan accomplishes this. However, Ackerman also notes that the text represents Jonathan as the initiator of the relationship between the two men. Ackerman suggests that this representation helps to alleviate concerns that David was involved in any coercive use of male-male sex to accomplish domination, such as we find threatened in Gen 19 and Judg 19 (two chapters in which threats of male-male rape play a role in the biblical plot). While this may be right, it's also worth pointing out that, by placing Jonathan in the position of initiator, the text puts Jonathan back in what can be seen as the more traditionally masculine position of subject, and David in the feminine position of object. Thus, a disavowed feminization that has been associated with Jonathan arguably resurfaces in the characterization of David, now the object of Jonathan's love. And when David later speaks of the "wonderful" nature of Jonathan's love for him, David's own manly status may therefore be called into question. Here, the object, normally coded as feminine in the ancient world, praises the love of the subject, normally coded as masculine. As a consequence, David's own manhood is potentially destabilized. Indeed, perhaps just this instability helps us understand how, at a later point in their story, David's own son Absalom can find it possible to challenge his father, once again using signifiers of gender, sexual practice, and symbolic unmanning (see Stone 1993, 1996).

It is therefore finally unclear whether the attempt to represent David as a pure, authentic embodiment of Israelite norms of manhood, and so to establish the greater suitability of David's house to rule Israel, is successful. Like *Paris Is Burning*, the story of the house of David and the house of Saul "both appropriates and subverts" gender norms. It appropriates those norms in order to try to discredit the house of Saul for its failure to embody gender norms with "realness." But it may subvert those norms, or at least offer openings for readers to subvert those norms, when, in the representation of David and his house, slippage and difference in the repetition of gender norms produce mixed gender messages. Such mixed messages may well provide opportunities for the resistant identification that Runions emphasizes in her book on Bible and film. For even if we believe (as I do) that the story of David comes to us from a world in which modern notions about gay identity and gay relationships were not presupposed in the conceptualization of homoeroticism, the presence in 1–2 Samuel of "ambiguously gendered characters" who love one another has long made the relationship between David and Jonathan a kind of "iconic text" (to use the phrase Runions applies to *Paris Is Burning*) for gay men who find in that relationship points of identification. Some gay readers do focus upon Jonathan as the stronger point for gay identification (e.g., Comstock

1993), perhaps confirming Ackerman's argument that the burden of the text's homoerotic feminization falls upon Jonathan rather than David. But to reflect for a moment anecdotally, I find it quite striking how often my gay male students speak, sometimes rather passionately, of David as the character with whom they more readily identify. While such identification could be dismissed as anachronistic, it might also be in part a consequence of the fact that the biblical books of Samuel, to appropriate again Runions's language, "perform genderfuck by setting up gender norms that are then repeated in ways that call those norms into question" (2003, 93). Thus, whatever the original intentions behind the text might have been, contemporary gay male identification with David and Jonathan is likely to remain one of the unpredictable effects of hybridity, ambivalence, and genderfuck in this story of war and competition between Israel's legendary houses.

Queer Reading at the Boundaries of Ethnic-Tribal Difference

I have suggested, then, that a queer reading of the story of the house of Saul and the house of David can usefully interpret that story by placing it alongside the film *Paris Is Burning*. Queer reading thus moves between Bible and film. However, any reflection upon *Paris Is Burning* necessarily raises questions about race, as reactions to the film by hooks (1992) and others indicate. Thus, a queer encounter between biblical literature and *Paris Is Burning* provides an opportunity to ask how a queer reading of the biblical text changes when matters of race and ethnicity are allowed to shape the nature of queer questions. To be sure, the queer readings of the Bible that have been produced to date have not often taken into account matters of race and ethnicity, as others have noted critically (e.g., Liew 2001). Nevertheless, the necessity of rethinking queer studies in relation to such matters is by now well established outside of biblical scholarship (see, e.g., among many other works, Muñoz 1999; Eng 2001; Somerville 2000; Ferguson 2003; Rodriguez 2003; Barnard 2004; McBride 2005; Johnson and Henderson 2005; Gopinath 2005). Indeed, some progress has been made along these lines even within biblical interpretation (see, e.g., Travis 2000; Monroe 2000; Cheng 2002; Bailey 2009; Liew 2009).

But how might matters of race and ethnicity be brought to bear on a queer reading of texts in which nearly all of the characters are Israelites? Even if we treat with some caution the assumed relevance for ancient literature of modern racial categories (cf. Nash 2003) and take as our starting point more complex processes of ethnic and national formation, we may wish to resist the tendency to think about Israelite ethnicity as a stable, substantive phenomenon. Just as queer accounts of gender and sexuality interrogate, rather than simply accepting, the supposed stability of heteronormative categories of sex and gender, so also the queering of ethnic identity must proceed with some critical suspicion toward normative categories. Thus it is important to underscore the fact that Israelite ethnicity is itself, today, a contested phenomenon. Certainly debates among historians and archaeologists lead one to doubt that anything like a fixed, stable Israelite identity can be located in the historical or archaeological record. The distinction between "Israelite" and "Canaanite," for example, is blurred by both historical and archaeological evidence (cf., e.g., Killebrew 2005; Finkelstein and Silberman 2001; McNutt 1999, 33–63) and, in some instances, the biblical texts themselves (Cohn 1994). Because the rhetorical construction of this distinction in both biblical literature and biblical scholarship sometimes utilizes sexual rhetoric, I have argued elsewhere that a queer reading of biblical texts might even find in the ambiguous figure of the "Canaanite" an unlikely point of identification (Stone 2004; 2005, 46–67).

However, Israelite ethnic and national identities are not only blurred externally. They are also fractured internally. "Biblical Israel," to focus for a moment on the textual phenomenon rather than a historical reality (cf. Davies 1995), is, after all, composed initially of a series of tribes, which ideally number twelve (though in fact that number is artificial and cannot account for all of the textual evidence). It also splits eventually into two nations, which are often enemies and rivals rather than allies and which ultimately suffer different fates. These internal literary fractures may well be related in some complex way to historical realities; for most historians now believe that the Israelites, far from being a unified ethnic entity, more likely originated from multiple and heterogeneous groups that only coalesced into something like a shared identity over time and through ongoing sociohistorical processes.

Now the story of the conflict between the house of Saul and the house of David is structured in part around these internal fractures. David is a member of the tribe of Judah, and his descendants eventually rule over the southern nation that bears the same name. Saul, on the other hand, belongs to the tribe of Benjamin. Geographically, Benjamin sits just to the north of Judah and just to the south of Ephraim, which is the largest and most significant of the northern tribes. In the narratives about Israel's eponymous ancestors in Genesis, Benjamin is one of only two sons born to

Rachel; and the other son, Joseph, is the father of Ephraim and Manasseh. Thus Benjamin, the tribe of Saul, seems to be more closely associated with the northern kingdom of Israel than with the southern kingdom of Judah, which was ruled by the Davidic dynasty. The story of conflict between the house of Saul and the house of David in the books of Samuel therefore contains hints of the conflicts between tribes that would eventually split unified Israel into two nations.

However, these conflicts may have shaped other sections of biblical literature as well. One example of such a section, which may have particular relevance for a queer reading, can be found in the closing chapters of Judges. Several scholars have suggested that the final form of the book of Judges is put together in such a way as to promote the interests of Judah and, in particular, Judah's Davidic dynasty (see, e.g., Brettler 1989; 2002, 109–16; Schneider 2000). Scholars who read the book in this fashion argue that this agenda is accomplished not only through positive representations of Judah in, for example, the first chapter of Judges but also through a polemic against Saul and his Benjaminite tribe. This polemic is particularly clear in the closing chapters of Judges, which contain several intertextual connections to the story of Saul (Amit 2000, 178–83). The tribe of Benjamin as well as the Benjaminite town of Gibeah, which is associated closely with Saul in the book of 1 Samuel, are represented quite negatively in Judg 19–21. Several other places that play important roles in the final chapters of Judges, such as Jabesh-gilead and Mizpah, are also important for the story of Saul. Moreover, the Levite's act of cutting the body of his *pilegesh*, the so-called "concubine," into twelve pieces and using those pieces to call together the tribes of Israel (Judg 19:29–30) is a striking parallel to Saul's act of cutting oxen into pieces and using those pieces to muster troops in 1 Sam 11:7.[1]

If scholars are right to have concluded from such intertextual connections that a polemic against Saul is taking place in Judg 19–21, it is not entirely surprising that motifs concerning the feminization of men, which we have already noted in connection with Saul's son Jonathan, appear in these chapters as well. In the opening scene of Judg 19, the *pilegesh* takes the step of leaving her husband to return to her father, thereby adopting the position of female sexual subject. Within the male-centered honor-

---

1. On the decision to leave *pilegesh* untranslated rather than adopting the more common translation "concubine," see Stone 2005, 193–94; cf. Schneider 2000, 128–30.

and-shame system presupposed by these texts, this action threatens to "unman" the Levite, who is assumed as male subject to be responsible for the women of his household (cf. Stone 1995, 1996, 2006; Yee 2007a). The Levite attempts to reclaim his manhood by reclaiming his *pilegesh* from the woman's father in Bethlehem, a city associated with David; and the woman's Bethlehemite father welcomes him with an extraordinary display of hospitality. This hospitality in Bethlehem contrasts with the dishonorable lack of hospitality that the Levite will receive in Gibeah, much as Abraham's hospitality in Gen 18 contrasts with the treatment his own visitors will receive in Sodom in a parallel story. Once the Levite leaves the Davidic town of Bethlehem, he explicitly avoids stopping at Jerusalem, which eventually will become the capital of David's kingdom, and stops instead at Gibeah, the town known as the home of Saul. There the men of Gibeah threaten to unman the Levite in a far more graphic fashion, through male same-sex rape. That is to say, they threaten to place that Levite in the position of object, which, in Israel as in many other cultures, is normatively reserved for women. Although the threatened rape of the Levite does not take place, the men of Gibeah do, as I have argued elsewhere (Stone 1995, 1996), symbolically feminize him by raping his *pilegesh*. Yet gender tables are turned on the Gibeahites and their Benjaminite kin when the Israelite tribes defeat them in battle. Because military "defeat is a feminine-associated event" (Chapman 2004, 167) in ancient Israel as elsewhere in the ancient Near East, the extended attention to this defeat in Judg 20 serves to highlight the feminization of Saul's tribe. The insult is only compounded in chapter 21 when the surviving members of that tribe have to be assisted and instructed by others in the quintessentially manly role of securing women. On one level, then, the closing chapters of Judges can be read as a polemic against the Benjaminites. However, the last five chapters are also knit together with the recurring observation that "in those days there was not a king in Israel," twice in this form (Judg 18:1; 19:1) and twice with the additional observation that "each man did what was right in his eyes" (17:6; 21:25). Thus, the negative representation of the premonarchic Benjaminites that takes place in these chapters is articulated with a glance toward Israel's monarchy that will follow in 1 Samuel, which arguably needs to be read as the continuation of Judges (cf. Jobling 1998). And, since the Benjaminites in general and the townspeople of Gibeah in particular are clearly behind the chaos that engulfs Israel in the closing chapters of Judges, a reader who has traveled through those chapters will hardly have reason to feel optimistic about a ruling house founded by the Benjaminite Saul of Gibeah. A monarchy associated with the hospitable city of Bethlehem, on the other hand, may inspire more confidence.

Now for my purposes, the point to underscore here is the way in which matters of gender, sexuality, ethnicity, and nation are thoroughly intertwined in these passages. The biblical texts I have noted arguably work together to elevate the reputation of the house of David by undermining the reputation of the house of Saul. The particular ways in which they accomplish this, however, involve something very close to ethnic slander. Saul's people, the Benjaminites, are represented in a negative light collectively, as dishonorable agents of chaos who attempt to unman others only to be defeated in turn. Political conflict and ethnic difference are represented negatively in terms of sexual violence and gender ambiguity.

Yet as with the passages in Samuel, so also in Judges this representation is not entirely "straight"-forward. While the Benjaminites are ultimately defeated, their military skills are recognized in the book, not only in chapters 20 and 21 but also in the story of Ehud the Benjaminite in chapter 3. Moreover, when the construction of Israel's ethnic identities in the books of Judges and Samuel is examined more carefully, it appears that the figure of David himself is not represented in unambiguous ways. For during the latter period of Saul's reign, David seems to be allied with those great enemies of Israel, the Philistines. On the one hand, this association with the Philistines locates David outside the boundaries of Israelite identity as such boundaries are represented in biblical literature; for, as David Jobling notes, "biblical tradition ... often (not consistently) casts the Philistines as the utterly 'other,' as alien in a higher degree than any of the rest of Israel's neighbors" (Jobling 1998, 197). Yet Jobling goes on to note that the Philistines are, within biblical discourse, also in certain respects feminized (216, 230–31). Thus David's surprising association with the Philistines seems to blur not only ethnic boundaries but gender boundaries as well. To be sure, biblical literature does not only associate David with the Philistines. It also distinguishes him at other points from the Philistines, most strikingly perhaps in 1 Sam 18 where he kills one hundred Philistines and takes their foreskins to Saul as a brideprice for Michal. Thus we see that, in matters of ethnicity as in matters of gender and sexual practice, biblical representations are in most cases neither entirely positive nor entirely negative but rather are characterized by contradiction and ambivalence.

Conclusion

I conclude, then, by returning briefly to the matter of queer reading between Bible and film. When I speak about "queer reading," I am sometimes asked for a definition of "queer" or a specification of method. However, rather than referring in any obvious way to a single method, a single subject matter, or a single set of readers who might be differentiated from other readers, the phrase "queer readings of the Bible" is better understood, in my view, as a diverse set of approaches to biblical interpretation that take as their point of departure a critical interrogation, or active contestation, of the ways in which the Bible is read to support heteronormative and normalizing configurations of sexual and gender practices and sexual and gender identities. One can certainly engage in queer readings of the Bible without worrying about film, and one can analyze Bible and film together without producing a reading that anyone would find it useful to call queer. But for a queer reading, the question to be asked about Bible and film is not whether it seems proper, in a methodological sense, to read Bible and film together. The question to be asked is whether one's reading undermines or complicates the ease with which biblical interpretation undergirds normative configurations of sex, gender, and kinship.

On the surface, at least, there are few parts of the Bible that are more beholden to notions of virile manhood than the narratives about David and Saul, structured as they are around military valor and the "traffic in women" (Rubin 1975). Given the Bible's ongoing influence, it would be easy to conclude that such narratives can only contribute to the continued power of virile, heteronormative manhood in the contemporary world. When one takes this biblical epic and places it alongside *Paris Is Burning*, however, it is possible to find in this story elements and dynamics that also work against dominant relations of sex, gender, and kinship. The effect is somewhat akin to an effect found in the film itself, where the shots of the ball children performing their roles in competitions for "realness" are juxtaposed to shots of other people in the so-called real world, going about their business as Cheryl Lynn's song "Got to Be Real," a gay disco anthem, plays in the background. The assumed naturalness of the gendered bodies moving in the latter shots is undercut by the similarities between those bodies and the ball performances that the viewer has already been watching. If we imagine replacing the shots in *Paris Is Burning* that are taken from outside the gay world with scenes from the biblical epic, we may, I think, catch a glimpse of the film's potential to undermine the Bible's contributions to stable notions of sex, gender, and kinship. A reading between Bible and film is unlikely, in itself, to topple heteronormativity. But if the space between virile biblical epic and contemporary drag ball is smaller than we usually imagine, the attempt to ground heteronormativity in appeals to biblical literature may prove to be less secure, less "straight"-forward, or less inevitable than many of those who make such appeals imagine.

Works Consulted

Ackerman, Susan. 2005. *When Heroes Love: The Ambiguity of Eros in the Stories of Gilgamesh and David*. New York: Columbia University Press.

Amit, Yairah. 2000. *Hidden Polemics in Biblical Narrative*. Translated by Jonathan Chipman. Leiden: Brill.

Bach, Alice, ed. 1996. *Biblical Glamour and Hollywood Glitz*. Semeia 74. Atlanta: Scholars Press.

———. 1997. *Women, Seduction, and Betrayal in Biblical Narrative*. Cambridge: Cambridge University Press.

Bailey, Randall C. 2009. "That's Why They Didn't Call the Book Hadassah!": The Interse(ct)/(x)ionality of Race/Ethnicity, Gender, and Sexuality in the Book of Esther. Pages 227–50 in Bailey, Liew, and Segovia 2009.

Bailey, Randall C., Tat-siong Benny Liew, and Fernando F. Segovia, eds. 2009. *They Were All Together in One Place? Toward Minority Biblical Criticism*. SemeiaSt 57. Atlanta: Society of Biblical Literature.

Barnard, Ian. 2004. *Queer Race: Cultural Interventions in the Racial Politics of Queer Theory*. New York: Peter Lang.

Berlin, Adele. 1983. *Poetics and the Interpretation of Biblical Narrative*. Sheffield: Almond Press.

Bhaba, Homi. 1994. *The Location of Culture*. New York: Routledge.

Brettler, Marc Zvi. 1989. The Book of Judges: Literature as Politics. *JBL* 108:395–418.

———. 2002. *The Book of Judges*. New York: Routledge.

Butler, Judith. 1993. *Bodies that Matter: On the Discursive Limits of "Sex."* New York: Routledge.

Chapman, Cynthia R. 2004. *The Gendered Language of Warfare in the Israelite-Assyrian Encounter*. Winona Lake, Ind.: Eisenbrauns.

Cheng, Patrick S. 2002. Multiplicity and Judges 19: Constructing a Queer Asian Pacific American Biblical Hermeneutic. Pages 119–33 in *The*

Bible in Asian America. Edited by Tat-siong Benny Liew and Gale A. Yee. *Semeia* 90–91. Atlanta: Society of Biblical Literature.

Cohn, Robert L. 1994. Before Israel: The Canaanites as Other in Biblical Tradition. Pages 74–90 in *The Other in Jewish Thought and History: Constructions of Jewish Culture and Identity*. Edited by Laurence J. Silberstein and Robert L. Cohn. New York: New York University Press.

Comstock, Gary David. 1993. *Gay Theology without Apology*. Cleveland, Ohio: Pilgrim.

Davies, Philip R. 1995. *In Search of "Ancient Israel."* 2nd ed. Sheffield: Sheffield University Press.

Eng, David L. 2001. *Racial Castration: Managing Masculinity in America*. Durham, N.C.: Duke University Press.

Exum, J. Cheryl. 1996. *Plotted, Shot, and Painted: Cultural Representations of Biblical Women*. Sheffield: Sheffield Academic Press.

Ferguson, Roderick A. 2003. *Aberrations in Black: Toward a Queer of Color Critique*. Minneapolis: University of Minnesota Press.

Fewell, Danna Nolan, and David M. Gunn. 1993. *Gender, Power, and Promise: The Subject of the Bible's First Story*. Nashville: Abingdon Press.

Finkelstein, Israel, and Neil Asher Silberman. 2001. *The Bible Unearthed: Archaeology's New Vision of Ancient Israel and the Origin of Its Sacred Texts*. New York: Free Press.

Gopinath, Gayatri. 2005. *Impossible Desires: Queer Diasporas and South Asian Public Cultures*. Durham, N.C.: Duke University Press.

Goss, Robert E., and Mona West, eds. 2000. *Take Back the Word: A Queer Reading of the Bible*. Cleveland, Ohio: Pilgrim.

hooks, bell. 1992. Is Paris Burning? Pages 145–56 in *Black Looks: Race and Representation*. Boston: South End Press.

Jobling, David. 1998. *1 Samuel*. BerOl. Collegeville, Minn.: Liturgical Press.

Johnson, E. Patrick, and Mae G. Henderson, eds. 2005. *Black Queer Studies: A Critical Anthology*. Durham, N.C.: Duke University Press.

Killebrew, Ann E. 2005. *Biblical Peoples and Ethnicity: An Archaeological Study of Egyptians, Canaanites, Philistines, and Early Israel, 1300–1100 B.C.E.*. SBLABS 9. Atlanta: Society of Biblical Literature.

Liew, Tat-siong Benny. 2001. (Cor)Responding: A Letter to the Editor. Pages 182–92 in Stone 2001.

———. 2009. Queering Closets and Perverting Desires: Cross-Examining John's Engendering and Transgendering Word Across Different Worlds. Pages 251–88 in Bailey, Liew, and Segovia 2009.

Livingston, Jennie. 1991. *Paris Is Burning*. Los Angeles: Off White Productions/Academy Entertainment. Videocassette (VHS), 71 min.

Lyne, Adrian. 1987. *Fatal Attraction*. Los Angeles: Paramount Home Entertainment. Videocassettte (VHS), 121 min.

McBride, Dwight A. 2005. *Why I Hate Abercrombie and Fitch: Essays on Race and Sexuality*. New York: New York University Press.

McCarter, P. Kyle, Jr. 1984. *II Samuel*. AB 9. Garden City, N.Y.: Doubleday.

McNutt, Paula. 1999. *Reconstructing the Society of Ancient Literature*. Louisville: Westminster John Knox.

Monroe, Irene. 2000. When and Where I Enter, Then the Whole Race Enters with Me: Que(e)rying Exodus. Pages 82–91 in Goss and West 2000.

Muñoz, José Esteban. 1999. *Disidentifications: Queers of Color and the Performance of Politics*. Cultural Studies of the Americas 2. Minneapolis: University of Minnesota Press.

Nash, Peter T. 2003. *Reading Race, Reading the Bible*. Minneapolis: Augsburg Fortress.

Newsom, Carol. 1989. Woman and the Discourse of Patriarchal Wisdom: A Study of Proverbs 1–9. Pages 142–60 in *Gender and Difference in Ancient Israel*. Edited by Peggy L. Day. Minneapolis: Fortress.

Olyan, Saul. 2006. "Surpassing the Love of Women": Another Look at 2 Samuel 1:26 and the Relationship of David and Jonathan. Pages 7–16 in *Authorizing Marriage? Canon, Tradition, and Critique in the Blessing of Same-Sex Unions*. Edited by Mark D. Jordan. Princeton: Princeton University Press.

Phelan, Peggy. 1993. The Golden Apple: Jennie Livingston's *Paris Is Burning*. Pages 93–111 in *Unmarked: The Politics of Performance*. New York: Routledge.

Rodriguez, Juana. 2003. *Queer Latinidad: Identity Practices, Discursive Spaces*. New York: New York University Press.

Rubin, Gayle. 1975. The Traffic in Women: Notes on the "Political Economy" of Sex. Pages 157–210 in *Toward an Anthropology of Women*. Edited by Rayna Reiter. New York: Monthly Review Press

Runions, Erin. 2003. *How Hysterical: Identification and Resistance in the Bible and Film*. New York: Palgrave Macmillan.

Schneider, Tammi J. 2000. *Judges*. Collegeville, Minn.: Liturgical Press.

Somerville, Siobhan B. 2000. *Queering the Color Line: Race and the Invention of Homosexuality in American Culture*. Durham, N.C.: Duke University Press.

Stone, Ken. 1993. Sexual Practice and the Structure of Prestige: The Case of the Disputed Concubines. Pages 554–73 in *SBL Seminar Papers, 1993*. Edited by E. H. Lovering. Atlanta: Scholars Press.

———. 1994. Sexual Power and Political Prestige. *BRev* 10.4:28–31, 52–53.

———. 1995. Gender and Homosexuality in Judges 19: Subject-Honor, Object-Shame? *JSOT* 67:87–107.

———. 1996. *Sex, Honor and Power in the Deuteronomistic History*. Sheffield: Sheffield Academic Press.

———. 2001a. Queer Commentary and Biblical Interpretation: An Introduction. Pages 11–34 in Stone 2001b.

———, ed. 2001b. *Queer Commentary and the Hebrew Bible*. Sheffield: Sheffield University Press; Cleveland, Ohio: Pilgrim.

———. 2004. Queering the Canaanite. Pages 110–34 in *The Sexual Theologian: Essays on Sex, God and Politics*. Edited by Marcella Althaus-Reid and Lisa Isherwood . London: T&T Clark.

———. 2005. *Practicing Safer Texts: Food, Sex and Bible in Queer Perspective*. London: T&T Clark.

———. 2006. The Garden of Eden and the Heterosexual Contract. Pages 48–70 in *Bodily Citations: Religion and Judith Butler*. Edited by Ellen T. Armour and Susan M. St. Ville. New York: Columbia University Press.

———. 2007. Gender Criticism: The Un-Manning of Abimelech. Pages 183–201 in Yee 2007b.

———. 2008. Bibles That Matter: Biblical Theology and Queer Performativity. *BTB* 38:14–25.

Travis, Irene S. 2000. Love Your Mother: A Lesbian Womanist Reading of Scripture. Pages 35–42 in Goss and West 2000.

Yee, Gale A. 2007a. Ideological Criticism: Judges 17–21 and the Dismembered Body. Pages 138–60 in Yee 2007b.

———, ed. 2007b. *Judges and Method: New Approaches in Biblical Studies*. 2nd ed. Minneapolis: Fortress.

PENDERECKI'S IRON MAIDEN: INTIMACY AND OTHER ANOMALIES IN THE *CANTICUM CANTICORUM SALOMONIS*

Heidi Epstein

In "The Song of Songs in the History of Sexuality" (2000), Stephen D. Moore vividly chronicles the queering of the Song within the allegorical commentaries of ancient and medieval church fathers (e.g., Origen, Bernard of Clairvaux, Denis the Carthusian, et al.). These writers reveled in playing the Shulamite for their triune lover God. Even though each celibate exegete has renounced "the sexual, the sensual, the fleshly, the female," each one "internalizes a feminine persona so completely that he speaks fluently in her voice, feels with her emotions, and throbs with her sexuality" (338). These "Christian cross-dressers" thus show a refreshing "lack of homosexual panic" that unfortunately did not last. In not-so-coincidental tandem with the nineteenth-century "invention" of homosexuality, more literalist commentators, schooled in modern, "scientific" approaches to textual criticism, "labored to straighten out the queer reading to which the Song had so long been subjected" (348). The result was a "homiletics of heteronormativity," and for Moore, the sociocultural discursive effects of this censorial interpretive trajectory "constitute yet another fascinating footnote in the infinitely intricate history of sexuality" (348–49).

Moore is understandably reluctant to dismiss premodern readings of the Song as somehow less critically sophisticated (because allegorical), given their modeling of queerer reading practices and relations to the divine for readers today. I propose that the "arduous task of queering the Song" (Moore 2000, 328)—indulged by the fathers, renounced by the "enlightened," and revived by biblical scholars today—might be enhanced by analysis of the Song's contemporary musical afterlives.[1] If we accept

---

1. I am looking at such settings in what will be a full-length study: *The Polyphonic*

New Musicologists' tenet that music is a body-sculpting, mind-molding discourse of expressive codes and gestures that mediates normative and "deviant" fabrications of sexuality, analysis of musical "commentaries" on the Song may produce new allegorical registers within the text, some of which, I contend, are queer. Engaging New Musicology to read musical treatments of the Song might therefore add further complexity and discursive breadth to the latest biblical, critical conversations about the Song's thematics. In turn, fluency in the latter polemics will guide the identification of noteworthy musical properties within musical settings thereof.

As a case study in such cross-fertilization, this essay enlists insights from New Musicology, queer biblical criticism, and feminist theory to analyze composer Krzysztof Penderecki's jarring "deconstruction" of the Song, such that Penderecki's musical exegesis becomes a set of performative practices that actually anticipates biblical scholars' more recent attempts to develop queerer "carnal allegories" of this text. Carnal allegories do not spiritualize the Song's sexual content but reconfigure its cultural meanings according to a variety of critical theories. These resistant readings in turn help to undermine the hegemony of, for example, heteronormative/sexist pleasures, aesthetics, and relational dynamics (cf. Boer 2000; Moore and Burrus 2003; Exum 2000; Brenner 2000; Black 2009). Following Moore's example, the interdisciplinary conversation that follows also archives yet another episode of the Song's formative career within the history of Western sexuality.

Introduction: Music, Subjectivity, and Sexuality

Since the late 1980s, New Musicologists (Brett, Kramer, McClary, Subotnik, Cusick, et al.) have ideologically problematized formalistic, "score-driven" analyses of musical works. Taking their cues from Theodor Adorno, these scholars reconceptualize music as a force field of competing social energies that inevitably modulates human subjectivity.[2] For example, and for the purposes of this paper, Susan McClary's designation of Western erotic music, from Monteverdi to Prince, as erotic map-

---

Shulamite: Modulating Subjectivity through Musical Settings of the Song of Songs. For a discussion of the Pixies' and Steeleye Span's settings of the same, see Epstein 2009.

2. For an overview of the history, objectives, scholars, and publications that constitute New Musicology, see Pasler and Duckles 2001; McClary 2001.

pings that circulate and interpellate listeners within their given cultural milieu[3] offers a useful interpretive lens through which to articulate the discursive power and significance of the biblical Song's musical afterlives, especially Penderecki's somewhat perturbing *Canticum canticorum Salomonis* (1970–1973). How does McClary arrive at this metaphor of erotic mapping? In light of Foucault, we know that sexuality and the erotic are discursively produced, and erotic music is no exception: the melodies, harmonies, rhythmic "gestures," and sonic "contours" of many musical works actively "map patterns through the medium of sound that resemble those of sexuality" (McClary 1991, 8). Musical compositions are thus reframed as "'fabrications of sexuality'" (8, quoting Heath) or as sonic composers of human sexual identity, because they proffer techniques of the self and constitute "models of the self performed" (McClary 1994, 77). The latter are concretized and mediated through melody, harmony, rhythm, and meter. As a semiotics of desire, music circulates social energies (Greenblatt 1989) and organizes bodily movement in the process. It inscribes porous flesh with culturally defined kinetic and affective social codes. In doing so, it teaches proper or improper ways to experience the body, thereby shaping human consciousness—one's corporeal sense of self. Ancient Greek sympotic songs, French courtly dances, Italian renaissance madrigals, opera, rock 'n' roll—all such musical innovations across the centuries "unleash [new] forms of physicality" which literally transform human embodiment (McClary 1995, 90).[4] Musical settings of the Song of Solomon are easily situated within these erotic cartographies and "pedagogies."

Additionally, some New Musicologists read the tonally harmonic system building that Western composers developed and experimented with across particular styles and historical periods as imbuing musical forms (sonata form, *da capo* arias, theme, and variations) with *narrative* plotlines that render these models of the self performed teleological; and such narrative unfoldings arguably simulate a form of sexual experience

---

3. See McClary 1991, 7–9.

4. McClary describes the socializing force of baroque courtly song and dance, for example, as follows: "As part of his absolutist agenda, for instance, Louis XIV employed dance and its supporting music to regulate—indeed, literally to *synchronize*—the bodies and behaviors of his courtiers. In accordance with Louis's priorities (motivated at least as much by political as aesthetic considerations), French musicians maintained dance at the center of their activities" (1995, 90).

as well, because a work's harmonic progressions and the formal sections
that these generate can be framed as episodes of tension-building foreplay,
climax, and release.[5] (Even purely instrumental works such as the sonata,
concerto, and symphony can be read in these terms.) In effect, all these
narrative and metaphorical evocations of sexuality and selfhood constitute extramusical, "vertical" readings on top of the perceived "horizontal"
unfolding of music's sonic, that is, "literal," developments, in a meaning-
making dynamic that I would denominate allegorical.[6] Such allegorical
potential is only perceptible, however, if music is understood as equal
among other very powerful "sources of the self" (Taylor 1992). Thus by
enlisting all these New Musicological interpretive keys, while Penderecki's
musical reconfiguration of the Song may or may not lend itself to uphold-
ing the text's standard allegorical messages, the signifying power and discursive effects of his seemingly "deviant" erotic mapping or model of selfhood produces an as-yet untapped, musically induced (and transmitted)
allegorical register within the biblical text.

What may obfuscate reception of the work's new allegorical thematics
is the *Canticum*'s cacophonous soundscape. For listeners unfamiliar with
the sound worlds of the twentieth-century musical *avant garde*, the *Canticum* seemingly dashes any desire for intimacy with the biblical Song's
sensual delights. But engagement of the above hermeneutics, if placed in
conversation with recent iconoclastic exegeses of the Song, may make the
music more alluring. I shall in fact characterize Penderecki's erotic codes
and gestures as positively queer. If queer designates "a flexible space for
the expression of all aspects of non-(anti-, contra-)straight cultural production and reception" (Doty 1993, 3), the *Canticum* constitutes such an

---

5. Narrative readings of key Western composers' works have been done by musicologists Edward T. Cone, Anthony Newcomb, Joseph Kerman, and Susan McClary,
among others (cf. Maus 2006 for a comprehensive bibliography). The sexual and sexist
overtones of such narratives are discussed more explicitly in McClary's readings. *Critiques* of narrative treatments of musical forms and meaning construction include
Abbate, Maus, Nattiez, and Kramer. Maus summarizes "failures of analogy" between
the music and literary narrativity: "no possible distinction between subject and predi-
cate; no capacity for various kinds of reflexive self-commentary; no past tense" that
can create "space between story and story-telling" (narration; Maus 2006, n.p.).

6. McClary makes musicological use of the term "allegory" from time to time. She
describes Adorno's reading of musical works as "allegor[ies] of personal development"
or "allegories of exquisitely wrought selfhood" (1998, 15). She discusses Monteverdi
and his forebears' "allegories of inwardness" (2004, 36).

expressive space within Western romantic/erotic discourse and conventions. It is the queerness of Penderecki's compositional palette—if we dare to reimmerse ourselves in its initially alienating sonorities—that makes this erotic mapping so charming, more specifically 1) its "prescient" evocation of postmodern love; 2) its provision of a musico-sexual "counterpleasure"; 3) its politically subversive[7] erotic temporality; 4) its enticement of queerer listening postures. Furthermore, thanks to these four carnally allegorical, discursive effects, Penderecki's model of the self-performed "confounds" not only "the categories that license sexual normativity" (Jagose 1996, 98) but those that license musical normativity as well. For the *Canticum* is queer not just in the nonnormative romantic lovers and love story that Penderecki sculpts in sound but in the composer's "antistraight" approach to musical composition. Details of Penderecki's place within music history, therefore, especially his tactical straddling of several compositional camps, shall occasionally fortify my queer characterization of his work.[8]

Before continuing, readers with access to academic databases may wish to taste some or all of Penderecki's pungent fruit at the online Classical Music Library that is provided through Alexander Street Press at the following Web address: http://clmu.alexanderstreet.com.

---

7. Queer theory has been constructively critical of both the terms "subversive" and "transgressive." For those who still believe in the subversive or transgressive power of minority-group identity politics for challenging the workings of an oppressive status quo, Butler, Foucault, and other queer theorists caution that "woman/man," "feminist/misogynist," "gay/straight," etc., are really "effects" of a "regulatory regime of differences." Therefore, even subversive or transgressive identities participate in regimes of classification and such "identity categories have come to be considered complicit in the very structures that their assertion was intended to overthrow" (Jagose 1996, 90). Butler explains that "identity categories tend to be instruments of regulatory regimes, whether as the normalizing categories of oppressive structures or as the rallying points for a liberatory contestation of that very oppression" (1991, 13–14). This is not to say, however, that political resistance is impossible or futile. What is called for though is "recognition of the precarious state of identity and a full awareness of the complicated processes of identity formation both psychical and social" and a sensitivity to the ways in which "the assertion of collective identities" may well "put into circulation effects in excess of its avowed intention" (91).

8. Here I take advantage of the broader application of the term "queer" beyond its usual "sexual register" to designate "anti-assimilationist and anti-separatist" strategies (Hennessy 1994, 86–87) within a wider variety of "identity constituting" and "identity fracturing discourses"; Sedgwick 1993, 9).

1. Love in the Key of Queer

Are these the sounds of love in the '70s? Composed in Communist Poland during the successive regimes of Gomulka and Gierek, and just after workers were slaughtered in a Gdansk shipyard,[9] Penderecki has given us cold lovers for a Cold War, an iron maiden behind an iron curtain. The couple's impenetrability—for listeners unfamiliar with the sound worlds of the twentieth-century musical *avant garde*—lies (I suggest) in five very general stylistic features of the piece:

---

9. In 1970 in a Gdansk shipyard, the Polish military opened fire on protesters who were outraged by sharp rises in food prices that were instituted by the Gomulka regime. Forty-two people were killed, a thousand arrested and some three thousand injured. Penderecki commemorated the 1970 Gdansk shipyard slaughter in his setting of the *Lacrimosa* (1980), which he dedicated to Lech Walesa and Solidarnosc and later incorporated into the *Requiem*. With the assignment of Poland to jurisdiction by the Soviets after World War II, the church "became the cherished trustee of the nation's history, culture, and traditions and of the collective memories of Polish people" (Borowik 2006, 718). Consequently, Penderecki's early religious works were often enlisted to honor the political suffering of his compatriots. His persistent setting of religious musical works in that supposedly post-Christian era and context also served political ends by increasing cultural resistance, so to speak, to Communist attempts to resocialize Poles out of their own history and culture and into a Communist civil religion (in resocialization in Poland, see Borowik 2006, 719–20).

Penderecki was in fact friends with Cardinal Stefan Wyszynski—heroic leader of the Polish Catholic Church from 1948 to 1981. Wyszynski had been imprisoned by the Communists from 1953 to 1956 and was particularly instrumental in mobilizing the antigovernment protests that intensified throughout the 1970s, when the *Canticum* was written. (The composer would later write a setting of the *Agnus dei* for Wyszynski's funeral in May 1981. It would form part of his *Polish Requiem* [1980–1984]).

Regarding Gomulka and Gierek, Wladyslaw Gomulka was head of the Polish United Workers' Party from 1956 to 1970, and consistently harangued the "church and intelligentsia" (Borowik 2006, 718). Edward Gierek succeeded him, serving from 1970 to 1980, during which time there was some amelioration in church-state relations. In both regimes, however, chronic wrangling best describes church-state relations (though with intermittent *rapprochements* and with appreciably less hostility than during the immediate postwar period of Soviet restructuring (1945–1956); cf. Monticone1986, ch. 1 (on Gomulka); ch. 2 (on Gierek).

Both leaders did open Poland's borders in varying degrees to allow freer cultural exchange between Eastern and Western artists, writers, and composers, and this allowed Polish composers like Penderecki to absorb the new techniques and experimental sounds of the likes of Stockhausen, Boulez, Nono, and Ligeti.

1. We never get to latch on to a melody that the lovers might share or exchange. Instead, lines usually assigned either to the male or female voice in the story blur imperceptibly in tangled choral confusions, offering no points of reference with which to follow the text. Voices and instruments, furthermore, traffic in rather unmelodious microtones[10] and *glissandi*—slurred speech that creates sensations of vertigo as parts slide up and down—the antithesis of melodic lyricism.

2. No steady meter is ever established that might offer a semblance of order "beneath" the music's surface metamorphoses. We have to attune ourselves instead to the episodic play of musical colors and textures to gain some semblance of form "beneath" the seemingly free flow of sounds.

3. Scrambling for some additional sense of structure, we may latch on to the recurring whole-tone and semitone sighing motifs (rehearsal nos. [RN] 1, 2, 29, 32, 33), but these just vacillate back and forth without "leading" us forward or giving us a sense of narrative progress. (Sighing motifs are classic musical tropes for evoking unfulfilled longing or ennui.)

4. Indeed, the overall mood of this piece seems one of acute romantic ambivalence rather than idyllic joy. Because its soundscape is not ordered by way of harmonic progressions but by sharply contrasting panels of sound ("sound mass densities"), we feel abducted by a series of musical mood swings. For these juxtapositions seem designed to underline mixed *verbal* messages. For example, there are two dirge-like warnings from the men's voices—"I swear daughters do not awaken my love 'til she is ready" (Song 2:7; RN 10; and Song 3:5; RN 24)—immediately followed by crazed rebuttals of leaping and bounding intervals; the first announces the beloved's full-court press (Song 2:8; RN 10); the second expresses the lovers' resumption of their hide- and-seek (Song 4:1a, 5–7; RN 24). But these unauthorized awakenings are quickly aborted as one slams abruptly into knuckle-rapping snares (end of RN 16) and the other is lethally

---

10. The use of microtones was an *avant garde* means of sharply challenging the naturalness of the twelve-tone, equally tempered division of the octave that Western tonality had established by the mid-eighteenth century. This generated a wider variety of pitches to work with. One basic example would be the use of quarter tones in a quarter-tone scale by dividing each of the twelve tones in half (Schwartz and Godfrey 1993, 13). Julian Carrillo actually divided the octave into ninety-five pitches in his "The Thirteenth Sound." Harry Partch developed a "forty-three-note approach" (Cope 2001, 64–65).

wounded (as I explain below) and deflates in wailing *glissandi* (end of RN 26).

5. Most disturbing of all perhaps is the brute encounter with what often becomes a lifeline in a difficult musical work—the human voices. Here they can sound inhuman and butcher the poetry; *consecutive* verses in the text are superimposed upon each other and sung simultaneously or their syllables are chopped up and tossed across multiple voice parts. Some words simply dissolve into breathy hissing and sputtered consonants (e.g., RN 9, 13, 14, 17).

We are a long way from Donna Summer/*Saturday Night Fever* romance. But this is where New Musicological hermeneutics are instructive. If we understand the composer's craft as arousing, manipulating, and channeling our desires, such that cultural norms of sexuality and of gendered behaviors are reinforced or transgressed through musical conventions, then perhaps Penderecki's eccentric language of love circulates more conflicted sonorities for expressing intimacy in a militarized, agonistic context—in effect, erotic mappings of Cold War love that can, in my view, be recycled to evoke the vicissitudes of postmodern love as well. Sociologist Eva Illouz's in-depth interviews with fifty American men and women on the subject of love found them deeply conflicted about the same, fuelled as they are by cynicism toward the old romantic codes and values that still circulate widely in pop culture and the media but that fall short as means for articulating their own experiences of love. Postmodern lovers are painfully aware that "[t]he experiential categories of everyday love in the realm of everyday life ... conflict with the hedonism, intensity and aestheticism that are the basis of the experience of being a postmodern consumer and viewer" (Illouz 1998, 178). Her interviewees' personal notions of love reflect "a certain exhaustion of the romantic paradigm of love, a systematic attitude of irony and unbelief, the demise of Love as a grandiose and threatening experience of the 'limits'" (183). Their disenchantment indicates that "[l]ove seems to have 'flattened' out in a culture where all forms of 'intensities' are actively encouraged and simultaneously demystified" (183). The romantic self is consequently haunted by, even as it cultivates, "an ironic semiotic suspicion" (182).

To me, Illouz's profile of the postmodern romantic self as a conflicted "collage" that also suffers from "a crisis of representation" offers one allegorical interpretation of Penderecki's tortured, sonically encoded romantic selves, his patchwork model of the self performed:

The contemporary romantic self is marked by its persistent, Sisyphus-style attempt to conjure up the local and fleeting intensity of the love affair [still trafficked by the mass media] within long-term global narratives of love (such as marriage), to reconcile an overarching narrative of enduring love with the fragmentary intensity of affairs. This splitting of the romantic self into incompatible narrative structures, the patching of self-contained, discontinuous affairs into narratives of life-long love, breaks the coherent, heroic self of modernity into a "collage" of conflicting narrative selves. And this collage, I want now to claim is accompanied with a crisis of representation which we may qualify as postmodern. ... [A] media-saturated [postmodern] culture deepens and complicates the relation between the ways in which we sustain our experience and the codes that are available to us to construct such experience. (Illouz 1998, 178–79)[11]

Musicologists have chronicled the more euphonious, gender-bending versions of such fragmented romantic selves within popular music. These love songs circulate a similar "ironic semiotic suspicion"—those of k.d. lang, Prince, Annie Lennox, and David Bowie, for example.[12] But it is crucial to note that these artists not only deconstruct but also creatively resynthesize old musical erotic conventions (McClary 2000, 152–59). On the one hand, their salvage operations both reflect and instill an acute awareness of the decentered, iteratively performative nature of Western gendered subjectivity, a reality that has inevitably rendered relational intimacy highly unstable and postmodern love complicated. Yet on the other, and in spite of all the latter uncertainties, these artists' musical bricolage still asserts love's viability. So, for example, McClary characterizes k.d. lang's campy, revamped torch songs as stylistic modalities for speaking of love in a postmodern universe. Lang "revels in the postmodern rubble":

---

11. Illouz's central project is to refute assertions that modern and postmodern romantic quests and narratives are radically discontinuous with each other in their expressive codes, representations, and definitions of love: "But this [postmodern] cultural configuration [outlined in her article] does not represent a decisively new qualitative turn or radical departure from modern regimes of representation of love and remains, in any case, to be systematically and empirically investigated. What seems to be new, however, is a certain exhaustion of the Romantic paradigm of love, a systematic irony and unbelief" (1998,183).

12. See here Leonardi and Pope 1996 on Annie Lennox; McClary 2000 and Walser 1994 on Prince; Mockus 1994 and McClary 2000 on k.d. lang; and Waldrep 2004 on Bowie.

"She doesn't entirely trust the language she has chosen, but she also knows
that she cannot speak from outside language; rather than opting for non-
communication, she sings on defiantly, demonstrating most poignantly
the pathos, the absurdity, the hilarity of uttering something as shop-worn
as an admission of love: love, which still somehow lingers on long after
cynical intellectuals have announced the demise of centered subjectivity"
(McClary 2000, 159).[13] If Lang sings "on the borderline between irony
and sincerity, between ambivalence and hope" (159), perhaps Penderecki's
erotic mapping of one of the West's most sacred, endlessly quoted templates for romantic relations—while enlisting signifying practices that
are hardly household musical codes—straddles similar moods and can
accommodate romantic ambivalence for listeners today, especially listeners for whom even scavenged pop vocabularies of heartbreak and ecstasy
just aren't queer enough.

Details of music history fortify my appropriation of this tale of love
as emblematically queer and postmodern. For it is a product of rebellion not just within postwar political/cultural history but within modern
music history as well. What Penderecki and other *avant gardists* wanted to
do was disrupt all our habits of thought about what music is—how time
and pitches "should" be organized. This would also require disrupting the
strict dichotomy that listeners maintain between music and noise.[14] Such a
radical reconfiguration of music *in se* inevitably stymies our hierarchically
binarized expectations of what musical pleasure and pain, consonance and
dissonance, and by extension, erotic or even sacred erotic[15] musical codes
"should" sound like.

---

13. See her analysis of "Still Thrives this Love" (2000, 157–59).

14. See Schwartz and Godfrey's summary of composers' "interest in 'noise' and
percussive timbres" (1993, 12–13). They cite wider cultural catalysts for the dissolution of this dichotomy that include Luigi Russolo's 1913 essay "The Art of Noises." See
also John Cage's essays on music, especially his "Credo" of 1937 (1961, 3–6).

15. Scholars use the term "sacred erotic" to categorize a long and varied repertoire
of artistic, literary, and musical imagery that depicts divine-human relations in sexual
terms. The cornerstone that authorizes the articulation of sacred devotion in such
profane, i.e., earthy, sexual metaphors, is in fact scriptural; in the Hebrew testament,
God describes Israel as his wife or bride, and hence the love poetry of the Song was
deemed an elaborate template for describing union with God via romantic tropes.
Some of the most famous examples that constitute sacred eroticism include the commentaries Moore explores; a plethora of medieval writings now classified as "erotic
Christ mysticism"; Bernini's statue of an ecstatically transfixed St. Teresa of Avila; the

Because Penderecki's initially impenetrable iron maiden and tormented knight enflesh all these romantic, aesthetic, and compositional ruptures, they may endear themselves to us if we hear them as "conflicting narrative selves," navigating multiple crises of representation that resonate with our own. Or if we hear the *Canticum* and its protagonists as a politically powerful, queer parable that resists multiple "regimes of the normal" (Warner 1993, xxvi); their shocking contours upend previous musical encodings and perpetuations of a supposedly "free, natural and primordial sexuality" and impress upon us (by "negative" example) an acute awareness that sexuality is a product of "discursive effects" (Jagose 1996, 98). Adopting New Musicology's attention to music's cultural semiotics and its discursive role in subject formation may thus encourage more positive reception of Penderecki's seeming defacement of the Song. And it is this rereading that sparks a conversation with biblical scholars' queering of its textual pitches. In my view, Penderecki's compositional subversions, and the dissonant sonic exegesis of the Song that these create, support and anticipate the latest resistant readings of the Song performed by (among others) critics Fiona Black, J. Cheryl Exum, Athalya Brenner, Stephen D. Moore, Virginia Burrus, and Roland Boer. All have cautioned readers against assuming that standard interpretations of this canonical heteronormative love story have been accurate. Not only do Penderecki's anomalous erotic codes warn us against thinking we know how the Song should sound, what range of sonorities are appropriate for its dissemination, but his nonnormative erotic gestures and sonic pleasures also tacitly participate in, *and urge us to discursively expand*, Stephen D. Moore's project of tracing the role of this biblical text in the history of Western sexuality (Moore 2000).

2. The *Canticum* as Counterpleasure

Moore himself, in collaboration with Virginia Burrus (Moore and Burrus 2003), expands the Song's role within the history of sexuality by teasing yet another transgressive thematic out of the Song—rereading its dream sequence/beating scene as a woman's S/M fantasy (5:2–7) and celebrating

---

holy sonnets of metaphysical poets John Donne and George Herbert; and musical settings of the Song by Heinrich Schutz, Lucrezia Vizzana, and Claudio Monteverdi, to name just a few.

not only the latter but also the Song's more general "erotics of deferral" (46). The Song's form and content (its beating scene, its refusal to satisfy readers' desire for teleological, narrative closure) thus become "counterpleasures" as conceptualized by philosopher Karmen McKendrick (1999). Counterpleasures are marked by four basic traits: 1) They "queer our notion of pleasure, consisting in or coming through pain, frustration, refusal." 2) They are performative or ritual practices of "exceptional intensity, refusing to make sense while still demanding a philosophical unfolding." 3) They are pleasures that "refuse the sturdy subjective center, defying one's own survival, promising the death not of the body, but for an impossible moment of the subject" (18–19). Moore and Burrus (2004) emphasize a fourth point as well: "Counterpleasures by their very nature pursue their goals—political as well as erotic—only by indirect routes; their structure is such as to thwart teleology at every turn" (41). In my view, Penderecki's lovers constitute an aural prototype of those counterpleasures that Moore and Burrus identify both in the Song itself and in Roland Boer's pro-porn X-egesis thereof (1999, 2000), and this decades before either McKendrick's model or queer readings of the Song developed. Furthermore, Penderecki's counterpleasurable semiotics of desire, his musical erotics of deferral, constitutes a set of less politically controversial performative practices than those of S/M or porn, offering an arguably more accessible taste of the "destabilizing power of perverse pleasures," pleasures that disrupt insofar as they have not been formulaically prepackaged and fed to us by mainstream consumerist/musical economies. Counterpleasures cannot be easily co-opted by the latter because they "are fragmented, indirect, multiple and nonsensically multidirectional" (McKendrick 1999, 11). The rhythms and configurations of erotic interaction in the *Canticum*'s personae and (non-)story line, like other nonteleological and therefore "inefficient" counterpleasures, constitute a messier tale of love in which, pleasurably enough, lovers never know what's coming next, chronically miscommunicate with each other, run into walls, yet still, when they least expect it, get filled to bursting with insatiable passion. In this "nonsensically multi-directional" erotic mapping, all fits of pique, no matter how severe, remain unconsummated. A brief reading of the interplay of music and text evokes the *Canticum*'s interminably counterpleasurable flow. I apprehend this dynamic at two different levels—in the interactions between the chorally diffuse(d) lovers and musical instruments within the *Canticum*, as well as in listeners' counterpleasurable auditory experience.

Musical Interlude

As the piece opens, the Shulamite woos her beloved with sighs of praise for his beauty (Song 1:2, 13; RN 1–3), but his reply (Song 1:15; RN 6) is delayed by the first of many instrumental interruptions—this time by a slow, sinister materialization of a tone cluster packed with long notes from the winds, percussion, and harmonium (RN 3). (It is precisely these erratic instrumental interjections that create such aural unpredictability for the listener throughout the piece, but these deferrals exude their own exotic charm and heighten sensory suspense; conch shells and *campanelli* [bell lyres] bedazzle the eardrums, and strings do kinky things with their bows[16] to chafe the nerves and quicken the pulse.) This first foreboding buildup culminates in a magic wand–like flourish from the celeste, keyboard percussion, and harp (RN 4) that will recur four more times throughout the piece; this *presto–change-o* gesture "coils" us in "Pavlovian anticipation" (McClary 1995, 84) as we strain to hear what comes next. Listeners' somatic tension is further heightened when the Shulamite "reappears" after another wave of this wand (RN 6), now supposedly praising her lover's beauty (Song 1:16) and expressing delight at being taken to her lover's wine cellar (Song 2:4–6; is this a memory or a possibility?), but she does so by way of wailing motivic cells that evoke hallucination. These distressing moans eventually dissolve into nasty snake-like rattlings from wire-brushed cymbals (RN 9) that spill into equally unpleasant, dirge-like admonitions from the tenors and basses not to awaken love too soon (Song 2:7; RN 10). True to this disorienting hurry-up/not-yet pattern, and in blatant disregard for the men's warning, a manic delegation of harp, harmonium, strings, and percussion immediately accelerates (RN 12) at breakneck speed to preface the Shulamite's shocking announcement that her lover is in fact coming (so much for keeping love at bay; Song 2:8b–9; RN 13). Whispered at first with intermittent instrumental squawks (Song 2:8b; RN 13–14), the instruments and voices suddenly erupt—mimicking the beloved's gazelle-like leaps and bounds with their own dramatic

---

16. Mirka catalogues Penderecki's signature innovation of "percussive" sound effects from the strings as follows: "legno battuto, col legno," playing the "highest possible tones on a given instrument obtained by pressing the string close to the bow ... striking the sound board ... scraping the tailpiece ... bowing, plucking, hitting one or more strings near or on the bridge or tailpiece ... striking the fingerboard with the palm of the hand, and the desk or the chair with the bow" (1997, 7).

leaps of sevenths, ninths, and thirds (Song 2:9; RN 15); the dynamics grow louder and louder as his physical proximity increases. But the pleasure in this episode comes through pain as the supposedly joyous sounds of imminent reunion feel more like aural strangling at the hands of frenzied rubbings from the voices and instruments.

All these counterpleasurable abrasions, these painful "pleasures of exceptional intensity that refuse to make sense," continue unabated: for that latest fools' rush of desire is beaten back when the wooden blocks, tam-tams, and *frusta* preemptively strike again (end of RN 16). Suckers for punishment, this tug-of-war actually repeats and closes with another percussive slap in the face; the Shulamite protests a third time *parlando* that "he is coming" (RN 17), but the resistance derails into yet another detour, as the celeste et al. waves its wand and the strings actually retune in open fifths as if to start the whole piece again (RN 18–19). Fittingly so, because the beatings—a cocktail of pain and frustration—have rekindled the lovers' passion. Desire hurts now though—the men sigh over and over *quasi-falsetto*—their highest vocal *tessitura* : "Arise and come my dove ... hiding in the rocks and cliffs" (Song 2:13–14), while "she" (i.e. sopranos, altos, and basses) chokes out in reply that she is his and defiantly calls him forth—*revertere* (Song 2:17; RN 20) as *crotali*[17] and metal blocks toll underneath. Another forceful instrumental interruption ensues; the woodwinds push forward and then give way to a round of acidic high notes from the strings followed by an abrupt flourish from the celeste (RN 21).

Where are we now? The strings writhe to and fro in ascending and descending *glissandi* that drag all parties onto a veritable moonscape (just before RN 21)—a surprisingly barren sonic locale for what turns out to be the infamous dream scene (prime locus of counterpleasure for Moore and Burrus). There, voices and strings slither and moan in a slow-motion search for the beloved, before melting into a dejected "he did not come" (Song 3:1–2). This latest episode of frustrated desire is sealed with a three-layer wall of long, low chords from the celeste et al. (end of RN 23), another warning from the men not to awaken love too soon (Song 3:5; RN 24), and then a final wall of fingernails-on-blackboard string gestures. But taboo incites counterpleasurable transgression as full choir and orchestra stage one last crazed uprising (RN 25–26)—pummeling us with the beloved's laudatory collage of breasts/gazelles/spice-laden mountains and hills

---

17. Crotali are small finger-cymbals

(Song 4:1a, 5–7). As we might expect from such sonic S/M, however, the revolt is crushed, and Penderecki dramatizes this "wounding" with *fortissimo* musical word painting (Song 4:9): "Vulnerasti cor meum, soror mea, sponsa," gasps the choir as it and the string section vertiginously dissolve into contrary motion *glissandi*. In this noisy, brutal, anticlimactic climax, have we witnessed the final counterpleasurable dissolution of the lovers' "sturdy subjective centers"?

Not quite. Since counterpleasures are fueled by "pain, frustration, refusal" and "thwarted" teleology, this wounding immediately mobilizes every ounce of choral and orchestral energy to keep desire—and hence the pleasurable promise of more excitation and frustration—alive (RN 27). As McKendrick explains, this latest infliction of eroticized pain "provokes a double response" (i.e., make it stop/keep going), which preempts closure ("There is nowhere one might 'get to'") and lets desire explode "beyond the orderly economy that would allow it to produce relaxation" (1999, 114). And so, one more crazed ode to her beauty (Song 4:10–11; RN 27) and one more prayer to the elements from the bride to keep her "garden" lush for his arrival (Song 4:16; RN 29), *though in fact between these two eruptions he had just deemed her "garden" closed* via decelerating musical *glissandi* that had seemingly drained the soundscape of all life (Song 4:12; RN 28). This tangled knot of unrequited love is sonically extended/exacerbated via one final tension-building instrumental exchange (RN 30–31)—a low moan from the woodwinds, a plodding pack of blocks, gong, and *pizzicato* strings take us we know not where, until finally we bump into another magic-wand flourish from the celeste et al. (RN 32). Listeners will recognize this gesture and also the musical sighing motifs that then follow to convey the text's closing verse (Song 5:1); all of these are the same materials first heard when desire flared at the beginning of the piece. Are we thus trapped, delectably enough, in what promises to be an endless cycle of erotic deferrals? Here Penderecki's poetic license will confirm this intuition, even as it too delivers one last counterpleasurable punch (RN 32): "*I come* to the garden," the beloved/choir sings in a garbled flow of syllables ("Veni in hortum meum, soror mea sponsa"), but listeners are fed (and apprehend) just *one* lone word from this verse's opening line: "Veni, veni," whisper the ever-receding, sirenic voices, and, without the score and full text in hand, the "mood" of this last caress seems as much imperative as declarative.

*   *   *

This counterpleasurable *ménage* between lovers and instrumental domi-
natrices evokes those painful sensations and dynamics that Moore and
Burrus identify Gregory of Nyssa (of all people) experiencing and pro-
moting in his homilies on the Song: "For Gregory, Shulamith, *c'est moi*. ...
Like the smitten woman (or so he imagines) Gregory knows that pain and
ecstasy coincide in desire, and that the only true goal for a lover is found
in love's unending detours and deferrals; thus the most violent frustration
of desire ... is reconceived by him as the source of the soul's deepest pleasure. Gregory not only rejoices in the agony of his own unfulfilled desire,
he actively wills that the pain be intensified" (Moore and Burrus 2003, 45).
While it is unlikely that Penderecki's "reading" of the Song was an attempt
to "unlock" for Christians "the infinite mysteries of divine eros," as Gregory's expositions did for his flock (45), the composer's soundscape nevertheless enfleshes, and facilitates a similarly counterpleasurable *and acutely
embodied experience of*, "love's unending detours and deferrals" (45).

Penderecki's aural perversity also fits the bill as a counterpleasure
because of the politically constructive function it serves. Although it must
be emphasized that the deepest pleasure in counterpleasures necessarily
transcends any use-value they hold in subverting capitalist economies
of (sexual) pleasure,[18] Moore and Burrus argue for a reconstrual of S/M
counterpleasures (among others) as allies rather than enemies of feminist sociopolitical objectives, precisely because counterpleasures thwart
the agenda of heteronormativity and its gender-stereotypical sexual roles
and behaviors. "As performative or ritual practices (overlapping complexly
with liturgy and asceticism), the counterpleasures may serve feminist ends
by exposing, intensifying, parodying, displacing, and dislodging obdurate
relations of power inscribed within gender (but not only gender)" (Moore
and Burrus 2003, 41). So too Penderecki's performative practices: rather
than composing an erotic mapping that reinscribes through *musical* conventions heterosexism's ideal of true love—that spiritual ground that will
sanction marriage, reproduction, and hence a properly contained sen-

---

18. McKendrick (1999) follows Raoul Vaneigem (*The Book of Pleasures*) in arguing that "the counterpleasures are conspicuously resistant to absorption by exchange
value" (11). Having said this, however, McKendrick insists that "pleasure is not subversive if we make of it something useful, even if that use is to subvert. ... There is an
explosive quality to these pleasures that goes beyond the possible aims of a subject"
(13). Assessing them for "effectiveness" of any sort is to misunderstand their "subject-
shattering" nature (12–13).

suality (33–34; an oppressive ideal that feminist utopian readings of the Song as odes to the joys of egalitarian, heterosexual love inadvertently reinforce)[19]—his music (like S/M but without the bruises) participates in a discursive "countereconomy" to heteronormativity: "s/m subverts heteronormative lack-based economies of desire, as the point is no longer to 'get' what you 'lack'—whether it be the phallus, a baby, or even your orgasm—not to 'get' anything or anywhere, in fact, bur rather to continue to *want*, ever more intensely, ever more insistently, and hence ever more pleasurably" (45). Moore and Burrus do not identify or include music per se when they encourage feminists to reconsider counterpleasures as tactically useful for feminist ends. (Though music does, of course, constitute part of liturgy.) Yet the discursive effects of the queer musical counterpleasures absorbed through Penderecki's erotic mapping constitute an interrogation of "obdurate relations of power" within gender and sexuality as the latter are codified more tacitly (paradoxically enough) in music.

The composer's poetic license may scupper the above musicobiblical exegesis, however. My depiction of the *Canticum* as counterpleasure collapses insofar as Penderecki does not set the beating scene from ch. 5 that is so central to these lengthy debates over the Song's potentially feminist or patriarchal or queer erotics. He chooses instead a portion from the gentler dream scene in ch. 3 (vv. 1–2). Penderecki does not in fact shy away from darker thematics in his religious works,[20] but it is possible that in setting and selecting verses from this classical sacred love story he does succumb to convention in suppressing its dissonant elements. But this is where the always-slippery relationship between music and text (and reader response) queers the project of musical meaning-construction in playfully polysemic ways. To me, the work's harrowing sonorities and jarring collisions of sound panels make the whole setting one long (albeit highly pleasurable) beating scene. That is to say, the music unleashes the violence the editing repressed; the sounds themselves—music's own body as it were—seemingly attacks the text's pleasantries or sadomasochistically queers them, and the entire work's (for some) grotesque musical accoutrements ravage the Shulamite's beautiful breasts, the embrace of her beloved's stalwart hands, their garden of delights—boxing listeners' ears in the process.

---

19. Moore and Burrus survey these theoretical blind spots in Kristeva, Ostriker, Exum and Black, Trible, Brenner, and Fontaine (2003, 25–30).

20. See here, for example, his settings of *The Devils of Loudon* and his highly unorthodox *Dies irae* (1967).

Also soundly trounced is any saccharine gratification of happy end-ings which hopeless romantics in the audience have been conditioned to expect from any musical settings of this old scriptural chestnut. The work's "erotics of denial" (Moore and Burrus 2003, 45) thus does double duty: it stymies musicocultural conditioning even as it counterpleasurably tenders other auditors' blissfully painful erotic resignation—their joyful surren-der to unsated desire. Reconfiguring the lovers' unnerving *cris de coeur* in these queerer terms, as erotic/representational practices of resistance, may sweeten the strains they bear.

3. Queered Erotic Rhythms, Interpersonal Repercussions

If the *Canticum*-as-counterpleasure is too much of a conceptual stretch (particularly without a musically rendered beating scene), we may ingest a less kinky *countercultural* pleasure through its musically transmitted meditation upon the text's own nonlinear temporality—a feature that many readers erase by assuming the lovers' game of hide-and-seek ends in joyful reunion. The latest generation of biblical critics has challenged this misreading for its censorial deployment by religious and political conservatives against "perverse" pleasures, desires, and values. Pen-derecki's musical setting strengthens such ideology critique precisely because, via music, the subversively discursive power of this nonlinear text will now be *corporeally registered* through the *Canticum's* circulation of irregular rhythms and its nonteleological organization of time and our lived musical experience. The *erotic* implications of the biblical text's own nonlinear temporality, emphatically foregrounded by today's bibli-cal critics, is here given queerer musical flesh that can kinetically manip-ulate our own. In other words, the musical setting redoubles the text's sociocultural discursive power as a weapon for denaturalizing the extant heteronormative menu of erotic ways to experience time's unfolding. As a socializing force, music can help immensely to denaturalize heteronor-mativity. For "music's ability to structure time—to immerse the listener in patterns that come to appear entirely natural and thus imperceptible to those who share their predilections"—is in fact "even more fundamental to the shaping of subjective consciousness" than its other figurations of "the body, emotions, social order, gender, desire and pleasure" (McClary 1998, 8). We do well therefore to interrogate the rhythms and meters within musical settings of the Song and ask, "What kinds of needs do these patterns satisfy?" (11).

Here again, twentieth-century compositional innovations like those of Penderecki carry queer valences, at least in the repertoire of musicoerotic conventions they afford. Part of the project of denaturalizing our notions of music itself (discussed above) involved emancipation from the oppressively "forward-moving, goal-oriented grammar of tonal music" (Schwartz and Godfrey 1993, 15), those "heroic narratives" conveyed through time via tensely building musical struggles (i.e., harmonic progressions), that would always eventuate in climactic, triumphant resolutions (McClary 1998, 22). (This same temporal build-up of tension and release imitates and inculcates heteronormative rhythms/patterns of sexual pleasure.[21]) Postwar composers, by contrast, chose instead to translate scientific assertions of time's relativity and/or sought to suspend (and thereby destabilize) our "natural" sense of time's unfolding (cf. Schwartz and Godfrey 1993, 34–35). Penderecki's restructuring of time does more therefore than facilitate biblical critics' calls to awaken readers from their narrative slumber. He queers extant patterns of erotic temporality, further hampering the Song's deployment to heteronormative ends. To borrow Judith Butler's terminology, his setting exposes listeners to a wider range of sensual resources with which to variegate the "ritualized production" of gender and sexuality within the "process of iterability" that composes human subjectivity (1993, 231).[22] Each audition, so to speak, of Penderecki's *Canticum* thus provides alternative means for self-fashioning.

---

21. Basic examples of such *double entendres* would include Bach's organ fugues, Brahms's symphonies, Tchaikovsky's Fourth Symphony, the music of Bizet's opera *Carmen*, and Beethoven's Ninth Symphony. See McClary 1991, 12–17, 53–79, 124–31; 2000, chs. 3 and 4, for in-depth discussions of some of these works. For broader readings of key Western composers' "heroic narratives," see Adorno 2006; Subotnik 1991; McClary 2007 (including a complete list of her many narrative analyses in the bibliography); and copious articles by Anthony Newcomb catalogued in Maus 2006.

22. These are Butler's terms for describing gendered subject formation: "Performativity cannot be understood outside a process of iterability, *a regularized and constrained repetition of norms*. And this repetition is not performed *by* a subject; this repetition is what enables a subject and constitutes the temporal condition for the subject. This iterability implies that 'performance' is not a singular 'act' or event, but a ritualized production, *a ritual reiterated under and through constraint*, under and through the force of prohibition and taboo, with the threat of ostracism and even death controlling and compelling the shape of the production, but not, I will insist, determining it fully in advance" (1993, 231; emphasis added).

I take seriously Butler's caveat that the performance of gender is not like putting on or taking off clothes (Jagose 1996, 87). I am not therefore reducing music's role

Listeners may perhaps be more familiar with those composers who, seeking non-Western sources of kinetic pleasure and alternative orientations to space and time, explored cyclical, highly repetitive, trance-inducing temporalities that they discovered at work in Eastern musics and spiritualities—a diverse "lineage" of musical experimentation conducted first by Debussy, Ravel, and Stravinsky, then intensifying in the work of minimalists Riley, Reich, and Glass and experimentalists Pauline Oliveros and Laurie Anderson—explorations of temporality that then reached even wider audiences through the more popular output of the Beatles and Led Zeppelin and even that of Madonna, Prince, Tupac and techno (cf. McClary 1998, 16–20). Particularly pertinent to this discussion, such sonic "reconceptualizations" of time's unfolding catalyzed a sexual revolution (16–20).[23] Given that Penderecki is setting one of the West's most famous romantic templates and sources of sensual pleasure, his quirkier rhythms similarly invite us to imagine different patterns of erotic interaction, deviating as they do not only from the "orientalist" rhythmic trajectory above (and its hypersexual pop spinoffs) but also from the more classically "phallic" Western erotic narratives of tension and release. The latter, moreover, have been soundly encoded and reinforced by previous, well-loved tonal settings of the Song—those of Monteverdi, Palestrina, and Vaughn Williams (even those popular Israeli folk renditions Athalya Brenner discusses as part of her own memory bank; 2000, 157–58). Penderecki's model of erotic temporality is decidedly queer in the way it defies categorization within even this binary model of Western versus Eastern, mainstream versus alternative erotic temporalities.

Accepting another "dance" with these offbeat lovers as a way to free ourselves momentarily from the programmatic demands of mainstream erotica may in turn spark a more general affection for the way not only its denaturalization of (erotic) time but also its other dissonant elements help

---

in subject formation to basic, voluntaristic, performative acts of musicians playing and audiences listening. Rather, music participates in the broader formative dynamic outlined above as a constrained, socializing discourse that continuously repeats and inculcates norms, taboos, etc., but also allows resistant slippages within these repetitions.

23. McClary is careful to specify that *black* musical styles and genres (especially blues) fused with and provided the "musical framework" underneath these "Asian characteristics" in the realm of pop music, and together these played a pivotal role in the sexual revolution of the 1960s (1998, 19).

to jam the socializing force of heteronormative cultural semiotics. That is to say, readers with intimate knowledge of the text's all-too-often overlooked dystopic elements—its nonnarrativity, its lack of happy ending, its couple's grotesque bodies (Black 2009)—might savor the shock value this rendition holds if it is enlisted as a cattle prod with which to jolt traditionalists and conservatives out of their ideological misuses of this power-wielding canonical text. Penderecki's seemingly discordant rendering of the text in musical space and time broadcasts a rather loud hermeneutic of suspicion that jogs us from our reading ruts—inviting us to go back and read the book again, more closely, with greater care. Sloppy readings of the text imprison its lovers within a politics of representation that discourages not only interpretive accuracy but also relational intimacy. Penderecki's music effectively frees the text's lovers from the same and affords them circulation within a more realistic, sonically disseminated model of intimacy. How so?

In her book *Carnal Knowing* (1989), Margaret Miles records the insidious relational damage that polarized visual representations of women as virgin-whore, angel-temptress have caused. Such images create repressive substitutes for flesh-and-blood women in people's imaginations that will then misguidedly predetermine one's relationships with actual women (10).[24] Tonally harmonious musical renderings of the Song's supposedly "happy" lovers can certainly be situated within a similarly pernicious genealogy. If we enlist Miles' logic on the politics of representation, musical, artistic, and exegetical caricatures of the Song's "happy" lovers actually generate *distance* between readers and the text's in-fact more disturbing content. Doing so then reinforces relational models of intimacy that "stabilize [false] assumptions and expectations" (10). Conversely, Penderecki's couple reconnects readers to that "complex and contradictory reality" that human intimacy inevitably entails—banishing those "cumulative representations" within other musical settings, artworks, and theologies that in effect make the story's actual lovers "disappear" (10). Listeners and biblical scholars might therefore warmly embrace Penderecki's rather time-warped

---

24. Miles explains: "Representations provide a shortcut, enabling immediate response without the laborious process of reflection that would be necessary if each person or situation were to receive an individual response. Moreover, representations often determine intimate as well as less personal relationships. Because the level of threat and the potential for pain in intimate relationships is very high, representations of the other are used to reduce her to manageability" (1989, 10).

erotic mapping as an emancipatory musical erotics, precisely because the composer short circuits the transmission of conventional gender roles and romantic scripts, even more powerfully here because music appeals so viscerally and holistically to both flesh and spirit. Nor can Penderecki's lovers be conscripted to support theological misrepresentations of the song's heteronormative, matrimonial moralities, still widely dispersed as we know through wedding sermons and marriage counseling. And so, despite alienating first impressions, the lovers' cattle-prod erotics make them winsome allies for queer political and hermeneutical agendas.

4. Cusick's Queer Ears: Music as Lover

Perhaps for some ears, however, these Cold War lovers still remain chillingly inaccessible. What last-resort strategies might temper this aural xenophobia? Given my love for this piece, I might try to solicit more affection for the *Canticum* by impressing listeners with deeper knowledge of the composer's innovative compositional techniques. Academic appraisals of modernist and *avant garde* works' greatness often involve drawing intricate charts and graphs that will reveal the more esoteric ingenuity of a composer's "architectonic" vision or meticulous system building as executed through their treatment of motivic cells, tone rows, and alternating sound-mass densities. However, rather than trying to plunge you inside the composer's mind, one New Musicologist, a lesbian who has no desire "to think straight," suggests breaking musicological rules and putting us flat on our backs instead—in a queer listening posture. Trained in traditional musicology, Suzanne Cusick questions the discipline's phallogocentrism, its "apparent preoccupation with the text-like nature of music, that is, with the grammar and syntax of pitches and durations" (1994a, 13). She attends instead to previously neglected musicoanalytical components—texture, timbre, bodily performance—and to music's erogenous—even "gynomorphic"—behaviors (1994b, 77).

By approaching both music making and reception as first and foremost mutually interdependent, performative, bodily events, Cusick literally and metaphorically retrieves and revalorizes the subtext, the musical body, the "music made flesh" (her term), that is all too often ideologically smothered beneath supposedly more valuable score-driven analysis of the composer's creative processes. Our bodily reactions to a work, not our intense scrutiny of a musical score, become the preferred matrix for musical understanding. This atypical analytical posture or starting point for musical analysis provokes a sexual metaphor with which to describe musical meaning making: spurning the masculinist Music-as-Score, Cusick approaches music as her sonically embodied Lover—that "active force which generates pleasure, which leads one body and soul into an alternate reality" (1994b, 74). No longer a textual object, Cusick embraces music's erotic powers as sexual subject, exploring "her" body "intersubjectively." She listens with reverent attention because her musical Lover "may have things to say that are totally different from what listeners expect to hear" (76–77). Cusick wants therefore "to allow the music her own voice ... her own wholeness of utterance, before analytical or cultural historical interrogation. ... Because I think both the essentializing and the dismembering strategies [of standard musicological analysis] feel akin to those violences as they are committed on the bodies and souls of real women, and because I am being serious when I say I love music, I cannot bear to do those things to a beloved" (76–77).

Of course, this more positive construal of Music-as-Lover requires postulation of a crucial interdependence between human sexuality and musicality. Cusick knows their intense confluence in her own lived experience but elaborates her intuitions more theoretically by consulting Michel Foucault and Judith Butler. Most simply defined, and minus its usual phallocentric trappings, sexuality denotes "a way of expressing and/or enacting relationships of intimacy through physical pleasure shared, accepted or given" (Cusick 1994b, 70). Power dynamics inevitably permeate such interaction. More accurately then, sexuality is the "circulation" of power, pleasure, and intimacy between bodies, as are music making and appreciation (71). Clearly this theoretical conflation of music and sex is only possible if, like Cusick, one rejects excessively genitalized definitions of sexual relations and redefines human sexuality as something much more diffuse (70–71); Cusick does so with relative ease precisely because, as a lesbian, she consciously resists the sexual power dynamics of the phallic economy (70–73).

Redefined in these terms, music is thus an extension, or even precondition, of Cusick's sexuality. Cusick uses the visceral image of "bleedthrough" to describe the intimate "proximity" of human musicality and sexuality: "If music isn't sexuality, for most of us, it is psychically next door" (70–71) This reality then informs her musicological pedagogy:

> I ask my students to open themselves to the music they hear, to let music do it to them, to become more intensely aware physically, emotionally,

intellectually of what's being done to them. I teach them to ask of the music, later, how it achieved that effect (and in more advanced courses, I try to teach them to ask it why). These interrogations are designed in effect to increase the actual intimacy of my students' subsequent encounters with that music or with any music, by increasing their knowledge of who it is, so to speak, who's been on top and by increasing their skill, through practice, in the art of being music's beloved. (Cusick 1994b, 74)

Elsewhere I have enlisted Cusick's notion of music as lover to write a feminist musical Christology, and Fiona Black has treated the biblical Song as her beloved via Roland Barthes' amatory hermeneutics.[25] Now Cusick's more holistic and "intersubjective" approach to musical works may grant Penderecki's musically incarnate biblical lovers a second hearing; if listeners dare to become "bottoms" to Penderecki's sonic "top," they can grow closer to this initially repellent and cacophonous soundscape, expanding thereby not only their lexicon of pleasurable erotic sonorities but also their available means of identity construction (however fluid and unstable identity construction proves to be, as queer theorists continually emphasize, in our postmodern context).[26] The lovers' initially eerie siren calls invite us to assume strange new listening positions and warm to the foreign touch of queerer pitches, utterances of the wholly Other. Indeed, lying on our backs and acquiescing to this unsettling interplay of power, pleasure, and intimacy might allow these perplexing lovers to diffuse a sonic translation of Iris Murdoch's famous line: "Love is the extremely difficult realization that something other than oneself is real" (1998, 215).[27] Biblical critics' resistant readings of the Song arguably translate its main thrust—its solicitation of myriad wrestlings with alterity—in similar terms.

And we may inch just a little closer to this iron pair if, adopting Cusick's sensitivity to phallic economies within musicological discourse, we admire more appreciatively Penderecki's contribution to *music history* by framing his compositional innovations as a form of resistance to the phallic economy of serious composition, one that an elitist "guild" of com-

---

25. See Epstein 2004; Black 1999.

26. Music's own fluidity and transience—the way evaporation grounds its nature as an expressive medium in and of itself—helpfully allegorizes the contingent, necessarily unreified nature of identity that queer theory foregrounds (Jagose 1996, 96).

27. Skerrett (1996, 91) cites Murdoch's aphorism in her own critique of an eros theologian/lover's misguided refusal to accept the existence of an Other's boundaries.

posers and critics tried in vain to champion over against both popular music's growing mass appeal and against Penderecki and other composers' return to tonality and other traditional compositional means after atonality's "irreversible" revolutionary coup. Cusick's alternative set of listening or analytic priorities is actually more appropriate for appreciating Penderecki's music, precisely because he rejected excessively intellectual and mathematical compositional processes that were hallmarks of the vanguard composers of his day,[28] particularly the strict serialism and purist aesthetic of the Darmstadt school.[29] Part of Penderecki's idiosyncratic style, according to Adrian Thomas, lay in his preference for the "immediate drama of extreme contrasts" and his music's "almost visceral expressivity," which contrasted with the far more cerebral compositional techniques of his other European contemporaries (2005, 180); Greek composer Iannis Xenakis, for example, conceptualized pieces using stochastic theories and Hungarian Gyorg Ligeti systematically deployed micropolyphony (180).[30]

---

28. Penderecki (1998) situates himself as follows: "I have gone my own way throughout my career. Even my avant-garde period was different from others. It was going against my colleagues from Darmstadt and Donaueshingen.... The escape from the avant-garde trap of formalism enabled me to turn back towards tradition. I was even called 'the Trojan horse' of the avant-garde. ... Malicious critics accused me of eclecticism" (16–17).

29. The term "Darmstadt school" was coined to delineate the compositional ethos and practices of a group of pioneering composers (Nono, Maderna, Stockhausen, Boulez) who for a time (c. 1950–1961) promoted their own compositional techniques (particularly strict serialism) as crucial musical ingredients for any serious, self-respecting composer of the day, especially during the annual Darmstadt summer schools. Christopher Fox comments: "the compositional techniques of the Darmstadt School were widely adopted by other composers anxious to be at the cutting edge of modernism. Darmstadt serialism may have grown out of expressive necessity but, like any philosophy for which historical inevitability is invoked, it soon hardened into dogmatic orthodoxy for its disciples. The activities of these zealots—Franco Evangelisti called them the 'dodecaphonic police'—has led in latter years to the use of 'Darmstadt' as a pejorative term, implying a desiccated, slavishly rule-based music. The adherence of the School's founders to their collegial aesthetic ended with the 1950s," as each of its founders went off in different musically innovative directions (Fox 2006).

30. Thomas concludes his exercise in contrasts as follows: "Whether Penderecki was ever a fundamentally radical composer is a matter for debate. His later career indicates that his is more conservatively grounded than the two non-Polish composers with whom he is often linked in the 1960s: Xenakis and Ligeti" (Thomas 2005, 180). Of his quest for synthesis, Thomas comments: "Those who viewed the sonoristic pieces as

Penderecki's musical recuperation of the sensual to resist the hegemony of the rational (while revalorized by someone like Cusick), provoked criticism from those who adhered to an arguably more "masculinist" aesthetic. Thus Haylock: "Krzsyztof Penderecki has for a long time been viewed with a certain amount of skepticism by the learned musical establishment. At a time when the elitist avant-garde scene was dominated by the intellectually imposing post-serialist and aleatoric preoccupations of Pierre Boulez and Karlheinz Stockhausen, Penderecki emerged as an out-and-out sensualist" (1994, 3). Other critics who in fact valued such "radical sonorism" as in and of itself iconoclastic were still disappointed when in the 1970s Penderecki diluted this signature feature that had earned him a place among 1960s *avant garde* composers—attempting instead to forge a synthesis between traditional musical forms and sounds and those of his earlier, more experimental works in the '50s and '60s (Thomas 2005, 240). Such hybridity created a "degenerative softening" in his musical palette and in the works of the 1970s and after (240).[31] It is not hard to detect in the evaluative criteria and value judgments attending Penderecki's reception— his problematically emotional/sensual rather than rational/"ascetic"[32] compositional aesthetic and practices—an age-old, gendered binarism to which both the categorization of concrete musical codes and musico-critical discourse were definitely not immune (now amply documented within New Musicological scholarship). With her queer ears and analyti-

---

representing the best of the Polish avant-garde were more likely to view Penderecki's new direction [in the 1960s and 70s] as a compromise too far" (181).

Schwartz and Godfrey (1993) summarize Xenakis's "stochastic method" as follows: "sound masses are shaped by mathematical probability (as expressed in Bernoulli's Law). The stochastic approach allowed Xenakis to calculate, as a function of probability, the shape and behaviour of composite masses of sound made up of many brief sound events. Thus his music is often dominated by enormous clusters or 'clouds' of small sound 'particles,' beginning, ending, and fluctuating in density as rain or hail does when striking against a hard surface [Xenakis's own analogy]" (179). (Xenakis was educated in architecture and engineering.) Ligeti's micropolyphony consists of "dense weaves of canons at the unison, in which lines move at different speeds and are not separately identifiable" (Griffiths 2006). See for example Ligeti's *Atmospheres* (1961).

31. Unfortunately Thomas does not cite his original sources for these negative reviews of Penderecki's work.

32. Mirka contrasts Polish musical expressivism with "the experimental 'asceticism'" of Western music in the 1950s (1997, 2).

cal techniques, however, Cusick allows us to reframe these phallocentric epithets—"degenerative," "softening," "sensual," "emotional"—as badges of honor within queerer compositional economies.

By listening again to Penderecki's *Canticum* with Cusick's queered hermeneutic of generosity, one that also acknowledges that these foreign sounds are in fact for him and others erotic and sensual, just simply outside the reigning phallic economies of orthodox musical idioms of the day (be these serialist or syrupy pop), the piece approaches us today as both invitation and question: Penderecki's hybrid musicality invites us to listen and relate to musical sound in new ways and to expand our repertoire of erotic sonorities and pleasures, hence our available sources of selfhood, in the process. Alternatively, and because Cusick makes our bodies the matrix of musical understanding, we are always free to reject the advances (or assaults) of any unsavory musical partners. And so, if Penderecki's erotic overture still remains a turn-off, even after we have given "her" a fair hearing, his erotic mapping may still haunt us as a question—"a ruddering interrogative," to borrow Kathleen Sands' term:[33] how hegemonically defined are your desires? (This may have been an urgent question in 1970s Communist Poland.) If, on the other hand, we've enjoyed every second of the counterpleasurable pain, then the text and music have "topped" us in ways of which Moore, Boer, Burrus and Cusick would approve.

GODLY VIBES, SCRIPTURAL SUBSIDIES: A QUEER ALLEGORICAL POSTSCRIPT

Having attempted to render Penderecki's postwar lovers and erotic mapping more ingratiating by virtue of the counterpleasurable, subversively offbeat, resourcefully postmodern, and aurally queer love story that intercourse with them affords, and teasing out in the process a new, musically induced, carnally allegorical model of the self performed from the biblical book, Cusick's closing directives above—her sensitivity to and emphasis upon the intimacy between human sexuality and musicality—suggest another untapped allegorical thematic within the Song, this time at the level of theology. As Solomon's song, this book's very name, plus its racy content and hallowed theological place within Jewish and Christian canons, allegorizes a sacred, visceral "bleed-through" between *music and*

---

33. See Sands 1994.

sex, this despite centuries of hypervigilance over, and theological invec-
tive against, this other couple's—music and sex's—dangerous affinities and
illicit collaborations.[34] The Song of Solomon—a text within a scriptural
canon—prototypically and serendipitously endorses the confluence of
music and sex as a matrix for deeply relational self-understanding. This is
a very different "carnal allegory" than Moore and Burrus's or Boer's, one
lying dormant yet staring us in the face for centuries.

It is perhaps not coincidental that this latent, rather unorthodox moral
of the story has emerged by enlisting Cusick's notion of Music-as-Lover to
wrestle more productively with Penderecki's peculiar setting of the Song.
It is as if his language of love creates a mode of negative resistance that
rivets our attention upon the intimate connection between musicality
and sexuality: in other words, Penderecki's *Canticum* flags their tacit conflation within the biblical book, precisely because his rendering of their
conjunctio sounds (for many listeners) so wrong, so problematic, anomalous. Devoting more sustained attention to *musical* settings of this sacred,
sexually charged Song—a heretofore neglected biblical afterlife—can
help remind readers of its often forgotten, yet originary, musicality. And,
in conversation with biblical critics' resistant readings of the same, such
interdisciplinary analyses can further elaborate the emancipatory power
of the Bible's own allegorical baptism of musicosexual pleasures. To boot
(and much to fundamentalists' dismay), theological projects that celebrate
this crucial nexus between music and sex now have a biblical precedent
for their apologetics, and the Song's renegade status in the canon acquires
even cheekier legitimacy.

WORKS CONSULTED

Abbate, Carolyn. 1991. *Unsung Voices: Opera and Musical Narrative in the
    Nineteenth Century*. Princeton: Princeton University Press.
Adorno, Theodor. 2006. *Philosophy of New Music*. Translated by Robert
    Hullot-Kentor. Minneapolis: University of Minnesota Press.
Black, Fiona C. 1999. What Is My Beloved? On Erotic Reading and the
    Song of Songs. Pages 35–52 in *The Labour of Reading: Desire, Alien-*

---

34. For a survey of such sexually charged, ecclesiastical aspersions cast upon
music as a dangerous woman and emasculating seductress, and upon women making
music (as being either virgins or whores), see Epstein 2004, part 1.

ation, and Biblical Interpretation. Edited by Fiona C. Black, Roland Boer, and Erin Runions. SemeiaSt 36. Atlanta: Scholars Press.

———. 2000. Beauty or the Beast? The Grotesque Body in the Song of Songs. *BibInt* 8:302–23.

———. 2009. *Artifice of Love: Grotesque Bodies and the Song of Songs*. New York: T&T Clark.

Black, Fiona C., and J. Cheryl Exum. 1998. Semiotics in Stained Glass: Edward Burne-Jones's Song of Songs. Pages 315–42 in *Biblical Studies/ Cultural Studies: The Third Sheffield Colloquium*. Edited by Cheryl J. Exum and Stephen D. Moore. GCT 7. Sheffield: Sheffield Academic Press.

Boer, Roland. 1999. Night Sprinkle(s): Pornography and the Song of Songs. Pages 53–70 in idem, *Knockin' on Heaven's Door*. London: Routledge.

———. 2000. The Second Coming: Repetition and Insatiable Desire in the Song of Songs. *BibInt* 8:276–301.

Borowik, Irena. 2006. Poland. Pages 718–22 in vol. 2 of *Encyclopedia of Politics and Religion*. Edited by Robert Wuthnow. 2 vols. 2nd ed. Washington, D.C.: CQ Press.

Brenner, Athalya. 1993. To See Is to Assume: Whose Love Is Celebrated in the Song of Songs? *BibInt* 3:1–20.

———. 2000. "My" Song of Songs. Pages 154–68 in Brenner and Fontaine 2000.

Brenner, Athalya, and Carole R. Fontaine, eds. 2000. *The Song of Songs: A Feminist Companion to the Bible*. FCB 2/6. Sheffield: Sheffield Academic Press.

Butler, Judith. 1991. Imitation and Gender Insubordination. Pages 13–31 in *Inside/Out: Lesbian Theories Gay Theories*. NewYork: Routledge.

———. 1993. *Bodies That Matter: On the Discursive Limits of "Sex."* New York: Routledge.

Cage, John. 1961. *Silence: Lectures and Writings*. Middleton, Conn.: Wesleyan University Press.

Cope, David. 2001. *New Directions in Music*. 7th ed. Prospect Heights, Ill.: Waveland Press.

Cusick, Suzanne G. 1994a. Feminist Theory, Music Theory, and the Mind/ Body Problem. *Perspectives of New Music* 32:8–27.

———. 1994b. On a Lesbian Relationship with Music: A Serious Effort Not to Think Straight. Pages 67–83 in *Queering the Pitch: The New Gay and Lesbian Musicology*. Edited by Philip Brett, Elizabeth Wood, and Gary C. Thomas. New York: Routledge.

Doty, Alexander. 1993. *Making Things Perfectly Queer: Interpreting Mass Culture*. Minneapolis: University of Minnesota Press.

Epstein, Heidi. 2004. *Melting the Venusberg: A Feminist Theology of Music*. New York: Continuum.

———. 2009. Sour Grapes, Fermented Selves: Musical Shulammites Modulate Subjectivity. *Bible and Critical Theory* 5:1–17.

Exum, J. Cheryl. 2000. Ten Things Every Feminist Should Know about the Song of Songs. Pages 24–35 in Brenner and Fontaine 2000.

Fontaine, Carole R. 2000. The Voice of the Turtle: Now It's *MY* Song of Songs. Pages 169–85 in Brenner and Fontaine 2000.

Fox, Christopher. 2006. Darmstadt School. *Grove Music Online*. Edited by Deane Root. Online: http://www.grovemusic.com (accessed 19 July 2009).

Greenblatt, Stephen. 1989. *Shakespearean Negotiations: The Circulation of Social Energies in Renaissance England*. Berkeley: University of California Press.

Griffiths, Paul. 2006. Ligeti, György. *Grove Music Online*. Edited by Deane Root. Online: http://www.grovemusic.com (accessed 19 July 2009).

Haylock, Julian. 1994. Program notes. On *Krzysztof Penderecki: Selections*. EMI Classics Matrix Series 5. EMI Records 7243 5 65077 2 3. Compact disc.

Heath, Stephen. 1982. *The Sexual Fix*. New York: Shocken.

Hennessy, Rosemary. 1994. Queer Theory, Left Politics. *Rethinking Marxism* 7 (3):85–111.

Illouz, Eva. 1998. The Lost Innocence of Love: Romance as a Postmodern Condition. *Theory, Culture, and Society* 15.3–4:161–86.

Jagose, Annamarie. 1996. *Queer Theory: An Introduction*. New York: New York University Press.

Kramer, Lawrence. 1990. "As if a Voice Were in Them": Music, Narrative and Deconstruction. Pages 176–213 in *Music and Cultural Practice, 1800–1900*. Berkeley: University of California Press.

Kristeva, Julia. 1987. A Holy Madness: She and He. Pages 83–100 in *Tales of Love*. Translated by Leon S. Roudiez. New York: Columbia University Press.

Leonardi, Susan J., and Rebecca A. Pope. 1996. *The Diva's Mouth: Body, Voice, Prima Donna Politics*. New Brunswick, N.J.: Rutgers University Press.

Maus, Fred Everett. 1998. Music as Drama. *Music Theory Spectrum* 10:56–73.

————. 2006. Narratology, Narrativity. *Grove Music Online.* Edited by Deane Root. Online: http://www.grovemusic.com (accessed 19 July 2009).

McClary, Susan. 1991. *Feminine Endings: Music, Gender, and Sexuality.* Minneapolis: University of Minnesota Press.

————. 1994. Paradigm Dissonances: Music Theory, Cultural Studies, Feminist Criticism. *Perspectives of New Music* 32 (Winter):68–85.

————. 1995. Music, the Pythagoreans, and the Body. Pages 82–104 in *Choreographing History.* Edited by Susan Leigh Foster. Bloomington: Indiana University Press.

————. 1998. Rap, Minimalism, and Structures of Time in Late Twentieth-Century Culture. The Norman and Jane Geske Lecture. Lincoln: University of Nebraska Press.

————. 2000. *Conventional Wisdom: The Content of Musical Form.* The Bloch Lectures, 1993. Berkeley: University of California Press.

————. 2001. II: Disciplines of Musicology, 11; Gender and Sexual Studies. *Grove Music Online.* Edited by Deane Root. Online: http://www.grovemusic.com (accessed 21 May 2008).

————. 2004. *Modal Subjectivities: Self-Fashioning in the Italian Madrigal.* Berkeley: University of California Press.

————. 2007. *Reading Music: Selected Essays.* Burlington, Vt.: Ashgate.

McKendrick, Karmen. 1999. *Counterpleasures.* New York: State University Press of New York.

Miles, Margaret. 1989. *Carnal Knowing: Female Nakedness and Religious Meaning in the Christian West.* New York: Vintage.

Mirka, Danuta. 1997. *The Sonoristic Structuralism of Krzysztof Penderecki.* Katowice: Akademia Muzyczna.

Mockus, Martha. 1994. Queer Thoughts on Country Music and kd lang. Pages 257–71 in *Queering the Pitch: The New Gay and Lesbian Musicology.* Edited by Phillip Brett, Elizabeth Wood, and Gary C. Thomas. New York: Routledge.

Monticone, Ronald C. 1986. *The Catholic Church in Communist Poland, 1945–1985: Forty Years of Church-State Relations.* New York: Columbia University Press.

Moore, Stephen D. 2000. The Song of Songs in the History of Sexuality. *CH* 69:328–50.

Moore, Stephen D., and Virginia Burrus. 2003. Unsafe Sex: Feminism, Pornography, and the Song of Songs. *BibInt* 11:24–52.

Murdoch, Iris. 1994. The Sublime and the Good. In *Existentialists and Mystics: Writings on Philosophy and Literature.* New York: Penguin.

Nattiez, Jean Jacques. 1990. Can One Speak of Narrativity in Music? *JRMA* 115:240–57.

Ostriker, Alicia. 2000. A Holy of Holies: The Song of Songs as Countertext. Pages 36–54 in Brenner and Fontaine 2000.

Pasler, Jann, and Vincent Duckles. 2001. I: The Nature of Musicology, 5; New Trends. *Grove Music Online.* Edited by Deane Root. Online: http://www.grovemusic.com (accessed 21 May 2008).

Penderecki, Krzysztof. 1975. *Canticum canticorum Salomonis quod hebraice dicitur.* Score. Krakow: Polskie Wydawnictwo Muzyczne.

———. 1994. *Krzysztof Penderecki: Selections.* EMI Classics Matrix Series 5. EMI Records 7243 5 65077 2 3. Compact disc.

———. 1998. *Labyrinth of Time: Five Addresses for the End of the Millennium.* Chapel Hill, N.C.: Hinshaw Music.

Sands, Kathleen M. 1994. *Escape from Paradise: Evil and Tragedy in Feminist Theology.* Minneapolis: Fortress.

Schwartz, Elliott, and Daniel Godfrey. 1993. *Music since 1945: Issues, Materials, and Literature.* New York: Schirmer.

Sedgwick, Eve Kosofsky. 1990. *Epistemology of the Closet.* Berkeley: University of California Press.

———. 1993. *Tendencies.* Durham: Duke University Press

Skerrett, Kathleen Roberts. 1996. When No Means Yes: The Passion of Carter Heyward. *JFSR* 12:71–92.

Subotnik, Rose Rosengard. 1991. *Developing Variations: Style, Ideology in Western Music.* Minneapolis: University of Minnesota Press.

Taylor, Charles. 1992. *Sources of the Self: The Making of Modern Identity.* Cambridge: Harvard University Press.

Thomas, Adrian. 2005. *Polish Music since Szymanowski.* Cambridge: Cambridge University Press.

Trible, Phyllis. 1978. *God and the Rhetoric of Sexuality.* Philadelphia: Fortress.

Waldrep, Sheldon. 2004. Phenomenology of Performance: David Bowie. Pages 105–40 in *The Aesthetics of Self-Invention: Oscar Wilde to David Bowie.* Minneapolis: University of Minnesota Press.

Walser, Rob. 1994. Prince as Queer Post-Structuralist. *Popular Music and Society* 18 (2):79–90.

Warner, Michael. 1993. Introduction. Pages vii–xxxi in *Fear of a Queer Planet: Queer Politics and Social Theory.* Edited by Michael Warner. Minneapolis: University of Minnesota Press.

QUEER THEORY AND HISTORICAL-CRITICAL EXEGESIS: QUEERING BIBLICISTS—A RESPONSE

S. Tamar Kamionkowski

Queer readings of the Bible feel like roller-coaster rides. (I love roller coasters!) The readings, when done well, can make my heart race and my guts twist. They can turn me in unexpected directions and even throw me for a loop. When I complete a queer biblical reading, I often feel as I do when I exit the roller coaster for the first time. I cannot recall the details of the ride, but I come off with a sense of intensity and disturbance that makes me both uneasy (or queasy) and elated.

As a lesbian, I delight in queer readings of the biblical texts. They speak to my personal experiences and I see myself reflected in biblical texts in new ways—my experience is given voice in the Bible. Queer readings also have a tendency to be fun, surprising, and sometimes even titillating. As a Jew who holds the Tanak as a sacred and dynamic text that provides the soil from which meaning making occurs, I struggle with queer readings. These interpretations challenge sustained identity, enduring meaning, or even a perch from which to gaze upon the world.

As a lesbian and a strongly identified Jewish biblicist, I find myself queer identified in that I embody or perform identities that would seem to be at odds with one another from the perspective of heteronormative culture. At the SBL, for example, I attend "traditional" sections such as Israelite Prophetic Literature and Theology of the Hebrew Scriptures alongside "subversive" sections like Ideological Criticism and Gender, Sexuality, and the Bible. The analogy is weak but I sometimes feel like I'm traveling between the synagogue and gay bars—unlikely to find a lot of the same people and somewhat closeted in each location. When I think of myself as a queer biblicist, I mean one who is queer and subversive by the very nature of occupying professional spaces that the academy has defined as oppositional to one another, not one who applies queer theory to the Bible. In other words, I blur the boundaries of "traditional = dominant regime" and "postmodern/queer = subversive." I embrace both historical criticism and queer readings.

I begin with this personal statement in order to provide the background from which I will be engaging primarily with the works of Stone and Guest (with some reference to Epstein and Runions). What happens when a queer biblicist (both traditional and postmodern) applies her lens to these essays?

Each writer provides a slightly different definition of queer readings of the Bible. However, the common thread is that each claims to approach the Bible as a text to be interrogated for the ways in which it is read to support the heteronormative-regulating regime. Stone, Epstein, and Runions (and Guest less so) approach the text as an Other to be interrogated even while the offensive may be directed more at the history of readers rather than the text itself. By positioning themselves as interrogators, they consciously stand "outside" to chip away at the "center." The political and social agenda of bringing down heteronormativity (an agenda that I share) is the primary aim of these authors, and it seems to me that the biblical text and other cultural media are tools, or the means by which the political agenda is addressed. I want to suggest, however, that these writers are also making important contributions to those scholars who do not share the same political agenda. I seek to widen the circle of those who might benefit from queer readings, even if they fail to understand heteronormativity.

The bridge I find useful is not cultural media (film, art, etc.) or theories of race, ethnicity, postcolonialism but rather Jewish textual interpretation. It is this hermeneutic that enables me to travel between the two worlds (traditional historical-critical and postmodern) and in so doing, to merge the worlds into a beautifully complex and messy universe.

The broader reading framework that informs my approach is a Jewish textual reading tradition that Jon Levenson first articulated among Jewish biblicists. "Whereas in the church the sacred text tends to be seen as a *word* (the singular is telling) demanding to be proclaimed magisterially, in Judaism it tends to be seen as a *problem* with many facets, each of which deserves attention and debate" (Levenson 1993, 55). He continues, "It is not only that Jews have less motivation than Christians to find a unity or center in their Bible; if they did find one, they would have trouble integrating it with their most traditional modes of textual reasoning. What Christians may perceive as gain, Jews may perceive as a loss" (55). A number of scholars of Judaic studies, outside of biblical studies, have independently argued that rabbinic interpretation allows for multiple perspectives and truths. In b. Sanh. 34a we read: "One biblical utterance is susceptible to many interpretations."

Susan Handelman (1982) argues that there are radical differences between rabbinic and patristic interpretation and that these early differences paved the way for two substantially different approaches to text. She argues that there is no stable, single text in Jewish thinking. The written Torah cannot be separated from the Oral Torah, and in fact, the tradition of Torah predates creation itself. Everything is interpretation, commentary.

Similarly, David Kraemer has written, regarding the Babylonian Talmud, "What is outstanding about the deliberations that the Bavli records is that they so often avoid any conclusion; more often than not they prefer to support competing views rather than deciding in favor of one view or the other" (1990, 6). He continues: "the form of the Bavli embodies a recognition that truth, divine in origin, is on the human level indeterminable. For this reason, at least in part, the Bavli considers alternative approaches to the truth but methodically seeks to avoid privileging one over another" (7).

Likewise, the redacted Bible recognizes multiple truth claims and sets them side by side, perhaps suggesting similarly that "truth" on the human level is indeterminable but that we must still strive to seek it. This approach to reading, which is based on the joy of commentary, open-ended argumentation, and the acceptance of multiple perspectives side by side is the framework from which queer readings may reach the most people.

While I thoroughly enjoyed all the essays, space will allow me to focus on only the works of Stone and Guest.

Ken Stone uses models of relationships and gender performance that are highlighted in the film *Paris Is Burning* to inform our reading of the Dtr texts regarding the houses of Saul and David. Rather than taking a document from the ancient Near East, he asserts that the knowledge we gain from *Paris Is Burning* can be applied to a biblical text—not because there is a direct line of influence but simply because the application of the model from the film "works" on the Saul-David narratives. As Stone points out, what makes this reading queer is that the models in the film highlight the performance of gender and challenge the heteronormative claim to a binary system.

Stone's reading accomplishes its goal of getting us to understand the competition between Saul and David from a new dimension. He shows

us how the competition between Saul and David is "a contest in the performance of gendered 'realness'" (83). The house of David predominates
because he performs "manhood" more successfully than does the house of
Saul. Ultimately, Jonathan is "read" as mimicking or imitating manhood.
He is an ambiguous character who embodies both manly and womanly
traits.

Stone describes his work as an "experiment" and as a "practice" (76).
He suggests that there is a rather arbitrary nature as to which texts outside the Bible are considered acceptable as texts for comparison or frame
working (e.g., twentieth-century anthropology of shame and honor). (I
am reminded of the work of Albright and his students, who used Egyp-
tian Execration texts alongside Nuzi documents and Akkadian law codes
to "prove" the historicity of the patriarchal narratives. The difference in
cultures and the time span is not radically different from setting the Bible
alongside modern film!) At the end of his essay, he writes: "But if the space
between the virile biblical epic and contemporary drag ball is smaller than
we usually imagine, the attempt to ground heteronormativity in appeals to
biblical literature may prove to be less secure" (95).

The analogies between the film and the royal narratives are indeed
striking and I believe that Stone accomplishes his goal. While he accomplishes the lessening of the divide, he does far more that interests me as a
biblicist and a lover of these texts. I now understand the conflict not just
as military, and therefore masculine, but also as a complex set of gender
dynamics and interpersonal relationships. *Stone's reading brings the text to
life and honors the text* by claiming that the epic is more than simply a story
of a rivalry for political and military power. Stone reveals the complexity
and shifting identities of the epic's characters.

Guest's study is a bridge between the interrogator and the identity
seeker. She is the writer who most explicitly suggests that she is looking
for a mirror of herself. She admits that she is deliberately interrogating
the text with her own agenda—but as the essay continues, *one discovers
that the agenda is not just to break down heteronormative structures but to
create a place for herself within biblical readings.* She writes that the lesbian and queer perspectives that she engages break "upon the traditional
and cherished norms of historical-critical exegesis with all the force of
several gate-crashers at a party from which they had long been excluded"
(10). Guest is the only writer to pause, or as she says: "press … the pause
button" (23). The pause allows for a moment identity formation—rather
than looking at the text as an Other to be "troubled," Guest enters into the

world of the text to find herself reflected in it. The trouble is the sophisticated awareness that she holds in recognizing that to see herself reflected in the text is to exclude others, such as transsexuals. The identity that she uncovers in the character Yael from the book of Judges is one of Yael with a penis, neither a woman warrior nor a male rapist. She is not-woman, not-man, but Yael with a penis—a gender blur. Guest's work furthers the spectrum of individuals who may find a place for themselves within the text. In so doing, Guest has accomplished two things: she brings into question the claim that the Bible is one of the most successful products of the heteronormative regime (as do other queer readers), but then she does not simply walk away. She takes the next step and suggests that since the Bible (or a reading of the Bible) offers identities that stand outside the norm, we might find something *useful* in the Bible—a perspective that deepens our reading of the Bible rather than alienating us from it.

Stone adds a valuable perspective to our exegesis of the Saul/David narratives and Guest carefully opens up the text to make room for those who have traditionally been excluded. In both cases, these subversive readings that invoke the concept of genderfuck (brought into biblical studies by Runions) and reference to drag balls have the potential to bring all students of the Bible closer to its complexities. While they may present themselves as breaking down the house, they build it up with newer materials and resources.

So I return to my earlier question: is the future of queer readings of the Bible going to make the most impact by serving as a political tool to bring down the regime of heteronormativity? I believe that queer readings will have a longer lasting impact and will speak to a greater audience if they are framed as a reading strategy that adds new layers to our appreciation of the Bible. This will require queer theorists to allow themselves to land for even a moment in the world of meaning making and, perhaps more challenging, it will require more traditional biblicists to heed the voice of Jewish textual tradition that "these and these are the word of the living God" (b. 'Erub. 34a).

Works Consulted

Handelman, Susan. 1982. *The Slayers of Moses: The Emergence of Rabbinic Interpretation in Modern Literary Theory*. Albany: State University of New York Press.

Kramer, David. 1990. *The Mind of the Talmud*. New York: Oxford University Press.

Levenson, Jon. 1993. *The Hebrew Bible, the Old Testament, and Historical Criticism*. Louisville: Westminster John Knox.

CAPITALISM, MASOCHISM, AND BIBLICAL INTERPRETATION

Teresa J. Hornsby

"The economic subject is an erotic subject." (Marcella Althaus-Reid 2000, 166)

"The erotic subject is an economic subject." (me)

This opening quote from Marcella Althaus-Reid's work *Indecent Theology* describes a *de facto*, exposed-to-the-light status between capitalism and the sexuality of human beings: human beings are economic subjects and human beings are erotic subjects. Yet, what it doesn't disclose is a covert and hegemonic aspect of that relationship: capitalism produces the human erotic subject. More, it produces not only heteronormative human sexuality but all of those sexualities that we call "subversive" or queer.

If sexuality and gender are constructed in collusion with capitalistic power, a shift in capitalism should create different sexual and gender normatives. For the purposes of this paper, I uncritically accept that 1) power produces sexual normatives; 2) the dominant form that this power takes in Western Euro cultures is neoliberal capitalism; and 3) Christianity (indeed, organized religion) is an arm of power that aids in this production. I will explore, then, how a shift in capitalism (from a closed, centrally powerful, and industrialized system [Fordism] to an open, globally diverse, and electronically based system) may involve a queering of gender normatives, particularly a valorization of submission.[1] This valorization

---

1. David Harvey (1990) has labeled this shift as "the postmodern condition." Social critics of the 1980s predicted a demise of industrialism, the rise of what Alvin

can be observed, I will argue, in postmodern theory and in contemporary theology, cinema, and biblical interpretation.

To begin, we should be familiar with at least basic notions of capitalism and the production of gender normatives, and with rudimentary Freudian masochism; though theoretical masochism does not originate with Freud, Freud wrestled with it throughout his life and never appears at ease with his conclusions. Every theorist thereafter, however, is responding to Freud, it seems.

1. Capitalism

A postmodern capitalism, according to David Harvey, is still capitalism—not unique, in that change is driven by producing capital, but special because of culturally produced specifics (Harvey 1990, vii). It is not a "new capitalism," nor is it a "post capitalism." The monster that is capitalism still thrives by producing and eating those who are anointed "other" and by pooping profit. At its core construction, capitalism is static in the fact that it must produce profit. It is dynamic in *why* (that is, to what cultural events it responds) and *how* it produces profit. A primary form of neoliberal capitalism is that profit margins can be made enormous by the exploitation of human beings—the less that is spent on labor costs, the higher the profit margin. While there are arguably more humane and moral ways to create profit and streamline labor costs, many transnational manufacturers know that they can pay extremely low wages with no fringe benefits to particular types of people. Historically, these "particular types" of people tend to be women and/or persons of non-European descent, for example, though there is fluctuation here depending on extenuating circumstances (class stratification, religious affiliations, or ethnicity, for example).

A mode of survival for this type of capitalism is that it must covertly produce those persons 1) whom the mainstream considers "other" and 2) who must accept that their value is no more than what the status quo deems it to be.[2] In other words, perception of otherness must be both external and internal. Not only must the dominant fiction define the one

---

Toffler refers to as a third wave economics' system. Other notable economic forecasters of this shift are Charles Reich, William Glasser, and Theodore Poszak.

2. For an accurate and more complex description of neoliberal capitalism, see Hennessy 2000, 74–78. Althaus-Reid (2000) also makes clear the relationships between capitalism and theology in the production of sexualities.

who is not "normal," the "abnormal" or "queer" person must also accept (and, perhaps, desire) his or her own situation. This is where Christianity comes in. As one of the primary items in the capitalist tool belt, Christianity has, since its origins, (re)produced the false dualisms necessary for power's sustenance and the creation of the other. Christian doctrine and biblical interpretation have always been complicit in securing the diminished value of women, of sustaining racial otherness and the otherness of the impoverished, the diseased, and, of course, the erotic other. Christianity also assists capitalisms in the production of internalized otherness. A masochistic impulse within certain types of Christianity is strong. It tells us that we (human beings) are not worthy of the things we are given; it tells us that suffering is not only "normal" but is to be desired; it espouses humility; it beatifies submission; it glorifies pain. This masochism is fundamental to a thriving capitalist system in that it produces those bodies that readily submit to power. It also instills a sense of privilege and justification (or righteousness) in those who align themselves with power; the suffering and exploitation of "others" is rendered "just" and "good."

In the past two centuries, capitalism has changed; industrialized cultures have experienced an acceleration of what Harvey refers to as the "compression of space and time" (Harvey 1990, 241). Because of a radical shift from the world where the 10 m.p.h. pace of horse-drawn carriages and wind-driven ships was the maximum speed, to the 800 m.p.h. thrust of the modern jet, to the instantaneous appearances made possible by the microchip and the internet, there has been an explosion of electronic commerce. Electronic commerce is a manifestation of postmodern capitalism, a capitalism born of human experiences in a compressed space and time. One stark way that postmodern capitalism differs from an industrial-based, or Fordian, capitalism is that a postmodern capitalist system is not dependent upon a production of "real" commodities; the financial system rests on the production of nontangibles. We are experiencing a Baudrillardian production of signs—images rather than commodities (Baudrillard 1995). Harvey writes,

> The interweaving of simulacra in daily life brings together different worlds (of commodities) in the same space and time. But it does so in such a way as to conceal almost perfectly any trace of origin, of the labour processes that produced them, or of the social relations implicated in their production. The simulacra can in turn become the reality. (Harvey 1990, 300)

Not only do we now produce invisible commodities, we have, as Harvey writes, effectively hidden labor processes that produce them. This shift to a postmodern, or simulacra, capitalism should be accompanied by an equally radical shift in constructed desire. Rosemary Hennessy has recognized that

> the dominant discourses of sexual identity in over-industrialized sectors, spun across national lines through media and travel industries, seem to be changing, albeit in uneven ways. ... The network of equations among sex, gender, sexual practice, and desire on which normative heterosexuality as a matrix of intelligibility came to depend under Fordism is being disrupted. (Hennessy 2000, 107)

As electronic commerce becomes principal within postmodern capitalism, power no longer needs the *many* bodies that industrial capitalism did in the production of physical commodities. In this capitalistic shift to the production of "simulacra," power needs subservient bodies—bodies that work independently, without external supervision. Theoretically, to police these new bodies, power must produce different sexual and gender normatives. Compulsory heterosexuality produces those physical bodies; yet, as the needs of power in the form of capitalism change, as populations grow and mix, and as technology reduces the need for sexual reproduction, greater submission to power becomes inevitable. In other words, fewer bodies are needed but those bodies must serve selflessly and partly independently of external regulation (because commerce no longer takes place wholly in the public sphere). Bodies must have a heightened and internalized "will to submit." Thus the production of a compulsory heterosexuality becomes less important since fewer physical bodies are needed.

This shift in capitalism, Harvey's "postmodern condition," rivals the revolutionary global changes of technologies of previous centuries (linguistic, agricultural, industrial, nuclear). Each of these revolutions produced varying constructions of normative desire. As power is more centralized, thus concentrated, the boundaries defining normative sexuality are more tightly drawn. A construction of desire necessary for the rise of postwar, pre-Internet (thus bounded and defined) monopolistic and colonial capitalism, a compulsory heterosexuality as it has appeared within the industrial age, should become obsolete (or at least rare) because that particular desire is no longer essential in the production of capital. As this shift occurs, we begin to see a heightened social acceptance (a movement toward the normative) of diverse sexualities and genders. My prediction is this: as the need for *definite* sexualities and genders becomes less important to the needs of capitalism, gender fluidity and masochism move to the center. Hennessy writes,

> The discrete asymmetrical opposition between male and female is being thrown into question, pressuring the imaginary logic of opposites and sex-gender equations that the prevailing heterogender system once relied on. In the media images generated in overdeveloped capitalist centers especially, more permeable, fluid, ambiguously coded sexual identities are allowed, even promoted. (Hennessy 2000, 107)

Hennessy's observations are predictable, I think, simply because there is a reduced need for the number of physical bodies but an increased need for more exploitable, more subservient bodies.

2. Producing Queer Bodies

At first glance, a heightened production of queer bodies may seem like a "good" thing—some may see it as more of "us," less of "them" or perhaps as a possibility for less hegemony. For example, Althaus-Reid makes the argument that Christianity needs an "indecent theology" (rather than a heteronormative one) to serve the needs of all people. By indecent theology, she means

> theologians who come out in their pursuit of honesty and engagement with the real and ... grab a blouse and a lipstick and per/vert the normative socio/theological script, unveil obscenity and are able to see, from sexual stories at the bottom of Rubin's sexual pyramid, tales of God and criticism of political systems. (Althaus-Reid 2000, 199)

Althaus-Reid claims that the experiences of those sexualities "at the bottom of Rubin's sexual pyramid" are necessary to forge a "real" relationship with the divine, "an encounter to be found at the crossroads of desire, when one dares to leave the ideological order of the heterosexual pervasive normative" (2000, 200).

While Althaus-Reid sees the inclusion of nonheteronormative, or queer, sexualities in central theological discourse as necessary, as a positive move forward in dismantling worldwide oppression, I would argue that this theoretical inclusion of indecency is capitalism's use of Christian theology to construct the types of sexual/economic subjects it needs. Christianity consistently takes a leading role in constructing subservient bodies, normative desires born of masochism; indeed, a masochistic impulse lies at the heart of Pauline Christianity: idealized suffering, willful self-sacrifice, glorified humiliation, and romanticized slavery. A look at recent interpretations of Pauline texts and contemporary representations of Christian suffering reveals a heightened sense of a Freudian "moral masochism" and its collusion in the production of normative sexual desires.

MASOCHISM

Freud's "moral masochism" emerges solidly in his final work on masochism, in which he expands on a previously introduced triune of masochisms: feminine, erotogenic, and moral masochism. "Feminine masochism" is assigned only to men and betrays a gendering of masochism in its desire to be beaten—an essentially "normal" quality in females but a perversion in males. Erotogenic masochism is a physical conflation of pain and sexual pleasure. And finally, moral masochism, according to Freud, is a desire to be punished; this particular brand of masochism becomes almost indistinguishable from internalized power. Moral masochism is not only an internalized need to be punished but, more importantly, a sense of joy in self-deprivation. We so desire punishment (so that we will be good people) that we do not allow ourselves to have it; we convince ourselves that we do not deserve the satisfaction of being disciplined. We can only savor the suspended, undeserved pleasure that pain might bring and we yearn, as Freud would say, "to be beaten by the father"—yet, as David Savran articulates in *Taking It Like a Man,* it is a Father whom we have internalized; we become slaves to our own "despotic superego that has internalized the Law, the Father, and the Word" (1998, 25). Here is the integration of masochism with a Christian ideal. All of Freud's masochisms (the feminine, the erotogenic, and the moral) converge in one place: this desire to be punished by the father. According to Freud, "Being beaten by the father is analogous to being loved [by the father] (in a genital sense). ... The wish to be beaten by the father is closely connected with [a wish] to have some passive (feminine) sexual relations with him" (Savran 1998, 31).[3] Savran

---

3. See Freud 1955, 198. A good summary of Freud on masochism, as well as other theories of masochism, can be found in Taylor 1997, 106–30.

notes that "desire for the father is transformed into a desire to submit to the cruelty of the father's will and all he represents" (32).

To be an ideal Christian, in this sense, means to take on a passive, culturally defined "feminine" role and to desire to take on whatever "our father which art in heaven" dishes out. That human beings become feminized in relation to God the Father in Christian Scripture is not new—the prophets see the men of Israel as God's wife; the church is Jesus' beloved; the "elect men" in Revelation are the brides of Christ.[4] The wrinkle I see in postmodern representations of the ideal or model Christian (Jesus Christ) and of perfect masculinity (Jesus Christ) is a positive demonstration of femininity. In other words, rather than depicting the feminine as lesser and in opposition to perfect masculinity (Christ), Christ's representations (linguistic and visual) are infused with elements of traditional femininity and a strong reverence for feminine and moral masochism. In contrast to modernist representations of the Christian ideal, feminine elements are presented as desirable.

A recent popular example of Christ's willingness to accept (or desire) the pain and humiliation imposed on us by "the father" is observable in Mel Gibson's ode to Christian masochism, *The Passion of the Christ*, or, as David Hein dubs it, "The Crucifixion."[5] Though it reveled in its bloody and sadistic brutality, Christians, particularly evangelicals, not only loved the film but vehemently insisted that it *must* be gruesome, that the depiction of the passion must be explicitly brutal and bloody. They defended the sadomasochistic spectacle at every turn. My first suspicion about the film was that it was perhaps one in a long line of war-propaganda films espousing the value and necessity of self-sacrifice. But I think the phenomenon betrays something beyond the temporal and geographically specific production of wartime hype; the eroticization of brutality on such a global scale provides a fleeting glimpse into a production of desire complicit with an evolving capitalism. The film and its receptors seem to say that to be a good Christian, to be worthy of forgiveness and of salvation, one must desire and willingly submit to the most brutal tortures. More, one must enjoy seeing others suffer horrific pain and see this pain as redemptive. In this film, Christ (as ideal Christian) is constructed as a sign of perfect

---

4. Tina Pippin has a delicious article on this called "The Joy of (Apocalyptic) Sex" (2006).

5. I thought I made this term up but I came across it recently in Moore 1996, 4.

masculinity. But that perfect masculinity is now assembled with a Freudian feminine masochism.

SOTERIOLOGY

Gibson's *Passion* is not, of course, proof of a heightened shift to a more
masochistic Christianity—rather, it is a bellwether that calls attention to
a distinct ideology of a mimetic call to suffer, as opposed to an emphasis on Christ's death as expiatory. This emphasis has "plung[ed] Christian
spirituality into a toxic brew of idealized masochism, authorized violence
and social domination" (Heim 2005, 20). Indeed, Gibson's *Passion* resonates with Christians who understand suffering in a way that Paul seems
to express in Rom 5:3b–4: "We boast (or "find glory"; καυχάομαι) in our
suffering (θλίψις), knowing that suffering produces endurance (ὑπομονή),
and endurance produces character (or "experience," one who has proved
him or herself; δοκιμή), and character produces hope (or "anticipation
of good things"; ἐλπίς)" (NRSV). Hope, as a vehicle for fulfillment, as an
escape from powerlessness, or as any generic promise of a better life, rests
on one's ability to suffer—not briefly, but unwavering, enduring suffering.
For Paul, this suffering is an honor (Phil 1:29).

Rather than focus on Jesus as apocalyptic teacher, Jesus as healer, Jesus
as social critic or Jesus as political revolutionary, the torturing and crucifixion of Jesus has become *the* thing for biblical interpreters. And for
theologians, we are called to mimic that suffering. Subservience and sub-
missiveness, the beaten, humble servant are images of Jesus that contemporary readers of Paul emphasize. Paul's call to mimic Jesus' tragic end
and his self-references as a suffering slave who delights in suffering, in
being a slave, in persecution, and in humiliation all for the sake of Christ
(e.g., Rom 8:18; 1 Thess 3:3–4; 2 Thess 1:4–5; 2 Tim 1:8; 2:12; 3:12; 1 Pet
2:21; 4:12–13, 16) are pushed to the forefront of popular Pauline theology.
Paul, according to current critics, was convinced that physical suffering
was central and necessary for his fledgling Christian communities.

One work treating the responses to the suffering of Christ is David Seeley's *The Noble Death*. Seeley finds strong parallels between Jesus' suffering
and death and the idea of the Hellenistic "Noble Death" as it occurs in 2
and 4 Maccabees and in other Greco-Roman works (Seeley 1990, 83–112).
He argues that Paul's summoning of Christians to imitate Jesus' suffering and death is not meant to be literal; it is the symbolic death of baptism. However, Seeley's symbolic appeal to the Noble Death model does

not strip Paul's theology of the cross from its masochistic elements. The most important of the four primary criteria of the Noble Death, according to Seeley, is obedience. For Jesus' execution to be a Noble Death, he had to submit obediently to God's desire that he be humiliated, that he suffer and die. Again, God is in the place of the sadistic father who requires the obedience of a son to the point of a brutal and public death.

Though Seeley argues that Paul looks to the Maccabean martyrdom as a way to construct the death of Jesus theologically, he misses by claiming that Paul merely wants Christians to suffer and die *symbolically*. Jerry L. Sumney agrees with Neeley but expands to say that the writer of Colossians sees Paul's own suffering as something that should inspire trust in him and that to suffer and die for your philosophy is noble and should be imitated (mimetic suffering; Sumney 2006, 272, 279). Joseph Hellerman argues that it is precisely the crucifixion (in its absolute excrucation) in which Paul lays claim to an extraordinary source of power, the power that lies within the person who is willing to be humiliated and to suffer to the point of death. More, Hellerman argues that it is Jesus' self-humiliation that would have resonated in the social context of Paul's readers. As a "loathsomely degrading" experience, the crucifixion was, for some, a public humiliation of God (Hellerman 2003, 428).

Though the critics above make strong cases for the centrality of suffering in Paul's community building, it seems to go against common sense that if you want to grow your community, the primary selling point should be a plethora of suffering; the centrality and promotion of suffering, humiliation, and pain seem problematic in a world that already has an abundance of those things. Some theologians have recognized this contradiction. Dorothee Soelle claims in her well-known essay, "A Critique of Christian Masochism," that Christianity is perverted by a radical theology of the cross; she maintains that positing a God who demands the salvific suffering and death of his son creates a God who is a "sadistic, ruling and omnipotent father" (Soelle 1975, 26–27). Soelle does not hold Paul responsible for this "perverse theology"; Soelle places Christianity's perversion squarely into the hands of later theologians who have misunderstood Paul's call to mimic the suffering and death of Jesus. So through our scholarship we (biblical scholars and theologians) work covertly to strengthen postmodern capitalism.

For example, the author of Luke-Acts (hereafter Luke) seems to echo a sentiment that the hope of Christ rests in his suffering, not upon his death (Luke 9:22; 17:25; 22:15; 24:46; Acts 3:18; 9:16; 26:23). But it seems that

modern critics are quick to see this as a valorization of suffering rather than
Luke's attempt to connect Jesus to prophetic Scripture. Luke, like Matthew,
Mark, and Paul, labored to explain how the Son of God should not only be
killed but die by crucifixion, a slave's death. The Christian architects elaborate on the suffering and the "slavery" to strengthen the connection to the
Suffering Slave, the anointed one who must suffer (e.g., Isa 49:1–7; 50:4–9;
52:13–53:12).[6] Paul makes the connection between the crucifixion and
slavery explicit in Phil 2:7–8: "[he emptied] himself, taking the form of a
slave, and humbled himself and become obedient to the point of death—
even death on a cross." Hellerman claims, however, that to associate Jesus
with slavery is to represent Jesus as symbolically willing to become "the
lowest of the low" for the Philippians. Rather, I would argue that "slave"
here in Phil 2:7 would remind readers of Isaiah's Suffering Slave.

According to Martin Hengel's take on Paul, Jesus' suffering *must* be
brutal, horrific, humiliating. Hengel argues that Christians cannot have an
authentic theology of the cross unless they, like Paul, embrace the reality
of the crucifixion: that "[Christ] died like a slave or a common criminal,
in torment, on the tree of shame. Paul's Jesus did not die just any death; he
was 'given up for us all' on the cross, in a cruel and a contemptible way"
(Hengel 1977, 90). The crucifixion must be more than a single event of
torture; it is a call for all to mimic the ideal, to suffer as Christ suffered, too
participate in the pain. Thus, Richard Gaffin writes, "suffering with Christ
is not only a precondition for a future share in his glory, but is also itself,
through his indwelling Spirit, a present manifestation of Christ's exaltation glory" (Gaffin 1979). Or as Merrill Proudfoot writes, "Paul knows suffering as a *participatio Christi*, not as an *imatio Christi* only" (Proudfoot
1963, 160). An emphasis on real suffering and pain for the willing victim
in modern theologies of the cross reveals a heightened valorization of
masochism; it is a peek into an ideological production of docile bodies.[7]

---

6. John Dominic Crossan has argued that nowhere do the Hebrew Scriptures pre-
dict that God's anointed one would die. An emphasis on the suffering would bypass
what Paul calls the scandal of the cross.

7. Theologian Emily Askew has recognized that to buy into sacrificial atonement
theology (and the identical discourse in television "makeover" reality shows) is to say
that "I must accept myself as broken and in need of restoration. I must accept that suffering, both mental and physical are par for the course for being made whole" (2009,
29).

The emphasis on Jesus and Paul's suffering and the necessity of it also reproduces culturally produced feminine markers, the passivity and silence of the slave, such as we see in Isaiah and in *The Passion of the Christ*: "He was oppressed, and he was afflicted, yet he did not open his mouth; like a lamb that is led to the slaughter, and like a sheep that before its shearers is silent, so he did not open his mouth." (Isa 53:7; cf. Phil 2:7–8, NRSV). Thus, the suffering and silent Jesus in biblical interpretations and in Gibson's representation of Christ as übermasculine rests on its feminine social markers and on its masochism. More, there is a thread in modern feminist biblical interpretation on the "goodness" of submission.

FEMINIST BIBLICAL CRITICISM: VALORIZING SUBMISSION

One specific example of how a valorization of submission plays out in contemporary feminist biblical interpretation appears in recent scholarship on Luke 10:38–42, an account of Jesus' visit to the home of Mary and Martha in Bethany. In this passage, Martha complains to Jesus that she has to do all the work while Mary is sitting at Jesus' feet, presumably listening to him.

Initial feminist readings of this passage critiqued the apparent praise of women's passivity; some, the standards being Elizabeth Schüssler Fiorenza (1983, 1992) and Stevan Davies (1991), saw this passage as a mandate from the early church to squelch women's activity and to urge women to submit to the authority of male leadership.

Responses to Schüssler Fiorenza took various forms. Adele Reinhartz argues that Luke is doing two things here: he is employing his "gotcha" literary technique, and he maintains, as quoted by Veronica Koperski, that "true service consists not of caring for physical needs but of ingesting, and digesting, the message of the gospel" (2002, 175). So, in other words, Reinhartz has shifted Mary's passivity of "receiving teaching" to the activity of learning and discipleship. In a similar vein, Turid Seim argues that "being at the feet of Jesus" should be understood as an empowering place for women (1994, 101).

Barbara Reid, on the other hand, suggests that Mary and Martha represent two types of female Christian service—that Martha is actually criticizing the fact that women were being made to accept the passive role of listener rather than a more active service ministry (Koperski 2002, 185). In this reading, Reid sees that we are not talking about individual women in the Gospels but rather that these women, as do the women of the Hebrew

Bible and intertestamental writings, represent whole communities. Yet what we should consider is that the communities each woman represents in this story and in all stories aren't the communities of early Christians but communities right here, right now.

You might ask, don't all believers read their scriptures to inform them of how to live their lives right now? Yes, but usually with personal intention toward spiritual growth, of being a better person, or of living a just life. My assertion is that interests of power are served in the determination of what a "better or just person" is. Is a good person submissive? Is a just person law abiding, not making waves? The area of concern has passed from the call for women's submission to a valorization of submission in general. For example, this is from a piece that is marketed as Christian marital advice:

> Submission is a word which can be described/defined as "willing conciliation." That means that the wife should be "willing," not coerced. Wives are to respect their husbands. Husbands are to be considerate of their wives. Both partners should be willing to "put the other's interests above his/her own" as Philippians 2 describes. The woman should be willing to submit to her husband not be unwilling or forced. The man should be a loving, servant leader—accountable and responsible to God and his family. A loving leader leads—doesn't manipulate or pressure. A submitter doesn't "take over." (Hoy n.d.)

These questions, such as "What is 'good'" or "What is right," are asked when one wrestles with passages such as Jesus' visit to the home of Mary and Martha. The answers tend to have nothing to do with early Christian women and everything to do with the modern citizen and her or his interactions with power. To talk about Mary's position at the feet of Jesus doesn't reveal much, if anything, about historical Christianity or the roles of women in a Greco-Roman milieu; rather, we create, in our encounters with this story, cultural attitudes about submission and our roles as a cog within capitalism. To quote Warren Carter, "Contemporary Biblical scholarship is divided in its assessment of the presentation of women in the text. Is the Biblical author an oppressor or liberator? Must the audience read with or against the text?" (Carter 2002, 214). To answer his final question, we always read with the text; indeed, we cannot do anything else. Even if we think we are reading against it, reading it as subversives, perhaps lifting up submission as a place of power, it is all in the service of power.

As an example of this, we see in R. Marie Griffith's book, *God's Daughters: Evangelical Women and the Power of Submission*, an eloquent and sensitive defense of how submission functions as power in the lives of evangelical women. Griffith writes the following:

> I have refused to interpret with undue haste the discourse of female submission as flatly or irrevocably oppressive. Such a depiction would disregard the complexities of evangelical faith and, worse, render these women's devotional lives unrecognizable to themselves. Instead, I have taken pains to credit their piety as a meaningful source of religious and social power, laden with copious practical strategies for inverting conventional hierarchies and enabling women to influence husbands— perhaps even change or save them—and alter their family lives, as well as to create newly whole and joyful selves. As women teach it to each other, Christian submission is a flexible doctrine intricately attached to control—of self and other—and freedom, rather than a rigid blueprint of silent and demoralizing subjugation. (Griffith 1997, 201–2)

While evangelical women may find power in submission, and certainly some feminist interpreters find power in a place of submission at the feet of Jesus, it is no coincidence that at the same time, electronic, lightning-fast capitalism needs docile and submissive subjects to function.

Thus, the literal interpretations of Paul's invocations to suffer and to be humiliated and the biblical interpretations of the power of submission betray a queering of normative Christianity or a normalization of queer masochism. Either way, the end product is an extraordinarily submissive body—a body that connects suffering with hope and humiliation with empowerment. This body, though not completely free from the bonds of compulsive heterosexuality, is patterned after the ideal Christian (Jesus), which allows much more movement in terms of gender normatives.

Postmodern Cultural Critics: Valorizing Masochism

Christianity, a key producer of gender normatives for an evolving capitalism, is shaping a new idea of the "person," one that is grounded in a masochistic ideal that, in the words of Savran, "allows the white male subject to take up the position of victim" (Savran 1998, 33) and, I would add, that transfers an illusion of power onto the victim—which is a critical move in the production of valorized masochism.

One of the first to assign power to the masochistic subject was Gilles Deleuze. Deleuze first argues that the sadist and the masochist are wholly separate philosophies. And of the two, Deleuze identifies the masochist as most powerful: "The masochistic hero appears to be educated and fashioned by the authoritarian woman whereas basically it is he who forms her, dresses her for the part and prompts the harsh words she addresses to him. It is the victim who speaks through the mouth of his torturer, without sparing himself" (Deleuze 1989, 22).

Though Cynthia Marshall is highly critical of Deleuze's separation of masochism from sadism and his dismissal of the reader, she, like Deleuze and following Jean Laplanche and Leo Bersani, renders masochism as essentialist. Marshall's thesis is this: the ego is unable to unify our complexity of selves; though it tries, it fails (Marshall 2002, 7–8, 35–47). In its attempt to bind together our selves into a whole, elements of our selves are always left out. Masochism then becomes necessary to shatter (not to destroy but to disperse) the unsuccessful quasiunified self. Marshall sees our desire to witness violent images (such as Gibson's *Passion*) as a masochistic drive that seeks to preserve, not destroy, our selves. Thus, for Marshall and others, masochism is no longer aligned with death, as Freud seemed to think, but is aligned with eros, the pleasure principle, and with the preservation of self.

Nick Mansfield, in *Masochism: The Art of Power*, recognizes that, as you can guess from the title, masochism is power. Mansfield's thesis is that masochism does not oppose power, it *is* power incognito. He grounds this assertion in his critique of Deleuze: even though Deleuze replaces Freud's "battering father" with an "oral mother," the male masochist still has the initiative. Mansfield writes, "Male power is to be destroyed in Deleuze's quasi-heroic alliance with the oral mother. Yet, this can only be brought about under conditions motivated and designed by male power, the power of the masochist himself" (1997, 73). The "art" of masochism is that it is able simultaneously to turn on itself (attempts at self-annihilation) as it creates and recreates its own power. Masochism has found in poststructuralism its host. Poststructuralism encourages the subversions of masochism where it collapses any distinction between pleasure/pain, power/powerlessness, activity/passivity, masculine/feminine, or a host of other binaries. Yet, as it appears to contest power, masochism "designed the possibility of a power that could operate in a permanent state of disavowal of itself" (98).

Mansfield concludes by saying that masochism, more than anything else, has shown that masculine power does not have to be phallic. It (masochism) is a trope of masculinity that shifts, turns on itself, and does whatever it needs to do to recreate itself, which is what power does. Mansfield writes,

> Masochism shows us that the assumption of a unidirectional disestablishment of power was not adequate in understanding another contradictory and self-denying power, a power that operated by mutilating itself in acts that ensured its strengthening and perpetuation, and that also consumed its antagonists, making them mere versions of itself, preempting its experiments and turning its politics into a type of art. (Mansfield 1997, 99)

What I find so provocative about Mansfield's work is that he valorizes masochism to the point that it is power itself, yet he recognizes that his own work (the literary text) is a poststructuralist vehicle for the continuation of that power. The only difference (and I suppose it's a big one) between Mansfield's ideas and mine is that I position capitalism as the central power that produces, reproduces and sustains masochism; Mansfield would argue that masochism is the prime mover. In both systems, though Mansfield never mentions this, Christianity would be one of the institutions that encourages the modern subject "in its perennial state of proto-panic and confession, [who] can never stop asking itself Am I mad? Am I sick? Am I a criminal?" (84). And, I would add, "Am I worthy to suffer shame?" (cf. Acts 5:41).

We can observe, in part, a presence of masochistic masculinity and the complicity of Christianity in Gibson's *Passion*, as well as in contemporary theologians' readings of Paul. Yet the valorization of masochism becomes most evident in works of postmodern psychologists, literary critics, film producers, theologians, feminist and queer Bible scholars, and other cultural critics who all come together at the site of "the powerful masochist." From Deleuze to Silverman, from Laplanche to Marshall, masochism is posited as a place of power. As masochism becomes synonymous with masculinity, and folks gravitate toward, no, idolize victimization, the necessity, or at least the centrality, of a heteronormative desire lessens. The absence of this desire creates space for queer desires.

3. Queer Heteronormativity

Some cultural critics have already named these alternative desires, these "queer heterosexualities." In her deconstruction of Freud and Lacan, Judith

Butler argues that since the phallus is representative—it is not a "real" penis and can designate any body part—then the phallus (as symbol of a heterosexual normative) through constant repetition and recreation can be subverted. Butler inserts (ha) the idea of a "lesbian phallus," an effective subversion of a heterosexual normative (Butler 1993, 57–65). What Butler effectively does is reveal that the phallus, as a symbol of power, is not at all dependent on a male, heterosexual body. As the phallus is liberated from the penis, bodies enjoy a respite from strict gender definition. What Butler doesn't say specifically, though Leo Bersani does, is that all of this subversive liberation from strict gender definition is dependent on a masochistic impulse (Bersani 1986, 41). If sex is potentially subversive as it threatens to undo a perception of self, then sexual pleasure must be perceived as masochistic—it is a finding of pleasure in one's own potential destruction. This, as we see in Marshall's and Mansfield's work, is a valorization of masochism.

Kaja Silverman also presents the "male lesbian"—a man who desires to be passive, to be dominated by a woman, takes on the role of a woman who desires other women, who seeks sexual gratification through passivity and without the penis (1992, 386).[8] Like Butler, Silverman separates the penis and the phallus and grounds eroticism in masochism: a subject is sexually aroused as she or he identifies with the suffering of an other. Savran argues that at the core of a masochistically produced capitalism lies the feminine male: a male who desires pain and humiliation, who seeks victimization and identifies as victim though he occupies a place of power. The male subject, according to Savran, "must tirelessly police himself and his desires while calling this submission 'freedom.' He must work rigorously to confound pleasure and pain, to welcome the severity of punishment. He must always be ready to discipline, that is, to scourge himself for his shortcomings and irresponsibilities" (1998, 25).

Butler's, Silverman's, and Savran's theoretical queer heterosexualities show the possibilities of how queer bodies may be constructed and that masculinity is not necessarily about the penis, though still grounded in heterosexuality. The "queerness" arises in the move away from compulsive heterosexuality, in the feminization of masculinity and in the masculinization of pain. Yet, all of these sexualities only emerge as the masochism becomes more central and foundational.

---

8. See also Schor 2001.

Conclusions

I know my examples here are far from exhaustive, given the space I have, but as we tend to accept the notions that economic situations have direct impact on constructions of gender, sexuality, class concerns, and so forth, it seems to be a given, then, that such profound changes in our economic system would indeed bring about change to our social structures. And changes in social structures depend on, and simultaneously produce, the ideologies that spring from and inform biblical interpretation. My simple thesis is that this new postmodern capitalism requires submissive subjects, and we, as postmodern biblical scholars, are doing our part to produce them.

Because of the needs of a dynamic and global capitalism, perceptions of modern Christianity aid in producing docile bodies—bodies that submit to power while being under the illusion of sexual freedom. The bodies, no longer required to reproduce sexually, can wander within wider, more elastic sexual and gender boundaries; that's the good news. Capitalism in whatever form is still capitalism: "While [postmodern sexualities] may disrupt norms and challenge state practices that are indeed oppressive, they do not necessarily challenge neoliberalism or disrupt capitalism" (Hennessy 2000, 109). These "more open, fluid, ambivalent sexual identities" (109) must be willing, no *eager* to suffer for this elasticity. Sure, it is a good thing that queer sexualities are being understood to be more "normative," but queer sexualities are manufactured and serve power just as much as any sanctioned sexuality. Queer sexuality does not subvert power nor is it produced apart from or over and against the ideological center. It is merely moving within that system. Heteronormativity has been queered, but it is still heteronormativity. It is the illusion and the promise of greater sexual liberation that keeps us bound.

Works Consulted

Althaus-Reid, Marcella. 2000. *Indecent Theology*. New York: Routledge.

Askew, Emily. 2009. Extreme Makeover and the Classical Logic of Transformation. Pages 15–34 in *You've Come a Long Way, Baby: Women, Politics, and Popular Culture*. Edited by Lilly J. Goren. Lexington: University Press of Kentucky.

Baudrillard, Jean. 1995. *Simulacra and Simulation*. Ann Arbor: University of Michigan Press.

Bersani, Leo. 1986. *The Freudian Body: Psychoanalysis and Art.* New York: Columbia University Press.

Butler, Judith. 1993. *Bodies That Matter: On the Discursive Limits of "Sex."* New York: Routledge.

Carter, Warren. 2002. Getting Martha Out of the Kitchen: Luke 10:38–42 Again. Pages 214–31 in Levine 2002.

Davies, Stevan. 1991. Women in the Third Gospel and the New Testament Apocrypha. Pages 185–97 in Levine 1991.

Deleuze, Gilles. 1989. Coldness and Cruelty. Pages 1–142 in *Masochism.* New York: Zone Books.

Freud, Sigmund. 1955. A Child Is Being Beaten. Page 198 in *The Standard Edition of the Complete Psychological Works of Sigmund Freud, Vol. 17 (1917–1919).* Edited by James Strachey. London: Hogarth.

Gaffin, Richard. 1979. The Usefulness of the Cross. Audio recorded January 1979. Posted May 2011. http://media1.wts.edu/media/audio/inrg1-copyright.mp3.

Griffith, R. Marie. 1997. *God's Daughters: Evangelical Women and the Power of Submission.* Berkeley: University of California Press.

Harvey, David. 1990. *The Condition of Postmodernity: An Enquiry Into the Origins of Cultural Change.* Cambridge: Blackwell.

Heim, Mark S. 2005. Cross Purposes. *ChrCent* 122 (6): 20–25.

Hellerman, Joseph. 2003. The Humiliation of Christ in the Social World of Roman Philippi. *BSac* 160 (640):421–23.

Hengel, Martin. 1977. *Crucifixion in the Ancient World and the Folly of the Message of the Cross.* Philadelphia: Fortress.

Hennessy, Rosemary. 2000. *Profit and Pleasure: Sexual Identities in Late Capitalism.* New York: Routledge.

Hoy, Lynette. n.d. Should Wives Really Submit? Christian Women Today. Online: http://christianwomentoday.com/advice/submission.html.

Koperski, Veronica. 2002. Women and Discipleship in Luke 10:38–40 and Acts 6:1–7. Pages 161–96 in Levine 2002.

Levine, Amy-Jill, ed. 1991. *"Women Like This": New Perspectives on Jewish Women in the Greco-Roman World.* SBLEJL 1. Atlanta: Scholars Press.

———. 2002. *A Feminist Companion to Luke.* FCNTECW 3. Sheffield: Sheffield Academic Press.

Mansfield, Nick. 1997. *Masochism: The Art of Power.* Westport, Conn.: Praeger.

Marshall, Cynthia. 2002. *The Shattering of the Self: Violence, Subjectivity, and Early Modern Text.* Baltimore: Johns Hopkins University Press.

Moore, Stephen D. 1996. *God's Gym: Divine Male Bodies of the Bible*. New York: Routledge.

Pippin, Tina. 2006. The Joy of (Apocalyptic) Sex. Pages 64–74 in *Gender and Apocalyptic Desire*. Edited by Lee Quimby and Brenda Brasher. London: Equinox.

Proudfoot, Merrill. 1963. Imitation or Realistic Participation: A Study of Paul's Concept of "Suffering with Christ." *Int* 17:140–60.

Reinhartz, Adele. 1991. From Narrative to History: The Resurrection of Mary and Martha. Pages 161–84 in Levine 1991.

Savran, David. 1998. *Taking It Like a Man: White Masculinity, Masochism, and Contemporary American Culture*. Princeton: Princeton University Press.

Schor, Naomi. 2001. Male Lesbianism. *GLQ: A Journal of Lesbian and Gay Studies* 7:391–99.

Schüssler Fiorenza, Elizabeth. 1983. *In Memory of Her*. New York: Crossroad.

———. 1992. *But She Said: Feminist Practices of Biblical Interpretation*. Boston: Beacon.

Seeley, David. 1990. *The Noble Death: Graeco-Roman Martyrology and Paul's Concept of Salvation*. JSNT 28. Sheffield: JSOT Press.

Seim, Turid. 1994. *The Double Message*. Nashville: Abingdon.

Silverman, Kaja. 1988. Masochism and Male Subjectivity. *Camera Obscura* 17 (May): 31–66.

———. 1992. *Male Subjectivity at the Margins*. New York: Routledge.

Soelle, Dorothy. 1975. *Suffering*. Philadelphia: Fortress.

Sumney, Jerry L. 2006. "I Fill Up What Is Lacking in the Afflictions of Christ": Paul's Vicarious Suffering in Colossians. *CBQ* 68: 664–80.

Taylor, Gary Wilson. 1997. The Discursive Construction and Regulation of Dissident Sexuality: The Case of SM. Pages 106–30 in *Body Talk: The Material and Discursive Regulation of Sexuality, Madness, and Reproduction*. Edited by Jane M. Ussher. London: Routledge.

LAZARUS TROUBLES

Jione Havea

And going near Jesus rolled away the stone from the door of the tomb. And straightaway, going in where the youth [Lazarus] was, he stretched forth his hand and raised him, seizing his hand. But the youth, looking upon him, loved him and began to beseech him that he might be with him. And going out of the tomb they came into the house of the youth, for he was rich. And after six days Jesus told him what to do and in the evening the youth comes to him, wearing a linen cloth over his naked body. And he remained with him that night, for Jesus taught him the mystery of the kingdom of God.[1]

LAZARUS TRAUMA

The John 11 storyline is traumatic: Jesus is away from Bethany when Lazarus falls ill. Dis-ease. Martha and Mary, the sisters of Lazarus, send words to inform Jesus that the one whom he loves affectionately (*philein*; 11:3, 11) is ill. Ache. The narrator and the sisters do not explain what they hope Jesus will do in response. Doubt. But we know that they, together with their brother, hold a special place in Jesus' heart, for he loves them unconditionally and sacrificially (*agapan*; 11:5). Hope.

---

1. Excerpt from *Secret Gospel of Mark*, which Morton Smith claimed Clement of Alexandria cited in a letter (Smith 1973, 447). Though scholars question the authenticity of the gospel and the letter (cf. Jeffery 2007; Esler and Piper 2006, 48), I am interested in the excerpt because of its queerness.

This chapter is a revision of "Lazarus, Darling, Come Out," presented at the joint session of the Gender Group and the Bible and Cultural Studies Section, Society of Biblical Literature, San Diego (17 November 2007). I am thankful to all who gave critical feedback on that occasion, as well as for research assistance from Peleti Lima.

Jesus takes his time to respond. Fear. Two days after receiving the message, Jesus leaves for Bethany. Apathy. By that time, Lazarus was already dead. Tears. We do not know when Lazarus died in relation to when Jesus received the message from his sisters, or how long Jesus and his disciples took to return to Bethany, but it is unambiguous that Jesus arrived four days after Lazarus had died. Loss.

Jesus goes to the home of Martha and Mary first. Questions. Then he goes to the tomb in the eyes and ears of onlookers, some of whom were his advocates but more who seem to be his antagonists, and calls Lazarus to come out. Rise. Then Jesus tells some of the people who were there to unbind Lazarus and let him go. Stagger. At that point, the attention of the narrator shifts from the raised body of Lazarus to the brewing resentment against Jesus by the Jews. Anguish. The story turns to Jesus as if the raised body of Lazarus was no longer needed. Neglect.

Jesus calls a dead body back to life. Power. Jesus did not let Lazarus rest in peace. Troubles. The story of Lazarus, a dead man who walks, is haunting. Lazarus troubles.

QUEERING LAZARUS, IN PRISON

The story of the raising of Lazarus has caught the attention of preachers, theologians, artists, and scholars, who interpret the story with a swarm of perspectives and appropriate it for a multitude of interests. Instead of repeating those findings, I have a simple goal for this chapter: to engage the story of Lazarus under the shades of experiences in the salt-water part of Oceania from where I come.

I will share some of the ideas of prisoners (or inmates) from the Pacific Islands who met me during 2007 in Parklea Prison, New South Wales, Australia (cf. Taylor 2004, 54). Regulars to my weekly visits agreed that I may share one of their names: 'Amini, Tu'ifua, Sāmiu, Sione (x2), Va'inga, Filisione, and Mafi (others came from time to time). I asked them to read John 11, to talk about Lazarus in the yard, to enact their understandings during our visits, in order to help me see the story in their tattooed, knifed, scarred, shot, pierced, and penetrated bodies. The prisoners also rapped a *ridiculous beat* titled "the gospel of Lazaroos," the lyrics to which changed every time they rapped it. (The titles of the following sections are phrases from their rap song.) I agreed not to rap their song (they said that I do not have the tongue to rap!) but to share some of their views about the Lazarus story and what I saw in their embodiment of the unwrapping of Lazarus.

There is of course no one prisoner understanding of the Lazarus story, just as there is no one native, indigenous, or Asian perspective (cf. Kang 2004). I honor the multiplicity of prisoners' views in this chapter, hoping to elude the imposition of dominating discourses toward legitimating perspectival control (cf. A. Jensen 2007).

This chapter will not echo the call by Jesus, "Lazarus, come out!" but queries "What da??" (cf. Althaus-Reid 2005, 7) on behalf of Lazarus. This chapter is about the troubles of Lazarus and how the story of Lazarus troubled us (as a group, for almost four months). I queer the story of Lazarus in the footsteps of Stephen Moore's understanding of "queer" as "a supple cipher both for what *stands over against* the normal and the natural to oppose, and thereby define, them, and what *inheres within* the normal and the natural to subvert, and indeed pervert, them—this opposition and subversion privileging, but by no means being confined to, the mercurial sphere of the sexual"[2] (Moore 2001, 18; cf. Althaus-Reid and Isherwood 2007; Stone 2001, 117). In this chapter, the mercurial sphere of the sexual overruns with the spheres of death out of respect for Lazarus and as suggested in one of the exchanges in Act 1 of Samuel Beckett's *Waiting for Godot* (premiered in 1953):

> Estragon: What about hanging ourselves?
> Vladimir: Hmm. It'd give us an erection.
> Estragon: (*highly excited*) An erection!
> Vladimir: With all that follows. Where it falls mandrakes grow. That's why they shriek when you pull them up. Did you not know that?
> Estragon: Let's hang ourselves immediately.

Lazarus, Your Sentence Is Death

Some of the prisoners I consulted are murderers; the relatives of the victims and their circle of friends agonize when my friends receive light sentences. But my inmate friends agonize when *pale faces* receive lighter

---

2. "I have said elsewhere that theology is a sexual act, and therefore to reflect on the theologian, her vocation, role and risks means to take seriously the changing geographies of Christian kneelings, and confessionary movements, and how they relate to positions of affection in Christian theology. In this way, queering who the theologian is, and what is her role and vocation is a reflection on locations, closely linked to the locale's events and spaces made of our concrete and sensual actions" (Althaus-Reid 2005, 11).

sentences for similar crimes.[3] In the prison environment, death stings at several levels, and my inmate friends emphasized the sting and stench of death in their understanding of the story of Lazarus.[4]

For the prisoners, John 11 is first of all a story of death, of confinement in a dark tomb from which family and friends are barred. Lazarus received the sentence of death, and he rots in seclusion, bound up with a cloth that would not let his body disintegrate even at death. The tomb and the wrappings of Lazarus trouble my death-dealing friends, one of whom squirmed restlessly on the ground like a fish out of water to illustrate how he imagined the rotting body of Lazarus. The story of Lazarus is simply about death, not because there is hope for resurrection but because death and death sentences are real. "Don't mess with death," the prisoners advised me, for the hope of people with life or death sentences is in death itself. Death is always at hand, and they do not fear death as much as I do (cf. Byrne 1991, 10–11).

---

3. Issues of race and color are unavoidable when dealing with people in prisons. While the prison population in New South Wales (NSW) is predominantly inmates with European roots, like the world outside the prison walls, the percentage of inmates with darker skin color is disproportionate to their population outside of prison.

The NSW Legislative Council on Social Justice (www.csa.nsw.gov.au) reports that in 2001, 19 percent of young detainees in Western Sydney were Pacific Islanders, and the number grew to 33 percent in 2002. In 2003, indigenous Australians made up 20.5 percent of the total Australian prison population (4,820 of 23,550) and 22 percent of the total NSW prison population (2,150 of 9,800) in 2005.

On October 21, 2007, indigenous Australians made up 20 percent of the male population, 30 percent of the female population, and 21 percent of the full-time prison population in NSW. This is appalling, given that indigenous Australians make up around 2.38 percent of the total Australian population.

This does not mean that people with darker skin colors are inherently lawbreakers but that the eyes of the law look more closely over their neighborhoods. Most afternoons at the block in the Sydney suburb of Redfern, for instance, where many indigenous Australians live, one will meet pairs of officers around every other corner. The eyes of the law watch intensely the streets where people with darker skin colors roam.

4. Outside of prison, the sting of death is strong against victims of Western colonization, which continues to deliver death sentences to many people and cultures throughout the world. This charge needs no explanation. But it still needs to be made because the colonizing nations of the West have yet to account for their destructive actions, because the ash heaps of colonization do not seem to affect how the world powers operate, and because the victims of Western colonization are mostly people with darker skin colors (so Dube 2006; Sugirtharajah 2003; Liew 2005). For people with darker skin color, the sting of death is real.

The inmates easily identify with Lazarus. The more violent criminals saw his death as a symbol for the chance to escape confinement, a view that scared small-time offenders who were not ready for death but who see the tomb of Lazarus as a figure for prison cells. Some were envious of Lazarus, imagining that he had a tomb all for himself. For them, it would have been cruel if Lazarus had a tomb-mate, as inmates have cell-mates, and he is raised but the other was not. Lazarus' resurrection thus troubled the prisoners who realize that though many have life sentences, a few of them, not all, will be released.

Where's the Love?

The death-dealing prisoners imagined that Martha and Mary were desperate when their brother fell ill. The story does not mention who was older than whom or who their parents were, so this was probably a family of three siblings.[5] The illness of one family member, male or female, would therefore be stressful to the other two siblings.

The sisters sent words to Jesus because he loved Lazarus (John 11:3). As North puts it, "what matters now is not who Lazarus is as much as how he stands in relation to Jesus; Lazarus is someone whom Jesus loves" (2001, 41). What kind of love did Jesus have for Lazarus? Did Jesus love Lazarus the same way as he loved his sisters?

Jesus relates differently to the sisters, and they respond to him differently. Martha is the busybody who hustles like an older sister to provide for Jesus and his friends (Luke 10:38–42), and she comes outside their home to meet Jesus upon his arrival (John 11:20). Mary is an indoors kind of sister (cf. Byrne 1991, 59), preferring to sit (Luke 10:39) and kneel (John 11:32) at the feet of Jesus; she anoints his feet and then wipes them with her hair at least once (John 12:3).[6] Mary likes the feet of Jesus. Jesus must have loved the sisters for the attention they gave to his needs, but he probably did not love them the same way because they attended to different needs, and their attention aroused different points of attention. When Jesus saw Mary weeping, along with the Jews with her, he was "greatly disturbed in

---

5. This is not to say that their parents were physically dead or literally murdered by the narrator. Rather, as in the case of prisoners, the parents may be alive but no longer involved in the lives of their children.

6. Cf. Matt 26:6–16 and Mark 14:3–11, where the feast was at the home of Simon the Leper and the woman is not named. Cf. Esler and Piper 2006, 45–74.

spirit and deeply moved" (John 11:33). Martha, however, did not come weeping to Jesus, nor was Jesus moved when he met her (John 11:20–27).

What may have been the basis for the sisters' claim that Jesus loves their brother? Did Jesus love Lazarus differently from his sisters? Or did he "dig" Lazarus like his sisters?

In the prison context, love is not associated with sexual practices. Prisoners have sex with one another, but that is not why they love one another. They have "wives" in each yard, and now and then someone gets raped, starting riots and further violence, but the prisoners do not see themselves as gay. The prison culture whirls in homophobia, even though prisoners (sometimes with guards) perform homosexual acts.[7]

In prison, love has something to do with the willingness to take the fall, to "do a walk" (which means going to beat up, even kill, someone on behalf of another) or to give up one's life for one's mates. Love is deadly. The absence of this kind of love from the story of Lazarus was noticeable to the inmates. They suspected that there might have been some *Ooh Lazarus loving* between Jesus and Lazarus, but they were saddened that there was no honest *O Lazarus, would I had died instead of you* (cf. 2 Sam 18:33b) *loving*. It is not such a big deal for the prisoners if Jesus had a sexual relationship with Lazarus (cf. Goss 2006; Smith 1973, 154) and/or with his sisters, but it is unacceptable that no one offered to "do a walk" for Lazarus.

To "do a walk" is no different from the "love command" that is assumed to have been one of the governing principles of the Johannine community. The key to understanding this love command is in John 15:13: "No one has greater love than this, to lay down one's life for one's friends" (cf. North 2001, 42–43). It is of course easier to state the love command than it is to do it. Many people loved Lazarus, but none showed *greater love* for him.

---

7. We need to rediscover God, as Althaus-Reid puts it, "outside the heterosexual ideology which has been prevalent in the history of Christianity and theology. In order to do that, it is necessary to facilitate the coming out of the closet of God by a process of theological queering. By theological queering, we mean the deliberate questioning of heterosexual experience and thinking which has shaped our understanding of theology, the role of the theologian and hermeneutics. That process requires from us not only honesty and courage, but also a critical engagement with Queer Theory, non-heterosexual and critical Heterosexual Theology. It also requires us to come clean about our experiences, which in some way or other always seem destined to fall outside the normative sexual ideology of theology" (Althaus-Reid 2005, 2; cf. Stone 2001, 112–15).

The sisters sent words to Jesus, who became emotional, but he did not do anything when Lazarus was ill. For my criminal friends, becoming emotional is not enough. So they doubt if anything that might happen afterward would be for the sake of Lazarus. Any tears that follow are crocodile tears, and any expression of sympathy later will be like someone who brings flowers to the funeral to make up for not taking the time to come while the deceased is still alive (in prison).

The prisoners were not convinced that Martha and Mary sent words to Jesus so that he would come and be a healer. Rather, they suggest that Martha and Mary called Jesus to *be there* for Lazarus, for if Jesus *was there*, Lazarus would not have died. Lazarus would have lived because he loves Jesus, and his love would have healed him: Lazarus would not have died in the presence of his lover. Both sisters, when they greeted Jesus, said the same thing, "Lord, if you had been here, my brother would not have died" (11:21, 32). So it is not that they thought Jesus could heal their brother. Rather, they trusted their brother to stay alive if Jesus was with him. Some of the Jews believed so too (11:37).

The love of Lazarus for Jesus, and the effect of the presence of Jesus for Lazarus, could have kept him alive, up and around, whereas the love of Lazarus for his sisters, and for others, relaxes him, permits him to lie back and die. So this was a story with multiple layers, and multiple degrees, of love. If we follow the storyline, there is no doubt that Lazarus died for the glory of Jesus. What love is greater? But where's love for Lazarus?

Yo' Jesus, What Took You So Long?

The inmates were dismayed that Jesus took his time to respond to the plea of the sisters.[8] What might the reason be for his delay? Jesus gives an explanation: "This illness does not lead to death; rather it is for God's glory, so that the Son of God may be glorified through it" (11:4b). And the narrator adds, "Accordingly, though Jesus loved Martha and her sister [who is not named here] and Lazarus, he stayed two days longer in the place where he was" (11:6–7). The prisoners were not satisfied with these explanations,[9] and they came up with four alternative explanations.

---

8. Compare Mark 5:21–43, where Jesus proceeds at once when he receives the plea concerning the death of Jairus's daughter, even though he was interrupted by the woman with a hemorrhage in vv. 25–34.

9. So Byrne: "Following upon the remark about Jesus' love in the preceding sen-

First, some of the inmates feel that Jesus did not truly love Lazarus
and his sisters (compare Esler and Piper 2006, 75–103). If he really loved
them, he would have dashed off as soon as he heard that the one he loved
was ill. Whether at night or during a storm, a true lover would hurry to
be with his or her beloved. At the far side of the Jordan (John 10:40–42),
"Jesus is a long way from Bethany when Lazarus falls ill" (Esler and Piper
2006, 8), but it was not as if Jesus and his disciples were on an island so
that they had to wait for a boat to take them across. The message from
the sisters came quickly, and Jesus too could have come quickly. His delay
in coming suggests that he did not care, which is unacceptable to the
inmates. This of course also says something about the prisoners themselves, for they cannot show up when the ones they love need them. They
were therefore projecting onto Jesus the disappointment of their loved
ones in them.

Second, given that many families and friends are ashamed to visit them
in prison, some of the prisoners suggest that Jesus may have been afraid to
see his beloved dying. To see Lazarus in his ailment would remind Jesus of
his own mortality, which he was not prepared to confront. To see Lazarus
in a vulnerable state would be like looking through the bars at another
inmate being knifed. There is nothing one can do but be silent, for to raise
the alarm might mean that one will soon receive a knifing. To be silent is
to not draw attention to oneself, but one is still expected to "do a walk" on
behalf of one's friend at another time. So the prisoners expect Jesus to "do
a walk" later for Lazarus.

Third, some of the prisoners suggest that Jesus might have been in a
situation from which he could not walk away, as in the case of gangsters
who trap one another into hanging out together as a group, a mob, resulting in each neglecting other more important people and responsibilities.
The one who leaves betrays the gang and that becomes a matter of life and
death. Such is gang culture. If that was the situation that Jesus was in, then
he could not break away easily, which would explain why he did not come
sooner to Lazarus.

Fourth, some of the prisoners thought that Jesus was just being a "regular guy." He did not hurry to Bethany because regular guys don't behave

---

tence, the delay comes as a severe surprise. It is not the response of a friend" (1991,
50). Source critics avoid this dilemma by imagining two accounts woven together in
John 11, one account declaring that Jesus came immediately after receiving the message from the sisters (see esp. Burkett 1994).

like that. He might care for Lazarus and his sisters, but it is not a guy-thing to announce and demonstrate love in public. Women do things like that, as the sisters did when Lazarus became ill. Real manly men do not do that. Self-control is what one expects from regular guys, and that is what Jesus showed here. (So when Jesus wept in 11:35 he was no longer manly.)

The four alternative explanations make Jesus' delay in coming easier to understand, but the prisoners would not justify him. They did not accept the explanations Jesus and the narrator gave, thus raising doubts about the Johannine agenda. They were suspicious of whatever Jesus said and did afterward. Was Jesus sincere? What was he covering up? For what was he compensating?

Come Back, My Dear Lazarus[10]

When I first entered prison, I was overwhelmed by the power of space. Prison space is not neutral, including the parts that are empty or designated as sterile. Prison space gasps under the tentacles of power and is controlling even over visitors; prison space feels like a pool of whirling power. When in prison, therefore, one has to confront the intersection of space and power.

Attention to space and power is high also on the agenda of postcolonial theorists (cf. Punt 2006), especially with regard to the occupation and fleecing of land spaces and the dispossession of the native people of occupied lands (so Robert Warrior and Norman Gottwald). Postcolonial theory attends closely to the exercise of power, calling for the dismantling of abusive powers and authorities as well as restitution for those.

Powers and authorities are of course necessary for orderly and meaningful life. But there are times when a limited number of people (fail to) exercise their powers and authorities for their own gain and interests. Powers and authorities are abused also when they are idolized or disinterested while underprivileged people are being abused.

In the story of Lazarus, Jesus is clearly the character with power and authority. John 11 is actually a story about Jesus in which Lazarus is a pawn "for God's glory, so that the Son of God may be glorified through" his illness (11:4), his death, and resurrection. Jesus speaks with authority

---

10. This is an allusion to the strife between Saul and David, and Saul's attempt to coax David back to his camp (cf. 1 Sam 26:21): Jesus is to Lazarus as Saul was to David.

about going back to Judea, where Jews earlier tried to stone him (11:7–8), in order to awaken Lazarus from sleep (11:11). Jesus sounds self-centered: "Then Jesus told them, plainly, 'Lazarus is dead. For your sake *I am glad I was not there,* so that you may believe. But let us go to him" (11:14–15). When Jesus and his disciples departed, his intention was clear: to raise Lazarus from the dead. Was this for the interests of Lazarus, Martha, and Mary also, or only for the interests of Jesus and God?

Martha believed that Lazarus would be resurrected on the last day (11:24), and she did not ask Jesus to raise him right away. Mary, however, did not say anything when she came to Jesus. She only wept, and her weeping greatly disturbed him (11:33, 38). If Jesus was not confident with his ability to raise Lazarus from the dead, Martha's urgings (so West 2003) and Mary's weeping pushed him forward. But those were not enough. He also needed to "do a prayer," which was suspect in the eyes of my prisoner friends: "Father, I thank you for having heard me. I knew that you always hear me, but I have said this for the sake of the crowd standing here, so that they may believe that you sent me" (11:42). While the prisoners believe in the power of prayer, they are only prayerful when they prepare for court hearings and for sentencing. Prisoners pray when their lives are in the balance, and they assumed the same was true for Jesus. The prisoners were therefore very disappointed because they expected Jesus to "do a walk" but he instead "did a prayer."[11]

Jesus offered a prayer that gave him power over death.[12] Then, like a ruthless master who would not let a poor slave die, Jesus called Lazarus back as if the hassles of life were preferable over the peace of death. The master called back a dead person to prove that he is "the real deal." Since the prisoners expected Jesus to "do a walk" for Lazarus, they were annoyed that Lazarus was called back to "do a walk" for Jesus instead. The power

---

11. "Nowhere else in the gospel tradition does Jesus pray to the Father before working a miracle. What we have here, however, is not strictly a prayer, but a thanksgiving, an act of communion with the Father which the bystanders are allowed to 'overhear'" (Byrne 1991, 78).

12. There are other interpretations of the prayer, ranging from suggesting that it was a show-off prayer to claiming that the prayer demonstrates the unity between Jesus and God. The prayer "is a confident acknowledgment that on this occasion, as always, Jesus has the ear of God" (North 2001, 102). What is often overlooked is how the prayer follows upon Martha's confidence in Jesus (so West 2003). Martha puts Jesus on the spot, making him ask something from God, and Mary's weeping excels him into action.

of the master grows in this story, and Lazarus receives the chance to die a second time.[13]

DEAD MAN STRIPPED

The tomb was opened, the stone rolled away, the prayer offered, then Jesus cries with a loud voice, "Lazarus, come out!"

In the two depictions of this moment by Rembrandt,[14] Jesus stands with authority on the stone as if he has conquered the power and space of death, with one of his arms raised. Jesus, the only one who is upright (pun intended) in the depictions, is the central figure in both works. Rembrandt presents the front of Jesus to the viewer in the earlier work and his right side in the later one, turning Jesus away from the viewer as if he is no longer the centering figure in Rembrandt's understanding of this story.

In Rembrandt's 1630–1631 oil painting *The Raising of Lazarus*, the lighting draws the viewer to the figure to the right of Jesus, whose arms rise as if in surprise: "Whoa, cool!" Whereas Jesus raises one arm, this character, who looks like a woman, raises both arms. If this character is Martha,[15] Rembrandt here highlights her place in the raising of Lazarus (so West 2003). It is toward this character that Lazarus faces, while his right arm reaches in the direction of Jesus, under the stone on which the uncovered feet of Jesus stand. Though the raised right hand of Jesus sug-

---

13. This echoes the anxiety of prisoners who spend days preparing for their sentencing, dress up, and come to court, to learn that the judge has delayed delivering the judgment. They have to go through the same pain later. Similar is the frustration of prisoners who receive tougher sentences after their retrial.

14. Both works by Rembrandt which I will discuss in this section are available online at *Olga's Gallery* (www.abcgallery.com). These works were produced two decades after Caravaggio's *Raising of Lazarus* (1608–1609; see Oates 2006 for a discussion of Caravaggio's work).

See Bal 1991 for suggestions on ways to "read" the works of "Rembrandt" (even though Bal did not discuss Rembrandt's works on Lazarus); Wilsey 2006 for the influence of the Protestant Reformation on Rembrandt (and Bach); and O'Kane 2005 on how artists are interpreters. See also Esler and Piper 2006, 131–45, for early Christian art depictions of a wand-bearing Jesus raising Lazarus, some intertexting this story with the Jonah story.

15. It could also be Mary, or another woman. Note that at the bottom left hand corner is another figure who appears to be a woman (her back is to the viewer).

gests the announcement of a blessing, his face suggests a slight expression of surprise: "Wow, did that really happen?" Could it be that the raised right hand of Jesus is a "stop it" gesture?

The reaction of other people in this painting, none of whom looks at the upright Jesus, affirms the Johannine agenda: the miracles and teachings of Jesus were in order that people may believe that Jesus is the son of God. The figures in the painting are more interested in the miracle than in the person of Jesus. However, could the disinterest in the presence of Jesus be an attempt to problematize the Johannine agenda?

In the 1632 etching *The Raising of Lazarus*, Rembrandt raises Jesus' left arm, turns him away from the viewer, and directs the face of Lazarus away from where Jesus stands. Jesus gathers in his robe and holds his right fist to his hip. It is through his posture that one may infer his emotions, since his face is not visible. In South Pacific island contexts, one may read Jesus' posture in two possible ways: first, Jesus is tired, frustrated, and annoyed, or second, Jesus is gaily showing off his abilities.

Concerning this work also, the viewer looks to the expressions of those who observe the event for reactions, a focal shift that underscores the importance of the response to the miracle of Jesus. Rembrandt provides the viewer with the effect of the power of Jesus on others, one of whom draws back with both arms raised, and in front of him, another one raises both arms and leans forward. In this later work, Rembrandt makes the impact of the raising of Lazarus more complex than in the earlier work.[16] In the 1630–1631 painting, the figure with raised arms may be a woman who leans forward as if to receive and embrace Lazarus. But in the 1632 etching, the figures with raised arms are male, and they express different reactions, one leaning forward as if in obeisance to Jesus through the raised head of Lazarus and the other drawing back as if in disbelief, amazement, or fear. In the 1632 etching also is one woman figure at the bottom right hand corner, leaning in the same direction as Lazarus.

I did not show these images to the prisoners, but I imagine that they would say that Rembrandt endorses the Johannine agenda. In both works, Rembrandt gives the impression that this story is not about Jesus or Lazarus but the effects of the work of Jesus on others. Rembrandt moves

---

16. Rembrandt's works provide far more than a snapshot of a biblical event. Rembrandt utilizes *chiaroscuro*, facial expressions, and figure arrangement to convey complex theological concepts to those who view them.

the focus away from Jesus and Lazarus to the reaction of the people. In this regard, Rembrandt is trapped by the drive of the Johannine agenda.

But something *telling* hides in the frame of the 1632 etching. The rounded frame of the etching accentuates the elongated figure of Jesus. The upward tapering of the frame draws the viewer to Jesus' raised hand, which seems to pull up the fluid body of Lazarus. Or, was Jesus reaching up to throw down the pots, tools, weapons, and other hangings from the ceiling, upon Lazarus? These hangings are within the reach of Jesus' raised left arm in the 1632 etching but beyond the reach of the right arm in the 1630–1631 painting. In this reading, the two characters with raised arms in the etching are reacting to what they thought Jesus was trying to do, that is, they saw him reaching for something with which to knock Lazarus back down. Why did Rembrandt raise Jesus' left arm? Was Jesus left-handed? Did Jesus plan to do something leftist to Lazarus? If the raised right hand in the painting suggests a blessing, what does the raised left hand in the etching suggest? Did Rembrandt think that the raising of Lazarus was problematic?

Wazzup wit' Jesus?

What upset the prisoners the most was that after Jesus raised Lazarus from the dead, he passed the responsibility for attending to Lazarus to other people. Jesus did not embrace Lazarus but called on other people to "Unbind him, and let him go" (11:44). Maybe Jesus was giving the responsibility to care for Lazarus to the community (so Perkins 2000), but this troubled the prisoners. They wanted Jesus to at least touch Lazarus, whom he loved.

Lazarus was untouchable in the eyes of Jesus, as well as for the narrator, in whose account nothing was done to the body of Lazarus. Lazarus had been dead for four days, so his body needed at least a good scrub and preferably some ointment and clothing (cf. Sanders 2007). But no one seemed to care about his body.

The neglect of Lazarus' body stands in the shadows of other biblical stories that attend to the body. The stories best known to the prisoners are the garden story, where God made garments to clothe Adam and Eve (Gen 3:21), and Michal criticizing David for parading in his nakedness (2 Sam 6:16–23).[17] How might God and Michal react to the neglect of the body of

---

17. See also the attention to the body in the stories of Uriah, whom David

Lazarus? The story of Lazarus also brings to mind the stories of the wife of Potiphar, who stripped Joseph of his garment (Gen 39:7–18), and the Beloved Disciple, who ran off naked from the garden of Gethsemane (Mark 14:51–52; cf. R. Jensen 1995, 22). In this connection, Lazarus is a reminder of Joseph and a figure of the Beloved Disciple (cf. Goss 2006, 560).

It troubled the prisoners that Jesus loved Lazarus but did not do what they expect of a lover. Jesus should have embraced his beloved. The prisoners consequently raised two questions: Wazzup wit' Jesus? Why didn't he give Lazarus a scrub? These questions are especially critical in light of the fact that Jesus gets bodily services in other Gospel stories: he is fed, washed, and his feet were anointed at least once. Jesus could have given or requested a scrub for Lazarus and, as in the parable of the Prodigal Son, asked for fresh clothes to be put on his beloved, the one who was dead but has now been raised (Luke 15:11–32). Jesus later washed the feet of his disciples, but not those of Lazarus.

If we follow the storyline, Lazarus was raised, unbound, and then let go, naked. That is not acceptable to my criminal friends, who look forward to their release from prison; and they expect their families and friends to greet, clothe, and celebrate them.

Jesus called Lazarus to come out and then left him hanging. This did not satisfy the prisoners, who understand the resurrection of Lazarus as a "coming out" kind of event (so Perkins 2000). Lazarus did come out. But Jesus did not come out fully. Resurrection should not be a wham-bang-get-out-of-here experience. Rather, as Heyward puts it, like coming out, resurrection is a lifetime process that has to do with spirituality. "Coming out [like resurrection] is a matter of making connections with one another, spiritually as well as sexually. It is an ongoing process of revelation and manifestation, of incarnation and epiphany" (Heyward 1995, 112).

GET PO'LAZARUS A BIKINI!

This chapter follows in the tracks of the *Secret Gospel of Mark* (see Smith 1973), which puts a linen cloth over the naked body of Lazarus. Since the prisoners I consulted are Pacific Islanders, an appropriate garment with which to clothe po'Lazarus would be a bikini.

---

instructed to wash his feet after returning from the battlefield (2 Sam 11:6–13), and Esther, who underwent twelve months of cosmetic treatment under the directions of a eunuch (Esth 2:12).

The bikini swimwear received its name from an island in the North Pacific Ocean, Bikini, where the United States tested atomic weapons in the 1940s and '50s. The bikini swimwear was released in the 1940s in Paris and it was named after Bikini Atoll on the reasoning that the burst of excitement the swimwear would cause would be like the nuclear device. There could be a second reason, which is that the design of the bikini, with a bottom and a top, suggests that it covers explosives at the bottom with the double top imaging the mushroom from the explosion.

I add a third, pidgin-like phonetic play: note how "bikini" sounds like "beginning." The bikini outfit needed for Lazarus therefore embodies the need for a new beginning for Lazarus. In other words, the bikini/beginning for Lazarus, and for people like Lazarus, involves a call for "the empire" to account for the "bikini atolls" that have been stripped and blown up in the interests of its government. In Oceania, the empire has at least two faces. At Bikini, in the Micronesian group to the north, the empire is the United States of America. But to the southeast, the empire is France, who tested its weapons in Mururoa.

Jesus ordered that Lazarus be stripped and released, naked; empires strip islands then leave them naked. Those empire nations, like Jesus in the biblical account, should no longer be allowed to test their explosions. For Lazarus to continue troubling, empire nations should be called to account for their explosions.

The prisoners' insistence that Lazarus be given a scrub and clothing, rather than being let go naked as in the biblical account, is affirmation that resurrection is a relational movement (Heyward 1995, 20; cf. Goss 2006, 548). This relational movement is mutual and not static. "It is a dynamic process generated by a shared assumption that all parties in a relationship can, and should be empowered through the relational process" (Heyward 1995, 87; cf. Goss 2006, 555).

The raising of Lazarus benefitted the mission of God, for many Jews believed Jesus because of Lazarus (John 11:45). Because of this, Lazarus was a marked man. The chief priest planned to put him to death again (John 12:10–11). The troubles of Lazarus increased after his resurrection, thanks to Jesus. For the troubles of Lazarus, my prisoner friends were also trouble.

WORKS CONSULTED

Althaus-Reid, Marcella. 2005. *The Queer God*. London: Routledge.

Althaus-Reid, Marcella, and Lisa Isherwood. 2007. Thinking Theology and Queer Theory. *Feminist Theology* 15:302–14.

Bal, Mieke. 1991. *Reading "Rembrandt": Beyond the Word-Image Opposition.* Cambridge: Cambridge University Press.

Burkett, Delbert. 1994. Two Accounts of Lazarus' Resurrection in John 11. *NovT* 36:209–32.

Byrne, Brendan. 1991. *Lazarus: A Contemporary Reading of John 11:1–46.* Collegeville, Minn.: Liturgical Press.

Dube, Musa W. 2006. Looking Back and Forward: Postcolonialism, Globalization, God and Gender. *Scriptura* 92:178–93.

Esler, Philip F., and Ronald Piper. 2006. *Lazarus, Mary and Martha: Social-Scientific Approaches to the Gospel of John.* Minneapolis: Fortress.

Goss, Robert E. 2006. John. Pages 548–65 in *The Queer Bible Commentary.* Edited by Deryn Guest et al. London: SCM.

Heyward, Carter. 1995. *Staying Power: Reflections on Gender, Justice, and Compassion.* Cleveland: Pilgrim.

Jeffery, Peter. 2007. *The Secret Gospel of Mark Unveiled: Imagined Rituals of Sex, Death, and Madness in Biblical Forgery.* New Haven: Yale University Press.

Jensen, Alexander S. 2007. Critical Theory, Feminism and Postcolonialism. Pages 192–206 in *Theological Hermeneutics.* London: SCM.

Jensen, Robin M. 1995. The Raising of Lazarus. *BRev* 11.2:20–28, 45.

Kang, Namsoon. 2004. Who/What Is Asian? A Postcolonial Theological Reading of Orientalism and Neo-Orientalism. Pages 100–117 in Keller, Nausner, and Rivera 2004.

Keller, C., M. Nausner, and M. Rivera. 2004. *Postcolonial Theologies: Divinity and Empire.* St. Louis: Chalice.

Liew, Tat-siong Benny. 2005. Margins and (Cutting-)Edges: On the (Il) Legitimacy and Intersections of Race, Ethnicity, and (Post)Colonialism. Pages 114–65 in *Postcolonial Biblical Criticism: Interdisciplinary Intersections.* Edited by S. D. Moore and F. Segovia. London: Continuum.

Moore, Stephen D. 2001. *God's Beauty Parlor and Other Queer Spaces in and around the Bible.* Stanford, Calif.: Stanford University Press.

North, Wendy E. Sproston. 2001. *The Lazarus Story within the Johannine Tradition.* Sheffield: Sheffield Academic Press.

O'Kane, Martin. 2005. The Artist as Reader of the Bible: Visual Exegesis and the Adoration of the Magi. *BibInt* 13:337–73.

Oates, Amy. 2006. The Raising of Lazarus: Caravaggio and John 11. *Int* 61:386–401.

Perkins, Benjamin. 2000. Coming Out, Lazarus's and Ours: Queer Reflections of a Psychospiritual, Political Journey. Pages 196–205 in *Take Back the Word: A Queer Reading of the Bible*. Edited by R. E. Goss and M. West. Cleveland, Ohio: Pilgrim.

Punt, Jeremy. 2006. Why Not Postcolonial Biblical Criticism in (South) Africa: Stating the Obvious or Looking for the Impossible? *Scriptura* 91:63–82.

Sanders, Beth. 2007. Heaven Scent. *ChrCent* 124 (5):19.

Smith, Morton. 1973. *Clement of Alexandria and a Secret Gospel of Mark*. Cambridge: Harvard University Press.

Steinberg, Leo. 1983. *The Sexuality of Christ in Renaissance Art and in Modern Oblivion*. New York: Pantheon.

Stone, Ken. 2001. Homosexuality and the Bible or Queer Reading? A Response to Martti Nissinen. *Theology and Sexuality* 14:107–18.

Sugirtharajah, R. S. 2003. *Postcolonial Reconfigurations*. St. Louis: Chalice.

Taylor, Mark Lewis. 2004. Spirit and Liberation: Achieving Postcolonial Theology in the United States. Pages 39–55 in Keller, Nausner, and Rivera 2004.

West, Mona. 2003. The Raising of Lazarus: A Lesbian Coming Out Story. Pages 143–58 in vol. 1 of *A Feminist Companion to John*. Edited by A.-J. Levine and M. Blickenstaff. FCNTECW 4. Cleveland, Ohio: Pilgrim.

Wilsey, John D. 2006. The Impact of the Reformation on the Fine Arts. *Faith and Mission* 23 (2):31–54.

Queering Early Christian Discourse:
The Ethiopian Eunuch

Sean D. Burke

I first focused my attention on the story of the Ethiopian eunuch in Acts 8:26–40 because of an interest in difference and how communities in general, and Christian churches in particular, negotiate difference as it relates to entrance into and participation in community life. It seemed to me that points at which multiple differences intersect would provide a particularly important locus for the negotiation of difference. The Ethiopian eunuch seems to embody just such an intersection of multiple differences, including differences of gender, social status, race, and perhaps sexuality and religious identity as well.

If I first focused my attention on the story of the Ethiopian eunuch because of an interest in difference, then it is an interest in ambiguity that has sustained my attention. Each time I tried to analyze a particular difference that the eunuch might embody, I discovered ambiguity. In the history of interpretation, the eunuch has been read as a man and as a castrato. He might indeed be different in terms of gender, but how does one identify his gender? The eunuch has been read as a high government official and as a slave. How, then, does one identify his social status? The eunuch has been read as a foreign Ethiopian and as a foreigner to Ethiopians. How, then, does one identify his race?

The text itself can be used to support each and every one of these readings, as well as multiple readings of the eunuch's sexual identity and his religious identity. How, then, is an interpreter to negotiate all these ambiguities? Over the centuries, interpreters have approached these ambiguities in at least four different ways. First, some have ignored the ambiguities and have interpreted the text as if each axis of the eunuch's identity were unambiguous. Second, some have noted the ambiguities but have concluded that they cannot be resolved. Third, some have attempted to resolve the ambiguities and to establish definitively each axis of the eunuch's identity. Finally, some have argued that although each axis of the eunuch's identity was clear in and of itself, the author of Acts introduced ambiguities into his identification in the story in order to serve some historical, literary, and/or theological purpose.

QUEERING

Queer theory provides a new and productive way to read ambiguities in identity. I think the most important insight in the work of queer theorists is that identity itself is a social construction produced through discourse (see, e.g., Jagose 1996, 75–83). Some may find this the most troubling aspect of queer theory, because identity categories have been employed not only as a basis for oppression but also as a basis for movements of liberation. While I do not deny that many have found in identity categories a rallying point for movements of social change, I think queer theorists are right to insist that identity categories remain arbitrary, totalizing, exclusionary, normative, and regulatory social constructions that function by denying difference and suppressing ambiguity. While identification with a particular identity category may function strategically as a means of resistance, the naturalization and normalization of identities—that is, the insistence that identities be recognized as natural, stable, fixed, and unitary—ultimately function in ways that oppress people.

Building on these theoretical insights, I define "queering" as the employment of a variety of strategies in order to deconstruct and to denaturalize identity categories. To deconstruct and to denaturalize identities is to demonstrate that what are claimed to be natural and normal essences are actually arbitrary and fluid social constructions. I do not employ queering as a means of deconstruction for deconstruction's sake. In the language of queer theorist Judith Butler (2004, 1–16), my goal in queering identity categories is to make it possible for more bodies to matter—for more bodies to be recognized as fully human.

If identities are arbitrary and fluid social constructions, then ambiguities in identity do not have to be approached as problems to be resolved nor as veils hiding fixed, stable, unitary identities. Instead, we can approach ambiguities in identity as potential sites for queering. Is it possible, then, to read the ambiguities in the identity of the Ethiopian eunuch of Acts 8:26–

40 not as problems to be ignored or resolved, but rather as sites within a particular early Christian discourse for queering identity categories?

ANCIENT MASCULINITIES

Eunuchs can be read as figures with the potential to queer constructions of what was one of the most important identity categories of antiquity: masculinity. The dominant Greco-Roman construction of masculinity was not simply a gender identity; rather, it was a complex effect of the intersection of multiple discourses of gender, sexuality, social status, and race. The possession of a penis and testicles was a necessary but not a sufficient condition for social recognition as a "man" (in Greek ἀνήρ and in Latin *vir*). Social recognition as a man depended on one's being perceived as embodying the positive terms in a series of binary oppositions: free/enslaved, native/foreign, superior/inferior, hard/soft, active/passive, dominant/submissive, inviolable/violable, impenetrable/penetrable, sexually insertive/sexually receptive, hairy/smooth, and self-disciplined/ruled by the emotions (Gleason 1995, 161; Kuefler 2001, 21; Moore 2001, 136–40; Williams 1999, 7). Thus, in the dominant Greco-Roman construction of identity, human beings could be divided not only into the categories of male and female but also into categories that Jonathan Walters (1993, 29) labels "men" and "unmen."

In order to earn and to maintain identification as a man, a free adult male citizen or native had to be perceived as one who dominated unmen—women, foreigners, slaves, and children. A free adult male citizen or native could forfeit identification as a man, therefore, if he were to be perceived as having been physically violated or sexually penetrated by another man or by an unman, thus marking him as "soft" or "effeminate" (Edwards 1993, 63–97; Halperin 2002, 32–44; Williams 1999, 172–224). The identity of unmen, however, functioned to naturalize and to normalize the physical violation and sexual penetration of certain persons by those identified as men, within boundaries produced by laws and social conventions (Cohen 1991, 133–73). As a slave advises his master in Plautus's *Curculio* (lines 36–37), a man may sexually penetrate anyone he wishes as long as he keeps away from married women (*nupta*), widows (*vidua*), virgins (*virgine*), youths (*iuventute*), and freeborn boys (*pueris liberis*).

An analysis of the discourses of the postexilic Torah, Greek-speaking Jews of the first century C.E., and the Palestinian rabbis suggests that Jewish constructions of masculinity differed from the dominant Greco-Roman construction. First, Jewish constructions of masculinity depended on what were identified as divinely sanctioned boundaries between male and female without reference to boundaries between men and unmen. As Daniel Boyarin (1995, 341–43) has argued, if the primary concern in the dominant Greco-Roman construction of masculinity was *hybris*—the usurpation of the attributes or activities of a man by an unman—the primary concern in Jewish constructions of masculinity was *hybrids*—the confusion or mixing of male and female. Second, Jewish constructions marked as deficient not only the masculinity of men who were sexually penetrated but also the masculinity of men who penetrated other men, on the grounds that they violated the divinely sanctioned boundaries between the categories of male and female. Finally, Jewish constructions of masculinity identified deviant sexual activities with foreigners, and thus the prohibition of such activities produced a distinction between Jews and Gentiles.

Eunuchs

Eunuchs had the potential to queer ancient constructions of masculinity because of their status as castrated males. Some scholars argue, however, that the word εὐνοῦχος does not always refer to a castrated male, but that it could also be used to refer to a (non-castrated) high official (see, e.g., Schneider 1964, 766). The results of philological analysis of εὐνοῦχος (as well as the Hebrew סריס and the Akkadian *ša rēši*) are inconclusive. Rather than the philological question of meaning, therefore, I pose a social-rhetorical question: what was the word εὐνοῦχος most likely to evoke among Greek-speaking audiences in the social-cultural context of the book of Acts? On the basis of my own analysis of the usage of the word in the Greek texts of Herodotus, Xenophon, Dio Chrysostom, Chariton, and Lucian, as well as in the Greek-Jewish texts of Sirach, Wisdom of Solomon, Judith, and Philo of Alexandria, I conclude that it is most likely that for Greek-speaking audiences—whether elite or nonelite and whether Jewish or non-Jewish—the word εὐνοῦχος would have evoked a castrated male. In fact, I have not been able to find one example in Greek texts from the fifth century B.C.E. to the second century C.E. or in Greek-Jewish texts from the second century B.C.E. to the first century C.E. in which εὐνοῦχος was used to refer to a person who was *clearly not* castrated.

The practice of castrating animals dates back to at least 2300 B.C.E. in Babylon, and the ancient Near East may have been the site in which male human beings were first castrated (Taylor 2000, 168–69). Castration may initially have been used as a means of humiliating enemies in war and of punishing criminals, but it soon came to serve another purpose in the context of the royal harem. Male slaves were castrated in order to render them fit to guard the sexuality of the women of the harem. The goal of castration was not to render these slaves incapable of sexually penetrating the women of the harem, but rather it was to render them incapable of impregnating the ruler's wives and concubines (Scholz 2001, 68–70; Taylor 2000, 35). This goal was best achieved not by removing the penis, which involved a higher risk of death, but rather by tying off, crushing, or removing the testicles.

There were two groups of eunuchs with which the audience of the book of Acts would have been most familiar. The first group was court eunuchs. This social institution most likely developed out of the role of eunuchs in the royal harem, where they came to be trusted not only by the women they guarded but also by their sons, some of whom grew up to be rulers themselves (Bullough 2002, 7; Llewellyn-Jones 2002, 41). The employment of court eunuchs is well documented for the courts of Persia, China, India, Rome, and Byzantium, and Hayim Tadmor (2002, 603–11) has made a strong case for their employment in Assyria as well. It is precisely their castrated status that made court eunuchs useful to rulers. In the fourth century B.C.E., Xenophon attributed to Cyrus the Persian the following rationale for choosing eunuchs as his bodyguards:

> as he knew that people are nowhere easier to overcome than at meals and drinking, in baths, and in bed and asleep, he looked for certain ones who were most faithful that he could have around himself at such times. And he held that no one would ever be faithful who loved another more than the one who required guarding. He believed, therefore, that those who had children or agreeable wives or boyfriends were by nature constrained to love these ones most. But as he saw that eunuchs lacked all these things, he held that they would esteem most highly such ones as could best make them rich, stand by them if they were wronged, and place them in offices of honor, and he held that no one could surpass him in bestowing such favors. Besides these things, as eunuchs are disreputable among other people, on account of this as well they need a master and defender; for there is no man who would not think himself worthy to have more than a eunuch in everything unless there were someone more powerful to prevent his doing so; but there is nothing to prevent even a eunuch from being superior to all in faithfulness to his master. (*Cyr.* 7.5.59–61; my translation)

Contemporary scholars have provided similar explanations for the employment of court eunuchs. Rulers valued them for their loyalty, but they also
considered them not to be threats because of their inability to establish
their own rival dynasties (Bullough 2002, 7). Rulers found eunuchs to be
absolutely dependent on their masters because they had not only been cut
off from their natal families, but they were cut off from the possibility of
establishing their own families by means of procreation (Patterson 1982,
319–20). Rulers also found the dependency of eunuchs on their masters
enhanced by people's general dislike of them (Scholz 2001, 115). Because
of their status as castrated males, rulers could use eunuchs as intermedi-
aries between public (male) and private (female) space (Patterson 1982,
318–19). Finally, an absolute ruler required the ultimate slave, and as
Kathryn M. Ringrose (2003, 7, 84, 202–11) has argued, the liminality, or
"in-betweenness," of the court eunuch made him the perfect slave.

The second group of eunuchs with which the audience of the book of
Acts would have been familiar was the *galli*, the self-castrated devotees of
the goddess Cybele. The distinctive characteristics of the cult of Cybele
developed in Phrygia in the seventh century B.C.E., and from there the
cult spread to the Greek world and ultimately to Rome (Roller 1999, 1–5).
According to Ovid, the self-castration of the *galli* was to be explained with
reference to the myth of Attis, a Phrygian youth who bound himself to the
goddess with a chaste love but then castrated himself after betraying her by
falling in love with a nymph (*Fast.* 4.215–46). The *galli* performed official
roles in the annual Roman festival of Cybele, and in ancient novels they
are also portrayed as mendicants who traveled throughout the Roman
East carrying a statue of the goddess and begging for money (Roller 1999,
319; Scholz 2001, 60–61).

The similarities between court eunuchs and the *galli* highlight two
constituent elements of ancient constructions of eunuchs. The first element is slavery. Court eunuchs had been subjected to involuntary castration as slaves; and while a *gallus* may have been freeborn, his voluntary
self-castration was described as producing a slave of Cybele (Scholz 2001,
107; Taylor 2000, 179–80). The second element is foreignness. The sources
of court eunuchs included foreign boys captured in war or sent to a ruler
as a tribute or a gift, and after castration was outlawed within the boundaries of the Roman Empire near the end of the first century C.E., it was
claimed that all eunuchs inside the empire were foreigners imported from
outside the empire (Taylor 2000, 141). In fact, this construction was so
strong that it persisted in the claim that Byzantine court eunuchs were

also all foreigners, even though it is clear that more and more of them were natives (Ringrose 2003, 10–11, 71–72; Tougher 2002b, 143–52). Likewise, no matter their actual origins, the *galli* were marked as foreign by the name of their group, their dress, and by the legal prohibition against the self-castration of Roman citizens (Borgeaud 2004, 65–66; Hales 2002, 90–93; Roller 1999, 228–34). Each of these constituent elements introduced ambiguities into the identities of eunuchs. One major difference between court eunuchs and the *galli* added to these ambiguities. The involuntary castration that produced court eunuchs was usually performed on prepubescent boys, while the voluntary self-castration of the *galli* typically occurred after puberty. Differences in the timing of castration resulted in differences in the physical and sexual characteristics of those castrated.

Eunuchs as Queering Figures

Eunuchs troubled the multiple discourses of gender, sexuality, social status, and race that produced ancient constructions of masculinity. In terms of gender, it was difficult even to identify a gender for eunuchs. Eunuchs castrated before puberty were variously gendered in ancient discourses as "effeminate males," "half-males," "girls," hybrids of male and female, and neither male nor female. The inability to stabilize the gender of such eunuchs troubled the boundaries between the categories of male and female. More than that, these eunuchs embodied the troubling proposition that the relatively simple procedure of castration could produce an irreversible loss of masculinity or even a loss of humanity, if recognition as human depends upon a stable gender identity. Eunuchs castrated after puberty were no less troubling. While they should have been excluded from social recognition as men by their lack of testicles, this lack was difficult to detect, and therefore they embodied the troubling possibility that one could be simultaneously identified as a man and as a eunuch.

In terms of sexuality, it might seem that eunuchs castrated before puberty could rather easily have been identified as "unmen" and hence as appropriate objects of sexual penetration. The intimacy of such eunuchs with women, however, raised the specter of the most troubling form of all passive sexual activity, cunnilingus, which amounted in Greco-Roman discourse to penetration by a woman (Parker 1997, 51–53). Eunuchs castrated after puberty were also troubling, because they had the capacity to penetrate the wives of adult male citizens without the risk of pregnancy (Kuefler 2001, 97–98). Since an adult male citizen who could not control his wife's sexuality risked his own identity as a man, a eunuch castrated after puberty had the frightening potential to unman a man by penetrating his wife.

Ancient constructions of masculinity depended on the naturalization of social status no less than on the naturalization of gender and sexuality. Aristotle naturalized the distinction between free and slave by claiming that some human beings are by nature rulers while others are by nature slaves (*Pol.* 1.1–2). Court eunuchs troubled this naturalized distinction. The sources of court eunuchs included freeborn boys who had been kidnapped, captured in war, or exposed to die. In terms of the discourse of natural slavery, were such freeborn, enslaved boys by nature rulers or by nature slaves? Court eunuchs also attained positions in which they exercised authority over freeborn persons. In such a situation, which one was the natural ruler, and which one was the natural slave? The *galli* also troubled this distinction. Was a freeborn *gallus* who chose to castrate himself in order to become a slave of the goddess by nature a ruler or by nature a slave?

Ancient constructions of masculinity also depended on a naturalized distinction between citizen/native and foreigner. This distinction functioned to racialize bodies—that is, it functioned to attribute to bodies unalterable and hereditary physical, mental, and moral characteristics based on shared factors usually related to environment and/or ancestry (see Isaac 2004). In terms of race, the identification of citizens/natives who were castrated as foreigners troubled this distinction, and such eunuchs embodied the troubling proposition that the relatively simple procedure of castration could produce the loss of one's citizenship or status as a native. Furthermore, in some ancient discourses, eunuchs as a group are called a γένος/*genus*, words that could function to racialize a particular group of bodies (Kamtekar 2002, 4–5). If castration could actually produce a "race," then how secure was the status as a citizen/native upon which one's claim to identification as a man depended?

Eunuchs thus have the potential to function as queering figures. I do not mean by this that eunuchs ought to be read as the ancient antecedents of people identified with a contemporary identity category, such as "gay," "transgender," or "queer," nor do I mean that ancient eunuchs had some sort of "queer consciousness." Rather, I am arguing that ancient discourses produced a social construction of eunuchs that had the potential to deconstruct and to denaturalize ancient constructions of masculinity. Wherever a eunuch is present as a figure in an ancient text, therefore, there is the potential for that eunuch to function rhetorically in ways that queer ancient constructions of masculinity. Such queering opens up space for contesting all identity categories, ancient and modern, in order that "transgressive" bodies may be recognized as fully human.

A Story of Ambiguities

The story of the Ethiopian eunuch in Acts 8:26–40 is marked by multiple ambiguities. At the beginning of the story (8:26), an angel of the Lord commands Philip to get up and to go κατὰ μεσημβρίαν, an ambiguous expression that can have a spatial meaning ("toward the south") or a temporal meaning ("at noon"). Rather than attempting to resolve this ambiguity, I read this expression as functioning rhetorically to make both the spatial and the temporal setting of the story ambiguous, or liminal, an appropriate space for a eunuch. Within the body of the story (8:30–35), Philip hears the eunuch reading Isa 53:7–8, a passage about a figure who is denied justice in his humiliation. It is the very ambiguity of this figure's identity that makes it possible for Philip to identify this figure with Jesus (Johnson 1992, 157). F. Scott Spencer (1997, 93–94) has suggested that this ambiguity might also make it possible for the eunuch to identify himself with this figure. Finally, at the end of the story (8:39), the spirit of the Lord has "snatched away" Philip, an action described by the verb ἁρπάζω. The use of this verb to describe an action of the Spirit is unique in the Bible, and it is also ambiguous, as the verb usually has negative connotations in both the book of Acts and the Septuagint (see, e.g., Pss 7:2; 10:9; 22:13; 50:22; 104:21; Ezek 18:7, 12, 16, 18; 19:3, 6; 22:25, 27; Acts 23:10).

Into the midst of these ambiguities enters a character identified as ἀνὴρ Αἰθίοψ εὐνοῦχος δυνάστης Κανδάκης βασιλίσσης Αἰθιόπων, ὃς ἦν ἐπὶ πάσης τῆς γάζης αὐτῆς. The juxtaposition of ἀνήρ and Αἰθίοψ immediately introduces ambiguity. Is Αἰθίοψ to be read as an adjective, thus producing one identification, "an Ethiopian," or is it to be read as a noun, thus producing two different identifications, "a man" *and* "an Ethiopian"? The juxtaposition of εὐνοῦχος and ἀνήρ introduces into the story the troubling of the boundaries between male and female. The juxtaposition of εὐνοῦχος and δυνάστης introduces into the story the troubling of the boundaries between men and unmen and the boundaries between free and slave. The juxtaposition of εὐνοῦχος and Αἰθίοψ introduces into the story the troubling of the boundaries between citizen/native and foreigner. The very presence of the eunuch in the story has the potential to subvert the norms upon which ancient constructions of identity depended. What makes this subversion so effective is that it is impossible to distinguish any of the eunuch's identities as "natural" or "performed." Is this a eunuch performing a man, or is this a man performing a eunuch? Is this a slave performing a powerful official, or is this a powerful official performing a slave? The eunuch *performs* multiple identities, but it is impossible to conclude that the eunuch *is* or *is not* any one of them.

The climax of the story brings with it yet more ambiguity. In 8:36, the eunuch says to Philip, "Behold, water; what is preventing me from being baptized?" The audience knows that there is much to prevent the eunuch from being baptized. He transgresses divinely sanctioned boundaries and threatens masculinity itself. Furthermore, his religious identity is indeterminable. How can one possibly determine the religious identity of a man who is a eunuch, an Ethiopian who is a foreigner, and a powerful official who is a slave? There is no way to determine his natal origin, nor is it possible to determine the status of his genitals and their meaning for Jewish identity. The crisis is resolved, however, in the ambiguous sentence in 8:38: "And he commanded the chariot to stop, and both went down into the water, both Philip and the eunuch, and he baptized him." The narrative logic certainly supports the reading that Philip baptized the eunuch. The ambiguity of the sentence construction, however, does allow a reader to imagine a reversal of subject and object. In a sense, the baptism represents Philip's conversion as much as it does the eunuch's.

QUEERING THE BOOK OF ACTS

It is a commonplace of interpretation of the book of Acts that Acts 1:8 functions as a programmatic statement for the book as a whole: "But you will receive power when the Holy Spirit has come upon you, and you will be my witnesses in Jerusalem and in all Judea and in Samaria and as far as the end of the earth." To conclude that this is *the* programmatic statement for the book of Acts, however, is to miss an important rhetorical link between Acts and the author's first volume, the Gospel of Luke. In each volume, the author articulates a programmatic statement of the ministry central to the volume in the form of a quotation from the Hebrew Bible. In Luke 4:18–19, the author places on the lips of Jesus a quotation from Isa 61:1; 58:6; and 61:2, and in Acts 2:17–21, the author places on the lips of Peter a quotation from Joel 3:1–5.

In light of this quotation from Joel 3:1–5, Acts can be read as the story of the expansion of a small community of Jewish Jesus-followers into a community in which the Spirit will be poured out upon *all* flesh (Acts 2:17), and *everyone* who calls on the name of the Lord will be saved (2:21). The story of the Ethiopian eunuch is rhetorically marked as an important turning point in the story of the book of Acts as a whole. The structure of the Ethiopian eunuch's story includes an angel speaking at the beginning of the story (8:26), the Spirit speaking in the middle of the story (8:29), and the Spirit acting at the end of the story (8:39). There is only one other story in the book of Acts with a similar shape, and that is the story of Peter and Cornelius (Acts 10:1–11:18). The relationship between the two stories has been a matter of great debate among scholars.

Reading the Ethiopian eunuch as a queering figure offers a new way to understand the relationship between the story of the eunuch and the story of Cornelius. The eunuch's story, with it queering of identities, settles the question of the expansion of the community's baptismal ministry. Once the eunuch has been baptized, how can Cornelius or anyone else be denied baptism? Since in 8:39 the eunuch goes on his way rejoicing, however, his story does not resolve the question of the implications of the expansion of the community's baptismal ministry for the life of the community as a whole. As Philip F. Esler (1987, 93–97) has argued, the central issue of the story of Cornelius, then, becomes the expansion of the community's table fellowship. The story of the Ethiopian eunuch sets in motion, and the story of Cornelius continues to develop, a trajectory that culminates in the decision of the leaders who meet in Jerusalem in Acts 15 and in the mission of Paul in the remainder of the book of Acts.

The genre and purpose(s) of the book of Acts have also been matters of great debate among scholars. I find it most productive to approach the book of Acts as a "story of origins," a term that I see not as a fixed genre but rather as a queering designation that deconstructs the binary oppositions of fact/fiction and past/present. The book of Acts is a work that draws on a variety of genres in order to tell a story of the past that has particular rhetorical functions in its audience's present. As Christopher R. Matthews (2004, 174) has argued, the goal of the author of Acts was "to produce an account of Christian origins that would show how those beginnings clarified and confirmed the social and cultural situation of Christians in [the author's] time."

Reading the Ethiopian eunuch as a queering figure has the potential to queer the book of Acts as a story of origins. First, such a reading takes a story

that has been identified as marginal to the book and demonstrates that it is
rhetorically productive to read it as central to the book. F. F. Bruce (1989,
378), for example, has argued that "this episode is isolated in the narrative
of Acts in the sense that it is unconnected with anything that precedes or
follows it. It is not woven into the fabric of the on-going narrative; if it were
removed, there would be nothing to indicate that anything of the kind had
ever stood there (Acts 8:26–40)." Reading the story in terms of the rhetorical
function of queering demonstrates that it plays a pivotal role in the fulfillment of the early Christian community's mission to expand its ministry.

Second, such a reading of the eunuch's story queers the binary opposition between the subjects and objects of conversion in this story of origins.
The book of Acts is not only the story of how a small community converted multitudes to faith in Jesus, but it is also simultaneously the story
of how that community itself was converted by its own mission. The early
Christians themselves had to be converted to the view that baptism and
table fellowship in Christ do not depend on a person's identity—Jew or
Gentile, male or female, man or unman, penetrator or penetrated, free or
slave, citizen/native or foreigner. In fact, they had to be converted to the
necessity of deconstructing and denaturalizing the very demand that each
and every body conform to identity categories, in order that all bodies
might matter.

Finally, such a reading of the eunuch's story queers the binary opposition between "inside" and "outside" in the interpretation of the book of
Acts. I suspect that some will criticize the application of "queering" to
biblical interpretation on the grounds that it is a strategy imported from
outside the text. I argue, however, that the application of queering strategies developed *outside* the text enables a reader to see queering strategies already inscribed *inside* the text. The author of Acts certainly did not
use the word "queering," but reading the story of the Ethiopian eunuch
through the lens of queer theory demonstrates the integral role queering
played in one early Christian discourse. Furthermore, while the author of
Acts may have been interested primarily, or even exclusively, in queering
religious identity (Jew/Gentile), he has bequeathed to subsequent readers
a story that has the potential to queer multiple identity categories.

CONCLUSION

The queering of identities played an important role in early Christian discourse. This insight needs to be applied to the study of other early Chris-

tian texts. Are there other "queering figures" in early Christian literature? Might it be productive to read other character groups, such as the "God-fearers," or other individual characters, such as Philip the "deacon" who acts more like an "apostle," as queering figures? This insight also needs to be applied to contemporary Christian discourses. In particular, I hope that members of Christian communities will consider the implications of the role of queering in early Christian discourse for the lives of contemporary persons who could be identified as flesh-and-blood queering figures, including lesbian, gay, bisexual, and transgendered persons. Are Christian communities today in need of ongoing conversion to a ministry of queering, in order that the Spirit might be poured out upon *all* flesh and *everyone* might be saved?

WORKS CONSULTED

Aristotle. 1972. *Politics.* Translated by H. Rackham. LCL. Cambridge: Harvard University Press.

Borgeaud, Philippe. 2004. *Mother of the Gods: From Cybele to the Virgin Mary.* Translated by Lysa Hochroth. Baltimore, Md.: Johns Hopkins University Press.

Boyarin, Daniel. 1995. Are There Any Jews in "The History of Sexuality"? *Journal of the History of Sexuality* 5:333–55.

Bruce, F. F. 1989. Philip and the Ethiopian. *JSS* 24:377–86.

Bullough, Vern L. 2002. Eunuchs in History and Society. Pages 1–17 in Tougher 2002a.

Butler, Judith. 2004. *Undoing Gender.* New York: Routledge.

Cohen, David. 1991. *Law, Sexuality, and Society: The Enforcement of Morals in Classical Athens.* New York: Cambridge University Press.

Edwards, Catharine. 1993. *The Politics of Immorality in Ancient Rome.* New York: Cambridge University Press.

Esler, Philip F. 1987. *Community and Gospel in Luke-Acts: The Social and Political Motivations of Lucan Theology.* New York: Cambridge University Press.

Gleason, Maud W. 1995. *Making Men: Sophists and Self-Presentation in Ancient Rome.* Princeton: Princeton University Press.

Hales, Shelley. 2002. Looking for Eunuchs: The *Galli* and Attis in Roman Art. Pages 87–102 in Tougher 2002a.

Halperin, David M. 2002. *How to Do the History of Homosexuality.* Chicago: University of Chicago Press.

Isaac, Benjamin. 2004. *The Invention of Racism in Classical Antiquity*. Princeton: Princeton University Press.

Jagose, Annamarie. 1996. *Queer Theory: An Introduction*. New York: New York University Press.

Johnson, Luke Timothy. 1992. *The Acts of the Apostles*. SP 5. Collegeville, Minn.: Liturgical Press.

Kamtekar, Rachana. 2002. Distinction without a Difference? Race and *Genos* in Plato. Pages 1–13 in *Philosophers on Race: Critical Essays*. Edited by Julie K. Ward and Tommy L. Lott. Malden, Mass.: Blackwell.

Kuefler, Mathew. 2001. *The Manly Eunuch: Masculinity, Gender Ambiguity, and Christian Ideology in Late Antiquity*. Chicago: The University of Chicago Press.

Llewellyn-Jones, Lloyd. 2002. Eunuchs and the Royal Harem in Achaemenid Persia (559–331 B.C.). Pages 19–49 in Tougher 2002a.

Matthews, Christopher R. 2004. Acts and the History of the Earliest Jerusalem Church. Pages 159–75 in *Redescribing Christian Origins*. Edited by Ron Cameron and Merrill P. Miller. Atlanta: Society of Biblical Literature.

Moore, Stephen D. 2001. *God's Beauty Parlor: And Other Queer Spaces in and around the Bible*. Stanford: Stanford University Press.

Ovid. 1951. *Fasti*. Translated by James George Frazer. LCL. Cambridge: Harvard University Press.

Parker, Holt N. 1997. The Teratogenic Grid. Pages 47–65 in *Roman Sexualities*. Edited by Judith P. Hallett and Marilyn B. Skinner. Princeton: Princeton University Press.

Patterson, Orlando. 1982. *Slavery and Social Death: A Comparative Study*. Cambridge: Harvard University Press.

Plautus. 1917. *Curculio*. Translated by Paul Nixon. LCL. Cambridge: Harvard University Press.

Ringrose, Kathryn M. 2003. *The Perfect Servant: Eunuchs and the Social Construction of Gender in Byzantium*. Chicago: University of Chicago Press.

Roller, Lynn E. 1999. *In Search of God the Mother: The Cult of Anatolian Cybele*. Berkeley: University of California Press.

Schneider, Johannes. 1964. εὐνοῦχος, εὐνουχίζω. *TDNT* 2:765–68.

Scholz, Piotr O. 2001. *Eunuchs and Castrati: A Cultural History*. Translated by John A. Broadwin and Shelley L. Frisch. Princeton: Markus Wiener.

Spencer, F. Scott. 1997. *Acts*. Sheffield: Sheffield Academic Press.

Tadmor, Hayim. 2002. The Role of the Chief Eunuch and the Place of Eunuchs in the Assyrian Empire. Pages 603–11 in vol. 2 of *Sex and Gender in the Ancient Near East: Proceedings of the 47th Recontre Assyriologique Internationale, Helsinki, July 2–6, 2001*. Edited by S. Parpola and R. M. Whiting. 2 vols. Helsinki: Neo-Assyrian Text Corpus Project.

Taylor, Gary. 2000. *Castration: An Abbreviated History of Western Manhood*. New York: Routledge.

Tougher, Shaun, ed. 2002a. *Eunuchs in Antiquity and Beyond*. London: Duckworth; Swansea: Classical Press of Wales.

———. 2002b. In or Out? Origins of Court Eunuchs. Pages 143–59 in Tougher 2002a.

Walters, Jonathan. 1993. "No More than a Boy": The Shifting Construction of Masculinity from Ancient Greece to the Middle Ages. *Gender and History* 5:20–33.

Williams, Craig A. 1999. *Roman Homosexuality: Ideologies of Masculinity in Classical Antiquity*. New York: Oxford University Press.

Xenophon. 1914. *Cyropaedia*. Translated by Walter Miller. LCL. New York: Macmillan.

Bodies *Del Otro Lado* Finding Life and Hope in the Borderland: Gloria Anzaldúa, the Ethiopian Eunuch of Acts 8:26–40, *y Yo*

Manuel Villalobos

"To survive the Borderlands you must live *sin fronteras* be a crossroads."
(Anzaldúa 2007, 217)

"Under the ground it doesn't matter which side of the border you're in."
(Anzaldúa 2007, 198)

In May 2004, Gloria Anzaldúa crossed over to the regions of the spirits, where *Coatlicue-Cihuacoatl-Tlazolteotl-Tonantzin-Coatlalopeuh-Guadalupe*, her favorite goddess, reigns. Her writings have become sacred for all of us who struggle to maneuver daily in various "borderlands," living queer, living undocumented, living in poverty, living in the martyrized South, living in all kinds of ambiguity, and finally, living as a *Mexicano "del otro lado."* Gloria Anzaldúa's words, metaphors, myths, and theory have forged a new gospel that transcends borders, announcing liberation for all the bodies that had been marked by sexism, racism, poverty, machismo, xenophobia, normalization, and homophobia.[1] Unfortunately, Anzaldúa's concepts of *Nepantla, Mundo Zurdo, mestizo/a, la facultad*, and the borderland have not yet crossed over into the biblical field.[2] In this essay, I attempt

---

1. See all the secondary bibliography that has been compiled by AnaLouise Keating in the third edition of Anzaldúa 2007, 247–55.

2. Some Latino/a theologians make brief reference here and there to Gloria Anzaldúa's work. Mayra Rivera's appropriation of Anzaldúa's concept of *los atrevesados* ("the crossed") has yielded a prophetic interpretation of the figure of Sophia (2006). Professor of English Alma Rosa Alvarez had opened a fruitful dialogue with some Chicano/a writers who had been marginalized due to their gender, politics, and

to cross the bridge in order to put into dialogue three bodies—Anzaldúa's body, the eunuch body of Acts 8:26–40, and my own body—and see how these bodies find life and hope in the borderland. These bodies belong to different cultures and epochs and have different *cruces*/crosses to bear. But these bodies who live in the borderland also remind us that a new way of being human might be possible when we cross borders, challenge institutions, and follow the Spirit who breathes new life into us.

1. Crossing Borders with Anzaldúa

Anzaldúa begins the preface to *Borderlands/La Frontera: The New Mestiza* with the following explanation of borderlands:

> The actual physical borderland that I'm dealing with in this book is the Texas–U.S. Southwest/Mexican border. The psychological borderlands, the sexual borderlands and the spiritual borderlands, are not particular to the Southwest. In fact, the Borderlands are physically present wherever two or more cultures edge each other, where people of different races occupy the same territory, where under, lower, middle and upper classes touch, where the space between two individuals shrinks with intimacy. (2007, preface to the 1st ed.)

These complex realities that Anzaldúa vividly describes made present a new territory, a new intellectual locale, a new spiritual space, a new psychic and psychological terrain (Pérez 2005, 3). As we might guess, borderlands are more than a geographical place on this side or that side of the contested dividing line. In the borderlands, all kinds of division, separation, and segregation occur at all levels. For as contradictory as this might appear, where there is a border, there is also a bridge that connects the outsider "us," the ones who "steal jobs," from the insider "US" who provide the "opportunities." No one denies that tremendous abyss that exists on both sides of the border. However, despite the billions and billions of dollars that Homeland Security has spent on building the border fence, Anzaldúa has debunked the notion that "we are safer than ever" and that our "borders are secure," as the Bush administration wished us to believe.

---

sexual orientation and liberation theology. She dedicated a full chapter to Anzaldúa's notion of the border. She "argues that Anzaldúa's establishment of this subject can be interpreted as a liberation theology project because it demonstrates a recuperation of history, sexuality and ultimately spirituality" (2007, 22). See also, Bedford 2004, 2005.

In the book *This Bridge Called My Back*, which she co-edited, Anzaldúa made visible the literature of women of color here in the United States. It is a book that celebrates Anzaldúa's crossing but also ours: "With *This Bridge* ... we have begun to come out of the shadows; we have begun to break with routines and oppressive customs and to discard taboos; we have commenced to carry with pride the task of thawing hearts and changing consciousness" (Anzaldúa 1983, v). In this historical crossing, together with her sisters of color, she challenges all oppressive institutions that have marginalized and disenfranchised women, that have kept "deviant" bodies well segregated, and that have arbitrarily claimed and marked out their territory.

Anzaldúa argues: "The U.S.–Mexican border *es una herida abierta* where the Third World grates against the first and bleeds" (Anzaldúa 2007, 25). This open wound that Anzaldúa pointed out would become her strength/weakness, dream/nightmare, reality/utopia, hope/despair, bridge/void, and love/hate. However, with this "open wound" Anzaldúa has marked the road to living without borders, where all kinds of bodies cross, where ideas transmigrate, and where we hope for a new way of being human. Her vision of new societal paradigms and a culture freed of prejudices, injustices, and violence is possible when each person accepts his or her own identity, history, and future. When all these people who have been shamed by the imperial system feel pride in their ancestry, know who they are and from where they have come, and can embrace the uncertainty of the future, then we can attend to Anzaldúa's invitation of celebrating *el día de la Raza*. "Estamos viviendo en la noche de la *Raza*, un tiempo cuando el trabajo se hace a lo quieto, en lo oscuro. El día cuando aceptamos tal y como somos y para donde vamos y porque—ese día será el día de la *Raza* ..." ("We are living in the Night of the *Raza*, a time when the work is being done quietly, in the shadows. The day when we accept who we are, as we are, and where we are going and why—that day would be the Day of the *Raza*" [109]).[3]

---

3. Translation is my own. One of the "problems" that scholars find with Anzaldúa's writing is the fact that she "crossed" not just borders but also languages. This "unnatural" practice of her writing has spawned a new way of communicating. One of the lasting effects of poststructuralism is our self-conscious use of language. Foucault's deconstruction of power-laden discourses, Derrida's insistence that language composes our consciousness itself, and Lacan's assertion that psychological development is predicated upon entrance into the "symbolic order" of language all plant identity,

The Day of *la Raza* is not a utopia or dream, it is real and possible. Yet to attain that goal, all those bodies that have been neglected need to start acting. There is no time for playing the victim. The journey of liberation has started, and we must dare to cross the mythological bridge that separates "us" from "them." "Basta de gritar contra el viento—toda palabra es ruido si no está acompañada de acción (*enough of shouting against the wind—all words are noise if not accompanied with action*). Dejemos de hablar hasta que hagamos la palabra luminosa y activa (*let's not talk, let's say nothing until we've made the word luminous and active*) … No nos podemos quedar paradas con los brazos cruzados en medio del puente (*we can't afford to stop in the middle of the bridge with arms crossed*)" (Anzaldúa 1983, iv). The new humanity must be forged in the fight of crossing many bridges as often as might be needed in order to recover our identity. Once we dare to march and cross the bridge we will find that in the borderland all bodies are connected and that we have a responsibility to each other not just for survival but as a way to envision a livable life. By crossing the bridge we can recover our *dignidad* and consciousness of being the children of the *Raza Cósmica*.[4]

1.1. *La Conciencia de la Mestiza*

One of the advantages of bodies that cross borders is their ability to mutate and be transformed in response to the reality in which they find them-

---

language, and power firmly on even ground (Ramsdell 2004, 166). Now we know that language forms ideas, concepts, and identity, and of course identity is a political matter. Anzaldúa become aware of the power of her writings. In her earliest essays (Anzaldúa 1983) she provides us with a translation, but later she decided to leave her writings untranslated. Claire Joysmith notices that Anzaldúa's magnum opus *Borderlands/La Frontera* remains untranslated into Spanish after twenty years, making it linguistically inaccessible to many: "How to translate it, of course, is a true challenge, as Gloria agreed years ago when we talked about it" (Anzaldúa 2007, introduction to the 3rd ed.). I provided the translation in order to make the essay more readable and digestible, hoping that Anzaldúa might forgive me for attempting to tame her "tongues of fire."

4. The idea of the *Raza Cósmica* belongs to the Mexican philosopher and educator José Vasconcelos (1966). He believes that humanity is moving toward the formation of the "fifth race," a kind of agglomeration of all the races in the world. In the *Raza Cósmica* there is no place for a superior race versus inferior race. All races are equal and must work in a harmonious way in order to form the new civilization. The influence of Vasconcelos in the works of Anzaldúa is obvious in her thoughts regarding the "mixture of all races" and in the "consciousness of the mestiza."

selves. This chameleonic ability has been our best ally to cope with the rigid established norm that labels and marks who is in and who is out. However, it is not enough merely to survive. We must resist the temptation of being assimilated by the system. We must embrace Anzaldúa's invitation to acquire a new consciousness where ambivalence is a *sine qua non* of being human. Living in the border territory could mean death for some who are not accustomed to dealing with "ambiguity" or for some who want to keep their boundaries well delineated at all times. On the other hand, the ambiguity of the *frontera* can be a sign of hope for those who dare to use their creativity in order to survive. Anzaldúa has promulgated that it is imperative to assimilate the in-between spaces the borderland offers us. "Border people are those in an in-between state, able to have two or three points of view because we've been in all these other spaces, worlds, and cultures" (Anzaldúa 1993, 21). It is in this complex reality that Anzaldúa gave voice to what it means to be a mixture, a hybrid, a real *mestiza*. Not all people can bear the weight of moving between worlds and cultures. Being on the periphery or margin is a devious behavior, yet those *mestizas/os* who manage to do it are rewarded with a new consciousness.

The consciousness of the *mestiza* is one of ambivalence and contradiction, ready to embrace changes and create new paradigms of family and society. The *mestiza* by her very nature is willing to travel into the unknown, allowing mystery to be revealed in each step. The power frequently inherent in religion has often diminished the *mestiza's* consciousness, for which reason she must constantly engage in a battle to circumvent or get rid of the oppressive systems that denied her humanity. In the process of recovering her consciousness, the *mestiza* must make some priorities in her life. "Despojando, desgranando, quitando paja" ("Rooting out, threshing, winnowing" [Anzaldúa 2007, 104; translation is my own]). The *mestiza* must "travel light" in order to have "room" for a new wisdom that might spring up on the side of the road quite unexpectedly. The *mestiza* does not romanticize the magical and mythical aspect of the borderland. Anzaldúa knows that the *mestiza's* consciousness has been contaminated by machismo, sexism, homophobia, and all kinds of oppression. Here the identity of the *mestiza* is on trial. She must prove her courage by judging her own culture. "This step is a conscious rupture with all oppressive traditions of culture and religion. She communicates that rupture, documents the struggle" (104). In the borderland territory, purification must happen at all levels. The uncertainty of walking among the wild beasts without roads or maps provides a magnificent opportunity for the *mestiza* to recycle her history and her story, to bring something new from the old. "She reinterprets history and, using new symbols, she shapes new myths. She adopts new perspectives toward the darkskinned, women and queers" (104). In the *mestiza's* borderland all persons are welcomed, all cultures are celebrated, and all languages are worthy.

Once that *mestiza* has recovered her consciousness, she becomes "abnormal," "dubious," "out of place," and "out of time." She is a sign of contradiction not only for herself but also for the society. "Cradled in one culture, sandwiched between two cultures, straddling all three cultures and their value systems, *la mestiza* undergoes a struggle of flesh, a struggle of borders, an inner war" (Anzaldúa 2007, 100). The *mestiza's* consciousness destabilizes the entire society. She has the power to turn the world upside down, but at the same time she has the power to construct something new, to give new meaning to her life, to envision new realities. "Deconstruct, construct. She becomes a *nahual*, able to transform herself into a tree, a coyote, and into another person" (105). Surprisingly and ironically the *mestiza* has found in her continuous transformation and mutation the strength for her daily battles.

With her new consciousness the *mestiza* acquires the ability to interpret and recreate her ancestor's myths. She celebrates her neglected and "superstitious" religion with pride. With her new consciousness the *mestiza* blessed the *Nepantla*[5] stage that announces to us that there is nothing wrong with being "in the middle," neither *here* nor *there*. *Nepantla*

---

5. *Nepantla* is a Nahuatl word meaning "place in the middle." The mythological aspect of *Nepantla* was described first by one of the earliest Dominican friars, Diego Dúran, to describe the "saddest truth" that the Indians were never completely assimilated into the Christian religion. Dúran provides the following anecdote: "Once I questioned an Indian regarding certain things. In particular I asked him why he had gone about begging, spending bad nights and worse days, and why, after having gathered so much money with such trouble, he offered a fiesta, invited the entire town, and spent everything. Thus I reprehended him for the foolish thing he had done, and he answered, 'Father, do not be astonished; we are still *Nepantla*.' Although I understood what that metaphorical word means, that is to say, 'in the middle,' I insisted that he tell me which 'in the middle' he referred to. The native told me that, since the people were not yet well rooted in the Faith, I should not marvel at the fact that they were neither fish nor fowl; they were governed by neither one religion nor the other. Or, better said, they believed in God and also followed their ancient heathen rites and customs. And this is what the Indian meant in his despicable excuse when he stated that the people still were 'in the middle' and were 'neither fish nor fowl'" (1971, 410–11).

and the borderland are two realities that convey conflict and struggle for people who are compulsive about "order," "demarcation," and separation. But for all the bodies who have been marked by the *mestiza's* consciousness, *Nepantla* becomes the site of transformation, the place where different perspectives come into conflict and where one questions the basic ideas, tenets, and identities one has inherited through one's family, one's education, and one's different cultures. *Nepantla* is the zone where one struggles to find equilibrium between the outer expression of change and one's inner relationship to it (Anzaldúa 2002, 548–49). People who become *nepantlera/o* have the ability to turn the chaos into order, the right into the left. In *Nepantla* anything can happen—even the absurdity of dreaming with a *Mundo Zurdo* (a left-handed world).

1.2. ANZALDÚA'S *MUNDO ZURDO*

Anzaldúa's crossing and her new consciousness demonstrates that boundaries are malleable places, where bodies can cross, people might get confused, and some bodies might collapse from the uncertainty of living in ambiguity. But for other bodies, being in *Nepantla* could be a blessing and liberation. Of course not all people would leave their secure and harmonious lives to enter into the absurdity of Anzaldúa's *Mundo Zurdo*. Even people who are already in the *marcha* toward new realities might be persuaded by pessimistic phrases like "Who can compare with the beast or who can fight against it?" (Rev 13:4b). We must resist the beast of passivity. For if we kill our imagination, visions, dreams, and myths, we sacrifice our own freedom. Instead, in the uncertainty of the future we can learn to recognize the opportunity to welcome Anzaldúa's *Mundo Zurdo*.

What exactly does Anzaldúa mean by *Mundo Zurdo*? She recognizes that even she does not really know. "I am confused as to how to accomplish this," she writes (Anzaldúa 1983, 208). However, el *Mundo Derecho*[6] is not an option for the millions of "nobodies" who have been deprived of living the reality of the dream because of our race, gender, economic situation, or religious beliefs. The inhabitants of Anzaldúa's *Mundo Zurdo* are

---

6. She does not talk about el *Mundo Derecho* (the straight world). I do not necessarily understand el *Mundo Zurdo* as being in opposition to el *Mundo Derecho*. El *Mundo Zurdo* is a place in the "middle" where all bodies that have been cast out live and find meaning for their lives.

the prohibited and the forbidden. "*Los atrevesados*[7] live here: the squint-eyed, the perverse, the queer, the troublesome, the mongrel, the mulatto, the half-breed, the half dead; in short, those who cross over, pass over, or go through the confines of the 'normal'" (Anzaldúa 2007, 25). Anzaldúa's *Mundo Zurdo* is a cry for justice for all: "I can't discount the fact of the thousands that go to bed hungry every night: The thousands that do numbing shitwork eight hours a day each day of their lives, the thousands that everyday get beaten and killed, the millions of women who have been burned at the stake, the millions who have been raped. Where is the justice to this?" (Anzaldúa 1983, 208). Indeed, Anzaldúa has touched the *punctum dolens* of our incurable wound.

Anzaldúa's *Mundo Zurdo* is a prophetic message for all those bodies that are suspended in the in-betweenness of life, all those whose humanity has been denied and whose bodies have been labeled second rate. But, the *Mundo Zurdo* is also a place where visions and dreams spring forth and where solidarity among the members is rooted. *El Mundo Zurdo* is "a vision place where people from diverse backgrounds with diverse needs and concerns co-exist and work together to bring revolutionary changes" (Keating 2002, 520). Furthermore, Anzaldúa's *Mundo Zurdo* is a site of transformation and liberation for all those bodies who are welcome nowhere and belong nowhere: "We are the queer groups, the people that don't belong anywhere, not in the dominant world nor completely within our own respective cultures" (Anzaldúa 1983, 209). In the section where Anzaldúa deals with her *Mundo Zurdo*, she points out in a footnote, "This section consists of notes 'Toward a Construction of *El Mundo Zurdo*,' an essay in progress" (208). I strongly believe that *el Mundo Zurdo* will never be complete. Using our allegorical imagination, we can compare Jesus' passion for the kingdom of God with Anzaldúa's *Mundo Zurdo* as two realities that have been inaugurated but that are still in progress. In order to see how Anzaldúa's *Mundo Zurdo* might be compatible with Jesus' kingdom of God, let us turn our attention to Acts 8:26–40.

---

7. In Spanish the word *atrevesado/a* has a variety of meanings. We used it for describing a thing that is collocated in a transversal way. This word is use to describe a person with a crossed or wandering eyes. Moreover, this word is used in some parts as synonym of *mestizo/a*. See Sánchez 2001. In Mexico among the gays this word is often used for describing someone who had been penetrated. It seems that Anzaldúa is playing with the multiple meanings of the word.

2. Crossing Borders with the Ethiopian Eunuch

The encounter between Philip and the Ethiopian eunuch recorded in Acts 8:26–40 reflects the struggles of the Christian community to minister to and to incorporate the Gentiles. The encounter, conversion, baptism, and total incorporation of the Ethiopian eunuch into the household of God implies a transgression of boundaries. The Ethiopian eunuch and Philip seem to be the main characters. However, if we look closely at the text, we find that this story really is more of a description of the action of the Holy Spirit who is transgressing and redefining borders. As of matter of fact, it is the Spirit who transforms the border, allowing all the bodies that inhabit *el Mundo Zurdo* to cross freely to God's salvation. In Acts 8:26–40, the spirit of God or the angel of God is behaving in a very Anzaldúan way. We can observe that in Acts 8:26–40 the border is not yet "fixed" but rather is movable. As of matter of fact, the border moves from the center to the periphery (from Israel to the unknown desert), from North to South (from Jerusalem to Gaza), from the pure male (Philip) to the deviant body (eunuch), from exclusivity to inclusivity. All those bodies are in constant movement, crossing and transgressing all kinds of borders. Philip crosses to the South, the Ethiopian eunuch crosses to the North, the Sprit crosses here and there. And these salvific moments are happening in *Nepantla*. What do I mean when I say that the Spirit is behaving in a very Anzaldúan way? Let us examine carefully the crossing of the Ethiopian eunuch.

Anzaldúa reminds us that most societies try to get rid of their deviants. Most cultures have burned and beaten their homosexuals and others who deviate from the sexual norm (Anzaldúa 2007, 40). In the case of our Ethiopian eunuch, the disgust that first-century people had toward his mutilated body would not be an exception. His body was neither real nor intelligible, his anomalous genitalia confined him at *el Mundo Zurdo*. Beyond this appearance of a eunuch in Acts, the only other time one appears in the New Testament is in Matt 19:12. In both cases, as I have argued elsewhere, the figure of the eunuch challenges the way that Israel understood the notion of masculinity, gender, and the body (Villalobos 2009). Israel labeled and classified mutilated bodies in the same category as the lame, blind, deaf, and all those bodies that had any skin problem. Perceived as unclean and incomplete, these bodies often were separated from the assembly and from the altar of God (Deut 23:2). We find this marginalization of eunuchs not only in the Bible but also in Josephus (*Ant.* 4.290–291) and Philo (*Spec.* 1.324–325), both of whom vigorously advocated for total separation from the community of those no-bodies or eunuchs who, the texts claims, were not only "effeminate" in their bodies but also in their souls. In the Talmud eunuchs are often ridiculed (b. Sanh. 152a), and they are crudely and pejoratively described as having no beard, smooth skin, and lanky hair (b. Yebam. 80b). These slanderous accusations against the eunuchs convey a single intention: the eunuchs are not "real men."

Why such hostility on the part of Israel toward the "body" of the eunuch? How did the eunuch's body become unreal? Israel's aggression toward the mutilated body of the eunuch was based in their understanding of the wholeness/holiness of the body. For Israel, a real man's body must include a penis. Only those men with healthy, functioning penises are real bodies (Berquist 2002, 36). "The possession of a penis and testicles was the *sine qua non* of morality and virtue. Those who did not possess them 'naturally' suffered from moral weakness and were incapable of 'virtuous' behavior" (Hester 2005, 19). Therefore the eunuch, due to his mutilation and castration, became unreal, invisible, cut off from the community and from the temple. So the story of the eunuch in Acts 8:26–40 depicts God turning upside down the entire household and challenging the new community to live without borders, embracing the *other* who lives in the South as a part of God's re-creation

2.1. The Border Is Transformed! "Neither the North Nor the South, but *Nepantla*!"

The notion of the "South" existed in our mythical imagination as being inferior in all aspects compared to the North, which symbolizes the superior and wealthier of the nations. With the Ethiopian eunuch, Luke inaugurates the first story of an individual's conversion that happened in *Nepantla*. This change of direction toward the south has the guarantee of God's presence. "An angel of the Lord" instructs Philip to go toward the south, to the road that goes down from Jerusalem to Gaza (Acts 8:26). In this crossing the eunuch can be seen as the first *mestizo* to destabilize the binary category of being neither from the North nor from the South. The eunuch is a *nepantlero* living in between two worlds. The Anzaldúan Spirit has empowered the *mestizo* eunuch with ambiguity; such a one is a perpetual outcast from his body, household, religion, and country. At the same time, this Anzaldúan Holy Spirit has the power to incorporate the *mestizo* eunuch in a new culture. This new creation in which the ambiguous body of the eunuch lives starts from the borderland and insignificant areas of the South, far away from the powerful institutions that are located in the North. However, the full incorporation of the Ethiopian eunuch happened neither in the South nor in the North, but in the middle of the road.

Jerusalem, and in particular the temple, is extremely important for Luke's notion of salvation and mission (see Chance 1988). But the temple and Jerusalem as a "holy city" and source of salvation, in this particular episode, have failed God's purpose of mission. In Acts 1:8 Jesus has promised the community that the power of the Holy Spirit will come upon them and has said that the disciples must be Jesus' witness throughout Judea and Samaria and ἕως ἐσχάτου τῆς γῆς ("to the ends of the earth"). The time has been fulfilled; God's saving act has started now. The Spirit "illegally" is transgressing and crossing borders. Neither the North (Jerusalem and the temple) nor the unknown South represents the sole locus of God's salvation for humankind any more. The Holy Spirit has taken very seriously Anzaldúa's invitation to meet her halfway (Anzaldúa 2007, preface to the 1st ed.) in order to incorporate the Ethiopian eunuch, who is crossing boundaries in the middle of the desert. The Spirit will go to the farthest borders, to the place where deviant people are located, to announce good news and invite them to celebrate their *nepantlero/a* way of life.

By allowing Philip and the Ethiopian eunuch to cross each other's lives, the *nepantlero* Spirit consecrates our *kairos,* "a time in between,"[8] a moment in which something special is going to happen. After all, it is not at the beginning of the day or at the end of the day that the crossing occurs, but in the ambivalence of the "noontime." The Greek phrase that usually is translated "toward the south" (κατὰ μεσημβρίαν) can also mean "about midday, at noon." Despite the fact that the phrase regularly appears in the Septuagint as a reference to time (Gen 18:1; 43:16; Deut 28:29; Jer 6:4), most scholars insist that here direction (toward the south) is intended. "Their reason is that the noonday sun makes traveling extremely difficult in the Middle East, something to be avoided if at all possible" (Gaventa 1986, 101). However, here we have an Anzaldúan Spirit whose activity is not restrained to the "normal time" of traveling. Also, Luke informs us in Acts 22:6 and 26:13 that Paul's encounter with Jesus occurred on another

---

8. To understand the notion of *kairos* as a time in between, see the several articles in Sipiora and Baumlin 2002.

road in the middle of the day. In God's *Mundo Zurdo*, everything is done contrary to the "norm," even how and when one travels. The Spirit's desire in meeting *los/as atrevesados/as*, those forgotten, those unwanted, those unwelcomed, those who are neither from here nor there, is marking a new way to travel. As long as there is an *atrevesado/a* struggling between life and death on the middle of the road, the Anzaldúan Spirit would meet him/her, even if it is noonday.

The queer Spirit has already directed God's salvation toward the south. Now the Spirit is going to break the norms of traveling, creating confusion and disorientation in the community. All members of the community must become the new *mestizos/as* in order to see God's salvation. This salvation might happen at any moment, even in deserted places where not a single sign of life is found. And noon is a particularly auspicious time for piercing supernatural revelation because of its association with brilliant, blinding light from above (Spencer 1997, 90). The true *mestizo/a* must be vigilant and watchful for God's theophanies, which do not necessarily occur in the "normal" time in the "right place" or with a "pure" body, but rather occur in the borderland and on the periphery. The God of the desert appears in radiance and beauty, hearing once again the cry of the oppressed in the middle of the desert.

We learn that the effeminate eunuch had come to Jerusalem to worship and was returning to his home. Philip, or to be more specific God, encounters the ambiguous eunuch in the middle of the road and in the middle of the day. The eunuch went to a place he did not belong (the temple) and where he could not find salvation. The *Mundo Derecho* is not for people like him. He is an outsider, marginalized for his lack of a penis. As Spencer suggests, "The results of this visit are not detailed, but the thrust of the eunuch's questions to Philip suggests a prior experience in the Jewish capital of receiving inadequate assistance in understanding the Jewish scripture ('How can I, unless someone guides me?' Acts 8:31) and of being denied full access into the fellowship of God's people ('What is to prevent me from being baptized?' Acts 8:36)" (Spencer 1997, 91). It is true that the North had failed the eunuch, but also his own culture and the beloved South had betrayed him. The eunuch could easily unmask his own culture, like Anzaldúa: "Not me sold out my people but they me. Because of the color of my skin they betrayed me. The dark-skinned woman has been silence, gagged, caged, bound into servitude with marriage, bludgeoned for 300 years, sterilized and castrated in the twenty century" (Anzaldúa 2007, 44). However, we are experiencing a new age, where the North and

South fuse to create an "in-between body," a hybrid who is capable of dealing with his/her bi-culture, bi-identity and bi-body.

Earlier in Acts we saw how the Spirit had pushed the mission to "the end of the earth" to reach the *others* who live on the *other side* of the bridge. By this historical crossing the Spirit would accomplish two tasks. On the one hand, the Spirit would challenge the entire community represented in the figure of Philip to cross over to the *other side (the south)* to embrace the *atrevesados/as*, those who do not belong to the house of Israel. On the other hand, the Spirit is providing the opportunity to those who live on the *other side* to cross to *this side (the north)* to experience recognition and salvation. Both sides and both bodies became sacred when they obey the Spirit of God and dare to cross over to each other's side. The challenge that the Spirit poses to these bodies and their respective communities is the challenge of honoring their own bodies, traditions, cultures, and territory. As Anzaldúa says, that challenge is about honoring ourselves "in ways that allow us to be changed by embracing that otherness rather than punishing others for having a different view, belief system, skin color, or spiritual practice" (Anzaldúa 2002, 4). The Holy Spirit promotes neither the North nor the South; rather, the Spirit is proposing a new way of interacting among bodies that live in borderlands. The community of this *nepantlero* Spirit must recognize in the *other* his/her own humanity in order eternally to end the us/them division. Anzaldúa correctly advises us that "as long as you're entrenched in a counter stance of 'us against them' you are locked in" (Anzaldúa 2005, 43). In *Nepantla* the Holy Spirit has unlocked both bodies that departed to different ways of praising the living God. The encounter and departure of these two bodies had happened as a result of reading the Scriptures.

2.2. And Behold, There Is an Ethiopian Eunuch Who Knows How to Read!

The Anzaldúan Holy Spirit moves Philip to "Go up and join that chariot" (Acts 8:29), and behold, there was a eunuch reading his Scripture! The body of the eunuch caused confusion, anxiety, and panic not only in the Greco-Roman culture but still today causes "anxiety" in some scholars who erroneously argue than Acts 8:26–40 does not really refer to a despised body, but rather to a powerful and important person. "This warns us not to consider the Ethiopian as a despised or deprived person—quite the opposite. He is a powerful, though exotic, court official, a well-placed and significant person who is receptive to the truth" (Willimon 1988, 71–72).[9] This could be a way to reinterpret this particular text, especially when we have some secondary sources that portray eunuchs favorably. For instance, Herodotus (*Hist.* 8.15) says that among barbarians, eunuchs were specially prized as servants because of their trustworthiness. Moreover, Luke portrays the Ethiopian eunuch as a court official in charge of the queen's treasure. "He not only possesses the expected accoutrements of an official of his rank (a chariot, servants [implied by the command in v. 38]), but also a copy of Isaiah. Beyond his obvious ability to read the biblical text, the language that is placed in his mouth shows him to be a highly educated and cultured individual" (Matthews 2002, 79). These details that Luke provides, as well as some secondary sources[10] in which some eunuchs are described as having a certain authority and power, could be misleading and might blind us from seeing the dehumanizing way in which the body of the eunuch is treated. The Ethiopian eunuch apparently does not qualify as a human since the gender of "his" body cannot be properly understood and so "his" entire humanity is at stake.[11] Even with all his "power" and

---

9. See also Haenchen, who states: "But the εὐνοῦχος of LXX, like both εὐνοῦχος and סָרִיס elsewhere, frequently denotes high political or military officers; it does not necessarily indicate castration" (1971, 310).

10. We need to be discreet and prudent in the way that we use the secondary sources in our own interpretation. Historians and moralists often change their own thoughts or contradict themselves. For instance, the same Herodotus (Hist. 8.104–106) informs us that a eunuch named Hermotimus in the Persian court of Xerxes enjoyed the king's highest favor. However, when opportunity presented itself, Hermotimus exacted vicious revenge on the rogue who had perpetrated his castration and enslavement and made him "to be as man … a thing of naught." Exercising his acquired authority, Hermotimus sought out this practitioner of "the wickedest trade on earth" and forced him publicly to castrate his own sons and they in turn their father. The second-century satirist Lucian of Samosata narrates a tale of a eunuch who applies for a chair of philosophy in Athens. His chief competitor said such people ought to be excluded not only from philosophy but also from temples and holy-water bowls and all places of public assembly. He goes on to declare it "an ill-omened, ill met sight if on first leaving home in the morning, one should set eyes on any such persons [a eunuch]." Markedly "smooth of jowl" (beardless) and "effeminate in voice," a eunuch was "an ambiguous sort of creature like a crow, which cannot be reckoned either with doves or with ravens," "neither man nor woman but something composite, patently incompetent to instruct young boys in philosophy" (Eunuch. 6.11).

11. Kuefler proves that Roman society portrayed the eunuchs in the same way that women were portrayed, and the stereotypes of their characters are virtually the

"ability" to read, he is still "sub-human, inhuman, non-human" (Anzaldúa 2007, 40) according to the criteria of his culture and religion. However, for the *nepantlero* Spirit who is crossing new species, and new readings, this eunuch with his scroll would find acceptance and recognition in the community of faith due to his interpretation of the Scriptures.

The way the Ethiopian eunuch reads the Scriptures begins in *Nepantla*. It is only in the ambivalence of time, surrounded by the uncertainty of the desert that the deviant body of the eunuch interprets his scroll in a liberating way. In a certain way, it is not only the bodies that cross boundaries, but also their own interpretation of their sacred texts that comes alive by transgressing the orthodox interpretation. When the Scripture is read and understood from the eunuch's *Nepantla* location, then the Bible becomes once again sacred and full of meaning. The ways the people of Jerusalem interpreted and appropriated this Scripture were not for him. Luke portrays the eunuch reading the Scripture and taking the initiative to be baptized. Although the eunuch is a marginal character in the narrative, in the end he is fully incorporated into God's *Mundo Zurdo* as a result of reading this scriptural text. The community is encouraged to see the eunuch's character with new eyes and not be deceived. "In the aura of such heavenly radiance, familiar sights may be eclipsed and fresh images may come into view, such as—'look!' (*idou*, 8:27)—a fellow-traveler who just happens to be reading scripture and needing illumination at the moment when Philip the evangelist-interpreter arrives on the scene and, again— 'look' (*idou*, 8:36)—a body of water in the desert (!) at the moment when Philip's companion is ready to be baptized" (Spencer 1997, 90).

The *nepantlero* Spirit makes the "invisible" body of the eunuch visible, audible, and tangible in the middle of the day in a desolate place. The Spirit has given him back his *facultad* to (re)interpret his scroll. According to Anzaldúa, *la facultad* is the capacity to see in surface phenomena deeper realities, to see the deep structure below the surface (Anzaldúa 2007, 60). With his newfound *facultad*, the Ethiopian eunuch is not reading just any Scripture or even worse reading a "clobber text," such as, "No one whose testicles have been crushed or whose penis has been cut off may be admitted into the community of the Lord" (Deut 23:2). According to Anzaldúa,

---

same as those of women: carnal, irrational, voluptuous, fickle, manipulative, and deceitful. "These are the vices also of the unmanly, and eunuchs are often referred to as *molles, effeminati, semiviri,* the whole hosts of terms used for unmanly men" (Kuefler 2001, 35).

those who are pushed out of the tribe for being different are likely to
become more sensitized (when not brutalized into insensitivity). Those
who do not feel psychologically or physically safe in the world are more
apt to develop this sense. Those who are pounced on the most have it the
strongest—the females, the homosexuals of all races, the dark-skinned,
the outcast, the persecuted, the marginalized, the foreign (Anzaldúa 2007,
60). By recovering his *facultad*, the eunuch's senses become so acute and
piercing that he is able to dismantle any false interpretation of the Scriptures that denies him full access to God's community. With his *facultad*
the eunuch, as Anzaldúa would say, not only can view events in depth,
"a piercing that reaches the underworld (the real of the soul)" (Anzaldúa
2007, 61), but also can interpret the Scriptures in his favor.

For Anzaldúa, *la facultad* it is a kind of survival tactic that people,
"caught between the worlds, unknowingly cultivate." (Anzaldúa 2007,
61). In Acts 8:26–40 this Ethiopian eunuch is using his "survival tactic" to
read Isaiah, the prophet of the eunuchs. "Let not the foreigner say, when
he would join himself to the LORD, 'The LORD will surely exclude me from
his people'; Nor let the eunuch say, 'See, I am a dry tree.' For thus says
the LORD: To the eunuchs who observe my Sabbaths and choose what
pleases me and hold fast to my covenant, I will give, in my house and
within my walls, a monument and a name better than sons and daughters; an eternal, imperishable name will I give them" (Isa 56:3–5). Arrang-
ing Acts 8:26–40 chiastically reveals both its nature as the pivot-point
of this text as well as important subsidiary ideas flagged through repetition on either side. "The hub of the eunuch narrative may thus be located
at Acts 8:32–35, dealing with the citation and discussion of Isa. 53:7–8"
(Spencer 1992b, 132). The eunuch as a *nepantlero* is flexible in his reading
and knows how to read his scroll in a revolutionary way. Moreover, he
knows how to ask the right question: "Tell me, is the prophet referring to
himself or someone else" (8:34). He is not asking why he was rejected by
Jerusalem, the Deuteronomistic tradition, or his own culture. He is constructing his own *nepantlera* hermeneutics and demands to know who
might be this unfortunate man whom the prophet describes with such
pity. Once the eunuch finds out that Jesus is also an *atrevesado*, citizen of
el Mundo Zurdo, whose body was humiliated and physically and sexually
abused, as I have demonstrated elsewhere (Villalobos, 2010, 126–219),[12]

---

12. See also Tombs 2006 and Conway 2006.

he is moved by the power of the Spirit to demand his own total incorporation into God's household.

3. Crossing Borders with Manuel Villalobos Mendoza

My earliest recollection of crossing borders and being situated as one *del otro lado/from the other side* happened while gazing upon Jesus' naked body. This incident took place during a Good Friday in a remote village of Mexico, where Jesus' body was displayed for veneration. All the "boys" and "girls" were lined up in order to kiss Jesus as a sign of respect and compassion. When I approached Jesus' body, without hesitation I kissed him on the mouth. The priest, irritated, "situated" me in my "place" by saying, "What are you doing? Are you *del otro lado/are you from the other side?*" Immediately, by instinct, I knew that being *del otro lado* was something that I should fear and avoid.

Academics have paid greatest attention to Anzaldúa's autobiographical writings, because autobiography especially gives voice to all those minority groups whose bodies and experiences of life had been confined to valleys of death. Anzaldúa's autobiographical writings have resuscitated the "smothered 'I'" (Gaspar de Alba 2004, 4) as a legitimate way to know and to reinterpret our reality, in my case to interpret the Bible. Some Latino/a theologians have argued that U.S. Latinos/as have "become invisible people, subaltern people. They have been left out of the master narratives; their voices and stories are silenced and covered" (Martinez-Vazquez 2003, 73). Despite this awareness, Latino/a scholars have themselves not incorporated into their own biblical interpretation the experiences of gays, lesbians, bisexuals, and transgender people (hereafter GLBT).[13]

I do not pretend to talk about or represent the experience of other GLBT Latinos/as who are out there struggling with the "mark of the beast," as Anzaldúa calls it. My coming out through my writings is for the purpose of coping with my own struggles of living in the borderland, as a *nepantlero* and as a *Mexicano del otro lado*. Yet now that I am in a "privileged position" of writing publicly about my own experience, a crowd of

---

13. Nickoloff correctly criticizes this intentional omission by a theology that pretends to be "inclusive" (2003). Miguel A. De La Torre is one of the few Latino scholars who has prophetically sympathized with the homosexual person and has offered a very liberating reading of the Bible (2002; 2007). Also, Carla E. Roland Guzman is sensitive to the homosexual person (2006).

voices tells me I don't have the right. I recognize my elementary-school teacher's voice deriding me because "eres un Indio, no sabes ni hablar/you are an Indio, you do not know how to talk." Even more painful, I recognize God's voice (as my grandmother used to call the priest) proclaiming with authority that "gente que es del otro lado merece morir/people from the other side deserve to die."

For silence to transform into speech, sound, and words, it must first course through one's own body. Because our bodies have been stolen, brutalized, and numbed, it is difficult to speak from and through them (Anzaldúa 1990, xxii). Yet here I am, a Mexicano *de este lado y del otro lado*, confessing and reclaiming some of the experiences that have influenced the way that I see not just the biblical text but my own body, the world, and God. Biblical scholars have in recent decades recovered their "personal voice in Biblical interpretation."[14] Autobiographical criticism timidly has appeared in biblical scholarship to announce that neither text nor reader is subject or object but rather that together they enter into a continuous dialogue of interpretation (see Kitzberger 2003). In autobiographical criticism, the body as an essential aspect of self and identity is seriously taken into account in the interpretative process. For this reason, I begin here with my body as a way to communicate my struggles in interpreting the biblical text from the many *lados* of exclusion.

Anzaldúa is right when arguing that it is difficult to speak through one's own body when we have suffered all kinds of exclusion. Perhaps for this reason it is difficult for me to write about my own crossing. From a young age I thought I had been born into the wrong place with the wrong people and at the wrong time. I did not fit in with the men around me because I did not like to do the things that males were "supposed" to do. I did not fit into my small village, a sense others constantly confirmed by mockingly asking, "¿Qué vas a hacer cuando seas grande no sabes hacer nada? What are you going to do when you grow up, you good for nothing?" In this environment I quickly developed my "survival tactic." By instinct I became a *nepantlero*, always moving and always negotiating my existence in two or more realities. I quickly realized that my village was not the place for me. I felt exiled from my own gender, my own people, and my own culture. Part of that alienating culture was my religion. Though at night I would hear my mother's prayer: "Dios te salve. A ti

---

14. See Kitzberger 1999.

llamamos, los desterrados hijos de Eva; a ti suspiramos, gimiendo y llorando en este valle de lágrimas/To thee do we cry, exiles, sons of Eve. To thee do we sigh, moaning and weeping in this valley of tears." How could I tell my mother that I was experiencing a kind of exile even though no one could actually expel me from my own village? I was living my exile in and with my own body, as Jean-Luc Nancy argues: "De ahí que no se trate de estar: 'en el exilio interior de sí mismo,' sino ser sí mismo el exilio" (Nancy 1996, 38). Since then, my body has became the place of my own exile; my experience and desires had been so alienated from my life that sometimes I had not even recognized myself. In order to survive in a homophobic culture and religion, I learned how to camouflage my feelings and desires, especially when other males described me and "situated" me as one *del otro lado*.

3.1. *Ser y Estar en el Otro Lado*

I narrated above how my earliest recollection of being *del otro lado* happened while attending the liturgical service on Good Friday. However, the process of *ser y estar en el otro lado* is possible only trough the continuous act of repetition. My *ser y estar del otro lado* is not something that was situated and accomplished once and for all. *Ser y estar en el otro lado* is the result of continuous repetition by other people, the community, the law, and religion. It is a reiteration. Once the priest dared to call me *del otro lado*, he opened a door to injurious language against my body with the intention of denying my existence. He inaugurated all the hegemonic discourse that the Catholic Church uses against people like me. Through his injurious speech, immediately I became not just *the other*, but also the sinner, the evil one, the sick one, the pervert, the immoral one, the inverted one, and the transgressor. Furthermore, the injurious speech that the priest used against me not only condemned me to be *the other* and to live *en el otro lado*, but also legitimated and indirectly blessed the logos of my choir colleague who taunted me after worship with the words "El Moreno es del otro lado, es del otro lado."

When we are oppressed in many ways we are forced to develop *la facultad* "so that we'll know when the next person is going to slap us or lock us away. We'll sense the rapist when he's five blocks down the street" (Anzaldúa 2007, 61). My acquisition of *la facultad* was soon manifested when I witnessed how some male members of my village raped and beat *uno del otro lado* who "provocó su hombría/provoked their manliness." At the time I did not know exactly why Solovino[15] was labeled as *del otro lado* or how he provoked their manliness. I thought perhaps it was because he lived across the Rio Lerma, in an opposite direction to my village. One day I was playing with my sister, and my older brother told me, "Yo creo que tú también eres *del otro lado*/I believe that you are also *del otro lado.*" I reminded him that we did not live on the *other side* of the river, so how could I be *del otro lado*? He did not explain to me what exactly *del otro lado* means. But his silence told me that we were not on the *same side*. I became an alien in my own family, I became *uno de los otros/one of the others*. Anzaldúa narrates that in her home town there was a girl who was called by the people *una de las otras*. "They called her half and half, *mita' y mita'*, neither one nor the other but a strange doubling, a deviation of nature that horrified, a work of nature inverted" (Anzaldúa 2007, 41). Being *del otro lado* or *uno de los otros* evoked emptiness in my heart. It was like walking under a sky without stars, where no one knew exactly what to do with me.

In my desire to know and meet a person *del otro lado,* one day I crossed the river searching for Solovino, hoping that he would explain to me how to live the life *del otro lado*. When I arrived at his house, I found him lashed to a weeping willow tree by his neck. There were no words between us, only a mystical silence. His tears and body were sufficient to tell me there was no place for the likes of us in our small villages. As if this realization were not enough, my brother appeared from the middle of nowhere at that very moment and harangued me, saying, "Dios los hace y el Diablo los junta," which literally means, "God creates them and the Devil puts them together," probably the equivalent of the English-language saying "Birds of a feather flock together." My brother made me swear that I would never cross to the *otro lado* and I would never talk with a person *del otro lado,* warning me that otherwise I would burn in hell. From that day on *Dios y el Diablo* were present in each moment of my life, if anything fighting more for my body than my soul. One the one hand, I would hear my mother telling me how special I was, how I was born when no one expected me, that I was a miracle of God. On the other hand, my brother and the priest never stopped reminding me that as one *del otro lado* I belonged to hell and deserved to die.

---

15. Fictitious name, but true story.

A few months after my "crossing" to *el otro lado del Rio Lerma*, I heard my dad telling my older brother that Solovino had "abandoned" his family and crossed the Rio Grande illegally to *el Norte*. If for the Greeks the Ethiopians and their lands were paradise, where "the rams grow their horns quickly. Three times a year their flock gives birth, and there no lord would ever go wanting, nor would his shepherd, for cheese or meat, nor for the sweet milk either, but always the sheep yield a continuous supply for their sucklings" (*Od.* 4.84), for us people *del otro lado del Rio Grande, el Norte*, would be a similar symbol not just of abundance but also of refuge.

Due to the economic and political situation, most of the males from my village cross to the *otro lado* or, as my mom says, "se van pal' Norte/ they go to *el Norte*." For months at a time my village becomes a no-man's land; only women, children, and old men remain. Once when I confessed to my grandmother Mina that as soon as I grew up I would likewise go to *el Norte*, she warned me that: "el Norte se come a los hombres/the North devours men." Later on, my mother told me that my grandfather Octavio, during the "Bracero Program" had crossed the Rio Grande, that he was "lost" to the family for almost twenty-five years, and that consequently my grandmother had had to raise my dad by herself. At that moment I understood my grandmother's well-known saying: "Pobre de Mexico tan lejos de Dios y tan cerca de los Estados Unidos/Poor Mexico, so far from God and so close to the United States." I could not explain to her that my crossing to *el Norte* would have a different purpose and goal. I did not want to cross *el Rio Grande* in order to achieve the American dream in my mind, bodies *del otro lado se van para el otro lado*/bodies of the other side go to the other side.

In my innocence, I believed that in *el Norte* people *del otro lado* lived in peace and harmony. *El Norte* became something sacred, appealing, and desirable. *El Norte* was like the lost paradise. After all, Solovino had escaped to *el otro lado,* hadn't he? Of course no one knew for sure if he was alive or dead. In the village no one talked about him, for his very existence had brought misfortune and shame to his family, his younger brother told me. A couple of years ago I met Solovino in Anaheim, California, and he confessed to me that he had been dead to his family and village since the day his dad told him, "Prefiero un hijo muerto, que un hijo del otro lado/I prefer a dead son to a son who is *del otro lado*." In Mexico like any other part of the world, the crime, violence, and aggression against people *del otro lado* is real and we experience it every day. Why such aggression? Because we people *del otro lado* have not yet been deemed human. On one of the few occasions that I went to a certain city in the state of Gua-najuato, I read in a public restroom: "Se prohibe la entrada a animales y homosexuales/Entrance forbidden to animals and homosexuals." At the time I thought that a homosexual was a kind of aggressive animal capable of inflicting contagion on humans. Then I understood that this word was used to describe people *del otro lado*. "Homosexual" was another word to fear, another word with the power to negate my existence.

In a homophobic culture, animals and homosexuals belong to the same category of nonhumans. Perhaps it was my continued desire to attain human status that helped me to cross to *el otro lado del Rio Grande*. Since early in my childhood the mythical idea of *el Norte* chased me like a ghost, until finally a little more than a decade ago "the spirit of adventure" snatched me like a Philip and I was found not in Azotus but in Tijuana. Unlike Philip, I was not preaching to all the cities but attempting to cross the fence. Unfortunately, *el Norte* soon disappointed me and revealed *otros lados* of exclusion, marginalization, segregation, exploitation, and dehumanization. I realized that people *del otro lado* are condemned to be like Cain, forever roaming without a country to call our own, fearing for our lives all the time, hiding our bodies from God's face, and always looking for the non existence *del otro lado*.

3.2. INTERPRETING THE BIBLE *COMO EN EL OTRO LADO Y DEL OTRO LADO*

"When they came up out of the water, the Spirit of the Lord snatched Philip away; and the eunuch no longer saw him, but went on his way rejoicing" (Acts 8:39). We do not know for sure what the Ethiopian eunuch did after his baptism. Unlike Philip, who is in Azotus preaching in all the cities, Luke or the community has once again attempted to silence the Ethiopian eunuch. However, "tradition has it that this eunuch went home and evangelized Ethiopia. We can at least be sure that he who went on his way rejoicing would not be able to keep his newfound joy to himself" (Barclay 2007, 80). I showed above the power that the word of God has when it is read in *Nepantla*.

A couple of years ago, when teaching in a major seminary in Ciudad Juarez (on the border with the U.S.), the bishop questioned my credentials and accused me of teaching "como en el otro lado, como protestantes/ like on the other side, like Protestants." When I confessed to him that I was not just teaching *como en el otro lado* but in fact was *del otro lado*, he expelled me from his diocese and I became a *persona non grata*. Once again I crossed to the United States and started the painful process not only of finding my voice but of embracing my *otros lados* through interpreting the Bible. However, biblical scholars often are not willing to recognize my interpretation of the Bible as valid, because they find my body and discourse illegitimate.

In the winter of 2004 I was invited to the Asociación Bíblica Mexicana to talk about the Bible and homosexuality. I knew that the audience, composed almost entirely of priests, would not easily listen to what I had to say. As soon as I presented myself as someone *del otro lado*, all their questions challenged my "credentials" rather than engaging my arguments. Finally, an irritated priest yelled at me: "¿Quién quiere escuchar tus joterías?/Who wants to listen to your joterías anyway?"[16] He unceremoniously reduced my interpretation of the Bible to worthless *joterías,* insisting that my hermeneutics did not follow the rigor of the historical-critical method. He continued: Your hermeneutics could be accepted in *el otro lado* (referring to the U.S.), but not here. Your interpretation and conclusions are contrary to "common sense." I could not get a word in edgewise to reply, so hotly were some of the participants debating among themselves.

In Mexico as well as in the United States, a *joto* is regarded with suspicion, and his/her *joterías* are difficult to accept, even among other *jotos.* When my *jotos* friends find out that I am primarily interested in issues of gender and masculinity in the Bible, they often accuse me of "seeing *joterías* where they are not." For them, it is difficult to understand that I, as an *atrevesado,* cannot see or think "straight" into the biblical text. They only half-jokingly conclude, "You should be incinerated or at least jailed for using the Bible for your own convenience." Ironically, our Mexican word *joto* was coined in a Mexican jail called El Palacio Negro de Lecumberri. This jail operated from 1900 until 1976 and was divided into sections, each section identified by a letter of the alphabet. All those bodies that were causing "gender trouble"[17] in society, as Butler would say, were confined to section "J" (pronounced "hota"). When the inmates of section J were noisy, the guard would says something like: "callen a los del área J/shut up to those inmates in area J." Eventually that became: "Callen a los jotos/shut up to the jotos" (pronounced "hoto"). Since then, the desire to shut up the

---

16. *Joto* is slang for "gay" person, thus *jotería* is what a *joto* does.
17. I borrow this phrase from Butler 1990.

joto and his/her *joterías* seems to have been part of the Mexican psyche as well as that of (hetero)sexual biblical scholars.

For me it is obvious that as a body *del otro lado* I must interpret the Bible *del otro lado* and write *del otro lado*, because for centuries myself and people like me have been deliberately left out of biblical interpretation. Therefore, my biblical interpretation is an act of justice that the Anzaldúan Holy Spirit has approved and legitimated as a valid one. In the story of the Ethiopian eunuch, the Anzaldúan Holy Spirit had set the rules not just to describe who is a real man, but rather who counts as a human. As a *mestizo del otro lado* I am now in a privileged position due to the inauguration of God's *Mundo Zurdo*. The old paradigms, which legitimated all kinds of abuses toward my body, have been unmasked by God's mighty power. Through my interpretation of the Bible I have started to reclaim my own body and challenge the "official" and "heteronormative interpretation of the Bible." I have taken Anzaldúa's invitation very seriously: "You don't need to obey the reigning god's laws … and accept fate as decreed by the church and culture" (Anzaldúa 2002, 542). Being exposed to *otros lados* here in the United States has helped me to embrace my own body and challenge the "official" and "heteronormative interpretation of the Bible." Being *del otro lado* has helped me to see things differently and interpret the Bible in a more liberating way: "Living between cultures results in 'seeing' double, first from the perspective of one culture, then from the perspective of another (549). I have already experienced and suffered enough because of the orthodox interpretation of the Bible. Now I need to recover and honor my orphan *logos* in order to rejoice with the God of the *mestizos/as*.

In the history of biblical interpretation, Anglo as well as Latino (hetero) sexuals have let their voices be heard in order to legitimate their *logos* as something sacred, valuable, and worthy to transmit life and hope. Yet, the voices and interpretations of other minority groups have been left out of the biblical discourse. In Mexico, a *joto* like me is not allowed to interpret the Bible because "I have my own agenda," as I am often told, meaning that my word is illegitimate, incapable of producing any "real meaning" in my biblical interpretation. "He is a bastard who speaks nonsense," they say of me, whereas their discourse and interpretation are classified and validated on the basis of "social location." In this context, my body and my *joterías* have become homeless and borderless.

The Mexican philosopher Leopoldo Zea insists that people from Latin America have been obligated and forced through the centuries to "bargain away" our humanity. In order to be able to legitimate ourselves as human beings, we have taken a foreign "word" (*logos*) for ourselves. That borrowed *logos* is the Western *logos* (Zea 1969, 9–31). For the Chicanos/as, language is an orphan tongue: "Somos los del español deficiente. We are your linguistic nightmare, your linguistic aberration, your linguistic *mestizaje*, the subject of your *burlas*. Because we speak with tongues of fire we are culturally crucified. Racially, culturally and linguistically *somos huérfanos*—we speak an orphan tongue" (Anzaldúa 2007, 80). As a *nepantlero del otro lado* I have been voiceless, searching always for my *In Xochitl in Cuicatl*,[18] which might help me in understanding my own life and reality. I, like other minority groups that live in *otros lados* and see in the word of God a call for freedom, I also had turned to the Bible. However, the Bible has been my "Text of Terror."[19]

The Bible has been used against bodies *del otro lado* without pity since her first crossing from Europe to our Aztec territory. Instead of giving hope, love, and compassion as the missionaries promised to our ancestors, it became a death book, announcing hell and eternal damnation to all the sodomites. This was actually the first impression that Cortés had about the body of the Indian. In his infamous report that Cortés made to Charles V, he declared: "We have come to know, for certain, that they are all sodomites and practice the abominable sin" (Garza Carvajal 2003, 138). One of the earliest misuses of the Bible against the Mexican "sodomites" is attributed to the Franciscan friar Bernardino de Sahagún, who "pastorally" recommended what to do with all of those who commit the *pecado contra natura*: "The sodomite is an effeminate, defilement, a corruption, filthy; a taster of filth, revolting, perverse, full of affliction. He deserves laughter, ridicule, mockery; he is detestable, nauseating, disgusting. He makes one acutely sick. Womanish, playing the part of the woman, he merits to be committed to flames, burned, consumed by fire, he burns; he is consumed by fire. He talks like a woman, he takes the part of the woman" (Guerra 1971, 29). Since then, cardinals, bishops, priest, pastors, and ministers abusing their power literally have followed Sahagún's advice regarding the homosexual person. For scholars who are confined to order and decorum in their biblical interpretation, to find good news for people

---

18. The idiomatic expression, *In Xochitl in Cuicatl*, which literally means "flower and song," has a metaphorical sense of poem, poetry, artistic expression, in a word, symbolism. For the Aztec philosophers or *Tlamatinimes*, *In Xochitl in Cuicatl* was a way to know truth on earth (León Portilla 1963, 75).

19. I borrow this phrase from Trible 1984.

del otro lado is impossible. However, the citizens of *Mundo Zurdo* that have been blessed by ambiguity are capable of converting the text of terror into a text of liberation.

When reading and interpreting the biblical text from *otros lados*, we can find not just liberation but even joy in our interpretation. One of the reasons that I found for rejoicing in my interpretation of the Bible is found in the Anzaldúan Spirit of Acts 8:26–40, who demands total inclusion of *all* people, especially the ones who live not only in the borderlands but at the very "ends of the earth." Luke artistically and devoutly emphasizes that the eunuch is from Ethiopia. "And look, there was an Ethiopian who had gone up to worship in Jerusalem. He was a eunuch, an official of Candace, queen of Ethiopia" (Acts 8:27). Luke shares the same prejudices that other Hellenistic writers had toward Ethiopia and its inhabitants. As Aaron Johnson notes, "Already in Homer the extreme remoteness of the Ethiopians, geographical and mythical, appears central to their representation in the Greek literary imagination" (Johnson 2006, 167). Greek writers believe that the Ethiopian land was at the "end of the world, … apart furthest of men, some beyond the setting sun, others beyond the rising sun" (*Od.* 1.23–24). The feast that inaugurates the *nepantlero* Holy Spirit is not simply for Jerusalem, the true Israelites, or the eunuchs but rather for all those whose humanity had been confined to the shadow regions of *el otro lado*.

The joy that the Ethiopian eunuch experienced begins neither in the *Norte* nor in the *Sur*, but rather in the borderland, where ambiguity reigns and ambivalence is celebrated as part of God's creation. Reading and interpreting the Bible *en el otro lado* often produces joy and life, for it is only when I embrace my ambiguity, my *Nepantla* stage, that my interpretation of God's word becomes sacred, capable of nourishing my soul and body, capable of sustaining me while yet in a homophobic culture and religion. People who have lived in the *frontera*, in the middle of the desert, know that we cannot survive by ourselves. Surviving the desert demands solidarity with other brothers and sisters who, despite suffering all sorts of discrimination, still find hope in their biblical interpretation. My joy and interpretation of the Bible cannot be isolated from the struggles of the community. There cannot be a full celebration in my interpretation of the Bible if someone still lives in oppressive structures. Anzaldúa reminds us that not all of us have the same oppressions, but we empathize and identify with each other's oppressions. We do not have the same ideology, nor do we derive similar solutions. Some of us are leftists, some of us practitioners of magic. Some of us are both. But these different affinities are not opposed to each other. "In el *Mundo Zurdo* I with my own affinities and my people with theirs can live together and transform the planet" (Anzaldúa 1983, 209).

My interpretation *del otro lado* provides the tools to enter into a deep dialogue with other races, cultures, and people, especially those who have been enslaved and reduced to nothingness. Nonetheless, my interpretation is not limited to the experience of people who live *en el otro lado* or are *del otro lado*, but rather there is an open invitation to recognize the "new Ethiopians" who are everywhere and exclaim, like the historian Herodotus, "The Ethiopians are the tallest and most beautiful people" (*Hist.* 3.20). My interpretation of the Bible must help me to praise the God who loves all cultures, especially those who live on the margins and periphery and dare to live without borders. My reading *del otro lado* must unmask the idolatrous slogans of "God bless America." In my biblical interpretation all cultures must be praised, celebrated, and accepted as a generous gift from God. In theological discourse the dialogue and solidarity among minorities must be advanced. I notice the brokenness and lack of real theological dialogue that still exists among the scholars who represent their respective cultures and communities of faith. Division among us does not help to leash the "Beast of heteronormativity" that waits each moment to devour God's creation. Let us take seriously Anzaldúa's invitation to build the *Mundo Zurdo*: "Arriba mi gente, toda gente arriba/In spirit as one, all people arising. Toda la gente junta en busca del Mundo Zurdo en busca del Mundo Zurdo/All the people united in search of the Left handed World" (Anzaldúa 2007, 214 [my translation]).

CONCLUSION

We have seen how the notion of borderland presents a unique opportunity for Anzaldúa, the Ethiopian eunuch, and myself to envision a new way to be human. Although each of these bodies' stories and experiences is unique, there is also a common thread among us. We have been marked as the "other," disavowed and disallowed from our own culture, religion, and society. However, the ambivalence of the borderland is precisely where Anzaldúa's *Mundo Zurdo* dwells; it is a site of transformation, where the stranger becomes a friend, the outsider becomes an insider, the sojourner becomes a citizen, the impure becomes holy, and bodies *del otro lado* find hope. Bodies who dare to live in borderlands are blessed by the notion of *la facultad* in order to see a new reality and reinterpret our myths and sacred books in a more liberating way.

Anzaldúa's theory, like a gospel, had crossed many disciplines, bodies, and borders to announce that God's Holy Spirit is found in *Nepantla* demanding inclusion for all. In this essay, I applied Anzaldúa's feminist and queer theory to our biblical text of Acts 8:26–40. We delighted as we discovered how the Anzaldúan Spirit benefited and preferred the dislocated and ambiguous people who live in borderlands. We celebrated that God is faithful to the ambivalent desert and that miracles of conversion and inclusion happen when we see and interpret the Bible through the *nepantlero/a* eyes. Writing about my own crossing was the most difficult part of this essay because it made me feel vulnerable. I did not find any maps, roads, or signs to indicate to me how to live in *el otro lado* or how to embrace *el otro lado* of my being. Despite the heteronormative interpretation that permeates our biblical text as a whole, I dared to find some joyful motif to celebrate the God who still cares for all *atravesados/as*. My hope is that through this paper, I might contribute to a fruitful dialogue between people from "this side" and people *del otro lado del Rio Grande*. My hope for this paper is that it will invite all people to walk with the guidance of the *nepantlero* Holy Spirit in order that we might praise God in our own ways (Acts 8:40).

Works Consulted

Alvarez, Alma Rosa. 2007. *Liberation Theology in Chicana/o Literature.* New York: Routledge.

Anzaldúa, Gloria. 1983. *This Bridge Called My Back: Writings by Radical Women of Color.* Edited by Gloria Anzaldúa and Cherríe Moraga. New York: Kitchen Table/Women of Color Press.

———, ed. 1990. *Making Face, Making Soul Hacinendo Caras: Creative and Critical Perspectives by Feminists of Color.* San Francisco: Aunt Lute.

———. 1993. Gloria Anzaldúa. Pages 19–42 in *Backtalk: Women Writers Speak Out; Interviews.* Edited by Donna Perry. New Brunswick, N.J.: Rutgers University Press.

———. 2002. Now Let us Shift … The Path of Conocimiento … Inner Work, Public Acts. Pages 540–78 in Anzaldúa and Keating 2002.

———. 2005. Daughter of Coatlicue: An Interview with Gloria Anzaldúa. Pages 41–56 in Keating 2005.

———. 2007. *Borderlands/La Frontera: The New Mestiza.* 3rd ed. San Francisco: Spinster/Aunt Lute.

Anzaldúa, Gloria, and AnaLouise Keating, eds. 2002. *This Bridge We Call Home: Radical Vision for Transformation.* New York: Routledge.

Barclay, William. 2007. *The Acts of the Apostles.* New Daily Study Bible. Louisville: Westminster John Knox.

Bedford, Nancy E. 2004. Escuchar las Voces de las Nepantleras: Consideraciones Teológicas desde las Vivencias de Latinoamericanas y "Latinas" en Estados Unidos. Pages 205–21 in *La Encrucijada del Género: Conversaciones entre Teología y Disciplinas.* Buenos Aires: Centro de Estudios Salesiano de Buenos Aires.

———. 2005. To Speak of God from More than one Place: Theological Reflections from the Experience of Migration. Pages 95–118 in *Latin American Liberation Theology: The Next Generation.* Edited by Ivan Petrella. Maryknoll, N.Y.: Orbis.

Berquist, Jon L. 2002. *Controlling Corporeality: The Body and the Household in Ancient Israel.* New Brunswick, N.J.: Rutgers University Press.

Butler, Judith. 1990. *Gender Trouble: Feminism and the Subversion of Identity.* New York: Routledge.

Chance, J. B. 1988. *Jerusalem, the Temple, and the New Age in Luke-Acts.* Macon, Ga.: Mercer University Press.

Conway, Colleen. 2006. Paul and the Virility of the Cross. Paper presented at the Annual Meeting of the AAR and SBL. Washington, D.C., November 18.

De La Torre, Miguel A. 2002. *Reading the Bible from the Margins.* Maryknoll, N.Y.: Orbis.

———. 2007. *A Lily among the Thorns: Imaging a New Christian Sexuality.* San Francisco: Jossey-Bass.

Dúran, Diego. 1971. *Book of the Gods and Rites and the Ancient Calendar.* Edited and translated by Fernando Horcasitas and Doris Heyden. Norman: University of Oklahoma Press.

Garza Carvajal, Federico. 2003. *Butterflies Will Burn: Prosecuting Sodomites in Early Modern Spain and Mexico.* Austin: University of Texas Press.

Gaspar de Alba, Alicia. 2004. Crop Circles in the Cornfield: Remembering Gloria E. (1942–2004). *American Quarterly* 56:4–7.

Gaventa, Beverly Roberts. 1986. *From Darkness to Light: Aspects of Conversation in the New Testament.* Philadelphia: Fortress.

Guerra, Francisco. 1971. *The Pre-Columbian Mind.* New York: Seminar.

Haenchen, Ernest. 1971. *The Acts of the Apostles,* Philadelphia: Westminster.

Hester, David. 2005. Eunuchs and the Postgender Jesus: Matthew 19.12 and Transgressive Sexualities. *JSNT* 28:13–40.

Johnson, Aaron P. 2006. The Blackness of Ethiopians: Classical Ethnography and Eusebius's Commentary on the Psalms. *HTR* 22:165–86.

Keating, AnaLouise. 2002. Forging El Mundo Zurdo: Changing Ourselves, Changing the World. Pages 519–30 in Anzaldúa and Keating 2002.

————, ed. 2005. *Entre Mundos/Among Worlds: New Perspectives on Gloria E. Anzaldúa.* New York: Palgrave Macmillan.

Kitzberger, Ingrid R., ed. 1999. The Personal Voice in Biblical Interpretation. New York: Routledge.

————, ed. 2003. *Autobiographical Biblical Criticism: Between Text and Self.* Dorset, England: Deo.

Kuefler, Matthew. 2001. *The Manly Eunuch: Masculinity, Gender Ambiguity, and Christian Ideology in Late Antiquity.* Chicago: University of Chicago Press.

León Portilla, Miguel. 1963. *Aztec Thought and Culture: A Study of the Ancient Nahuatl Mind.* Translated by Jack Emory Davis. Norman: University of Oklahoma Press.

Martinez-Vazquez, Hjamil A. 2003. Dis-covering the Silences: A Postcolonial Critique of U.S. Religious Historiography. Pages 50–78 in *New Horizons in Hispanic/Latino(a) Theology.* Edited by Benjamin Valentin. Cleveland: Pilgrim.

Matthews, Christopher R. 2002. *Philip: Apostle and Evangelist; Configuration of a Tradition.* Leiden: Brill.

Nancy, Jean-Luc. 1996. La Existencia Exiliada. *Archipiélago: Cuadernos de Crítica de la Cultura* 26–27:34–40.

Nickoloff, James B. 2003. Sexuality: A Queer Omission in U.S. Latino/a Theology. *Journal of Hispanic Latino Theology* 10:31–51.

Pérez Emma, Gloria. 2005. La Gran Nueva Mestiza Theorist, Writer, Activist-Scholar. *NWSA Journal* 17 (2):1–10.

Ramsdell, Lea. 2004. Language and Identity Politics: The Linguistic Autobiographies of Latinos in the United States. *Journal of Modern Literature* 28:166–176.

Rivera, Mayra. 2006. God at the Crossroads: A Postcolonial Reading of Sophia. Pages 238–53 in *The Postcolonial Biblical Reader.* Edited by R. S. Sugirtharajah. Oxford: Blackwell.

Roland Guzman, Carla E. 2006. Sexuality. Pages 257–64 in *Handbook of Latina/o Theologies.* Edited by Edwin David Aponte and Miguel A. De La Torre. Saint Louis: Chalice.

Sánchez, Aquilino. 2001. *Gran Diccionario de Uso del Español Actual.* Madrid: SGEL.

Sipiora, Phillip, and James S. Baumlin, eds. 2002. *Rhetoric and Kairos: Essays in History, Theory, and Praxis.* Albany: State University of New York Press.

Spencer, F. Scott. 1992a. The Ethiopian Eunuch and His Bible: A Social-Science Analysis. *BTB* 22:155–65.

———. 1992b. *The Portraits of Philip in Acts: A Study of Roles and Relations.* Sheffield: Sheffield Academic Press.

———. 1997. *Acts.* Sheffield: Sheffield Academic Press.

Tombs, David. 2006. Torture, Trauma, and Truth: The Scandal of Crucifixion. Paper presented at the annual meeting of the AAR and SBL. Washington, D.C.

Trible, Phyllis. 1984. *Texts of Terror: Literary-Feminist Readings of Biblical Narratives.* Philadelphia: Fortress.

Vasconcelos, José. 1966. *La Raza Cósmica: Misión de la Raza Iberoamericana. Notas de Viajes a la América del Sur.* Madrid: Aguilar.

Villalobos, Manuel. 2009. Eunucos por el Reino. *Qol* 50:43–68.

———. 2010. Abject Bodies in Mark's Passion Narrative: A Butlerian Interpretation by a Mexicano Del Otro Lado. Ph.D. diss., Garrett Evangelical Theological Seminary.

Willimon, William H. 1988. *Acts.* Atlanta: John Knox.

Zea, Leopoldo. 1969. *Filosofía Americana Como Filosofía Sin Más.* México: Siglo XXI.

THE CORINTHIAN WOMEN PROPHETS AND TRANS ACTIVISM: RETHINKING CANONICAL GENDER CLAIMS

Joseph A. Marchal

Over two decades ago, feminist biblical scholar Antoinette Clark Wire posited that Paul and Corinthian women had different experiences of their status before and after joining this community in Corinth. More recently, it has come to the attention of queer theorists that trans folk have different experiences of their status than expected by the medical and psychological establishment, both before and after changes in and through behavior, dress, expression, and surgery. Though dissimilar in a variety of ways, these two dynamics are strikingly analogous in matters of being, becoming, and belonging. Most prominently, arguments about suffering, authority, and normalcy are key in both domains. These kinds of arguments draw my attention, not only because I have been trained rhetorically as a feminist scholar, but also because I seek to recognize and contest the normalizing force of such arguments by developing strategies at the intersections of queer, postcolonial, and feminist approaches.

In the first century interaction, Paul attempts to manage or form the community at Corinth according to certain narratives about suffering and status. These arguments themselves are also claims to a certain authoritative status that, ironically, suggests Wire, also affects the manner in which the arguments have been and should be received by those with other kinds of status. In the contemporary rhetorical interaction, medical and psychological professionals frame the meaning of transsexuality as the result of a disorder and work to "certify" certain trans people[1] as legitimate and

---

1. Except for cases where I will discuss the dominant perspective in the medical and psychiatric fields that treat transsexuality as a disorder, in this paper I opt for the more generalized, inclusive, and, some might say, political term "trans" to refer not just to transsexuals but also to a range of people who cross gender-normative bound-

worthy subjects for treatment. These claims by doctors, alternately echoed and challenged by trans people (Whittle 2006, xiii-xv), also involve arguments about particular kinds of suffering and their meaning for human identity. Furthermore, they instill specific kinds of status and authority upon the speakers, in both chilling and potentially liberatory fashions. Given these dynamics, putting these two interactions in contrapuntal conversation could prove profitable for rethinking what precisely is involved in gender, community, and identity, particularly as they relate to processes of initiation, conversion, or transition (for the first or the twenty-first century).[2] In the end, this should demonstrate the additional and unexpected utility of feminist sociohistorical modeling for feminist and/or LGBTIQ communities as well as the possibilities for a continually relevant queer and feminist practice of biblical studies.

The relevance of such an effort should become clearer as we recognize that we are even now being formed socially as subjects of certain orders by reference to canonical texts, both religious (the Bible) and medical (the *DSM-IV*).[3] If we have reasons to be suspicious of either (or both), then a critical engagement with how Paul and certain forms of psychology argue and attempt to shape their domains could provide a resource for our strategic practices today. My essay proceeds to present four points of view on two rather different, but oddly connected, historical and rhetorical situations. In both cases, we will consider the dominant scripts, presented by Paul and medical authorities, as well as ways to resist and

---

aries or categories. This will, of course, not satisfy all informed readers, as some transsexuals prefer not to think politically about their identity, or politically in this fashion, or even desire to identify as transsexual. In more common or accepted parlance, *transgendered* is a more general umbrella term for all those who live "in-between" genders, while transsexual typically refers specifically to those who seek surgery and/or hormone treatment to transition into another gender. As my contrapuntal analysis proceeds, I hope it will become clear why I prefer to use "trans people" or "trans folk" when referring to a number of parties, including those who alter their mode of behavior, style, dress, comportment, or physicality. On the origins and use of the term "trans," see Whittle 2006, xi-xii.

2. On contrapuntal styles of reading, see, for example, Said 1993, 18–19, 32–33, 66–67.

3. The *DSM-IV* is the established colloquial and professional shorthand for the fourth edition of the *Diagnostic and Statistical Manual of Mental Disorders*, about which I will elaborate further below.

resituate such scripts, given insights from the Corinthian women prophets and trans activism.

1. The Dominant Script Presented by Paul

One might not expect it for a feminist and queer analysis of 1 Corinthians, but the focus of my essay will for now remain on the letter's opening chapters, where Paul first attempts to formulate his views of communal belonging.[4] First Corinthians 1–4 delivers a compelling succession of reversals, dissociations, descents, and redefinitions in order to ensure authority for Paul and argue for a standard of sameness for the community.

One key gesture for achieving these goals is the unexpected reversals Paul develops, especially in terms of foolishness and wisdom. Paul argues that the divine works through the folly of Paul's words and makes the wise foolish (1:20–25). Though the argument is ostensibly humbling to Paul, it prioritizes the divine work this "fool" does. In fact, Paul acts as an arbiter of who else in the community is ready for this wisdom, highlighting that some are ready, given their mature, complete, or perfected status (2:6).[5] This exercise is also marked by exclusion, since the wisdom is obscure and secret (2:7) when it is received through a spiritual conduit (2:10–13). Yet, in Paul's arguments to follow, the community being addressed with these words is not yet in this stage of development. To Paul, they are infants or children, still fed with milk; they cannot yet be addressed as those spiritually mature people described above (3:1–2).[6] From his own point of view, Paul has attained the appropriate level of status to judge this, since he is the deity's coworker (3:9) and the community's one and only father (4:14–15).

Paul continues to argue for this authoritative status through his own manifest weaknesses (2:2–3) and difficulties. The dissociating and rever-

---

4. For elaborations on the "usual suspect" passages in 1 Corinthians from queer, or at least lesbian and gay, perspectives, see, for example, Martin 2006; Hearon 2006.

5. Since the full statement in this verse contrasts this kind of wisdom with that of the rulers, some scholars see this as an indication of the apocalyptic, and therefore anti-imperial, nature of Paul's message. See, for example, Horsley 2000.

6. Strangely enough, the term chosen to describe the community as childish (*nēpiois*, 3:1) stresses that element of immaturity where one cannot yet speak, or can but without appropriate forethought or reflection. Such claims about subjects who are immature, childish, or less linguistically advanced echo long-standing claims about the abilities of non-gender-conforming people as well as imperial and colonial rationales based on ethnic difference. For reflections on the latter, see Marchal 2009.

sal arguments fit Paul's self-presentation as one who suffers a catalogue of woes: he is hungry, homeless, beaten, slandered, and persecuted (4:11–13). The image of Paul's suffering self is constructed so that he can rather directly exhort the community to "become imitators of me" (4:16) in this letter (Castelli 1991). Describing a lowered or debased status in this fashion allows Paul to argue for voluntary sacrifices from the community, since he is "holding up his own voluntary sacrifice as a model" (Wire 1990, 36). As a result, the paradigm he presents of himself to the community is recurrently disciplined by a descend-to-ascend, suffer-to-gain pattern (Wire 1990, 58–71; Marchal 2005).

In this fashion, Paul builds upon the previous reversals, dissociations, and resignifications of weakness and foolishness to create a new vantage point from which to argue. This is essential to the plan of 1 Corinthians, as following Paul's lead will be his solution to a number of communal troubles. At nearly every turn, the letter's "answers" for the community will be formed through these rearranged conditions of suffering and status. According to Paul's view of the community, membership involves imitating his sacrifice, a willingness to suffer, and a generalized descent into a range of difficulties in this life. The letter represents his attempt to normalize this view of communal identity and construct particular meanings out of a situation he molds in terms of certain kinds of status and suffering. As will become clear, this is only one half of the story.

2. Resisting/Resituating the Dominant Script: The Corinthian Women Prophets

The unique contribution of Wire's study of this letter is found in the way she conceived of Paul's arguments within a rhetorical interaction. Paul seeks to convince others; therefore, he must find ways to appeal to them. This indicates that one can *read through* the arguments Paul makes in order to reconstruct the potential perspectives of other parties in the audience (Wire 1990, 1–11; cf. Kittredge 2003). Since several of his arguments seem to be directed to women prophesying in the Corinthian assembly, Wire endeavors to explicate their potential perspectives. This provides a very different point of view on these opening chapters.

Again, the idea of wisdom is key. In using the Greek words for "wise" or "wisdom" twenty-six times in these first four chapters, Paul seems to be responding to the Corinthians' own interest in wisdom. Paul begins his argument acknowledging that the Corinthians see life in the community differently than he, as they have knowledge, speaking abilities, and all kinds of spiritual gifts (1:5, 7), things he sought to resignify and reverse above. He contrasts himself with the audience in many places, indicating that they are enjoying gains or benefits in communal life. This occurs upon joining the assembly, though, as Paul exhorts the audience to remember their station in life at the time of their "call": neither wise, powerful, nor well-born (1:26).

Reexamining these rhetorics for critical insights on social locations, Wire conducted a multifactored analysis, selecting wisdom, power, honor, servitude, ethnicity, and gender as the six categories to measure relative status in the community, both before and after joining (Wire 1990, 62–63, 273–74). For the prophetic women in the community, Paul's comments in 1:26 make clear that they lacked the first three elements in the list: wisdom, power, or the honor of noble birth. Since it seems unlikely that any of these women were Roman or had the rather limited privileges granted to Jews, their ethnic status would have been low, like their gendered status. Finally, given Paul's arguments about slavery later in the letter (7:17–24), it is possible that some of the women in the community were themselves slaves. Wire explains that "the social status of the Corinthian women prophets at the time they were called seems to be mixed on one indicator—free/slave—and low in every other indicator" (Wire 1990, 65).[7]

By the time Paul writes, though, the Corinthian women prophets, and others with them, seem to have a different sense of their status. As indicated in his mocking comparison in 4:8–10, Paul addresses the audience as believing they are already knowledgeable, strong, wise, fulfilled, and honored. Their ability to speak with wisdom involves elevation in the first three categories measuring relative social status: wisdom, power, and honor. Furthermore, if passages of initiation or baptism like Gal 3:28—"neither Jew nor Greek, neither slave nor free, not male and female"—reflect views of membership in communities like Corinth, as indicated by Paul's partial quoting of it in 1 Cor 12:13, then communal life seems to have involved some mitigation of the latter three categories as well. (Indeed, Wire and other feminist interpreters of Paul maintain that the "tensions" in his letters are indicative of his own negotiation of those who interpret this con-

---

7. We would do well to note the judicious tone of Wire's suggestions about relative social status across a range of factors. This should also be an indication that Wire preserves elements of difference from within the category "women" or "women prophets" and does not treat them as a monolithic group. Rather, Wire attempts to reconstruct (some of) their potential positionality as a contrast to the possible status of Paul.

cept of communal initiation differently than he.) Thus, for the prophetic women, joining the community would create the distinct impression of an upward swing *out of* social conditions that caused considerable suffering (Wire 1990, 66; *contra* the later views of Martin 1995).

As a free male able to travel in the empire, Paul exhibits a degree of status in the gender and servitude categories, and as one with Pharisaic training, he enjoys some status within his ethnic group. The education and influence that likely accompanied this status also ensure that he often would have been received as one with a degree of wisdom, honor, and power in this ethnic group. Though Paul's status measures relatively high in each of these six factors, this stature would also have changed upon his shift to join this developing movement. In the non-Judean context of the Corinthian community, the wisdom that is sought is not exactly commensurate with his education or background, as indicated by his struggles to redefine wisdom and foolishness in 1:18–31. Apparently now Paul's power and honor are also challenged, likely by those who were born in a lower station in terms of gender, ethnicity, and/or servile status. These changing conditions explain how Wire can claim, "our best documentation of status loss for a male believer is that of Paul" (Wire 1990, 66).

Paul's particular focus on the conundrum of the cross corresponds to his downward shift in social status. His theological concept stresses the divine as debased and foolish for the sake of believing members, while justifying a communal organization where such members should conform to Paul's model of voluntary suffering and sacrifice.[8] Given their differences in the social experiences of joining the assembly, the women and Paul look at the same Christic event, but from two different vantage points. Whereas the cross is an act of suffering descent for Paul, it is likely already seen as a victorious exaltation to the Corinthian women, who experienced joining the assembly as an elevation or an abrogation of status (Wire 1990, 68–69).

This difference has distinct social effects and social roots. For many, if not most, of the assembly at Corinth, life in a kyriarchally arranged imperial system involved oppression and subordination on a number of levels.[9]

---

8. As Wire claims, "There is a close parallel between Paul's view of his status loss and his view of what God is doing in Christ" (1990, 67).

9. The term "kyriarchy," based on the Greek word for "lord," was coined by Elisabeth Schüssler Fiorenza. Rather than a simplified, dualistic analysis of power in gendered terms (patriarchy), kyriarchy highlights how multiple and mutually influential structures of domination and subordination function together, evident not only in

Unlike Paul, the women would have suffered for being quite low in this structure. It is hard to imagine the appeal of a message that argues for further, voluntary losses and sacrifice. On the contrary, given the socio-political context, it seems much more likely that women, peasants, and/ or slaves in the community would have felt "called out of lowness, not into it" (Wire 1990, 31). Participation, even leadership, in this community could have alleviated some of the suffering of these social-status conditions, if only in this community functioning as a potential alternative to its own contemporary kyriarchal order. In fact, the effects of initiation or "conversion" could have been seen as an indication of divine presence and plenitude, rather than a call to descend into another sequence of sacrificial suffering. In Paul's system, the upward trend has not yet occurred, rhetorically, socially, or theologically; for the Corinthian women prophets, it already has. It is easy to see how the practice of prophecy grew out of, or reinforced, such views.

3. THE DOMINANT SCRIPT PRESENTED ABOUT TRANS IDENTITY AND PRACTICE

Moving from this first-century setting to a more contemporary context, similar dynamics persist in the presentation of certain dominant scripts about gender, identity, normalcy, and community. Though there have been a variety of accounts of people crossing gendered lines since antiquity, the concept of a "transsexual" identity itself had contorted, convoluted, and confused origins in the domain of the sexological sciences of the previous century. Ironically, it is these inconsistent and varying sets of arguments that will eventually coalesce to construct a singularly authoritative source for the naming and classification of a medicalized identity. The physician Magnus Hirschfeld implemented the term *seelischen Transsexualismus*, "spiritual or psychic transsexualism," as early as 1923, yet he mostly used the term to describe a form of sexual inversion, rather than the desire, practice, or identification with crossing gender (Hirschfeld 1923, 15; cf.

---

sexism but also in racism, classism, ethnocentrism, heterosexism, colonialism, nationalism, and militarism. For an introductory definition to this neologism, see Schüssler Fiorenza 2001, 1, 118–19, 211; 1999, ix. Indeed, the interpretive tasks of this essay—suspicious assessment, analysis of oppressive dynamics, historical remembrance, and the goal of transformation action—are clearly drawn from Schüssler Fiorenza's program for emancipatory interpretation, evidenced in both of these works.

Meyerowitz 2002, 15–30). In Hirschfeld's schema, the identification or desire to cross gender—what we might now call trans—was lumped with cross-dressing, transvestism, and homosexuality.

The specific desire for surgery in order to alter the sex attributed at birth was not classified as transsexualism until 1949, when David O. Cauldwell coined the medical category *psychopathia transexualis* (Cauldwell 1949, 276–80; cf. Meyerowitz 2002, 41–45). Though Cauldwell was able to identify this condition as separable from homosexuality and transvestism, he refused to endorse sex reassignment surgery, SRS, as treatment. This would not come until endocrinologist Harry Benjamin began working with those who wished to be/become female—in today's parlance, MTFs, male-to-female trans people. Benjamin's work was in part inspired by Hirschfeld and the early twentieth-century European sexological consensus regarding universal bisexuality (see Califa 1997, 52–57). Under this theory, all humans have a blend of male and female elements and live somewhere on a continuum between them. Benjamin argued that transsexuals, alongside homosexuals, intersexed, and transvestites, fall into the middle of this continuum, with transsexualism being an extreme or "genuine" form of transvestism (Benjamin 1966). In this focus, he defined "true transsexuals" over against transvestites exclusively in terms of the desire to remove the male genitalia:

> For them, the sex organs, the primary (testes) as well as the secondary (penis and others) are disgusting deformities that must be changed by the surgeon's knife. This attitude appears to be the chief differential diagnostic point between the two syndromes (sets of symptoms)—that is, those of transvestism and transsexualism. (Benjamin 1966, 13–14)

Thus, from the start of this discourse, the construction and identification of the authentic transsexual is primarily oriented around the authority of the scientist, the medicalized point of view, and the procedures they administer and guard, almost as if the condition or the person did not exist previous to this discourse.[10]

---

10. For similar reflections on the role of medicalized authority in constructing and constituting the acceptable bounds of an ambiguous embodied identity—in this case, intersexed or intersexual—see Kessler 1998; Dreger 1998; and the work of the Intersex Society of North America, www.isna.org. For reflections on these topics and queer approaches to Paul's letters, see Marchal forthcoming.

The enduring influence of Benjamin can be measured by the establishment of the Harry Benjamin International Gender Dysphoria Association (HBIGDA) in 1979 and the routinized application of their standards of care since. These standards revolve around the desire for SRS and the sanctioning of an official authority to determine appropriate subjects for this care. According to HBIGDA, surgical treatment could not be given "on demand" to those seeking it, requiring two clinical behavioral scientists to recommend SRS only for those diagnosed with gender identity disorder, GID. Thus, in 1980 the third edition of the *Diagnostic and Statistical Manual* of the American Psychiatric Association, *DSM-III*, listed transsexualism on a list of mental disorders under the umbrella of GID.

Though transsexualism is no longer listed as a mental disorder in the *DSM-IV*, the contours for treatment as well as the rare access to expensive options like SRS are still routed through the requirement for the customer/patient to be diagnosed as suffering from a gender identity disorder (Califa 1997, 263; Bornstein 1994, 13–15). To be certified as suffering this disorder, one must show signs not only of "a strong and persistent cross-gender identification" but also of "persistent discomfort about one's assigned sex" (APA 1994, 534). Those judging the prospective transsexual look for common narratives about being "trapped in one's own body" or of unbearable suffering and pain at their current condition (Bornstein 1994, 66; Stone 2006, 231).

The search for unhappiness and rejection reaches close to absolutist levels, since "medical people are unable to countenance castration or penectomy unless the genetic male in question eschews any penile pleasure and utterly rejects his 'useless' organ" (Califa 1997, 58). In the case of FTMs, doctors and therapists look for potential patients to confess "that I hate my breasts, that the desire for surgery comes from desperation" (Spade 2006, 331). Even as some doctors do not speak today of trans people in the previous terms of sickness or disease, they still operate with the grounding assumption that pain is a—if not the—major factor in identifying a disorder that, in turn, delineates what counts as a trans person: a desperately unhappy and disordered person. Even seemingly sympathetic studies of the history of treatment and technology operate with the belief that "the demand for sex change represents the desperation of the transsexual condition: after all, who but a *suffering* individual would voluntarily request such severe physical transformation" (Hausman 1995, 110, emphasis added).

Candidates for SRS and other forms of treatment not only need to demonstrate discomfort and pain but must also show a willingness and an ability to live "normally" as the other gender. The standards for care from HBIGDA require that the candidates for this diagnosis/identity consult with the same therapist or clinician for several months and "live as" the other gender for one to two years: MTFs as women, FTMs as men (Bornstein 1994, 15; Meyerowitz 2002, 273). The medical and psychiatric slippage between cross-gender identification and cross-dressing is apparent at this stage, since the "life test" portion of the treatment is mostly marked by the candidate dressing differently and taking a correspondingly different name. Within this phase of the treatment, gender-identity programs might deny candidates access to further services for a variety of reasons:

> age, a history of psychiatric illnesses, homosexuality, fetishism, sado-masochism, a criminal record, inability to tolerate hormones, a medical history of cancer, possessing a face or body that the surgeon believes will never pass muster as a member of the gender of preference ("somatically inappropriate"), poverty, employment in the sex industry, a refusal to aspire to be a feminine woman or a masculine man, or uppitiness. (Califa 1997, 224–25)

Similar categories of normalcy emerge in the very few studies done to test the effectiveness or satisfaction derived after SRS: giving points for "gender-appropriate" heterosexual cohabitation or marriage—MTFs with males, FTMs with females—and job advancement, while subtracting them for "non-gender-appropriate" relationships, jail time, decline in employment level, or psychiatric treatment (Meyer and Reter 1979, 1011–15). The processes involved in determining a positive trans identification or a healthy transition are themselves calibrated to a series of norms for gender, sexual, physical, and economic status.

These standards and norms, then, produce a model that operates mostly as a univocal justification for limiting access to specific identities and specific forms of care. One's status as trans is not based upon self-identification of a cross-gender desire or an intermediate-gender practice; rather, it is conferred by certain authorities able to properly certify someone as a transsexual. Medical, psychological, and behavioral professionals create and interpret standardized materials from the DSM-IV or the HBIGDA to select who counts as a real, true, or genuine transsexual. In the discourse that currently sets the conditions for how we identify and define transsexuality, these are the only authorities that indicate whether one is "deserving" of the status they grant. Thus, if one seeks the communal approval or the supports offered through these modes of social, medical, and economic power, one must to learn to align oneself and one's concepts about the self and gender in conformity with this model.

4. RESISTING AND RESITUATING THE DOMINANT SCRIPT: TRANS ACTIVIST VOICES

The experiences and more-recent activism and theorization of trans people and their allies challenge and reformulate these arguments. In order for feminist critique to live up to its claims, we must continue to develop a queer, feminist analytic that takes trans voices seriously and a praxis that contributes to trans safety, support, and sustenance. To achieve this, my essay will, among other things, turn to the resources provided by a queer theorist and a trans activist, both of whom identify as feminist: Judith Butler and Kate Bornstein.[11]

Since SRS and other treatment options require fitting within the *DSM-IV* definition of gender identity disorder, trans people are submitted to a process that necessarily pathologizes and stigmatizes their identity as a disordered condition. Butler highlights that such arguments about trans folk take on "the language of correction, adaptation, and normalization," forwarding the idea that they are somehow flawed or damaged and thus in need of repair (Butler 2004, 77).

This model for what trans identity is and what trans experiences mean was not created by trans people; it was developed by and is still maintained by the practitioners who are also the gatekeepers to treatment (Stone 2006, 227–32; Spade 2006, 320–21). The demands of insurers and medical professionals have created a regulatory apparatus whereby trans people—or

---

11. For some of the reservations members of the trans community have with Butler's earlier work, especially *Gender Trouble*, see K. Namaste 1996, 183–203; Stryker 2006, 10–11; Prosser 2006, 257–80. Though Butler does not directly refer to these reservations, concerns, or even critiques, it does seem that her later work, especially *Undoing Gender*, contains attempts to address them and/or revise and reshape her previous work in light of similar concerns. For some cautions about the practicality of Bornstein's vision of a larger, transgendered solidarity, see Califa 1997, 245–62. For some reflections on the tense relationship between queer, feminist, and trans studies—and/or queer feminist views of trans—see Prosser 2006.

in their view, candidates for the transsexual identity—must first pass a series of tests (see above; Butler 2004, 90–91; Spade 2006, 315–32). As a result, if someone self-identifies as trans and desires access to those services that facilitate their transition, one will have to rehearse and perform the expected role. This apparatus does create a small opening for a trans in need, via a deceptive but strategic repetition of the medical model. Yet, as Butler cautions,

> The only way to secure the means by which to start this transformation is by learning how to *present yourself in a discourse that is not yours,* a discourse that effaces you in the act of representing you, a discourse that denies the language you might want to use to describe who you are, how you got here, and what you want from this life. (Butler 2004, 91, emphasis added)

In order to gain the status of the identity one has already realized or chosen, the trans person has to be socialized into altering one's everyday rhetorical practice, specifically "by sacrificing one's claim to use language truthfully" (Butler 2004, 91). This is just one facet of the conundrum that certain norms of transsexuality place on the trans person who departs from what is expected in these norms but who still needs the services provided by and through the same norms.

Furthermore, acceptance of the use and performance of the gender identity disorder also does violence to others. Queer and trans activists have argued that the GID diagnosis has taken over some of the same stigmatizing weight that the *DSM*'s previous pathologizing diagnosis of homosexuality had. Indeed, in practice the application of information from the *DSM-IV* has particularly targeted queer and trans youth for "treatment." The manual's entry on GID argues, "By late adolescence or adulthood, about three-quarters of boys who had a childhood history of Gender Identity Disorder report a homosexual or bisexual orientation, but without concurrent Gender Identity Disorder" (APA 1994, 536). Implementing the entry on GID diagnosis as a claim about etiology, an entire homophobic and transphobic therapeutic industry has cropped up in an attempt to treat and eliminate the trans and queer pathology, especially in young males (Califa 1997, 264–65; Butler 2004, 78, 89).

Even if we were to isolate and challenge such forms of hate masquerading as medicine, the norms represented by the diagnosis have a powerful way of generating other forms of violence, both internalized and externalized. It has already been demonstrated that queer and trans youth are particularly vulnerable once such arguments about a normal kind of gender identity permeate a society. The increased incidence of suicide and suicide attempts among queer and trans youth should give further pause to those who consider these claims to be a part of healthy social- ization (Sedgwick 1993, 1–3; Butler 2004, 78, 98–99). This is occurring in a society where violence against those whose gender does not strictly conform, including especially trans people, is both tolerated and all too common, as the prominent cases of Brandon Teena, Tyra Hunter, Gwen Araujo, and Lawrence King make sadly clear.[12] Given these continuing conditions, though the gender identity disorder diagnosis in some senses "recognizes" a trans identity, one could ask, with Judith Butler, whether the diagnosis itself does violence, "whether the diagnosis of transgen- dered youth does not act precisely as peer pressure, as an elevated form of teasing, as a euphemized form of social violence" (Butler 2004, 99). In this case, the rhetorical practices of scientific authorities have aided in forming communities where violence is socially normalized.

While there is no self-evident solution to this current conundrum of access to services almost exclusively through a normalizing and stig- matizing apparatus of social and material violence, it has led to the more active, publicly political presence of trans people. Activists have ques- tioned why the APA or the AMA are the authoritative experts on their lives, when they have consistently failed even to consult with trans people in developing diagnostic and treatment materials (Wilchins 1997; Califa 1997, 221–44; Meyerowitz 2002, 283–86).[13] Trans activists ask what anyone should when encountering such a dominant script: from whose perspective is this written? According to trans activists like Kate Born- stein, medical and psychiatric professionals erase, or at least miscon- strue, the origins of trans status and suffering by ignoring this question

---

12. On violence against trans people, young and old, see the overview provided in Califa 1997, 230–37. On the more recent case of Gwen Araujo, see Butler 2004, 6, 98–99. On the shooting of Lawrence King on February 12, 2008, and the violent tar- geting of people based on gender identity or expression, especially "biological males," see the recent work of GenderPAC: www.gpac.org and www.50under30.org. For the suggestion that "genderbashing" might more accurately describe the phenomenon typically labeled "gaybashing," see V. Namaste 2006, 584–600.

13. On the emergence in recent decades of trans studies as it relates to the rise in trans activism, see Whittle 2006, xi–xvi; Stryker 2006, 1–17.

of perspective. The definitive source for trans information should not be the authorized clinician but the trans person. As Bornstein forcefully declares, "I am transsexual by choice, not by pathology" (Bornstein 1994, 118; cf. Stryker 2006, 1–2).

The medicalized claims about pain being internal in origin ignores that a large source of pain and even violence is from an external source: one's peers and the surrounding culture. The problem is displaced from the violence of certain medical standards and wider gender norms onto a "disorder" that is apparently internal to the one suffering under these norms (Bornstein 1994, 83; Butler 2004, 99–100). It is not the status or identity of being trans that causes pain and suffering, but our normalizing and stigmatizing reactions to this form of being and belonging. To Bornstein and Butler, the repetitive insistence that one must fit into certain gender norms, including choosing one of two fixed and polarized genders, causes suffering—and not only for trans people (Bornstein 1994, 8, 58, 121; Butler 2004, 81). In order to have a gendered identity, one is socially compelled to perform repetitively, even fastidiously, the authorized norms. Once Bornstein recognized the vigilance with which one must police the self in order to fit into one or the other group, she rather irreverently suggested that gender also works like a cult (Bornstein 1994, 103–5). In hitting upon such an image, Bornstein highlights the communal dynamics of identity and identifies that these norms require that one "religiously" express gender.

A vital alternative for Bornstein is to openly claim the name of trans or transgendered. But, the medicalization of trans identity both prevents and stipulates against such open identification, causing further pain and suffering. As Sandy Stone has observed, "it is difficult to generate a counterdiscourse if one is programmed to disappear" (Stone 2006, 230).[14] In order to best fit into their "new" gender, then, trans folk are told by their doctors and therapists to lie about their trans status as well as about their lives before transitioning.

> Transsexuality is the only condition for which the therapy is to lie. This therapeutic lie is one reason we haven't been saying too much

---

14. For further reflections on the problematic dynamics of visibility for trans men, see Green 2006, 499–508. Green nicely sums up the impossible constancy and burdensome normalization of secrecy: "in order to be a good—or successful—transsexual person, one is not supposed to be a transsexual person at all" (501).

about ourselves and our lives and our experiences of gender; we're not allowed, in therapy, the right to think of ourselves as transsexual. (Bornstein 1994, 62)

Giving voice to one's status, and the experiences of living as trans, breaks this silence and prevents the erasure that the medicalized model attempts to perform. Of course, the normative model contains within itself the insight it attempts to erase: that there are those who do not conform to this vision of gender and normalized identity. When one reads against the grain of this model, one realizes it is premised upon the existence of these nonconformists, those on whom the model especially tries to operate. The history of the diagnosis and its applications are resources for resisting the diagnosis.

From this perspective, trans is no longer defined as a disordered or pathological status, nor affixed to the professionalized verification of internalized suffering or pain. Establishing, or perhaps resurrecting, a practice of trans determination and description resists and resituates the diagnostic arguments. Unlike the dominant model, which requires the authorizing force of external expertise and the certifying surgical moment to move the subject out of the "not yet," recent trans theories and practices demonstrate that people are *already* living as trans, already disrupting the authorizing and normalizing structures. Such a praxis of resistance and rethinking could itself be the organizing nexus around which trans is variously defined. If trans could describe "anyone whose performance of gender calls into question the construct of gender itself," the trans person is more properly viewed as acting and active, rather than acted upon, by whatever set of social forces (Bornstein 1994, 121). When the community resists such normalizing gestures, they can develop their own rationales for why they should never be forced to suffer such violence, whether in the clinics or in the streets, in our schools or in our homes.

5. Reflections on This Rhetorical Juxtaposition and Some Initial Conclusions

What could be gained by reading these two rhetorical situations contrapuntally? The process of identifying the normalizing contours of two different dominant scripts, while resituating and resisting them in terms of other perspectives, allows the analyses of these two interactions to inform and reinforce each other. An engagement with these dominant scripts is especially relevant to feminist and queer forms of analysis, as the scripts make authoritative claims to normative categories of identity and community. We must learn to sharpen and refashion our analytic abilities in order to better identify and assess oppressive forms of argumentation, in whatever contexts they appear. In this regard, the process of applying critical evaluation and suspicious resistance in itself becomes a resource for the development of such skills.

Beyond such potentially strategic outcomes, this analysis has also explored a number of connections, if not exact parallels, between these seemingly disconnected rhetorical contexts. Both of these dominant scripts operate to authorize certain figures in a hierarchical and paternalistic structure: Paul and medical or psychological professionals. In their discourse they are the sole arbiters able to judge whether others are deserving of or have attained a specific status: community member or transsexual. In doing so, they construct these identities in a normalized fashion, molding specific and exclusive models for how one might fit the identity. Both constructions also help to constitute who "counts" as part of an officially sanctioned community; being the identity means belonging in the group.

Furthermore, both sets of dominant scripts especially focus on the aspect of suffering in ascertaining the normative communal identity. For Benjamin the revulsion at one's genitals and any accompanying forms of suffering are what differentiate "authentic" transsexuals from others. In Paul's schema, suffering in this world is not only characteristic of one who truly comprehends the cross, but it also redeems if one conforms oneself to this sacrificial model. Both sets of arguments also promise that fitting this model will result in the achievement of a new, better status: a "normal" person, in gender and/or in accordance with divine will. Thus, both narratives have their focal point in the act of suffering. Both follow a pattern whereby one should conform to a downward experience or descending status, in order to achieve an upward experience or an ascending status. Both argue that the authorities in this schema, Paul or the doctor/therapist, are the main conduits for effecting this hoped-for reversal—from down to up, low status to high. To achieve the desired identity and its corresponding status, one must go through these authorities and the normalized standards they maintain.

Yet, when we recall that all arguments are made in an interactive context, we recognize that there were other perspectives and other parties. While we have access to those who resist and resituate such arguments in the twenty-first century, the first-century context requires that we develop skills to reconstruct submerged voices and pose alternatives. Neverthe-less, these challenges to the dominant scripts refuse and reformulate in similar ways. The Corinthian women prophets and trans activists offer perspectives that significantly depart from those who seek to speak for or construct them in certain ways. Neither group waits for the authorizing structure to grant them a certain status or identity: these women already see themselves as members of the Corinthian assembly, while trans folk increasingly choose self-description and determination over external pathologization. Neither identity is dependent only upon surgical inter-vention or epistolary affirmation. Indeed, both show signs of living these identities in ways that do not easily conform to the models offered by the dominant scripts.

An encounter with trans folk and the Corinthian women prophets especially reformulates the relationship between status and suffering pre-scribed by normalizing authorities. First, there is no necessary connection between attaining the status of their identity and experiencing specific forms of suffering. Second, both parties seem to describe their experience as *already* living a particular status or identity. The self-described trans person does not wait for an authorizing diagnosis, while the Corinthian women are already experiencing wisdom and prophetic power. Neither group is looking to move downward in a hierarchical structure nor expe-riencing this process of being and becoming as a loss or lack. In joining the Corinthian assembly and/or identifying the desire to cross or transcend gender, both groups seem to achieve a heightened sense of satisfaction or an elevated position. Finally, those that resist such a script about suffering would likely disagree with dominant claims about its source. The causes for their suffering are neither within them—internalized pathology—nor according to divine will—the debasement of the cross. Rather, suffering comes from outside themselves in the wider norms and structures of dom-inating power, even as these norms and structures differ in between the first- and twenty-first-century contexts. The violence both groups expe-rience is the expression of different elements of kyriarchal power: those norms that govern expectations and positions in terms of gender, ethnic, imperial, and economic status, among others.

The utility of this particular contrapuntal analysis can be further demonstrated in the confluence of religious and scientific discourses that occurs even now in the deployment of normative gender identity diag-noses. In her reflections on trans identity and this diagnosis, Butler high-lighted the work of George A. Rekers, a behavioral-science professor who advocates therapeutic intervention for young males who fail to conform to gender norms through the GID diagnosis (Butler 2004, 89–90). Rekers works not only to combat homosexuality in young males but also to instill a heteronormative sexuality so that they might become "proper" husbands and fathers. Interestingly enough, Rekers also argues for "the positive therapeutic effects of religious conversion for curing transsexualism … and on the positive therapeutic effect of a church ministry to repentant homosexuals" (Rekers 1996, 11–20). In many ways, Rekers's arguments correspond to the dominant scripts offered in both the *DSM-IV* and Paul's letters. His therapy/ministry portrays itself as the turning point for those suffering an unbearable, even unthinkable, abnormality, offering an opportunity to enjoy the status of a Christian, patriarchal, and heteronormative position, of which he is the arbiter and authority. Rekers's diagnostic argumentation not only echoes the confused muddle of the early sexological combination of homosexuality with transsexualism, but also combines the processes and effects of behavioral therapy and of Christian conversion.

However, the preceding analysis of the experiences of being, becoming, and belonging in both the contemporary trans and the ancient Corinthian communities might significantly problematize such arguments. Rather than conversion being the "solution" for trans- or homosexuality, it is distinctly possible that critical reflection upon trans identification is the solution for rethinking the meaning of conversion. Scholarly reconstructions of the Corinthian women prophets indicate that "conversion," or joining the assembly, was not a reversal but a process of actualization. Trans practices of support, survival, and sustenance function similarly: becoming is not a process of rejecting or debasing one's self but of slowly performing and enacting the self. One is not moving down in order to go up; one is moving into the identity and the community. The experiences and critical reflections on trans identity and practice question whether stringent norms and the defense of fixed boundaries should be the sole means for defining membership in a community, whether it be "Christian" or not.

Indeed, the causes of suffering might just be connected to such calcified claims about what religious conversion or communal membership should mean. The most common narratives developed and shaped by medicalized authorities have been alternately, if often critically and self-consciously, mimed by trans people looking for services and support routed through the transition delineated and guarded by such authorities (cf. Stone 2006, 225–30; Spade 2006, 325–28). Butler, Bornstein, and others cited above have articulated the potential problems with even resistant repetitions of such (auto)biographic narratives in the reinforcement of normalizing impulses. Yet, critics must also be able to recognize the potential influence of religious tropes on the narratives evident in science and society at large. The language used to describe, even prescribe, gendered identity shares features with biblical conceptualizations.

For example, the transitional or baptismal formula Paul cites and saves is initially introduced as a practice of the community members who have "put on"—*enedusasthe*, entered into, or clothed themselves with—*Christos* (Gal 3:27; cf. Rom 13:14). Just as Bornstein noted the "religious" way in which we must persistently "put on" gendered norms, Stone similarly highlights the specific repetition, enjoined by medical authorities, of an "'oriental,' almost religious narrative of transformation" in trans narratives about transition and initiation (Stone 2006, 222). Key to this narrative is the change of clothing and comportment necessary to cross an absolutized and dichotomous borderline of gender, a practice that Stone even links to the influence of this Pauline notion of baptism: entering into membership through a change of clothing—*enduein* (Stone 2006, 227, 234). The viewpoint reflected in these rhetorical practices approaches difference in exoticizing terms, sees borders as key markers of this difference, and imbues transcendent authority to those pioneers who can guide one across such borders. Such constructions bear obvious marks of the imperial-colonial contexts in which Pauline and sexological claims were, and continue to be, produced (cf. Halberstam 1998, 141–73; Stryker 2006, 14; Stone 2006, 222, 226, 229). Thus, the norms for entering into gender are also enmeshed within the dynamics of race, ethnicity, empire, and economy.

Not only does the expression of *enduein* function on geographic terms of crossing, but it also intersects with claims about the demonstration of an interiorized identity through externalized practice. For Paul, he will know if his audience is true and obedient in belonging by the adoption of the practices he recommends—that would be *his* meaning of baptism. The process of transition functions similarly for medical authorities, as a subject in both domains attempts to insert one's body into the meaning generated by these paternalizing authorities through certain signs on the surface. The "life-test" portion of the protocol emphasizes the importance of this outward appearance. The crossing import of dress practices, in either context, simultaneously reinforces the authority of the protocol, by following it, and contradicts it, by demonstrating that one can move and live across this policed line without the administration of exclusively protected treatments—emphasizing suffering, obedience, hormones, or surgery. The meanings and processes of crossing are far less constrained than the authoritative options presented in such dominant scripts, while the ambiguous relations between practices and identifications could make manifest the potential proliferation of positionalities at cross-purposes with an essentializing installation of borders or boundaries in, on, or through bodies.

The contemporary environment in which we speak about gender shares features with the thought-world generated by biblical argumentation. Yet, this does not mean that the meaning and practice of this argumentation is entirely predetermined, as the examples of the Corinthian women prophets and trans theorists and activists should make clear. The present contrapuntal reading provides an opportunity to disrupt and resituate what this kind of putting-on might still mean. The meaning of entering into a Christic community, for instance, need not be fastened to "putting on gender" as a discrete identity, set aside and segmented from others, as the anointing import of *christos* might suggest. Yet, gendered belonging can also be viewed as something more *chrisma*-tic, "rubbed or smeared on" as an outward indication of one's complex relation to the processes of identification. Indeed, gender cannot be put on as something set apart and solitary, particularly as it is dynamically, idiosyncratically, but ineluctably intertwined in the operations of norms surrounding sexuality and status, race and ethnicity, economy and empire.

Engaging with trans folk or the Corinthian women prophets could, then, christen new visions of communal being and belonging. The overlap and borrowing between the domains of science and religion show that critics faithful to the spirit of human community should take up not the cross but a series of crossings. These crossing are not over lines of the absolutized, dichotomous variety but work between and within different disciplines, seemingly disparate histories, and eclectically effective contexts; where the complex intermingling, alliance, and identification of matters queer, trans, religious, and feminist flourish. If taken seriously, then, critical perspectives from trans folk or the Corinthian women prophets might just revivify religiosity, not threaten it. If nothing else, concepts of belonging and initiation/conversion into a new community or identity could be radically altered for the better if dynamics of suffering and sacrifice were reconsidered along these lines. The reconstructions of Corinthian women prophets and the resistant reformulations of trans people both function to question how necessary and inherent such dynamics are to the creation of community. Both are alternate sources of authority for these processes.

Such outcomes help to explain the utility of this potentially queer con-trapuntal analysis of ancient Corinthian and contemporary trans activist communities. These modes of analysis help to make us more savvy about recognizing and engaging dominant, normalizing forms of argumenta-tion, wherever they may appear. This alone, I believe, would make it a worthwhile disciplinary practice. Yet, it also demonstrates the advantages of critical assessment of the foundations of our practices, whether they are based on a Pauline or scriptural authority or a medicalized or scientific basis. Such advantages become even clearer when the rhetorics of religion and science are intertwined, as they so often are in wider social arguments regarding gendered and sexualized normativity. This is especially power-ful considering that science and religion each so often carry such defini-tive weight in argumentative contexts both public and personal. Thus, it seems especially important to navigate and question how religious and scientific ideas might influence each other. In developing certain concepts as legitimate, appropriate, and authoritative, each might indirectly prepare the way for other related arguments, similar in style and—unfortunately—in effect.

This might suggest a new kind of accountability for religious stud-ies, particularly for those who deal with "foundational" materials that currently hold ancient and/or scriptural authority. Perhaps now the field should be prepared to trace and contest the range of effects of these mate-rials, in ways both obvious and more indeterminate. This calls for further suspicious assessments and a critical awareness of other potential voices. Thus, we might contest problematic uses of the text and its authority with-out reinstalling its canonicity. Such strategic queerying demonstrates the potential utility of both resisting and reusing or redeploying such tradi-tions. We cannot ignore such arguments precisely because they are being used to establish and/or reassert authority and a range of normalizing enforcements.

These kinds of strategies would have been harder to articulate without the socio-historical modeling performed by Antoinette Clark Wire. In the face of falsely foundationalist-styled claims—far too prominent in certain arguments about gender identity and sexuality—such feminist rhetori-cal reconstructions provide an ancient basis for queer and trans schol-ars to argue that such resistant practices have a history, and one learned through the engagement of canonical religious texts, no less! This analysis hopefully also demonstrates that women's history need not only be for women. Queer theorists could benefit from greater familiarity with this kind of historical enterprise, while feminist scholarship would considerably improve its import and impact if it addressed itself more often to the challenges of LGBTIQ subjectivity and community. Grappling with queer theory and trans identity and activism in turn illustrates how attentive analyses of ancient rhetorical interactions might have continuing relevance and applicability. Since we so often encounter arguments emanating from those domains currently accepted as the twin sources of authority— science and religion—it is imperative that we develop just such modes for challenging authoritative texts from either domain, especially when they prize or even inspire suffering and pain. So many forms of suffering need not continue, nor are they necessary to create or achieve certain kinds of status. If biblical studies were to heed such calls to ensure the safety, survival, and social justice of those marginalized and oppressed by normalizing rhetorical practices, it would indeed be a relevant and transformative disciplinary practice.

Works Consulted

APA (American Psychiatric Association). 1994. *Diagnostic and Statistical Manual of Mental Disorders*. 4th ed. Washington, D.C.: American Psychiatric Publishing.

Benjamin, Harry. 1966. *The Transsexual Phenomenon*. New York: Julian Press.

Bornstein, Kate. 1994. *Gender Outlaw: On Men, Women, and the Rest of Us*. New York: Vintage Books.

Butler, Judith. 2004. *Undoing Gender*. New York: Routledge.

Califa, Pat. 1997. *Sex Changes: The Politics of Transgenderism*. San Francisco: Cleis.

Castelli, Elizabeth A. 1991. *Imitating Paul: A Discourse of Power*. Louisville: Westminster John Knox.

Cauldwell, David O. 1949. Psychopathia Transexualis. *Sexology* 16:276–80.

Dreger, Alice Domurat. 1998. *Hermaphrodites and the Medical Invention of Sex*. Cambridge: Harvard University Press.

Green, Jamison. 2006. Look! No, Don't! The Visibility Dilemma for Transsexual Men. Pages 499–508 in Stryker and Whittle 2006.

Halberstam, Judith. 1998. *Female Masculinity*. Durham, N.C.: Duke University Press.

Hausman, Bernice L. 1995. *Changing Sex: Transsexualism, Technology, and the Idea of Gender*. Durham, N.C.: Duke University Press.

Hearon, Holly E. 2006. 1 and 2 Corinthians. Pages 606–23 in *The Queer Bible Commentary*. Edited by Deryn Guest et al. London: SCM.

Hirschfeld, Magnus. 1923. Die Intersexuelle Konstitution. *Jahrbuch für Sexuelle Zwischenstufen* 23:3–27.

Horsley, Richard A. 2000. Rhetoric and Empire—And 1 Corinthians. Pages 72–102 in *Paul and Politics: Ekklesia, Israel, Imperium, Interpretation; Essays in Honor of Krister Stendahl*. Edited by Richard A. Horsley. Harrisburg, Pa.: Trinity.

Kessler, Suzanne J. 1998. *Lessons from the Intersexed*. New Brunswick, N.J.: Rutgers University Press.

Kittredge, Cynthia Briggs. 2003. Rethinking Authorship in the Letters of Paul: Elisabeth Schüssler Fiorenza's Model of Pauline Theology. Pages 318–33 in *Walk in the Ways of Wisdom: Essays in Honor of Elisabeth Schüssler Fiorenza*. Edited by Shelly Matthews, Cynthia Briggs Kittredge, and Melanie Johnson-Debaufre. Harrisburg, Pa.: Trinity.

Marchal, Joseph A. 2005. Mutuality Rhetorics and Feminist Interpretation: Examining Philippians and Arguing for Our Lives. *Bible and Critical Theory* 1.3.

———. 2009. Mimicry and Colonial Differences: Gender, Ethnicity and Empire in the Interpretation of Pauline Imitation. Pages 101–27 in *Prejudice and Christian Beginnings: Investigating Race, Gender, and Ethnicity in Early Christian Studies*. Edited by Elisabeth Schüssler Fiorenza and Laura S. Nasrallah. Minneapolis: Fortress.

———. Forthcoming. Bodies Bound for Circumcision and Baptism: An Intersex Critique and the Interpretation of Galatians. *Theology and Sexuality*.

Martin, Dale B. 1995. *The Corinthian Body*. New Haven: Yale University Press.

———. 2006. *Sex and the Single Savior: Gender and Sexuality in Biblical Interpretation*. Louisville: Westminster John Knox.

Meyer, Jon, and Donna J. Reter. 1979. Sex Reassignment: Follow-up. *Archives of General Psychiatry* 36:1011–15.

Meyerowitz, Joanne. 2002. *How Sex Changed: A History of Transsexuality in the United States*. Cambridge: Harvard University Press.

Namaste, Ki. 1996. "Tragic Misreadings": Queer Theory's Erasure of Transgender Subjectivity. Pages 183–203 in *Queer Studies: A Lesbian, Gay, Bisexual, and Transgender Anthology*. Edited by Brett Beemyn and Mickey Eliason. New York: New York University Press.

Namaste, Viviane K. 2006. Genderbashing: Sexuality, Gender, and the Regulation of Public Space. Pages 584–600 in Stryker and Whittle 2006.

Prosser, Jay. 2006. Judith Butler: Queer Feminism, Transgender, and the Transubstantiation of Sex. Pages 257–80 in Stryker and Whittle 2006.

Rekers, George A. 1996. Gender Identity Disorder. *Journal of Human Sexuality* 1:11–20.

Said, Edward W. 1993. *Culture and Imperialism*. New York: Vintage.

Schüssler Fiorenza, Elisabeth. 1999. *Rhetoric and Ethic: The Politics of Biblical Studies*. Minneapolis: Fortress.

———. 2001. *Wisdom Ways: Introducing Feminist Biblical Interpretation*. Maryknoll, N.Y.: Orbis.

Sedgwick, Eve Kosofsky. 1993. *Tendencies*. Durham, N.C.: Duke University Press.

Spade, Dean. 2006. Mutilating Gender. Pages 315–32 in Stryker and Whittle 2006.

Stone, Sandy. 2006. The *Empire* Strikes Back: A Posttranssexual Manifesto. Pages 221–35 in Stryker and Whittle 2006.

Stryker, Susan. 2006. (De)Subjugated Knowledges: An Introduction to Transgender Studies. Pages 1–17 in Stryker and Whittle 2006.

Stryker, Susan, and Stephen Whittle, eds. 2006. *The Transgender Studies Reader*. New York: Routledge.

Whittle, Stephen. 2006. Foreword. Pages xi–xvi in Stryker and Whittle 2006.

Wilchins, Riki Ann. 1997. *Read My Lips: Sexual Subversion and the End of Gender*. Ithaca, N.Y.: Firebrand.

Wire, Antoinette Clark. 1990. *The Corinthian Women Prophets: A Reconstruction through Paul's Rhetoric*. Minneapolis: Fortress.

THE STRAIGHT MIND IN CORINTH: PROBLEMATIZING CATEGORIES AND IDEOLOGIES OF GENDER IN 1 CORINTHIANS 11:2–16

Gillian Townsley

> ... attack the order of heterosexuality in texts and assault the so-called love, the heroes of love, and lesbianize them, lesbianize the symbols, lesbianize the gods and the goddesses, lesbianize the men and the women. (Wittig 1992, 87)

Monique Wittig burst onto the French literary scene in 1964, at the age of twenty-nine, with the publication of her first novel, *L'opoponax*, for which she was awarded the Prix Medicis, one of the most prestigious literary awards in France. With her subsequent novels and theoretical essays functioning alongside her radical politics, she was foundational in the development of post-Beauvoirian French feminist philosophy, a movement that she would come to epitomize alongside the better-known figures of Luce Irigaray, Julia Kristeva, and Hélène Cixous. Although she moved to the United States in 1976, it was Judith Butler's reading and critique of her work in *Gender Trouble* (Butler [1990] 1999) that brought Wittig to the attention of academic feminist circles throughout North America, the United Kingdom, and Australasia. Subsequently, in 1992, Wittig published *The Straight Mind*, the first and only collection of her essays, many of which were previously published between 1980 and 1990 in *Feminist Issues* and *Questions Feministes*.[1] However, Wittig's influence in the field of queer theory has been significant but not altogether straightforward. While Butler critiqued much of Wittig's theoretical framework, Teresa de

---

1. The title comes from her essay "The Straight Mind," first read to the MLA Convention in 1978, included in this collection.

Lauretis is open about the influence of Wittig's theories on her own (de Lauretis 2005, 51).

In this essay, we will explore the notoriously problematic Pauline text 1 Cor 11:2–16 in light of Wittig's philosophy of gender. The majority of studies on this passage focus either on the surface matter of correct attire for worship that occasions Paul's arguments—primarily the historical issue of whether or not the issue concerns hairstyles (Isaksson 1965; Murphy-O'Connor 1980; von Gielen 1999) or head coverings (Oster 1988; Gill 1990)—or on the exegetical matters concerning Paul's use of such terminology as *kephale* "head" (Bedale 1954).[2] The result has been the spawning of countless articles, with scholars divided on every issue.

But on a deeper level, this passage also raises fundamental questions of gender and sexuality.[3] This essay proposes that in order to make progress on deciphering this text, an approach is needed that critically examines these gender issues, both in an examination of the content of Paul's argument and also in terms of the ideological positions taken by scholars themselves. Utilizing Wittig's theory of gender to *re*read this Pauline passage—intersecting biblical studies and poststructuralist theory—creates a marginal zone of critical inquiry, something that Butler reminds us is required when examining the complex issue of gender (Butler [1990] 1999, xxxii).[4] Such an exploration has the potential to enable a new que(e) rying of this passage, thus hopefully shedding some new light on this troublesome passage of the New Testament. However, such a reading will also potentially do more than this; it will also trouble the heteronormative categories of gender presumed by most readers of the text, que(e)rying the text in such a way as to affirm Wittig's point that "a new personal and

---

2. One should also see Grudem 1985, 2001, and the rebuttal in Cervin 1989, as well as Gundry-Volf 1997 and Dawes 1998, for a full discussion on this issue. This key concept will be examined in the second part of this chapter.

3. For an excellent overview of the issues and a shift towards a gender-critical approach to this passage, see Vander Stichele and Penner 2005.

4. Butler says of her own methodology, which is informed through the political convergence of feminism and philosophy, that "this inquiry seeks to affirm those positions on the critical boundaries of disciplinary life. … The complexity of gender requires an interdisciplinary and postdisciplinary set of discourses in order to resist the domestication of gender studies or women studies within the academy and to radicalise the notion of feminist critique" (Butler [1990] 1999, xxxii). Page numbering refers to the 1999 (tenth anniversary) edition of *Gender Trouble*. For more discussion on Butler and 1 Cor 11:2–16 in particular, see Townsley 2006.

subjective definition for all humankind can only be found beyond the categories of sex (woman and man)" (Wittig 1992, 19–20).

WITTIG'S MATERIALIST LESBIANISM

Wittig's theory of gender is known as materialist lesbianism. Taking as her point of departure Karl Marx's concept of the sexual division of labor in the family, Wittig analyzed the situation of women in terms of political economy. Refuting Marx's assumption that this division is natural, she identified women as a social category, an ideological construct, but even more than that, building on the materialist feminist analysis of Christine Delphy, a political class, the product of an economic relation of exploitation.[5] She declared, for example, that "There is no sex. There is but sex that is oppressed and sex that oppresses" (Wittig 1992, 2). Building also upon the work of Simone de Beauvoir, she exposed the oppressive relation between gender and subjectivity in language and culture. The title of her 1980 essay, "On ne naît pas femme"—"One is not born a woman"— was a clever play on the famous quote from de Beauvoir that "On ne naît pas femme: on le devient"—"One is not born but becomes a woman" (de Beauvoir 1949, 13; 1953, 295). As de Lauretis observes, "Almost the same words and yet such a difference in meaning. ... In shifting the emphasis from the word *born* to the word *woman*, Wittig's citation of de Beauvoir's phrase invoked or mimicked the heterosexual definition of woman as 'the second sex,' at once destabilizing its meaning and displacing its affect" (de Lauretis 2005, 53).

Seeking the disappearance of women as a class, Wittig posed the reconceptualization of the subject as "the lesbian," a figure who exceeds the categories of sex and gender, who is not a product of a social relationship with a man, and who is thus "*not* a woman" (Wittig 1992, 20). She argued that women need to extract themselves from the "myth of woman"[6] that

---

5. Although Wittig critiques both dialectics and materialism, citing their lack of recognition of the political dimension of the division between the sexes, she does not reject an overall Marxist framework. She acknowledges her debt to the analyses of Christine Delphy and Colette Guillaumin in this regard and accepts Delphy's phrase "materialist feminism" as an apt descriptor of her own approach (Wittig 1992, xiv, 16–18).

6. Wittig acknowledges that this concept was first described by de Beauvoir (de Beauvoir 1953, 25, 174, etc.).

is imposed upon them by the dominant discourse of heteronormativity; the idea that women are a "natural" group that exist in relation to men—a relation that she describes as "servitude" and that "implies personal and physical obligation as well as economic obligation" (20). For Wittig, the only way to escape this myth, and to destroy the category of "woman," is through lesbianism. She states that "the refusal to become (or to remain) heterosexual always meant to refuse to become a man or a woman, consciously or not" (13). She further explains that "lesbianism provides for the moment the only social form in which we can live freely. Lesbian is the only concept I know of which is beyond the categories of sex (woman and man), because the designated subject (lesbian) is *not* a woman, either economically, or politically, or ideologically" (20).[7]

While acknowledging the historical difficulty of the individual subject, particularly within Marxism (Wittig 1992, 16–19), Wittig also discusses the importance of language as the means of producing such political and personal transformation (30–32). How gender functions at the grammatical level in language—in the reinforcement of heterosexuality and the appropriation of the universal by men—is of central importance for Wittig. She suggests that gender enforces upon women a particular category, depriving them of the authority of speech, denying them universality, and ultimately stripping them of subjectivity (81). She declares that "language casts sheaves of reality upon the social body, stamping it and violently shaping it" (78).

However, Wittig also suggests that language is neutral; it is raw material lying there to be used by the writer to create something new (Wittig 1992, 71). Words are likened to the Trojan horse—a "war machine" by which the author can shock the reader into an awareness of how language operates in the domain of ideology (71–73). Literature thus has the potential "to pulverize the old forms and formal conventions" that buttress heteronormativity and the domination of women (69).[8] For Wittig, the act of

---

7. Butler describes Wittig's lesbian as "a third gender" (Butler [1990] 1999, 26), and notes that this figure is "neither female nor male, woman nor man … a category that radically problematizes both sex and gender as stable political categories of description" (Butler [1990] 1999, 144). However, Butler has some major difficulties with Wittig's theory; her critique of Wittig was widely accepted but has also since been described by Wittig scholars as a *mis*reading. For a fuller discussion see Townsley 2007.

8. This idea of violence is critiqued by several feminists, such as Englebrecht 1990,

writing is a political act "of unwriting and rewriting" in order to specifically demonstrate that the category of "women" is not a natural group but a historical creation of the dominant phallogocentric point of view (Shaktini 2005b, 158). Gender, then, can—and indeed, "must"—be destroyed through the power of language (Wittig 1992, 81).

With this brief description of Wittig's gender theory in mind, we can turn to the task of que(e)rying 1 Cor 11:2–16. Primarily, I want to consider Wittig's challenge to "attack the order of heterosexuality in texts" and to "lesbianize the men and the women"—as stated in the quote at the start of this paper. The rest of this essay, then, will fall into two parts. First, by exploring various *mis*readings and *re*readings of both Wittig and 1 Cor 11:2–16, we will consider the possibility that the "problematic"[9] men in the Corinthian congregation may be comparable with Wittig's "lesbian" figure.[10] Second, we will focus on the notoriously problematic verse 1 Cor 11:3 and the "order of heterosexuality" that underpins it, seeking to reveal some of the heteronormative ideologies that are often ignored in the infamous *kephale* "head" debates that surround this verse.

THE "LESBIAN" MEN OF CORINTH

As we noted above, it was Butler's reading and critique of Wittig that was the catalyst for increasing awareness of her work outside of France. However, while many Wittig scholars argue that Butler's critique of Wittig is, in fact, a *mis*reading, as we shall see, other scholars found Butler's reading incisive. One such scholar is Daniel Boyarin, who utilized Wittig's theory in two articles exploring early Christian formulations of gender (Boyarin 1998, 2003). In his initial analysis, the crucial biblical text for Boyarin is 1 Cor 11:2–16, where he suggests, "Paul makes practically explicit his theory of gender as produced in the sexual relation" (Boyarin 1998, 123).[11] His

---

96. For Wittig's defense of her view see Wittig 2005, 45. See also the discussion in Shaktini 2005b, 150–52.

9. To take MacDonald's description of the women at Corinth and reassign it (1990, 164).

10. Permission to reprint parts of my article from the journal *Hecate*, where much of this material first appeared, is gratefully acknowledged (see Townsley 2007).

11. However, Boyarin opts in his second article to omit any reference to 1 Cor 11:2–16, perhaps implying that he has reconsidered the usefulness of this passage. In addition, we ought to note that very few scholars find this passage so clear, com-

initial premise is that early Christianity is a culture in which gender did not operate in a way that would produce so-called natural sex and suggests that this idea is exemplified by the theories of Wittig (118).

Boyarin's focus is primarily on Paul and his response to the Corinthians regarding whatever it was that they were up to that disturbed him so greatly. Citing key verses from this passage, he explains how Paul combines two systems of conceptualizing gender, one in which there is an explicit hierarchy (vv. 3, 7–9) and one in which there is none (vv. 11–12). The absence of hierarchy does not necessarily correspond to a practical equality, however; rather, Boyarin suggests it points to a representation of androgyny existing on the level of the spirit. Boyarin says, "Paul could never imagine a social eradication of the hierarchical deployment of male and female bodies for married people" (Boyarin 1998, 123). It is this qualification of marriage that seems to be the crucial factor here. Boyarin observes that for Paul, "it is (hetero)sexuality, therefore, that produces gender ... any possibility of an eradication of male and female and its corresponding social hierarchy is only possible on the level of the spirit, either in ecstasy at baptism or perhaps permanently for the celibate" (123). The key point for Boyarin is that "spiritual androgyny is attained only by abjuring the body and its difference" (121). As long as women renounce their sexuality and maternity—that which makes them specifically female—they may attain a level of autonomy and creativity on the spiritual sphere. Turning to an examination of Philo, Boyarin explains further: "As the category 'women' is produced in the heterosexual relationship, so in Philo a female who escapes or avoids such relationships escapes from being a woman" (121–22).

Boyarin thus anticipates his connection between this early Christian thinking[12] and Wittig's theory of gender. He makes this connection even more clearly when he states that "by escaping from sexuality entirely, virgins thus participate in the 'destruction of sex,' and attain the status of the spiritual human who was neither male nor female" (Boyarin 1998, 122). He finds the parallels between the views on gender found in the stories

---

menting rather that Paul is being "obscure" and "contradictory" (Scroggs 1972, 297), "inarticulate, incomprehensible, and inconsistent" (Bassler 1992, 326–27).

12. We ought to note here that Boyarin describes Philo as "one of the foundational thinkers for the version of Judaism that was to become Christianity," calling his work "a generative and important source for later orthodox Christian thinking" (Boyarin 1998, 119).

of Philo, along with other early Christian writings such as *Joseph and Asenath, Paul and Thecla*, et cetera, and the feminist philosophy of Wittig "stunning" (1998, 126; 2003, 25). He notes that Wittig herself makes such a connection when she states that "the category of sex ... turns half of the population into sexual beings, for sex is a category which women cannot be outside of. ... Some lesbians and nuns escape" (Wittig 1992, 6–7). Boyarin suggests, therefore, that "Wittig's lesbian is another version of the woman of Hellenistic Judaism or early Christianity made male and thus free through celibacy. ... Metaphysically speaking, nothing has changed" (Boyarin 1998, 127; 2003, 25). Philo's "virgins" and Wittig's "lesbian" are therefore almost—but not quite[13]—identical in that they are *not* women. Boyarin is openly reliant on Butler's analysis of Wittig. He declares that Butler "demonstrates clearly" that Wittig's call for the destruction of the category of sex is dependent on the same metaphysics, and thus the "same masculinist ideologies of transcendence," as Philo (1998, 126–27; 2003, 25). In citing Butler's critique of Wittig's adherence to the metaphysics of substance, he defends his conclusion that Wittig's position "ends up being almost entirely a reflection of the patristic ideology of freedom as pregendered and of nongender as male" (1998, 127; 2003, 25).

At this point we need to ask a few questions. Recalling that Boyarin is openly reliant on Butler's analysis of Wittig, what if, rather than being "incisive" (Boyarin 1998, 127), Butler's analysis of Wittig is instead a *misreading*, as many Wittig scholars claim? How would that affect Boyarin's reading of the theology implicit in 1 Cor 11:2–16? If we were to *reread* Wittig's theory in a way consistent with those who defend her work—and thus seek to hear Wittig's voice more clearly than Butler's[14]—might another reading of this passage emerge? Would we perhaps find that while Boyarin's reading accurately reflects a Philonic-Pauline view of gender, a *rereading* of both Wittig and the text reveals a view of gender character-

---

13. Boyarin notes "the enormous difference that sexual pleasure is not denied Wittig's lesbian" (Boyarin 1998, 127; 2003, 25). However, see comments below by Wittig scholars that suggest that this is irrelevant—Wittig's lesbian is not about desire in any case.

14. Of course, in doing so, we also reveal several of the central debates existing within feminism itself—the divide between Anlgo-American and French feminism, and the divide between essentialist and social-constructionist theories of gender—or "difference" and "equality" feminisms—that runs through both. See the discussions in Fuss 1989 and Schor 1995.

ized by the Corinthians themselves—those whose voice is *not* heard in
Boyarin's discussion? Remembering that for Wittig writing is a political
act of unwriting and rewriting, perhaps this is a strategy we can emulate.
If we *re*read this passage in such a way as to hear what we might call the
"subdominant voices" of both Wittig and the Corinthians,[15] rather than
the dominant points of view of both Butler and Paul, this "troublesome"
passage may yet prove open to further que(e)rying.

In order to affirm this possibility, let us consider the words of de
Lauretis; as one of those scholars who found Butler's analysis of Wittig to
be a *mis*reading, she points primarily to Butler's failure to understand the
figural, theoretical character of Wittig's "lesbian" and says,

> These critiques mainly failed to see that Wittig's "lesbian" was not just
> an individual with a personal "sexual preference" or a social subject
> with a simply "political" priority, but the term or conceptual figure for
> the subject of a cognitive practice and a form of consciousness that are
> not primordial, universal, or coextensive with human thought, as de
> Beauvoir would have it, but historically determined and yet subjectively
> assumed—an eccentric subject constituted in a process of struggle and
> *interpretation*; of *translation, detranslation*, and *retranslation* ... a *rewrit-
> ing* of self in relation to a new understanding of society, of history, of
> culture. (de Lauretis 2005, 55, emphasis added)

Wittig's "lesbian," then, is not so much the "cognitive subject" that Butler
posits (Butler [1990] 1999, 26)—with all the Cartesian connotations inherent in such a figure—but rather a conceptual figure whom de Lauretis
describes as an "eccentric subject ... a subject that exceeds its conditions
of subjection, a subject in excess of its discursive construction, a subject
of which we only knew what it was not: not-woman" (de Lauretis 2005,
52, 56). She goes on to add that this lesbian "is figured in the practice of
writing as consciousness of contradiction ... a consciousness of writing,
living, feeling, and desiring in the noncoincidence of experience and language, in the interstices of representation" (57–58). Subjectivity in such
lacunary spaces is therefore eccentric in that it involves a displacement, or
a disidentification; a leaving of the conceptually and/or politically familiar
for that which is unknown, "a place from which speaking and thinking are

---

15. To rephrase Boyarin's use of the concepts "dominant" and "subdominant" fic-
tions (Boyarin 1998, 12, 24).

at best tentative, uncertain, unauthorized" (53). This displacement—this reconceptualization of the subject—is not a static, singular event however; it inevitably entails "a constant crossing back and forth, a remapping of boundaries between bodies and discourses, identities and communities" (53).

Dianne Chisholm further clarifies this issue: "It should now be clear that Wittig's 'lesbian body' does not represent a real, physical, or political body; it does not imag(in)e lesbian persons nor even lesbian erotic experience. Rather, it *acts* as a body-metaphor; a *catachresis*, a metaphor without a literal referent that serves to conceptualize a radically different body/body politic, to think beyond representations of the conventional, naturalized body" (Chisholm 1993, 204). In addition, Karin Cope reminds us that Wittig's lesbian subject "is not a seamless whole, the One of patriarchal male 'major' subjectivity" (Cope 1991, 78). Rather, she states, "the lesbian 'I' is a 'minor' subjectivity; fragmentary and fractured" (78). She cites Wittig's own comment that "the minority subject is not self-centered as is the straight subject. ... This [involves] a constant shifting which, when the text is read, produces an out-of-the-corner-of-the-eye perception; the text works through fracturing" (Wittig 1992, 62). Cope goes on to say that "the power of minority subjectivity comes from multiplying sites of difference—so that even a 'major' subject is revealed to be different from itself, fragmentary and fractured, minoritized, as in the so-called death of the subject. ... When *the* subject is dead, subjects, however fragmented and fragmentary, remain to write and be written" (1991, 78).

And, finally, it is appropriate to hear the comments of Namascar Shaktini, renowned Wittig authority and compeer. She suggests that one reason why Anglo-American feminists have misread Wittig is that they have not paid enough attention to her self-acknowledged debt to the French linguist Emile Benveniste and his theory of the speaking subject.[16] In brief, Benveniste posits the indeterminateness of the concept "I," saying, "There is no concept 'I' that incorporates all the I's that are uttered at every moment in the mouths of all speakers. ... It is a term that cannot be identified except in ... an instance of discourse and that has only a momentary reference. ... *I* and *you* do not refer to 'reality' or to 'objective' positions in space or time but to the utterance, unique each time, that contains them. ... [They are]

---

16. Again, this raises the issue of the distance between Anglo-American and Continental philosophical discussions.

'empty' signs that are nonreferential with respect to reality'" (Benveniste 1971, 226, 219). Shaktini thus makes the connection between Benveniste's "I" and Wittig's "lesbian" in that they are both "empty signs" able to be filled only in specific instances of discourse (Shaktini 2005, 157).

With these *re*readings of Wittig's "lesbian" in mind, we are ready to *re*read 1 Cor 11:2–16. As we have already noted above, this text is notoriously difficult; biblical scholars have debated the various hermeneutical, theological, and historical aspects of this text with little consensus emerging on any of the issues (Thiselton 2000, 800–806). This passage allows for—and even encourages—an approach that accepts contradictions, multiplicities, and "out-of-the-corner-of-the-eye" perceptions. It is a passage replete with lacunae, "empty signs," and "eccentric" subjects who defy definition.

Elsewhere I have argued that it is crucial in terms of a gender analysis to ensure adequate attention is given to the Corinthian men in this passage (Townsley 2006).[17] Too many analyses of this text have either ignored the presence of the men in Paul's argument, or declared that their role in his argument is purely hypothetical, and have focused solely on the behavior of the "problematic women" (MacDonald 1990, 164).[18] Yet both textually and historically there is no reason to suppose that Paul is not also addressing the men's behavior alongside that of the women. A *re*reading of this passage, then, can take into consideration the possibility that the men—by playing with the established sign systems of clothing and coiffure—are as involved in "gender-scrambling" (Redick 1994, 39) behaviors as the women.[19] Consequently, these men may be as "eccentric" as, if not more so, their female counterparts. As contradictory, unthinkable figures, ignored or deemed hypothetical, viewed as effeminate and thus mislabeled as "homosexual,"[20] these men may be reflecting a subdominant view of gender. And as such, it might even be possible to liken them to Wittig's "lesbian" figure.

---

17. Thiselton also makes this point (2000, 800, 805).

18. Many scholars writing on 1 Cor 11:2–16 either deem the role of the men in Paul's argument as hypothetical (for example Fee 1987) or ignore their presence altogether (for example Dowling and Dray 1995).

19. Paul may well be *more* concerned with the behavior of the women, but I am not concerned with the historicity of this passage, only with issues of gender.

20. See the discussion in Barrett 1971; Scroggs 1972; and Murphy-O'Connor 1980. This is a whole new area for discussion; see my unpublished Ph.D. dissertation chapter and 2007 SBL International Meeting paper " 'Horror of Homosexualism': Paul's Response to a Corinthian Conflict?" (Vienna, 2007).

A consideration of first-century Mediterranean views on masculinity reveals that for anatomical males, masculinity is not a given but something that needed constant attention and maintenance (Gleason 1990; Martin 1995; Moore and Anderson 2003). Within the Stoic view of sexuality, men and women were arrayed along a continuum "according to their metaphysical perfection … along an axis whose telos was male" (Laqueur 1990, 5). If they did not maintain the appropriate gender behaviors, men risked slipping down this scale toward effeminacy, and in the words of the Stoic contemporary of Paul, Musonius Rufus, this would be "to appear as women, and to be seen as womanish, something that should be avoided at all cost" (frag. 21).[21]

However, there are also some examples of male behavior in Mediterranean contexts that do not fit with this dominant view of gender. As noted elsewhere, gender-role reversal was an important component in various religious festivals celebrated by the Greeks, particularly those regarding Heracles and Dionysus (Townsley 2006). The male worshippers of these gods would engage in "ritual transvestism," donning feminine apparel in order to "show themselves off as ambisexed beings, striving to transcend gender categories" (Frontisi-Ducroux and Lissarrague 1990, 228–29). With regard to the followers of Dionysus, many observers regarded this ritual transvestism as a shameful activity (Livy 39.15.9; 4.21).[22] Such language of shame is exactly how Paul describes the Corinthians' behavior (11:4–7, 13–15). And such language reflects the dominant view of sexuality, as we might expect.

But for those followers, whose writings we do not have, to be dressed as women, "to be seen as womanish," was not something shameful (Farnell 1971, 5:160; Loraux 1990, 21–35). Remembering that the Corinthians were primarily Mediterranean in their religious background and cultural environment, it would seem that an alternative, subdominant view of sexuality is operating here. Boyarin does in fact note some exceptions to this dominant view of gender. With no elaboration at all, Boyarin simply notes—in brackets—that "there were valued female characteristics and metaphors for male Christians as well" (Boyarin 1998, 126) and—in a footnote—that

---

21. See in particular the essays by David Clines, Diana Swancutt, and Jennifer Glancy in Moore and Anderson 2003 for more on ancient constructions of masculinity in relation to Paul.

22. We must remember, however, that the cult of Dionysos was also denigrated because of its debauchery, not just its practices of cross-dressing.

"there are representations in late antique Christianity of males 'becoming female' as well" (Boyarin 2003, 35 n. 9).[23]

The Corinthian male worshippers, then, by virtue of their "shameful" behavior, may well be additional examples of men who challenged the accepted gender hierarchy and who are thus examples of the contradictions and noncoincidences of experience and language that we can only see out of the corner of our eyes; easily missed, fragmentary and fractured, tentative, uncertain, unauthorized, those who abide in the interstices of representation, on the boundaries of identity—and as such, those whose voices are seldom heard, those whom we would want to highlight here. The Corinthian men may thus be described as conceptual, theoretical "lesbians": men who have challenged the dominant institution of heteronormativity, who experience disidentification and displacement—who radically symbolize a reconceptualization of the subject. Perhaps we could rephrase Boyarin and conclude that the men of Corinthian Christianity are another version of Wittig's lesbian, made *not*-men and free through the taking-on of the female.

KEPHALE—HETERONORMATIVE POLITICS OF THE BODY

Having considered the possibility of "lesbianizing" the "problematic" men of Corinth, we can now turn to a closer exploration of the text itself. As the author of this passage, Paul is using rhetoric in order to effect some change in the Corinthians' behavior. Yet, many scholars suggest that an analysis of the tone in this passage reveals that Paul is not altogether certain of his own stance on this issue, is struggling to work out his own theology of gender, and is thus "convoluted" and "confused" in his argumentation (Bassler 1992, 326–27).[24] As a piece of rhetoric, this text appears to be slippery indeed; Paul uses praise (v. 2, in contrast to v. 17), references to metanarrative (Gen 1 and 2), threats of "shame" and "dishonor" (vv. 4–6, 14), references to "Nature" (v. 14), and he concludes with a somewhat frustrated appeal to the example of other churches (v. 16). Paul is clearly hoping to influence the behavior of these men and women who are "praying and prophesying" in such a way that is somehow both in line with the

---

23. Although Boyarin doesn't mention his sources for these comments, we might note the work done in this area by Harrison 1990, 1992 and Burrus 2000.

24. Many other scholars make similar comments; see n. 12 above, and Schüssler Fiorenza 1983, 228; Brooten 1988, 296; Hays 1997, 183; Gorman 2004, 264.

traditions that he has taught them (v. 2) and yet also no longer within the bounds of what some others, including Paul himself, deem acceptable.

Wittig's theory asks us to consider how language operates in the domain of ideology. Given the instability that is evident in this text, and the slipperiness with which Paul handles this subject, what do we observe with regard to ideology? The passage is replete with ideological content and has been the source of much ongoing discussion regarding gender issues in both feminist and conservative circles, in both pastoral and academic settings. Paul's statements on gender in these verses are grounded in theological language, conveying to many readers, historically and currently, a sense of cosmological truth going beyond any specific cultural context, reinforcing certain notions of social order. As we noted earlier, Wittig warns us about the power of language to act upon the social reality. In particular, ideology—defined by Wittig as "the discourses of the dominating group" (Wittig 1992, 25)—seeks primarily to reinforce heterosexuality. Wittig suggests that this is done through a rhetoric that "envelops itself in myths, resorts to enigma, proceeds by accumulating metaphors, and ... poeticize[s] the obligatory character of the 'you-will-be-straight-or-you-will-not-be'" (Wittig 1992, 28). Such a description could hardly be more apt to the passage at hand and, in particular, to the specific verse to which we now turn and seek to trouble, 1 Cor 11:3:

Θέλω δὲ ὑμᾶς εἰδέναι ὅτι παντὸς ἀνδρὸς ἡ κεφαλὴ ὁ Χριστός ἐστιν, κεφαλὴ δὲ γυναικὸς ὁ ἀνήρ, κεφαλὴ δὲ τοῦ Χριστοῦ ὁ θεός.

But I wish you to know that the head of every man is Christ, and the head of woman is man,[25] and the head of Christ is God.

Immediately after the *captatio benevolentiae* with which he opens this passage (v. 2),[26] Paul outlines a series of three parallel pairs of relationships that center on the word κεφαλή, "head": every man and Christ, woman and man, and Christ and God. At the center of this triptych we

---

25. There is some debate here over the translation of γυνή and ἀνήρ; this can be seen in the difference between various translations; the REB, NIV, and NJB opt for "man/wife" whereas the NRSV opts for "husband/wife"—although only here in the middle clause of v. 3.

26. So think many commentators and scholars, eg., Barrett 1971, 247; Fee 1987, 500; Schrage 1995, 499; Collins 1999, 395. However, some see an ironic or even sarcastic tone present; see Moffatt 1938, 149; Hurd 1983, 182–83.

find the fundamental pairing of woman and man, a pairing around which the whole passage itself revolves. And it is here, in this pairing, that Paul headlines a theology of gender which could easily be read as reinforcing heteronormativity: κεφαλὴ δὲ γυναικὸς ὁ ἀνήρ, "(and) the head of woman is the man." If we opt for the NRSV translation, "The husband is the head of his wife," this even further reinforces the connection with heteronormativity, as it is within the specific institution of marriage that heteronormativity is buttressed; the addition by the NRSV of the possessive "his" could be seen to further reinforce this notion. Certainly in its binary opposition of man and woman—or husband and wife—and in its sense of hierarchy, this statement in v. 3 appears to affirm such a heteronormative ideology. In order to probe deeper into this ideology, this paper will examine the concept of κεφαλή at the center of the text. An examination of the scholarship in this area not only reveals the polemical nature of the debate but also points to its political nature, perhaps nowhere more obviously than in the United States,[27] providing us with some fascinating insights into what we might call the politics of the body. It is in debate over what Paul meant by his statement κεφαλὴ δὲ γυναικὸς ὁ ἀνήρ, "the head of woman is the man," that we find politics and bodies/heads clash. As Wittig states, the subjugation of women by men is a *political* fact, but one that is often concealed behind a "body of discourses" (Wittig 1992, 5).

In considering the middle pairing of κεφαλὴ δὲ γυναικὸς ὁ ἀνήρ, we begin by recalling how Wittig describes the relationship between man and woman. Wittig reminds us of the "myth" of women, a crucial concept underpinning heteronormativity in which women form a "natural group" existing in a "subservient" relationship to men (Wittig 1992, 9–11). Women are perceived as "natural" in that they are seen as sexual beings defined by the capacity to give birth and thus have a relationship with men based on physical, personal, and economic obligation, a relationship that Wittig deems artificial and purely political in origin. In particular, she notes that this is centered on the marriage relationship and describes it thus: "The category of sex is the product of a heterosexual society in which men appropriate for themselves the reproduction and production of women [the raising of children and the work of domestic chores] and

---

27. While scholars from other countries have contributed to the debate, the situation in the United States seems particularly polarized. See, for example, the comment by Peter Kivisto that "there is something unique about the American scene" with regard to religion and politics (1994, 223).

also their physical persons by means of a contract called the marriage contract" (6).

The key element within this relationship, according to Wittig, is the Marxist notion of "domination" (Wittig 1992, 4).[28] This concept conveys the idea that between various groups in society there exists a power dynamic where one group exerts control over the other, be that economic, political, social, or sexual, *and* that this control—or domination—be accepted as "natural," based on the supposed differences between the groups.[29] Wittig employs this term to describe the relationship between the sexes. As she puts it, "This thought which impregnates all discourses, including common-sense ones—Adam's rib or Adam *is*, Eve is Adam's rib—is the thought of domination. Its body of discourses is constantly reinforced on all levels of social reality and conceals the political fact of the subjugation of one sex by the other" (5). In her analysis, men are the "ruling class who have determined that their domination be viewed as "natural" given the "natural" differences between the sexes. And, as noted above, this relationship is therefore a heterosexual one, based on the reproduction of the species, and is legitimized through the marriage contract. Wittig likens this to the relationship between employer and worker, at best, and slave owner and slave, at worst.[30]

At this point, we need to consider what many commentators regard as the key word of the whole passage, and certainly of this verse, κεφαλή.[31] For

28. Marx and Engels say, "The ruling ideas are nothing more than the ideal expression of the dominant material relationships, the dominant material relationships grasped as ideas: hence of the relationships which make the one class the ruling one, therefore, the ideas of its dominance" (Marx and Engels [1845] 1938, 39).

29. This rule, or power, is maintained through a web of beliefs, and institutional and social relations, that the Marxist intellectual Gramsci calls "hegemony" (Gramsci 1992).

30. Wittig says, "Compare this contract [that of marriage] with the contract that binds a worker to his employer" (Wittig 1992, 6); "The category of sex is the category that ordains slavery for women" (8); "We are escapees from our class in the same way as the American runaway slaves were when escaping slavery" (20).

31. Not all scholars would agree, of course; Belleville argues that "it is actually δόξα [glory] and not κεφαλή that provides the key to understanding Paul's train of thought" (2003, 215). While scholars generally acknowledge that by far the most common usage of κεφαλή is in its *literal* sense as a physical head of a person or animal, it is the *metaphorical* sense of the word that is debated. This is complicated in 1 Cor 11:2–16 because it would seem that Paul is employing the term deliberately for its polyvalent potential—and it is difficult for readers to determine when he is referring

if, as some scholars suggest, this word can be understood metaphorically to mean *authority over*, then perhaps Paul has placed something akin to the Marxist notion of dominance at the center of the relationship between "husband and wife." However, the debates within evangelical circles over the meaning of κεφαλή are legendary;[32] as Thiselton states in his commentary, "The history of claims about the meaning of κεφαλή is immense and daunting" (2000, 812).[33] The traditional metaphorical meaning for κεφαλή is, as already noted, *authority over*, and is usually pitted against the meaning *source, origin*, often suggested as a more egalitarian interpretation. Scholars have tended to argue strongly for one meaning or the other, often making statements that completely contradict those of other scholars and that thus appear impossible to reconcile.

For example, at the forefront of the *authority over* position, Wayne Grudem declares that, in light of his survey of 2,336 examples, it is "very difficult to accept anyone's claim that *head* in Greek could not mean 'ruler' or 'authority over'" and further, as "no instances were discovered in which κεφαλή had the meaning 'source, origin,' ... it would seem wise to give up once for all the claim that κεφαλή can mean 'source'" (Grudem 1985, 52–53). By contrast, Gordon Fee states that "the metaphorical use of *kephale* 'head' to mean 'chief' or 'the person of the highest rank' is rare in Greek literature ... this metaphorical sense is an exceptional usage and not part of the ordinary range of meanings for the Greek word. Paul's understanding of the metaphor, therefore, and almost certainly the only one the Corinthians would have grasped, is 'head' as 'source,' especially 'source of life'" (Fee 1987, 502–3). Others who hold this *source* view make equally bold statements; the opening sentence of Catherine Clark Kroeger's discussion of this issue asserts that "the concept of *head* as 'source' is well

---

to the physical head of a person and when he is referring to "head" in a metaphorical sense; Collins, for example, states that Paul "plays on the multiple meanings of 'head'" (1999, 396).

32. See in particular the debates between Grudem 1985, 1990 and Cervin 1989, and the response to this debate in Perriman 1994. See also the response in Grudem 2001 to Kroeger 1987, 1993. Other scholars who have made significant contributions to the debate are Bedale 1954; Fitzmyer 1989, 1993; Dawes 1998; and Belleville 2003.

33. Thiselton also comments that "the translation of this verse has caused more personal agony and difficulty than any other in the epistle, not least because of the huge array of research literature and lexicographical data which presses controversially and polemically for diverse translations of κεφαλή" (Thiselton 2000, 811). See his thorough examination of the various meanings of κεφαλή (812–22).

documented in both classical and Christian antiquity and has long been accepted by scholars" (Kroeger 1987, 267).

On a deeper level, however, such polemic points to the political nature of the debate that is concealed behind the discourse and thus rarely addressed. Scholars who tend to follow the *authority over* position are invariably conservative in their views on the nature of the husband-wife relationship, seeing women's subordination as a central aspect of marriage and as a limiting factor within church ministry. It is not surprising, therefore, to see Grudem on the board of directors for the Council of Biblical Manhood and Womanhood (CBMW), an organization that grew out of a concern with, amongst other things, "the widespread uncertainty and confusion in our culture regarding the complementary differences between masculinity and femininity ... the increasing promotion given to feminist egalitarianism ... and behind all this the apparent accommodation of some within the church to the spirit of the age" (Piper and Grudem 1991c, 469).[34] On the other hand, scholars who prefer the *source, origin* option tend to be more egalitarian in their approach to the roles of men and women in marriage and church ministry.[35] Again, we are not surprised to see that Kroeger was on the board of directors as president emerita, and Fee on the board of reference, for the organization Christians for Biblical Equality (CBE), an organization that was formed after some members of the Evangelical Women's Caucus (EWC) felt that this group was moving in a direction they perceived as "unbiblical"—specifically its affirmation of lesbianism.[36]

Both of these groups (CBMW and CBE) were formed in 1987[37] and are still active twenty years later.[38] Both claim to be evangelical in nature,

---

34. See also the CBMW website, http://cbmw.org.

35. Grudem labels many followers of the *source, origin* option as "Christian feminist," but he also notes that others who do not generally endorse Christian feminism have also supported this view of κεφαλή (1985, 39).

36. CBE was initially affiliated with the international organization Men, Women and God: Christians for Biblical Equality, based in London. See their website for a full account of their history and core values: http://www.cbeinternational.org (cited 22 May 2007).

37. However, they disagree about the effect of one upon the other in their establishment; CBE states that the CBMW grew out of opposition to CBE, while CBMW states that it was formed independently; see the history section of the CBE website, and also Piper and Grudem 1991a, 403.

38. According to an e-mail from Marissa Cwik, research coordinator for CBE,

affirming the divine inspiration of the Bible and seeking a biblical approach to contemporary issues;[39] and both are concerned about preventing the breakdown of marriage and family and have a "welcoming but not affirming" approach to homosexuality/lesbianism.[40] Yet these organizations are diametrically opposed when it comes to the ideology underlying their views on the nature of men and women and how they are to relate to each other socially, politically, economically, and spiritually. Given the influence of the scholars involved in these organizations, at least within Western evangelical circles, with regard to matters pertaining to male-female relationships, marriage, and ministry in general, and for understanding 1 Cor 11:2–16—and other Pauline κεφαλή passages[41]—in particular, it is important to explore the underlying political ideologies of these groups further in order to reveal what has tended to be concealed or at least not made explicit.

CBMW

Central to the differences between these two groups is debate over the meaning of κεφαλή and the concept of *headship* that has come into

---

"membership has grown since our incorporation as a nonprofit in 1989." She makes the interesting point, however, that this membership is "constantly changing." She explains that "while there is a core of individuals who remain committed as CBE members, there is also another significant portion of individuals who join CBE only for a period of time … to learn as much as they can as their paradigm shifts and as they address the issues that initially inspired their membership." She suggests that the best indicator of CBE's influence is thus not membership but "the ongoing changes in church and nonprofit policies that increasingly embrace women's leadership" (e-mail dated May 26, 2007). The CBMW, however, state in an e-mail that they are not a membership organization: "The only members of CBMW are our council members … who serve as the governing body" (e-mail dated June 7, 2007).

39. See each organization's statement of belief. Clearly what we are dealing with here, then, are groups that are *both* on the conservative wing of a "left-right" political/theological spectrum—hence the epithet "egalitarian" rather than "liberal" when describing CBE.

40. To borrow the title from Stanley Grenz's book as promoted on the CBE website (Grenz 1998).

41. The word κεφαλή is found not only in 1 Cor 11:2–16 but also in Eph 5:23. It also appears throughout Ephesians and in Colossians in relation to Christ, who is "head over everything," for example (Eph 1:22). For discussion on the meaning of κεφαλή in Ephesians, see Dawes 1998.

common parlance in evangelical circles;[42] as Grudem states, "This discussion [on κεφαλή] is of considerable interest today because of its relevance to women's and men's roles in marriage" (Grudem 1990, 3). The foundational document for the CBMW is the Danvers Statement, which begins with the affirmation that "both Adam and Eve were created in God's image, equal before God as persons and distinct in their manhood and womanhood" (Piper and Grudem 1991c, 469–72). It goes on to expand on this distinction by declaring that "Adam's headship in marriage was established by God before the Fall," with the subsequent call for husbands to exercise "loving, humble headship" and wives to exercise "intelligent, willing submission" (470). A quick glance through Piper and Grudem's book, *Recovering Biblical Manhood and Womanhood: A Response to Evangelical Feminism*, which was especially commissioned as a project of the CBMW and which expands on the Danvers Statement, illustrates the centrality of 1 Cor 11:2–16, and in particular 11:3, in the argument for the particular style of marriage and family that they affirm.[43] What emerges is an understanding of κεφαλή as *authority over* and a concept of *headship* that therefore creates a picture of the family with the husband/father as the leader, sole breadwinner, and ultimate decision maker. The role of the woman is restricted to "motherhood" and "vocational homemaking" (469).[44]

This binary role division, seen as based in the divinely ordained distinctions between the sexes, is further elaborated upon in one particular article concerned about "the unisex mentality that is gaining popularity in our society today" (Rekers 1991, 294–95). Throughout this article there is much talk of "our culture" and "our society" and of the various roles in the family, church, and wider community that men and women are to take. These tend to illustrate a particular image reminiscent of 1950s white, middle-class America; masculine sex-roles include financially supporting

---

42. There is no term *headship* in the Bible, of course, but the usage of the concept implies an explicit theology that is rather more developed than the text can support. Both the CBMW and CBE Web sites have much to say about the topic of *headship*, leadership, submission, equality, and other related issues.

43. No other scriptural passage comes close with regard to references. There are eighty-nine references to the passage itself and to verses within it (twenty-one for 11:3 alone). Only 1 Tim 2:8–15 compares, with thirty-nine references (eighteen for 2:12 alone) (Piper and Grudem 1991c, 546–47).

44. Women are specifically challenged to choose full-time home-making and "God's business" over and above career and "secular employment" (Piper 1991, 56).

one's children, abstaining from sexual relations with males, playing professional sports on all-male teams, serving in combat, living in a fraternity,
wearing a suit and tie, and opening doors for women and girls. Feminine
sex-roles include wearing modest clothing, abstaining from sexual relations
with females, wearing a dress, living in a sorority, wearing make-up, and
shaving underarms or legs. Women are certainly *not* seen as contributing
financially, playing sports of any kind, engaging in combat, or even wearing
trousers (307). This hardly conjures up an image of multicultural America
or of those who live in poverty and who cannot afford a suit and tie, let
alone to go to college.

In considering the political nature of this particular image of the
American family as white, middle-class, nuclear, and heterosexual, we
ought to note that a Marxist approach, such as that which Wittig is partly
dependent upon, argues that the nuclear family is the basic economic
unit of capitalist society. Examining this link between capitalism and the
nuclear family, with the father as its head, we might also note that the
word "capitalism" originates from the Latin word for "head," *caput*. For
Marx, this concept of "head" is of "paramount importance" (Press 1977,
336 n. 18). As a materialist, Marx insisted that the dynamic of production
and consumption, and the way in which they have become separated from
each other in human society, is the root cause of alienation and oppression. He explains it thus: "As in the natural body, head and hand wait upon
each other, so that the labor-process unites the labor of the hand with
that of the head. Later on they part company and even become deadly
foes" (Marx [1859] 1904, 283).[45] This separation between production and
consumption, between the head and the body—the hand—is widened in
capitalist society and, as already noted, is expressed most fundamentally
in the patriarchal nuclear family.

The marriage relationship, according to Marx and Engels, consists of
both the original division of labor—that of the sexual act—and the notion

---

45. For Marx, this analysis was central to his critique of Hegel, who places consciousness—the head—at the center of man's existence. Rather than reifying this separation between the head and the body, Marx was highly critical of it, arguing that a
Hegelian politics of "the head" gives rise to an authoritarianism that allows for monarchy, for example, and other social hierarchies that he despised; see Marx [1843–1844]
1970. Thus Marx "regarded it as his greatest achievement, and the cornerstone of his
materialism, to have taken this philosophy of the head, and as Engels said, 'placed it
on its feet'" (Press 1977, 336).

of private property, about which they say, "the nucleus, the first form ... lies in the family, where wife and children are the slaves of the husband" (Marx and Engels [1845] 1938, 21). In his later book, *The Origin of the Family, Private Property and the State*, Engels discusses the emergence of the nuclear family as the basic economic unit of capitalist society. The monogamous family, as he describes it, is "based on the supremacy of the man" (Engels [1884] 1942, 125) and enables the preservation and inheritance of property (135, 138). For those in the "possessing classes," this supremacy is based on the obligation the man is under to earn a living and support his family; "that in itself gives him a position of supremacy without any need for special legal titles and privileges. Within the family he is the bourgeois and the wife represents the proletariat" (137). For the proletariat, he notes, for whom industry has taken the wife out of the home and into the factory, making her a breadwinner for the family, "no basis for any kind of male supremacy is left" (135).[46] Wittig's statement, "The category of sex is the category that ordains slavery for women" (1992, 8), therefore echoes Engels's statement that "the modern individual family is founded in the open or concealed domestic slavery of the wife" ([1884] 1942, 137).

Engels goes on to forecast that

> the peculiar character of the supremacy of the husband over the wife in the modern family ... will only be seen in the clear light of day when both possess legally complete equality of rights. Then it will be plain that the first condition for the liberation of the wife is to bring the whole female sex back into public industry, and that this in turn demands that the characteristic of the monogamous family as the economic unit of society be abolished. (Engels [1884] 1942, 137–38)

This, in many ways, is precisely what happened after the second wave of feminism in the 1970s in the West (Popenoe 1993, 527–55).[47] As women

---

46. The exception to this, he notes, is "the brutality toward women that has spread since the introduction of monogamy" (Engels [1884] 1942, 135). Given the widespread problems of domestic violence in society, this ought not to be ignored. It is an issue touched upon by Piper and Grudem's book only briefly (Piper and Grudem 1991b, 62; Piper and Grudem 1991c, 114, 501 n. 13), although a search on the CBMW website offers more current resources, such as Powlison, Tripp, and Welch 2003, 265–76 (cited 4 September 2008).

47. Popenoe notes, "In 1960, 42% of all families had a sole male breadwinner; by 1988, this figure had dropped to 15%. ... In 1960, only 19% of married women (hus-

demanded economic freedom and returned to the workforce, this was met
with strong resistance by those whose "supremacy" was threatened, and
we see the emergence in the United States of groups such as the CBMW,
seeking a return to "traditional family values."[48] The decline of the family
was widely touted, but in particular it was the decline of the *nuclear* family
that caused concern.[49] Engels's comments are echoed by those who, one
hundred years later, observed what was occurring in American society:

> Reacting strongly to the lingering male dominance of this family form, as
> well as to its separate-sphere removal of women from the labor market,
> the women's movement came to view the traditional nuclear family on
> very negative terms. ... Today, those who believe in less male dominance
> and greater equality for women ... share the views of the women's move-
> ment in favoring an egalitarian family form, with substantial economic
> independence for wives. (Popenoe 1993, 535)

"Traditional family values" was a core issue for the Republican party during
the 1980s, and although U.S. Vice-President Dan Quayle's political speech
on "family values" in 1992—with his infamous aside about the television
character Murphy Brown, who chose to have a baby out of wedlock—led to
an outcry from liberal and feminist groups, and damaged the Republican
presidential campaign of that year, it remained an important platform in

---

band present) with children under 6 years of age were in the labor force full- or part-
time or were looking for work. By 1990, that figure had climbed to 59%" (1993, 531).

48. Other groups include the American Family Association (1977), Focus on
the Family (1977), Christian Voice (1978), Concerned Women for America (1979),
Moral Majority, headed by Jerry Falwell (1979)—formed out of the Christian Voice;
revived in 2004 as the Moral Majority Coalition—Family Research Council (1981),
and the Christian Coalition, headed by Pat Robertson (1989)—formed out of the
Moral Majority. The Traditional Values Coalition, which includes many of these
other groups, typifies the stance of these groups with its commitment to patriotism
and opposition to "deviant" sexual behaviors—those that do not fit the pattern of the
nuclear family. See their website for more details: http://www.traditionalvalues.org/
defined.php (cited 22 May 2007).

49. The majority of children were still being raised by at least one natural parent,
but in single-parent, blended-family or gay/lesbian structures. Popenoe states, "Recent
family decline is more serious than any decline in the past because what is breaking up
is the nuclear family, the fundamental unit" (Popenoe 1993, 527). Note that changes in
the structure of the family are perceived as *decline*, rather than, for example, *diversity*
or *progress*.

American politics during the 1990s.[50] During the 2000s this has been coupled with an upsurge in patriotism in light of the September 11 attacks. The Traditional Values Coalition (TVC), for example, regularly posts articles that conflate their perceived "enemies" in sensational fashion: in response to some strong critiques of the Bush government, the TVC posted the comment that "a dangerous Marxist/Leftist/Homosexual/Islamic coalition has formed—and we'd better be willing to fight it with everything in our power."[51] More recently, in light of transgender man Thomas Beatie's pregnancy, TVC Executive Director Andrea Lafferty stated in a press release, "Americans face rising gasoline prices; and brave American soldiers are being killed on the battlefield to fight Islamic terrorism—while U.S. Rep. Robert Andrews (D-NJ) holds a hearing today on 'discrimination' against drag queens and she-males in the workplace. What's wrong with this picture?"[52] Such a conflation of political, religious, and sexual identities as the "other" highlights the straight, white, Christian, capitalist ideal that lies behind the conservative view of the "traditional family."

Bodies, and in particular those of women—but also those who, like Thomas Beatie, do not conform to the male "norm"—are to be controlled; reproductive, economic, and marital freedoms are highly regulated. Abortion, divorce, premarital sex, cohabitation, transgender pregnancy, and homosexuality are all opposed in the promotion of "family values." Groups that support these options, as well as affordable childcare, sex education, and parent-friendly employment laws, for example—which they also label as "family values"—are vilified and seen as not only anti-Christian but also anti-American.[53]

---

50. See Kivisto 1994, 223–27, and others in that special issue of *Sociology of Religion*, for a discussion on the New Christian Right (NCR) during the 1990s. See also Arnold and Weisberg 1996, 194–220.

51. See http://www.traditionalvalues.org/modules.php?sid=2533.

52. See the press release "Americans Face Energy Crisis While House of Representatives Holds a She-Male Hearing!" (June 26, 2008); http://www.traditionalvalues.org/modules.php?sid=3348 (cited 4 July 2008).

Immediately after the birth of Beatie's baby (on July 3, 2008), Andrea Lafferty stated, "This bizarre she-male pregnancy was little more than a publicity stunt to push forward the homosexual and transgender political agenda in our culture. ... The news media must not kow tow to the whims of the homosexual/transgender community in redefining the reality of male and female." See the press release, "She-Male Gives Birth to Baby Girl" (July 3, 2008); http://www.traditionalvalues.org/modules.php?sid=3355.

53. Such groups as Planned Parenthood (PP; 1916), Parents and Friends of Les-

CBE

But what of the—comparatively—more liberal view? What ideologies of the body underlie the position of those who support an egalitarian reading of the text? The statement of faith for CBE, entitled "Men, Women and Biblical Equality Christians for Biblical Equality," opens with the declaration that "the Bible teaches the full equality of men and women in Creation and in Redemption" and declares that both men and women "were created for full and equal partnership ... [and share] jointly the responsibilities for bearing and raising children and having dominion over the created order."[54] What this means in practice is developed more fully in the literature available on the CBE Web site and in their academic journal, *Priscilla Papers*. As with Piper and Grudem's book for CBMW, the CBE material reveals that considerable attention is given to the concept κεφαλή and how it is to be understood, particularly in relation to the topics of marriage and women in ministry. What emerges in these articles is an understanding of κεφαλή as *source, origin*, in the sense of that which is the "beginning of life" or "point of origin," and that which is thus "productive of growing life" (Kroeger 2006, 5). The husband is therefore seen as a "servant provider of life" and of "growth and development" (Bilzekian 2008). With regard to the issue of "roles" within marriage, Marissa Cwik, the research coordina-

---

bians and Gays (PFLAG; 1972), and People for the American Way (PFAW; 1981). See comments about these groups, labeled as "leftist" and "crank" (PFAW) or as being behind the "abortion industry" (PP), on http://www.traditionalvalues.org/modules. php?sid=2583. TVC also declares on their website that "hate" and "discrimination" are part of TVC's "core values." Liberal groups have played with the "family values" phrase with such slogans as "hate is not a family value" and "poverty is not a family value"; for a history of the first slogan, see Hasian and Parry-Evans 1997, 27–42; for the second, see Jim Wallis's speech for the Sojourners "Call for Renewal" Conference in 2006, found at http://www.sojo.net/index.cfm?action=sojomail.display&issue=060629#3. The situation is similar in New Zealand; a recent conference was held in Dunedin, entitled "Family Breakdown in NZ—the cost—what can we do?" (November 10, 2007). One of the speakers was Bruce Logan, a representative of the conservative Christian lobby group Family First.

54. See "Men, Women and Biblical Equality Christians for Biblical Equality," on the CBE website, "Biblical Truths," nos. 1–2; http://www.cbeinternational.org/new/about/biblical_equality.shtml. Piper and Grudem comment on this statement, saying, "The difference in approach from the Danvers Statement [the equivalent statement of faith from the CBMW] is signalled at the outset ... men and women are *not* equal in significant ways" (1991a, 407).

tor for CBE, states that "we firmly believe that each individual and couple should have the freedom to make the choice for themselves [regarding women in the workplace, childcare, etc.] based on a mutual decision and guidance from the Holy Spirit and not have a choice regulated to them based on cultural constructs of gender roles."[55] CBE thus have a more open view of "family," recognizing and seeking to empower extended families, single- and dual-headed households, and blended and divorced families, and are liberal on matters such as women in the workforce.[56]

Nevertheless, as with CBMW, CBE's view of "family" is also strictly heterosexual. One of their core beliefs, as expressed in their statement of faith, declares that they believe "in the family, celibate singleness and faithful heterosexual marriage as God's design."[57] No less than their more conservative counterparts, bodies are still to be tightly regulated with regard to sex and desire; heterosexuality is the only normative expression of sexuality.[58]

The CBE website has links to articles on various topics, and the article on homosexuality by Catherine Clark Kroeger, who was a board member and president emerita of CBE, is representative of the CBE position on this issue. She writes on the supposed link between an affirmation of women's equality and endorsement of homosexuality, arguing that biblically this is not the case.[59] Rather, she argues, it is biblical to be in favor of women's equality but against homosexuality. She states that "although the Bible

---

55. E-mail correspondence (dated June 14, 2007).

56. E-mail correspondence with Marissa Cwik; she states that "CBE stands in support of the family, and by that we mean both the nuclear and extended family. ... CBE makes a conscientious effort to provide resources that empower all these definitions of 'the family'" (dated June 14, 2007).

57. See the "Statement of Faith" section of their website, http://www.cbeinternational.org/new/about/who_we_are.shtml. E-mail correspondence with CBE also confirms this: "CBE believes that marriage is reserved for heterosexual couples. In that light, we provide resources that are geared to heterosexual families" (e-mail dated June 14, 2007).

58. See, for example, the following articles available from CBE, which all affirm heterosexuality as the norm and homosexuality as unbiblical: Mickelsen 1988; Van Leeuwen 1997; Belleville 1998.

59. Piper and Grudem articulate such an anxiety, arguing that "to us it is increasingly and painfully clear that Biblical feminism is an unwitting partner in unravelling the fabric of complementary manhood and womanhood that provides the foundation not only for Biblical marriage and Biblical church order, but also for heterosexuality itself" (1991b, 84).

contains a handful of references to same-sex eroticism, nowhere is there given any sign of approval to homosexual be-havior [*sic*]. Rather, there is loving sympathy for the individual but condemnation of the conduct" (Kroeger 2004, 3).

It is in Kroeger's discussion of Paul, however, that we see her main reason for rejecting homosexuality. The gender hostility that was directed toward women in the ancient world, according to Kroeger, is clearly associated with a positive view of homosexuality.[60] It is also something that she suggests is overturned in the New Testament, particularly by Paul. She refers specifically to 1 Cor 11:11–12, saying that "Paul deals with this repugnance [fear of women's sexual anatomy] when he writes that woman had issued forth from man, and now men came forth from women, in an interdependent cycle" (Kroeger 2004, 7). Elsewhere she has argued that the entire passage of 1 Cor 11:2–16 is Paul's attempt to address these negative attitudes to women. For example, his "recycling" of the Genesis creation account is to highlight "women as a gift from God and a treasure for man," to show that in contrast to the Greek creation myths, woman "was created for a positive purpose" (Kroeger and Kroeger 1979, 214). She also notes that "the concepts of woman as the glory of man and 'neither the man without the woman nor the woman without the man' (v. 11) were important ones in combating the sex segregation which the Greeks themselves saw as a contributory factor in homosexuality" (217). She concludes this earlier article by saying, "Zeus, Apollo, Hercules, Eros, and even Aphrodite might opt for the love of boys; but Paul frames a positive endorsement of heterosexuality and an integrated Christian community, one body in the Lord" (218).

To rephrase things, we might say that according to Kroeger, the Greeks had a negative view of women, which if it did not directly lead them to embrace "homosexuality,"[61] was at least in some ways coupled with such a view.[62] The CBE position, by contrast, rejects this negative view of women

---

60. There are difficulties regarding the differentiation between orientation and behavior, of course; suffice to say that Kroeger seems unaware of the importance of these nuances.

61. To use the terminology of the organizations such as CBE and CBMW, anachronistic as this may be. See the discussions in Boswell 1980; Halperin 1990; Sedgwick 1990; Richlin 1993. Brooten 1996 provides an excellent overview of the issues.

62. While the ancient writings we have suggest that Mediterranean society may have had a positive—or, more likely, mixed—view of male-male sexual relations, they

and thus also rejects homosexuality, embracing heterosexuality instead. These two positions are thus diametrically opposed. If we bring Wittig into the discussion at this point, we note some interesting connections and contradistinctions with these two positions. As with CBE, Wittig rejects the negative view of women she observes in Western society. However, in contrast to CBE, she argues that this is an intrinsic part of heteronormativity, and thus she rejects heterosexuality and embraces homosexuality, although, unlike the Greek view, her focus is on lesbianism.[63] We could also add here a fourth position, such as that reflected by the CBMW, which might be said to hold a negative—or, perhaps, "restrictive"—view of both women *and* homosexuality.

Such a spectrum of views on these issues highlights the complexity of the political and ideological positions and the inadequacy of a "left-right" dichotomy. Despite the enormous gaps between CBE and CBMW with regard to male and female roles, and their views on headship—be it a stance on κεφαλή that insists on the meaning of *authority over* or one that prefers the *source, origin* option—there is nonetheless a subscription to the overriding framework of heteronormativity, the belief that heterosexuality is the fundamental norm within which the male/female dynamic ought to operate, ultimately within what Wittig calls the "obligation" of marriage (Wittig 1992, 6).

Throughout this examination of both the conservative and the egalitarian views on κεφαλή, with a focus on the organizations CBMW and CBE as representative of these views, we have revealed some of the ideologies underlying the debate. The debate over what Paul meant in 1 Cor 11:3 when he stated that "the head of woman is man" is not just a debate over the *authority over* or *source, origin* options. Despite appearances, it is not simply a matter of sifting through 2,336 examples of κεφαλή in Greek literature—nor of making oversimplistic generalizations about ancient Greek misogyny. Most scholars realize that they have biases, but few appear to reflect on the interests served by these biases. This lack of critical ideologi-

---

certainly indicate a negative view of female homoeroticism (Brooten 1996, 2). For a discussion on the connection between homophilia and misogyny in the contemporary context, see Bonnet 2001.

63. Wittig's focus on the "lesbian" figure has been critiqued for excluding gay men (Hennessy 1993, 971). However, Hale suggests that this view misreads Wittig as a lesbian separatist; for him the issue with Wittig lies more with whether or not gay men count as men in her view (Hale 1996, 118 n. 6).

cal engagement serves to further oppression, with certain economic and social advantages gained and reinscribed. While the debate over κεφαλή could look like a debate between conservative and egalitarian value systems, that's only the surface part of it; divergent views on κεφαλή show how such differences sustain a heterosexual normativity and the unquestioning reinscription of the nuclear family unit within capitalism.

CONCLUSION

This paper has explored Wittig's materialist lesbianism in relation to 1 Cor 11:2–16, with the aim of problematizing some of the categories and ideologies of gender that emerge from this text. By moving beyond the traditional conventions of sex and gender, and the traditional approaches to this passage, we have attempted a new que(e)rying of both. In other words, we have attempted the act of "unwriting and rewriting" the text— and the scholarship on the text—seeking both to "lesbianize the men" and to "attack the order of heterosexuality" underpinning, in particular, the debates over the meaning of κεφαλή in the text. Wittig's theories of gender both challenge and allow us to go beyond the categories of "man" and "woman," giving voice to subdominant expressions of sexuality normally unnoticed and most certainly unallowed in a heteronormative framework. By revealing the deeply "compulsory" nature of this framework within certain areas of biblical scholarship,[64] we have at least taken a step toward troubling such an ideology. In conclusion, we might remember that the purpose of such troubling is not merely to engage in flights of theoretical fancy; writing, *un*writing, *re*writing, reading, and *re*reading are *political* acts. As Wittig scholar Louise Turcotte concludes, "This meeting of theory and politics is fundamental for all political struggle, and it is precisely what makes Wittig's thought so disturbing" (1992, xii). The "lesbian men of Corinth" may disturb some people; others may be disturbed by the politics lying behind scholarly debates over ancient word meanings. But when we consider the use of 1 Cor 11:2–16 to buttress notions of male "headship" and/or authority, and to reinforce heteronormativity as a divinely ordained paradigm, then perhaps the more we can disturb—or trouble— this situation the better.

---

64. To make reference to Adrienne Rich's concept of "compulsory heterosexuality" (1980). Wittig also makes reference to Rich's concept (Wittig 1992, 44).

Works Consulted

Arnold, Laura W., and Herbert F. Weisberg. 1996. Parenthood, Family Values, and the 1992 Presidential Election. *American Politics Quarterly* 24:194–220.

Barrett, Charles K. 1971. *A Commentary on the First Epistle to the Corinthians.* 2nd ed. London: A&C Black.

Bassler, Jouette M. 1992. 1 Corinthians. Pages 321–29 in *The Women's Bible Commentary.* Edited by Carol A. Newsom and Sharon H. Ringe. London: SPCK; Louisville: Westminster John Knox.

Beauvoir, Simone de. 1949. *Le Deuxiéme Sexe: L'expérience Vécue.* Paris: Gallimard.

———. 1953. *The Second Sex.* London: Jonathon Cape.

Bedale, S. 1954. The Meaning of κεφαλή in the Pauline Epistles. *JTS* 5:211–15.

Belleville, Linda. 1998. *A Biblical Perspective on Sexuality.* Covenant Communications Occasional Paper 6. Chicago: Evangelical Covenant Church.

———. 2003. KEFALH and the Thorny Issue of Head Covering in 1 Corinthians 11:2–16. Pages 215–31 in *Paul and the Corinthians: Studies on a Community in Conflict; Essays in Honour of Margaret Thrall.* Edited by T. J. Burke and J. K. Elliott. NovTSup 109. Leiden: Brill.

Benveniste, Émile. 1971. *Problems in General Linguistics.* Translated by Mary E. Meek. Coral Gables, Fla.: University of Miami Press.

Bilzekian, Gilbert. 2008. I Believe in Male Headship. Christians for Biblical Equality. Online: http://www.cbeinternational.org/new/free_articles/male_headship.shtml.

Bonnet, Marie-Jo. 2001. Gay Mimesis and Misogyny: Two Aspects of the Same Refusal of the Other? Pages 265–80 in *Homosexuality in French History and Culture.* Edited by J. Merrick and M. Sibalis. New York: Harrington Park Press.

Boswell, John. 1980. *Christianity, Social Tolerance and Homosexuality.* Chicago: University of Chicago Press.

Boyarin, Daniel. 1998. Gender. Pages 117–35 in Taylor 1998.

———. 2003. On the History of the Early Phallus. Pages 3–44 in *Gender and Difference in the Middle Ages.* Edited by S. Farmer and C. B. Pasternack. Medieval Cultures 32. Minneapolis : University of Minnesota Press.

Brooten, Bernadette. 1988. Response to "Corinthian Veils and Gnostic Androgynes" by Dennis Ronald MacDonald. Pages 293–96 in *Images of the Feminine in Gnosticism.* Edited by Karen King. Philadelphia: Fortress.

———. 1996. *Love between Women: Early Christian Responses to Female Homoeroticism.* Chicago: Chicago University Press.

Burrus, Virginia. 1995. *The Making of a Heretic: Gender, Authority, and the Priscillianist Controversy.* Berkeley: University of California Press.

———. 2000. *Begotten, Not Made: Conceiving Manhood in Late Antiquity.* Stanford, Calif.: Stanford University Press.

Butler, Judith. (1990) 1999. *Gender Trouble: Feminism and the Subversion of Identity.* 10th anniv. ed. New York: Routledge.

Cervin, Richard. 1989. Does κεφαλή Mean "Source" or "Authority Over" in Greek Literature? A Rebuttal. *TJ* 10:85–112.

Chisholm, Dianne. 1993. Lesbianizing Love's Body: Interventionist Imag-(in)ings of Monique Wittig. Pages 196–216 in *Reimagining Women: Representations of Women in Culture.* Edited by S. Neuman and G. Stephenson. Toronto: University of Toronto Press.

Clines, David. 2003. Paul, the Invisible Man. Pages 181–92 in Moore and Anderson 2003.

Collins, Raymond F. 1999. *First Corinthians.* SP. Collegeville, Minn.: Liturgical Press.

Cope, Karin. 1991. Plastic Actions: Linguistic Strategies and *Le corps lesbien. Hypatia* 6 (3):74–96.

Dawes, Gregory. 1998. *The Body in Question: Metaphor and Meaning in the Interpretation of Ephesians 5:21–33.* Biblical Interpretation 30. Leiden: Brill.

Dowling, Robin, and Stephen Dray. 1995. *1 Corinthians: Free to Grow.* Crossway Bible Series. Leicester: Crossway Books.

Engels, Friedrich. (1884) 1942. *The Origin of the Family, Private Property and the State: In the Light of the Researches of Lewis H. Morgan.* London: Lawrence & Wishart.

Englebrecht, Penelope. 1990. "Lifting Belly is a Language": The Postmodern Lesbian Subject. *Feminist Studies* 16:85–114.

Farnell, Lewis R. 1971. *The Cults of the Greek States.* 5 vols. Chicago: Aegean Press.

Fee, Gordon. 1987. *The First Epistle to the Corinthians.* Grand Rapids, Mich.: Eerdmans.

Fitzmyer, Joseph. 1989. Another Look at ΚΕΦΑΛΗ in 1 Corinthians 11.3. *NTS* 35:503–11.

———. 1993. *Kephale* in I Corinthians 11:3. *Int* 47:52–59.

Frontisi-Ducroux, Françoise, and François Lissarrague. 1990. From Ambiguity to Ambivalence: A Dionysiac Excursion through the "Anakreontic" Vases. Pages 211–56 in Halperin, Winkler, and Zeitlin 1990.

Fuss, Diana. 1989. *Essentially Speaking: Feminism, Nature and Difference*. New York: Routledge.

Gielen, M. von. 1999. Beten und Prophezeien mit unverhülltem Kopf? Die Kontroverse zwischen Paulus und der korinthischen Gemeinde um die Wahrung der Geschlechtsrollensymbolik in 1 Kor 11,2–16." *ZNW* 90:220–49.

Gill, David W. J. 1990. The Importance of Roman Portraiture for Head-Coverings in 1 Corinthians 11:2–16. *TynBul* 41:245–60.

Glancy, Jennifer. 2003. Protocols of Masculinity in the Pastoral Epistles. Pages 235–64 in Moore and Anderson 2003.

Gleason, Maud W. 1990. The Semiotics of Gender: Physiognomy and Self-Fashioning in the Second Century C.E. Pages 389–415 in Halperin, Winkler, and Zeitlin 1990.

Gorman, Michael. 2004. *Apostle of the Crucified Lord: A Theological Introduction to Paul and His Letters*. Grand Rapids, Mich.: Eerdmans.

Gramsci, Antonio. 1992. *Prison Notebooks*. Translated by Joseph A. Buttigieg and Antonio Callari. New York: Columbia University Press.

Grenz, Stanley. 1998. *Welcoming but Not Affirming: An Evangelical Response to Homosexuality*. Louisville: Westminster John Knox.

Grudem, Wayne. 1985. Does ΚΕΦΑΛΗ ("Head") Mean "Source" or "Authority Over" in Greek Literature? A Survey of 2,336 Examples. *TJ* 6:38–59.

———. 1990. The Meaning of κεφαλή ("Head"): A Response to Recent Studies. *TJ* 11: 3–72.

———. 2001. The Meaning of κεφαλή ("Head"): An Evaluation of New Evidence, Real and Alleged. *JETS* 44:25–65.

Gundry-Volf, Judith M. 1997. Gender and Creation in 1 Corinthians 11:2–16: A Study of Paul's Theological Method. Pages 151–71 in *Evangelium-Schriftauslegung-Kirche: Festschrift für Peter Stuhmacher Zum 65. Geburtstag*. Edited by O. Hofius and J. Adna. Göttingen: Vandenhoeck & Ruprecht.

Hale, Jacob. 1996. Are Lesbians Women? *Hypatia* 11.2:94–121.

Halperin, David M. 1990. *One Hundred Years of Homosexuality and Other Essays on Greek Love*. New York: Routledge.

Halperin, David M., J. Winkler, and F. Zeitlin, eds. 1990. *Before Sexual-*

ity: The Construction of Erotic Experience in the Ancient Greek World. Princeton: Princeton University Press.

Harrison, Verna. 1990. Male and Female in Cappadocian Theology. *JTS* 41:441–71.

———. 1992. The Male Woman: A Feminine Ideal in the Early Church. *JTS* 43:231–34.

Hasian, Marouf A., and Trevor Parry-Evans. 1997. "A Stranger to Its Laws": Freedom, Civil Rights, and the Legal Ambiguity of *Romer V. Evans (1996). Argumentation & Advocacy* 34.1:27–42.

Hays, Richard. 1997. *First Corinthians.* Interpretation. Louisville: John Knox.

Hennessy, Rosemary. 1993. Queer Theory: A Review of the *differences* Special Issue and Wittig's *The Straight Mind. Signs* 18:964–73.

Hurd, John C. 1983. *The Origin of I Corinthians.* Macon, Ga.: Mercer University Press.

Isaksson, Abel. 1965. *Marriage and Ministry in the New Temple: A Study with Special Reference to Mt. 19.13–12* [sic] *and 1. Cor. 11.3–16.* Copenhagen: Gleerup Lund.

Kivisto, Peter. 1994. The Rise or Fall of the Christian Right? Conflicting Reports from the Frontline. *Sociology of Religion* 55:223–27.

Kroeger, Catherine Clark. 1987. The Classical Concept of *Head* as "Source." Pages 267–83 in *Equal to Serve.* Edited by Gretchen Gabelein Hull. London: Scripture Union.

———. 1993. Head. Pages 375–77 in *Dictionary of Paul and His Letters.* Edited by G. F. Hawthorne and R. P. Martin. Downers Grove, Ill.: InterVarsity Press.

———. 2004. Does Belief in Women's Equality Lead to an Acceptance of Homosexual Practice? *Priscilla Papers* 18 (2):3–10.

———. 2006. Toward an Understanding of Ancient Conceptions of "Head." *Priscilla Papers* 20 (3):4–8.

Kroeger, Richard, and Catherine Clark Kroeger. 1979. St. Paul's Treatment of Misogyny, Gynephobia, and Sex Segregation in First Corinthians 11:2–6 [sic]. Pages 213–21 in volume 2 of the *SBL 1979 Seminar Papers.* 2 vols. SBLSP 18. Missoula, Mont.: Scholars Press.

Laqueur, Thomas. 1990. *Making Sex: Body and Gender from the Greeks to Freud.* Cambridge: Harvard University Press.

Lauretis, Teresa de. 2005. When Lesbians Were Not Women. Pages 51–62 in Shaktini 2005c.

Loraux, Nicole. 1990. Herakles: The Super Male and the Feminine. Pages 21–35 in Halperin, Winkler, and Zeitlin 1990.

MacDonald, Margaret. 1990. Women Holy in Body and Spirit: The Social Setting of 1 Corinthians 7. *NTS* 36:161–81.

Martin, Dale B. 1995. *The Corinthian Body.* New Haven: Yale University Press.

Marx, Karl. (1843–1844) 1970. *Critique of Hegel's "Philosophy of Right."* Translated by A. Jolin and J. O'Malley. Edited by J. O'Malley. Cambridge: Cambridge University Press.

———. (1859) 1904. *A Contribution to the Critique of Political Economy.* Chicago: Charles H. Kerr.

Marx, Karl, and Friedrich Engels. (1845) 1938. *The German Ideology.* London: Lawrence & Wishart.

Mickelsen, Alvera. 1988. Can Homosexual Sex Be Sanctified? *The Standard*, October, 12–15.

Moffatt, James. 1938. *The First Epistle of Paul to the Corinthians.* London: Hodder & Stoughton.

Moore, Stephen D., and Janice C. Anderson, eds. 2003. *New Testament Masculinities.* SemeiaSt 45. Atlanta: Society of Bibical Literature.

Murphy-O'Connor, Jerome. 1980. Sex and Logic in 1 Corinthians 11:2–16. *CBQ* 42:482–500.

Oster, Richard. 1988. When Men Wore Veils to Worship: The Historical Context of 1 Corinthians 11.4. *NTS* 34:481–505.

Perriman, Andrew C. 1994. The Head of a Woman: The Meaning of ΚΕΦΑΛΗ in 1 Cor 11:3. *JTS* 45:602–22.

Piper, John. 1991. A Vision of Biblical Complementarity: Manhood and Womanhood Defined according to the Bible. Pages 31–59 in Piper and Grudem 1991c.

Piper, John, and Wayne Grudem. 1991a. Charity, Clarity, and Hope: The Controversy and the Cause of Christ. Pages 403–22 in Piper and Grudem 1991c.

———. 1991b. An Overview of Central Concerns: Questions and Answers. Pages 60–92 in Piper and Grudem 1991c.

———, eds. 1991c. *Recovering Biblical Manhood and Womanhood: A Response to Evangelical Feminism.* Wheaton: Crossways Books.

Popenoe, David. 1993. American Family Decline, 1960–1990: A Review and Appraisal. *Journal of Marriage and the Family* 55:527–55.

Powlison, David, P. D. Tripp, and Edward T. Welch. 2003. Pastoral Responses to Domestic Violence. Pages 265–76 in *Pastoral Leadership for Manhood and Womanhood*. Edited by W. Grudem and D. Rainey. Wheaton, Ill.: Crossway.

Press, Howard. 1977. The Existential Basis of Marxism. *Philosophy and Phenomenological Research* 37:331–44.

Redick, Alison. 1994. Review of Judith Butler, *Bodies That Matter*. *Lambda Book Report* 4 (2):39.

Rekers, George A. 1991. Psychological Foundations for Rearing Masculine Boys and Feminine Girls. Pages 294–311 in Piper and Grudem, eds., 1991.

Rich, Adrienne. 1980. Compulsory Heterosexuality and Lesbian Existence. *Signs* 5:631–60.

Richlin, Amy. 1993. Not before Homosexuality: The Materiality of the *Cinaedus* and the Roman Law against Love between Men. *Journal of the History of Sexuality* 3:523–73.

Schor, Naomi. 1995. French Feminism Is a Universalism. *Differences* 7:15–47.

Schrage, Wolfgang. 1995. *Der erste Brief an die Korinther*. EKKNT 7.2. Neukirchen-Vluyn: Neukirchener.

Schüssler Fiorenza, Elisabeth. 1983. *In Memory of Her: A Feminist Theological Reconstruction of Christian Origins*. London: SCM; New York: Crossroad.

Scroggs, Robin. 1972. Paul and the Eschatological Woman. *JAAR* 40:283–303.

Sedgwick, Eve Kosofsky. 1990. *Epistemology of the Closet*. Berkeley: University of California Press.

Shaktini, Namascar. 2005a. Introduction. Pages 1–6 in Shaktini 2005c.

———. 2005b. The Critical Mind and *The Lesbian Body*. Pages 150–59 in Shaktini 2005c.

———, ed. 2005c. *On Monique Wittig: Theoretical, Political, and Literary Essays*. Urbana, Ill.: University of Chicago Press.

Swancutt, Diana. 2003. "The Disease of Effemination": The Charge of Effeminacy and the Verdict of God (Romans 1:18–2:16). Pages 235–64 in Moore and Anderson 2003.

Thiselton, Anthony C. 2000. *The First Epistle to the Corinthians*. Grand Rapids: Eerdmans; Carlisle, U.K.: Paternoster.

Townsley, Gillian. 2006. *Gender Trouble* in Corinth: Que(e)rying Constructs of Gender in 1 Corinthians 11.2–16. *Bible and Critical Theory* 2.2:17.1–17.14.

———. 2007. Wittig's "Lesbian" and the Corinthian Men: Problematizing Categories of Gender in 1 Corinthians 11.2–16." *Hecate* 33 (2):56–73.

Turcotte, Louise. 1992. Forward: Changing the Point of View. Pages vii–xii in *The Straight Mind and Other Essays*. Boston: Beacon.

Van Leeuwen, M. Stewart. 1997. To Ask a Better Question: The Heterosexuality-Homosexuality Debate Revisited. *Int* 31:143–58.

Vander Stichele, Caroline, and Todd Penner. 2005. Paul and the Rhetoric of Gender. Pages 287–310 in *Her Master's Tools? Feminist and Postcolonial Engagements of Historical-Critical Discourse*. Edited by C. Vander Stichele and T. Penner. SBL Global Perspectives on Biblical Scholarship. Atlanta: Society of Biblical Literature.

Wittig, Monique. 1992. *The Straight Mind and Other Essays*. Boston: Beacon.

———. 2005. Some Remarks on *The Lesbian Body*. Pages 44–48 in Shaktini 2005c.

The Pastor and His Fops: Gender Indeterminacy in the Pastor and His Readers[*]

Jay Twomey

The history of Christian interpretations of the Pastoral Epistles bears witness to moments in which representations of gender and authority in these texts lose their patriarchal moorings, thanks to the curious intervention of a reader. Sometimes this reader is, no surprise, a woman, struggling within or against the heavily policed confines of the Pastor's version of Christianity. There are a number of interesting protofeminist responses to the Pastor's misogyny, starting with Sor Juana Inez de la Cruz, Anne Hutchinson, Anna Maria van Schurman, Margaret Fell, and Mary Astell in the seventeenth and eighteenth centuries.[1] One could go even further back in the tradition—Saint Teresa of Avila (sixteenth century), and perhaps even Marcella (fourth century).[2] These women engage in a number of intriguing exegetical practices partially to undermine, or circumvent, the Pastor's denial of women's religious agency. Certain men, too, for instance, Abelard and even Jerome (insofar as we know about Marcella through Jerome), seem invested in readings that blunt the force of some of the Pastor's more egregious moments.[3] A thorough reception study of even marginally feminist critical uses of the Pastorals would illustrate the ways in which some of the tradition's most unpalatable source texts have been, and

[*] Thanks to Julia Carlson, Trish Henley, Lisa Meloncon, Laura Micciche, and Gary Weissman for their helpful comments on an earlier draft of this paper.

1. Juana Inés de la Cruz 2005, 282–83; Hutchinson (see the trial transcript in Hall 1990, 314–16); Schurman 1998, 132–33; Fell 1989, 12; Astell 2002, 80–82.
2. Teresa of Avila 1957, 1:344; for Marcella, see Jerome's *Ep.* 2.6 (*NPNF*[2] 6:255).
3. Jerome, *Ep.* 2.6 (*NPNF*[2] 6:255). Abelard doesn't so much challenge the Pastor as suggest that verses like 1 Tim 2:11–12 are equally relevant to men (2003, 135).

can be, undermined or redeployed by savvy readers.[4] My purpose, though, is to think about the ways in which apparently patriarchal readings of the Pastoral Epistles, and in this case readings by men, can be construed so as to undermine, or in fact queer, these texts, despite their good patriarchal intentions to the contrary.

Queer(ing) Reception

In this paper I am not directly concerned with queering the Pastoral Epistles themselves. My aim, rather, is to show that a certain history of readings has already done so, and in fact continues to do so still. Maybe one reason for the instances of gender instability in such interpretations as I'll discuss is that our exegetes recognize, unwittingly, that there's something oddly overdetermined about the Pastor's own construction of gender. As Robert Goss and Deborah Krause argue in *The Queer Bible Commentary*, the Pastor's letters serve in part to construct "an idealized, hypermasculine Church" (Goss and Krause 2006, 688).[5] His instructions to Timothy and Titus, they argue, correlate "hard bodies with pastoral power [and] underscores his call for male ecclesial leadership and control. He conceives the larger, ecclesial organization as an extended family, led by a pumped-up, hardened leadership ... a hierarchy of stronger male bodies ... displaying their authority over women, children and slaves" (688). Goss and Krause write of gay male bodybuilding in their reading of the Pastor, and their rhetoric playfully reflects, and profits from, this juxtaposition. Gay male bodybuilding, they claim, is a striving after "masculine status and the ideology of dominance" in a heteronormative culture, one that, as in the ancient Mediterranean world, still determines power in terms of penetration (689). The fact that the Pastorals manifest an anxiety about male authority may have something to do with the way Pauline women were

---

4. See the relevant passages on women's readings in my *Pastoral Epistles Through the Centuries* (2009). Margaret Thickstun (1991, 1995), in studies of Mary Astell and Margaret Fell, also provides a model for just such a reception project. Thickstun's work is deeply indebted to Elisabeth Schüssler Fiorenza, who also reflects (see e.g., 1992, 20–24; 1983, 26–27) upon women's subversive readings of the Pastorals and other texts. Dennis MacDonald's work (1983) on the Thecla traditions would similarly be a good place to begin. See also Newsom and Ringe 1998, xix–xxi; Ruether 1998.

5. The Pastor's emphasis upon the bishop as paterfamilias, the strict limitations upon women's dress and religious agency, and the various references to male physicality (e.g., 1 Tim 4:8 or 2 Tim 2:1–7) all contribute to this reading of the letters.

penetrating the power structure of the early church.[6] On the other hand, Jennifer Glancy, Jouette Bassler, and others are surely right to say that even on the face of it the Pastorals represent a fraught concern over alternative masculinities (Jesus' for instance, or John the Baptist's, or Paul's)—which were already central to the Christian tradition (Glancy 2003, 249; Bassler 1996, 81).

In any event, I am speculating here on the legibility of only partially obscured traces in the Pastorals themselves in order to engage, more pointedly, in what Alexander Doty calls "queer reception."[7] For Doty, "queerness ... is a quality related to any expression that can be marked as contra-, non-, or anti-straight" (1993, xv), a definition that, for all its democratic blandness (xv)[8] allows for an open-ended reading of the interpretive gender instabilities I am interested in and "recognizes the possibility

---

6. See Dennis MacDonald's argument that the *Acts of Paul and Thecla* bear witness to an asceticism in some strands of Pauline Christianity that freed some women from the household economy and that the Pastorals were written, at least in part, to counter (1983).

7. I prefer the term *queer reception* to *queer commentary* (Berlant and Warner, 1995) if only because it seems to me to emphasize the relationship between texts—in this case the Pastorals and a commentary upon them—more fully. Scholars engaging in queer readings of biblical texts can clearly trouble those texts in any number of ways, for instance by outing biblical characters, à la Nancy Wilson's *Our Tribe* (2000, 112), producing "queer" juxtapositions (Ken Stone has even defined queer, in part, as that which calls "to mind unorthodox combinations and transgressive juxtapositions of things normally kept apart" [2001, 31]), or recontextualizing homophobic biblical content. This last critical strategy has a long history—it's how Margaret Fell, for instance, eviscerates the Pastor's restrictions on women. In recent scholarship, such arguments are historical-critical in nature and say that prohibitions on male homosexuality are about power dynamics manifested as sexual activity, rather than sexual desire (see Long 2006, 8–11). Jacques Berlinerblau goes so far as to suggest that key homophobic biblical texts are simply incomprehensible, their meaning forever lost to modern understanding (see, for example, his discussion of Lev 18:22 in 2005, 104). In Stephen Moore's phrase, this approach is a kind of strategic "task of defamiliarization" (2001, 135).

8. Wayne Koestenbaum, in a "gay reading" of Oscar Wilde, remarks that "gay male reader response criticism" is quite a "pedestrian" idea. But he also can describe this work as resistance, "reading resistantly," "reading [as] a hunt for histories that deliberately foreknow or unwittingly trace a desire felt not by author but by reader" (1990, 177). My use of Doty's term "queer reception" is akin to this resistant reading, except that (unlike both Koestenbaum and Doty) I am not especially hunting for traces of erotic desire.

that various and fluctuating queer positions might be occupied whenever *anyone* produces or responds to culture" (3).

Anyone—even Gore Vidal. Or especially Gore Vidal? Vidal is in some ways the inspiration behind this paper, even if I will focus mostly on other texts. Until I read his *Live from Golgotha*, the (at least apparently) counterpatriarchal readings I came across in my work on the reception of the Pastorals had seemed quite intriguingly unexpected, but not theoretically linkable. Vidal's novel is ostensibly a New Testament rewrite—the description on the back characterizes it as "the Gospel according to Gore." But it's actually a raucous, farcical retelling of Paul's story, narrated in the first person by Timothy. Paul and Timothy are gay lovers—"sackmates, off and on ... for some fifteen years" (Vidal 1992, 173)—or rather, Paul is gay and Timothy is stridently bi, and both are wildly promiscuous in a world teeming with promiscuity. Among Timothy's other partners: Priscilla and Nero. The conceit of the novel is that a future Hacker is erasing the history of Christianity (somehow available, almost quaintly now, only on tape) and a number of media corporate executives from the '90s have figured out how to return to the past both to salvage the greatest story ever told and to film it, yes, "live from Golgotha." So described, the book may, unfortunately, sound just awful, and it has been panned by fans of Vidal as well as foes. Given that the novel was published just as Bill Clinton took office, it is probably best understood as a campy, coarse rebuke of the Reagan/ Bush I years—the years of the Moral Majority, of the AIDS epidemic, of the telescandalists.

But I would argue that Vidal's decision to focus his gospel retelling on Timothy and Paul is a savvy one. It is only Timothy, we're told, who can save the gospel truth from a Hacker who—if I might analogize—is to Jesus as the Pastor is to Paul. That is, Vidal's narrative assumes both that the Paul and Timothy we know from Acts and the Epistles are the product of a malicious intervention and that Christianity is, or might come to be, nothing other than the Gospel of Timothy—which is the Gospel of Paul as reported to Timothy, which is the Pastor's more-or-less obscure "deposit" of faith and tradition (1 Tim 6:20; 2 Tim 1:12, 14). In the end this may be a relatively heavy-handed way of saying that the Pastor is deeply implicated in the Christian tradition's understanding of social order. But what matters most from my perspective is that the "true story" about Paul and Timothy, in the novel, is the story of the instability of identity, especially gender identity. Timothy, at different moments in his sexual escapades, is or is potentially boy, girl, eunuch, husband, wife, bottom, top. His gender and sexuality shift from context to context, not always happily, of course, but with significant fluidity nonetheless. By the novel's end this instability becomes theological, as one of the visitors from the future tries (unsuccessfully, as it happens) to get Timothy to agree to the notion of a female God. "Such a little thing," this character argues, "to say [that Jesus] was the son of the Goddess and not of God, a slight matter of gender" (Vidal 1992, 225). All this, in conjunction with the novel's emphasis on performance—did I mention that Paul juggles and tap dances?—makes *Live from Golgotha* an interesting point of departure for a rethinking of the Pastoral Epistles and their readers in what we could call a closeted queer(ed) tradition in the history of heteronormative Christian reception.

Examples of ostensibly patriarchal readings of the Pastorals that undermine, or destabilize, normative constructions of gender and sexuality are available across the interpretive tradition. Unfortunately, none to my knowledge are quite as campy as Vidal's book. But such readings deserve attention as critical resources for antimisogynistic, antihomophobic projects within New Testament and biblical reception studies; they can serve as tactical evidence, internal to the tradition, of what Jacques Berlinerblau calls counterexegesis, that is, interpretive practices that "destabilize dominant conceptions of 'what the Bible says'" (2005, 106). Berlinerblau's polemical manifesto for "secularlists" (2005, 106) endorses reading strategies undertaken in various biblical-studies projects before and since his *The Secular Bible* was published.[9] In this essay I focus pretty exclusively on the counterexegetical options available (unconsciously? ironically?) within a relatively traditional reception history of the Pastorals. In doing so I draw inspiration from George Aichele's sense that the Bible is "a copy without an original, a map without a territory" (2006, 200). Aichele, borrowing a concept from Larry Kreitzer, suggests that Bible scholars should "reverse the hermeneutical flow" (198; see Kreitzer 2002); that is, they should shatter the controlling force exerted by the biblical canon, and then read biblical passages in "strange ... schizophrenic alignments with a wide array of noncanonical texts" (200). I want to extend this strategy to readings in the reception history of the Bible as well, taking Aichele's sense of the canon very broadly to include voices in the theological mainstream.

---

9. See, for instance: Sherwood 2000; Moore 2001; Runions 2003; Stone 2005; Cushing Stahlberg 2008.

Some Queer(ed) Fathers

Voices such as Augustine's. One of Augustine's most frequently cited passages from the Pastorals is 1 Tim 5:6, according to which "the widow who lives for pleasure is dead even while she lives."[10] Rarely concerning himself with the larger context of 5:6, Augustine cites this verse often when writing to actual widows, like Proba (*Ep.* 130 [*NPNF*[1] 1:460]), or about them, like his mother Monica, whom he takes as the model of Pastoral widowhood (*Conf.* 9.22 [*NPNF*[1] 1:137]). But in citing the Pastor, he more typically tries to apply this discussion of widowhood to all Christians. So, in his comments on Ps 132, for instance, he asserts that "the whole Church therefore is one widow, whether in men or in women, in married men or married women, in young men or in old, or in virgins: the whole Church is one widow, desolate in this world, if she feel this, if she is aware of her widowhood: for then is help at hand for her" (*En. Ps.* 132 [*NPNF*[1] 8:620]). Reading the church, including obviously the men of the church, typologically as feminine is not unusual, of course, although implications of such imagery are frequently overlooked.[11]

Perhaps more interestingly, with regard to Augustine's specific appropriation of 1 Tim 5:6, is that current scholarship on the widows in the Pastorals suggests that the Pastor worried about an office of widows that may have granted a certain zone of nonpatriarchal freedom to women, and he seems to have wanted, in the words of Dennis MacDonald, to "decimate [that] office" (1983, 75). Hence he restricted the age of enrollment to sixty and excluded all women with any family who could take care of them. Most pertinent to v. 6, there is also an apparently sexual dimension to these restrictions. Just what it would mean for "widows to live for pleasure" is unclear, but given the Pastor's concerns about women as dangerously appetitive sexual beings elsewhere in these letters (1 Tim 5:11; 2 Tim 3:6; Titus 2:3–5), one might conclude that even elderly women are a source of some specifically sexual anxiety. Or, as Jouette Bassler implies, illicit sexuality may be but a metonym for "autonomy" generally (Bassler 2003, 140). Reading such feminist New Testament perspectives back into Augustine's use of the verse, we note that the men Augustine has in view

---

10. Unless otherwise noted, all biblical citations are from the NRSV.

11. See Kalbian, *Sexing the Church*, for a discussion of a number of female metaphors for the church, including that of the widow (2005, 30, 113–15) in traditional and contemporary Catholicism.

are constructed as potentially (and dangerously) active and independent women who are apparently willing to abdicate all autonomy to serve under (divine) masculine authority in the name of their faith. Interestingly, in his treatises on the *Excellence of Widowhood*, Augustine even extends the wifely concern with masculine pleasure (drawing upon 1 Cor 7:34) to widows: "whatever attention she would otherwise give to things concerned with pleasing her husband, a Christian who is not married should reclaim and redirect to the purpose of pleasing the Lord" (1996, 129). So the church, even its male congregation, is a widow—desolate, continent, and yet still servicing the needs of her lord and master.[12]

Another major, early reader of the Pastorals, John Chrysostom, in his commentary on 2 Tim 3:6[13] regarding "little" or "silly women" (*gynaikaria*), remarks: "He who is easily deceived is a silly woman, and far removed from being a man. For it is characteristic of women to be deceived. Rather, not a characteristic of women, but of silly women" (*Hom. 2 Tim.* 8 [*NPNF*[1] 13:505]).[14] In Chrysostom's reading, "silly women" appears in fact to be a category of behavior, a status. Thus, an easily deceived person can be characterized, perhaps regardless of his or her actual gender, as a silly woman. This entails, clearly, the gendering of an *in*capacity as feminine.[15] And yet, as an exegetical maneuver, Chrysostom's reading may also undermine the Pastor's rigid gender stratification. The language of deception in Chrysostom's commentary at this point seems self-consciously to echo that of 1 Tim 2:13–14,[16] linking Eve to the silly women of 2 Tim 3:6–7. Adam was not deceived, the Pastor assures us. But Chrysostom is not so sure. An Eve, a silly woman, is one deceived, even if that one is … well, an Adam. Not that Chrysostom would articulate Adam's fault in this way. Adam is truly

---

12. See Power on Augustine's view of marriage as a version of the "master-slave relationship" (1996, 122).

13. "For among them are those who make their way into households and captivate silly women, overwhelmed by their sins and swayed by all kinds of desires, [7]who are always being instructed and can never arrive at a knowledge of the truth."

14. Ὥστε γυναικάριον ὁ εὐεξαπάτητος, καὶ ἀνδρὸς πόρρω. Γυναικῶν δὲ τὸ ἀπατᾶσθαι, μᾶλλον δὲ οὐδὲ γυναικῶν, ἀλλὰ γυναικαρίων. Many thanks to Richard Layton for advice on the translation.

15. The feminizing of psychological and emotional aspects of the human being does not originate with Chrysostom, of course. For a concise review of Hellenistic and Jewish uses of the topos of "silly" or "little women" in particular, see Collins 2002, 251.

16. "For Adam was formed first, then Eve; and Adam was not deceived, but the woman was deceived and became a transgressor."

deceived, yes, but his deception is less blameworthy than Eve's since he was deceived by an "equal" while she was deceived by a creature of lower status (*Hom. 1 Tim.* 9 [*NPNF*[1] 13:435]). Somehow, Chrysostom's reading of the Pastor's gender typology has less to do with the order of creation among humans than with the ontological ranking of different species. Essentially, Chrysostom denies the Pastor's misogynistic anthropology, at least at the moment of Adam's deception, and in the process radically opens gender to the variability of experience.

Now, Chrysostom obviously thinks that women subsequent to the fall are necessarily subordinate and inferior to men. But in a curious instance of metanoia, Chrysostom suggests that somehow the prelapsarian Eve may have been Adam's superior (given her apparent "power [*arche*] over the man"), despite texts such as the Pastorals and 1 Cor 11:9, etc., to the contrary (*Hom. 1 Tim.* 9 [*NPNF*[1] 13:435]). It would be interesting to apply the trope of the "silly woman," for example, that is, to queer, other deceived men mentioned in Chrysostom's works, as when he notes that otherwise faithful men can be "easily deceived" by authentic prophecy simply because prophecy "supplies the proof of its own truth not at the time when it is spoken, but at the time of the event" (*Hom. 1 Cor.* 29 [*NPNF*[1] 12:169]), or when he speaks of the "good deceit" performed upon Isaac by Jacob and upon Jeremiah by God himself (*Hom. Col.* 6 [*NPNF*[1] 13:284]).[17]

To give just a few further, brief examples: Anselm, in his "Prayer to Saint Paul," seems to toy with 1 Tim 2:15[18] in imagining Paul as a nurse and mother.[19] He asks "who are the sons you are in labor with, and nurse, / but those whom by teaching the faith of Christ you bear and instruct" (in Gaventa 2007, 15). In context, the Pastor's aim is to offer some minor consolation to women who are strictly limited in their religious agency. Anselm's poetic reflections upon Paul's maternity here effectively invert the Pastor's gendered priorities by rendering (or at least allowing us to

---

17. Blake Leyerle has noted that elsewhere Chrysostom similarly destabilizes gender categories by presenting certain men as "'feminized' … passive objects of the [divine] gaze" (1993, 173).

18. "Yet she will be saved through childbearing, provided they [i.e., the children] continue in faith and love and holiness, with modesty."

19. Caroline Bynum would link such imagery with an "ambivalence about authority" (1982, 113) and specifically teaching authority. Imagery of Paul as a mother is also drawn from a variety of other Pauline sources, including: 1 Thess 2:7; Gal 4:19; 1 Cor 3:2. See Gaventa 2007 for a full study of such images in Paul's writings.

read) male religious authority, including the giving of instruction in the faith, as maternal. Calvin implicitly genders Catholicism—or rather those who are "content with the sort of 'implicit faith' the papists invent" (*Institutes* 3.2.5, 1960, 1:548)—as feminine, on the basis of 2 Tim 3:6–7. But if Margaret Davies is right to suggest that the Pastor's goal in this passage is to tap into the insecurities of his Greco-Roman male audience regarding their ability to control or protect their women as sexual beings (1996, 78), then perhaps one could interrogate Calvin's anxieties about Papist impulses in Protestant circles. To what extent do these anxieties regender, or indeed queer, Protestants as women subject to creeping "Papist"—but in context, nevertheless, specifically masculine—influence?[20]

BECOMING WOMEN

There might well be dozens of other examples of readings that destabilize what in the Pastorals are proffered, stable gender identities. The point would not be to list them, of course, but to examine them in their contextual, historical differences and then deploy them as a subversive tradition within the tradition, an alternative semiotic mechanism[21] for troubling heteronormative assumptions about the Pastor's hypermasculinity. In the rest of this paper I would like to focus on one additional example, but in greater detail than I have above. The text I'm interested in is a popular eighteenth-century commentary, Philip Doddridge's *The Family Expositor*, cited by Jonathan Edwards, among other major figures of the period. Readers of Doddridge's comments on the Pastorals are informed that 1 Tim 2:9—regarding women's dress—pertains to men as well.[22] Inquiring minds are referred to an early seventeenth-century Flemish commentary

---

20. Elsewhere, Calvin worries that the idea of sacraments could play a role in the minds of some Protestants who, like the women of 2 Tim 3, might be too willing to indulge their "curiosity" (*Institutes* 4.19.1, 1960, 2:599).

21. I am borrowing from the subtitle of George Aichele's *The Control of Biblical Meaning: Canon as Semiotic Mechanism* (2001).

22. "[W]omen should dress themselves modestly and decently in suitable clothing, not with their hair braided, or with gold, pearls, or expensive clothes." John Wesley's comments on this verse come to the same conclusion. He argues that "you cannot be clear before God unless you throw aside all needless ornaments, in utter defiance of that tyrant of fools, fashion; unless you seek only to be adorned with good works, as men and women professing godliness" ("On Obedience to Pastors," *Works*, 1831, 7:116; cf. "On Dress," *Works*, 1831, 7:15–26). Wesley's men stand in apparent equality

by Willem Hessels van Est, a.k.a. Estius, who "very justly observes, that this [passage] concludes with yet stronger force against foppery in men" (Doddridge 1756, 5:450). This assertion is based, apparently, upon a slight misreading of Estius. True, in his discussion of v. 9, Estius mentions "men who have a fondness for bodily ornament" and indicates that "it is proper for this sex to pay less attention to such matters" (Estius 1841, 155).[23] But contrary to The Family Expositor's assertion, Estius's remarks do not conclude his discussion of 1 Tim 2:9 itself but rather of the authorities he adduces in his commentary on this passage. He has just cited Prudentius' Hamartigenia and attributes these remarks about "men with a fondness for bodily ornament" to that early Christian poet, and not to Paul (i.e., to the Pastor). Indeed, Estius's remarks about 1 Tim 2:9 would seem to argue for a rather stricter separation of gender identities. He would like to believe that the Apostle is an equal-opportunity critic when it comes to potential crises in his churches. So in v. 9, he says, Paul calls attention to a specifically feminine vice—excessive concern for dress and the body—just as in the previous verse he had commented upon a bane of masculinity by charging that men should pray "without anger or argument" (2:8). Men are prone to combativeness, and women try to catch their eye. It's as though Estius had conceived of the Pauline congregation as a kind of brutish mating ritual. Yet, his commentary is not without its own interesting nuances. Estius assures his readers among women of status that they need not cast away their bling altogether, so long as they shun merely vain display (155), and he cites Prov 31:22 in support: "she makes herself coverings; her clothing is fine linen and purple." So, while Estius places his discussion of 1 Tim 2:9 in the context of authorities who *do* worry about male ostentation, his own reading of the verse does not go there, and instead presents—from the perspective of an intersectional analysis—a crossing of traditional gender identities with specific class distinctions.

Doddridge's *The Family Expositor*, then, may get Estius slightly wrong. Yet Doddridge insists that this (mis)reading involves a "very just observation." Read strictly in context, the implication of Doddridge's exegesis is fairly clear: on the face of it, the verse in 1 Timothy is specifically geared toward women; hence, if men are included in its injunction, then they are, to some degree, womanly men. They are fops. Doddridge is articulat-

---

with the women of the congregation, as though the Pastor had been speaking to the church as a whole, regardless of gender.

23. Thanks again to Richard Layton for his translation advice.

ing common eighteenth-century anxieties about the relationship between ostentation, gender, and political authority. As scholars of seventeenth- and eighteenth-century theater note, foppery is a symptom of the shifting basis of political and economic power. It was, as Thomas King puts it, produced by "struggles against spectacularity" (2004, 229).[24] That is, a mercantile economy was in the process of re-allocating authority from royal or aristocratic patronage to the privacy of the individual subject. Spectacularity as a sign of royal prerogative, of proximity to aristocratic grandeur, loses its significance in the process. According to Susan Staves, "as the aristocracy lost power and self-confidence, ... magnificence no longer seem an appropriate virtue" (1982, 426). The fop is thus an awkward reminder of sources of power arising from what King calls "residual pederasty": the willing self-subjection of men to the royal patron, "to the spectacle of sovereignty" (2001, 110). As a defensive displacement, men whose style resembles what, in the cultural imagination, is a kind of "pederastic display" (115) become "effeminates displaying their subjection in order to court patronage and placement" (110), the "other against which [an] emergent, privatized political nation defined itself" (King 2004, 6).

Now, the fop is not necessarily homosexual. Indeed, as Staves and King both note, the theatrical fop is, more often than not, apparently asexual (Staves 1982, 415).[25] But like the biblical eunuchs outed by Nancy Wilson (1995, 128–29), fops, regardless of their actual sexual orientation, and regardless of any histories of actual sexual activity, are queer—or, as King puts it, "foppery is still queerness" (King 2004, 236).[26] The fact that eighteenth-century fops are also available to scholarly inquiry largely as

---

24. Thanks to Doug Harrison for suggesting I take a look at the eighteenth-century debates about fops and mollies.

25. Contemporary sources sometimes seem to assume, in fact, that the fop is heterosexual. A mid-eighteenth-century *Dictionary of Love*, for instance, says in its entry on the fop that he is someone who "fancies every woman that sees him cannot help dying for him" (Anonymous 1777, n.p.). Religious texts from the period frequently associate foppery with ostentation, ceremony, vanity, affectation, superfluity, insincerity, and the like. Robert Fellowes, in *A Picture of Christian Philosophy*, considers foppery in terms of the adulteration of Christian truth: "A good Christian will glow with an honest zeal to preserve the religion which he venerates from any contaminating mixture, either from hypocrisy or from bigotry; from that foppery of worship which mocks the supreme intelligence" (1798, 37).

26. This is so, King argues, because foppery, even "in the absence of sexual encounters of any sort," marks "problematic desires and misoccupations of social and

theatrical constructs leads us back to Doddridge, almost inevitably you might say, by way of Judith Butler's *Gender Trouble*. The fops of 1 Tim 2:9 are those womanly men of Doddridge's world who, along with ostentatiously dressed women, are told by the Pastor (in Doddridge's paraphrase) to

> adorn themselves only with decent apparel, with modesty and sobriety, neither exceeding in the article of unnecessary and inconvenient expense nor in the least degree entrenching [infringing] on the strictest decorum. I have many reasons, both relating to themselves and others, to wish that they may not place their ornament so much in plaited hair, or gold or pearls, or rich and costly garments, but in what is itself infinitely more valuable and much better becomes women [i.e., good works]. (Doddridge 1756, 5:451)

This is queer advice indeed. Doddridge's exposition appears confused, internally contradictory. The focus in the verses in question is on women, and clearly Doddridge is speaking of women in his paraphrase. But given his use of Estius, he has (obliquely at least) men in view too, those fops who, if they are to cease in their foppery, can do so only by "becoming women," so to speak. It may well be that in attempting to take a stab at eighteenth-century foppery, Doddridge inadvertently opens up 1 Tim 2:9 to an understanding of gender and sexuality as performative—or in this case, as performance proper. Staves notes, without pursuing the idea, that the fop is "the avant-garde of sex role change" (1982, 412), which is to say, in an *almost* anachronistic sense: drag.[27] The performance of drag, Butler

---

bodily spaces in all social subjects and cannot be assigned to any particular sexual subjectivity" (2004, 236).

27. *Almost* because, as King argues, there's a historical linkage on the English stage between foppery and gender-bending theatrical performances (2001). With regard to Stave's comment about sex-role change, it is interesting to note that some scholars emphasize a strict linkage of clothing and behavior to gender and sex in the early modern period. Will Fisher, in *Materializing Gender*, notes that "in early modern English culture, clothing was often seen as integral to a person's [gender] identity" (2006, 11). Similarly, Thomas Laqueur discusses a preenlightenment, but nevertheless long-enduring, "anxiety, expressed in the language of the body, that men ... consorting closely with women" might actually "become women"—and vice versa (1992, 125). In context, Laqueur is referring specifically to Castiglione's *Book of the Courtier* [1528]. I would not argue in any definitive way that such anxieties are entirely traceable in Doddridge's *Family Expositor*. Still, in his introduction, Doddridge worries

notes, induces "the recognition of a radical contingency in the relation between sex and gender in the face of cultural configurations of causal unities that are regularly assumed to be natural and necessary" (2006, 187). As is well-known, Butler goes on to remind us that what is parodied in this performance is not an ontological, original, necessary unity of sex/gender/sexual orientation. Rather "the parody is *of* the very notion of an original" (188). Doddridge's reference to "foppery in men" has no original either, not in the Pastorals at any rate, and barely at all in the commentary he cites. Like foppery itself, like ostentatious dress, it is merely a masking of the naked truth that we might take for granted but that the readers of *The Family Expositor* would likely have been scandalized to acknowledge (even in the fine print of a footnote): that the gender identities bequeathed to posterity by the Pastor are but uneasy constructs; that what the Pastor (in a scriptural text that is a *locus classicus* of patriarchal Christianity) suggests is constitutive of women turns out to apply equally to men.

CONCLUSION

I said earlier that the scholarship on theatrical foppery leads back to Butler, but I could just as easily have said that it returns us to Vidal, who, as Dennis Altman claims in *Gore Vidal's America*, "was a social constructionist before the term entered the academic discourse on sexuality" (2005, 14). Vidal's refusal to accept for himself the label homosexual has bothered some, but it arises from his personal insistence that any linkage of identity and sexuality is untenable.[28] Doddridge's recognition, brief and inchoate though it is, that gender traverses bodies without being located in them, feels more like a reaction to Vidal's Timothy than to the Pastor's unruly women. Perhaps the distance between these late first-century Epistles, this late twentieth-century novel, and the mid-eighteenth-century commentary (remarking, apparently, upon both) is not quite as great as it seems. And at any rate, Doddridge's concerns and confusions are still with us. A recent online screed against the Harry Potter books, for instance, argues

---

about the development, and influence, of what we might call foppish rhetoric. The "neglect" of the "masculine eloquence" of the Greeks, he writes, has produced that "enervate, dissolute and puerile manner of writing which is growing so much on the present age" (1756, 1:v).

28. Bert Archer's *The End of Gay* links, albeit in passing, Vidal to the work of Foucault on gender identity and sexuality (2004, 179).

that "[f]undamental Christians are opposed to crossdressing, perversion, and immodest clothing (1 Tim 2:9)."[29] The author, like Doddridge, appropriates a comment about women's clothing in the Epistle in order to articulate, albeit unclearly, his or her anxieties about gender distinctions and especially distinctions most pertinent to men. Not being a fan, I can't say whether or not "immodest clothing" is much of an issue in the series; it seems pretty evident, though, that the gown-like garments worn by certain male characters are what this rant has in view. Men in wizard's robes are perverse men are womanish men are ... fops, and their attractiveness to young readers, especially young male readers,[30] is deeply troubling to this author, worried as she or he is that the series' various improprieties "will appear EXCITING."

In this essay I have been inquiring into readings in which the female object of a scriptural admonition is regendered by an interpreter as male. I designed this inquiry at least partially in reverse, starting with Gore Vidal and working through a number of relevant readings more or less to trouble Pastoral Epistles themselves. Clearly, some examples of regendering, of queer reception, can be discussed as instances of a historical tradition of allegorical hermeneutics, that is, as texts that otherwise have little or nothing to do with gender issues.[31] But I would argue that a strategy of queering these readings, of exploiting even apparent gender insecurities and instabilities, can help destabilize the kind of conservative, restrictive sense of tradition that, for instance, the Pastor sought to impose upon his community.

WORKS CONSULTED

Abelard, Pierre, and Heloise Abelard. 2003. *The Letters of Abelard and Heloise*. Translated by Betty Radice. New York: Penguin.

---

29. http://www.pbministries.org/Parachurch/sorcery/sorcerers_stone_part1.htm.

30. Further on, the document, which barely mentions girls or women, worries yet again about the dangers of males appearing too feminine: "growing boys and men should have short hair."

31. Caroline Bynum, writing on the gendering of religious symbols in medieval texts, cautions that "[h]owever religious symbols 'mean,' they never simply prescribe or transcend social status. ... Gender related symbols, in their full complexity, may refer to gender in ways that affirm or reverse it, support or question it" (1986, 2).

Aichele, George. 2001. *The Control of Biblical Meaning: Canon as Semiotic Mechanism*. Harrisburg, Pa.: Trinity.

———. 2006. Recycling the Bible: A Response. Pages 195–201 in *The Recycled Bible: Autobiography, Culture and the Space Between*. Edited by Fiona Black. SemeiaSt 51. Atlanta: Society of Biblical Literature.

Altman, Dennis. 2005. *Gore Vidal's America*. Malden, Mass.: Polity.

Anonymous. 1777. *A Dictionary of Love* [Based on Jean François Dreux du Radier's *Dictionnaire d'Amour*, 1741]. London: J. Bew, J. Wilkie, G. Riley, and W. Caville.

Archer, Bert. 2004. *The End of Gay: And the Death of Heterosexuality*. New York: Da Capo.

Astell, Mary. 2002. *A Serious Proposal to the Ladies*. Edited by Patricia Springborg. Orchard Park, N.Y.: Broadview.

Augustine. 1996. *Marriage and Virginity*. Edited by John Rotelle. Translated by Ray Kearney. Hyde Park, N.Y.: New City Press.

Bassler, Jouette. 1996. *1 Timothy, 2 Timothy, Titus*. Nashville, Tenn.: Abingdon.

———. 2003. Limits and Differentiation: The Calculus of Widows in 1 Timothy 5:3–16. Pages 122–46 in *A Feminist Companion to the Deutero-Pauline Epistles*. Edited by Amy-Jill Levine. New York: T&T Clark.

Berlant, Lauren, and Michael Warner. 1995. What Does Queer Theory Teach Us about X? *PMLA* 3:343–49.

Berlinerblau, Jacques. 2005. *The Secular Bible: Why Nonbelievers Must Take Religion Seriously*. New York: Cambridge University Press.

Butler, Judith. 2006. *Gender Trouble: Feminism and the Subversion of Identity*. New York: Routledge.

Bynum, Caroline. 1982. *Jesus as Mother: Studies in the Spirituality of the High Middle Ages*. Berkeley: University of California Press.

———, ed. 1986. *Gender and Religion: On the Complexity of Symbols*. Boston: Beacon.

Calvin, Jean. 1960. *Institutes of the Christian Religion*. Edited by John McNeil. Translated by Ford Lewis Battles. 2 vols. Philadelphia: Westminster Press.

Collins, Raymond. 2002: *1 and 2 Timothy and Titus: A Commentary*. Louisville: Westminster John Knox.

Cushing Stahlberg, Lesleigh. 2008. Modern Day Moabites: The Bible and the Debate about Same-Sex Marriage. *BibInt* 16:442–75.

Davies, Margaret. 1996. *The Pastoral Epistles*. Sheffield: Sheffield Academic Press.

Doddridge, Philip. 1756. *The Family Expositor: Or, a Paraphrase and Version of the New Testament.* 6 vols. London: John Wilson.

Doty, Alexander. 1993. *Making Things Perfectly Queer: Interpreting Mass Culture.* Minneapolis: University of Minnesota Press.

Estius, William. 1841. *In omnes D. Pauli Epistolas item in Catholicas commentarii.* 4 vols. Mainz: Franciscus Kirchheim.

Fell, Margaret. 1989. *Womens Speaking.* Edited by Christine Rhone. London: Pythia Press.

Fellowes, Robert. 1798. *A Picture of Christian Philosophy.* Warwick: Sharpe.

Fisher, Will. 2006. *Materializing Gender in Early Modern English Literature and Culture.* Cambridge: Cambridge University Press.

Gaventa, Beverly. 2007. *Our Mother Saint Paul.* Louisville: Westminster John Knox.

Glancy, Jennifer. 2003. The Protocols of Masculinity in the Pastoral Epistles. Pages 235–64 in *New Testament Masculinities.* Edited by Stephen Moore and Janice Capel Anderson. SemeiaSt 45. Atlanta: Society of Biblical Literature.

Goss, Robert, and Deborah Krause. 2006. The Pastoral Letters: 1 and 2 Timothy, and Titus. Pages 684–92 in Guest et al. 2006.

Guest, Deryn, et al., eds. 2006. *The Queer Bible Commentary.* London: SCM.

Hall, David D., ed. 1990. *The Antinomian Controversy, 1636–1638: A Documentary History.* 2nd ed. Durham, N.C.: Duke University Press.

Juana Inés de la Cruz, Sor. 2005. *Sor Juana Inés de la Cruz: Selected Writings.* Translated by Pamela Kirk Rappaport. New York: Paulist Press.

Kalbian, Aline. 2005. *Sexing the Church: Gender, Power, and Ethics in Contemporary Catholicism.* Bloomington: Indiana University Press.

King, Thomas. 2001. The Fop, the Canting Queen, and the Deferral of Gender. Pages 94–135 in *Presenting Gender: Changing Sex in Early Modern Culture.* Edited by Chris Mounsey. Lewisburg, Pa.: Bucknell University Press.

———. 2004. *The Gendering of Men, 1600–1750: The English Phallus.* Madison: University of Wisconsin Press.

Koestenbaum, Wayne. 1990. Wilde's Hard Labor and the Birth of Gay Reading. Pages 176–89 in *Engendering Men: The Question of Male Feminist Criticism.* Edited by Joseph A. Boone and Michael Cadden. New York: Routledge.

Laqueur, Thomas. 1992. *Making Sex: Body and Gender from the Greeks to Freud.* Cambridge: Harvard University Press.

Leyerle, Blake. 1993. John Chrysostom on the Gaze. *JECS* 1:159–74.

Long, Ronald. 2006. Introduction: Disarming Biblically-Based Gay Bashing. Pages 1–18 in Guest et al. 2006.

MacDonald, Dennis. 1983. *The Legend and the Apostle: The Battle for Paul in Story and Canon*. Philadelphia: Westminster.

Moore, Stephen. 2001. *God's Beauty Parlor: And Other Queer Spaces in and around the Bible*. Stanford: Stanford University Press.

Newsom, Carol, and Sharon Ringe, eds. 1998. *Women's Bible Commentary*. Louisville: Westminster John Knox.

Power, Kim. 1996. *Veiled Desire: Augustine on Women*. New York: Continuum.

Ruether, Rosemary. 1998. *Women and Redemption: A Theological History*. Minneapolis: Fortress.

Runions, Erin. 2003. *How Hysterical: Identification and Resistance in the Bible and Film*. New York: Palgrave Macmillan.

Schurman, Anna Maria van. 1998. *Whether a Christian Woman Should be Educated and Other Writings from her Intellectual Circle*. Edited and translated by Joyce L. Irwin. Chicago: University of Chicago Press.

Schüssler Fiorenza, Elisabeth. 1983. *In Memory of Her: A Feminist Theological Reconstruction of Christian Origins*. New York: Crossroad.

———. 1992. *But She Said: Feminist Practices of Biblical Interpretation*. Boston: Beacon.

Sherwood, Yvonne. 2000. *A Biblical Text and Its Afterlives: The Survival of Jonah in Western Culture*. New York: Cambridge University Press.

Staves, Susan. 1982. A Few Kind Words for the Fop. *Studies in English Literature* 22:413–28.

Stone, Ken, ed. 2001. *Queer Commentary and the Hebrew Bible*. Cleveland: Pilgrim.

———. 2005. *Practicing Safer Texts: Food, Sex and Bible in Queer Perspective*. New York: T&T Clark.

Teresa of Avila. 1957. *The Complete Works of Saint Teresa of Jesus*. Vol. 1. Edited and translated by E. Allison Peers. 3 vols. New York: Sheed & Ward.

Thickstun, Margaret Olofson. 1991. "This Was a Woman That Taught": Feminist Scriptural Exegesis in the Seventeenth Century. *Studies in Eighteenth-Century Culture* 21:149–58.

———. 1995. Writing the Spirit: Margaret Fell's Feminist Critique of Pauline Theology. *JAAR* 63:269–79.

Twomey, Jay. 2009. *The Pastoral Epistles through the Centuries*. Malden, Mass.: Wiley-Blackwell.

Vidal, Gore. 1992. *Live from Golgotha*. New York: Random House.

Wesley, John. 1831. *The Works of the Rev. John Wesley*. 14 vols. London: John Mason.

Wilson, Nancy L. 1995. *Our Tribe: Queer Folks, God, Jesus, and the Bible*. San Francisco: HarperSanFrancisco.

Gazing at the Whore:
Reading Revelation Queerly*

Lynn R. Huber

In a 1998 issue of *Rolling Stone*, photographer David LaChapelle stages Madonna in a scene that suggests a modern Whore of Babylon.[1] The background of the two-page spread is a stylized magenta and blue sunset. The pop star is stretched out in the foreground and behind her is a magenta dragon showing its teeth. Madonna, the Whore, appears to be emerging out of or hovering on the surface of waters that reflect the sunset. The black lingerie and the black leopard print tights contrast with her white skin and long blond hair. Her right hand is raised as though she holds an invisible goblet, but a ball of fire moves toward the edge of the frame as though she has just released it from her hand. Necklaces, bracelets, and rings adorn her body, as she looks into the eyes of the viewer.

The image of the Great Whore from Revelation has captured the imaginations of artists throughout history. Her image can be found in the pages of medieval manuscripts, in the watercolors of William Blake, in the multimedia works of outsider artists, on film, in political cartoons, and myriad places where the artistic imagination has carried her. While LaChapelle's version may not be the most literal reading of Revelation's image (e.g., the

---

* I want to thank Kent L. Brintnall, Gail R. O'Day, Robert von Thaden Jr., and Stephen D. Moore for their comments on earlier drafts of this piece and Mel AhMu for her support and encouragement.

1. This image can be viewed under the entry for David LaChapelle at www.artnet. com, an online gallery and auction site. The image, which is titled "Madonna: Furious Seasons," is part of a collection of photos entitled "Excess." This photograph is not the only one of LaChapelle's works that evokes the Apocalypse. Themes of destruction and the end of the world are seen throughout his photographs, which are viewable at the above site or the artist's own website, www.davidlachapelle.com.

dragon has only one head) and it may not even be a conscious appro-priation of the text, it alludes to the possibility of a queer reading of the text. An openly gay artist, known for images that challenge heterosexist norms, places a queer icon in the role of the Great Whore. Although we can label LaChapelle's image a queer reception of the Whore, the image is not without its complexity.[2] One viewer might argue that LaChapelle subverts the meaning of Revelation by presenting the sexually powerful Madonna-Whore as a positive image, as an image to be admired by (queer) viewers. Another reader might contend that the image actually buys into Revelation's rhetoric: Madonna, the modern image of a sexually power-ful woman, is depicted as an insidious threat because of her beauty and allure. In this way, LaChapelle's rendering of Revelation points to the fact that there are multiple possible queer readings of any one text, as well as hinting at the complexity inherent within Revelation's image of the Whore.

That Revelation's image of the Great Whore yields to multiple inter-pretations is one reason why it is arguably one of the more controversial, yet popular, images in a text teeming with controversial passages. Some feminist and queer critics find the image objectionable, if not abhorrent, even though scholars generally highlight the image's role in Revelation's anti-imperial rhetoric. In the following, I offer a queer-lesbian reading of the Whore as an entry point into the larger question of whether and how Revelation might continue as part of the queer imaginary.[3] While some have argued that Revelation has little or nothing to offer queer readers, I suggest that used critically this text should continue to contribute to queer conversations. Specifically, given Revelation's engagement with the topic of empire, the text and its image of the Whore can play a role in conversa-tions about how queer individuals, specifically those of us living in the United States, position ourselves in relation to the very empire that seeks to control and commodify us.

LOOKING AT APOCALYPSE

Written toward the end of the first century c.e. within the context of the Roman Empire, Revelation offers a narrative account of one man's vision of Jesus Christ and "the things that will happen soon" (Rev 1:1). As John

2. The language of "queer reception" is taken from Alexander Doty.

3. While I understand the reading I offer as falling within the category of queer, I do privilege a lesbian perspective, since that reflects my reading location.

moves through his narrative, intended to be read aloud (1:3), he not only describes what he sees, but he prompts his audience to see along with him. He does this by using the grammatical imperative "Look!" (ἰδού) through-out the text (4:1–2; 6:2, 5, 8; 7:9; 14:1, 14; 19:11). These Greek imperatives seem awkward to some, since they are typically paired with the phrase "I saw" (εἶδον).[4] Despite this, they effectively prompt the audience to see what John has been allowed to see, including the Whore.

Addressed to seven churches in seven cities of the Roman province of Asia Minor, Revelation is typically read as a critique of imperial power (Carey 2008). This region initially came under Roman power in the second century B.C.E. and over the next two centuries the cities of the province would compete with one another for the attention of Rome. To this end, the cities embraced the practice of honoring Roman emperors, living and dead, and even the city of Rome itself as divine, erecting temples to show their devotion (Friesen 2001). Reflecting the complex nature of impe-rialism, which employs a variety of strategies (political, religious, eco-nomic, social, etc.) to accrue and maintain power over others, John's cri-tique of empire is multifaceted (Moore 2006, 97–121). For instance, John addresses the empire's control of all trade and commerce (13:16–17) and its material excesses (18:9–19), along with its use of violence, especially against those who refuse to follow its demands, namely, the followers of God and the Lamb (e.g., 6:9–11; 17:6).[5] Most egregious, according to John, is the empire's blasphemy—its arrogant claim to power and authority that belongs to God (e.g., 13:5–6; 18:7–8). In light of the "sins" of the empire, Revelation pushes its audience to choose between devotion to manifesta-tions of empire, which John characterizes as beasts (Rev 13), and devotion to God and the Lamb.

Not reticent about employing dualisms and violence as tools of per-suasion (e.g., 16:10–11), Revelation has historically made interpret-ers uncomfortable. The book continues to evoke negative assessments, including among some feminist biblical scholars (Jack 2001; Pippin, 1992,

---

4. Consequently, some English translations, including the NRSV and the NIV, diminish the imperative used in the text by smoothing out what appears to some as a redundancy.

5. While this has prompted modern scholars to debate whether John's audience experienced violent religious persecution at the hands of the state, many scholars agree that Rev responded to some form of perceived persecution or sense of impend-ing persecution (Collins 1984, 84–110).

1999). One the most sustained critical treatments of Revelation, a piece especially pertinent to this essay, is the entry on "Revelation/ Apocalypse" in *The Queer Bible Commentary*. In it, Tina Pippin and J. Michael Clark assert that a redemptive reading of the text is not possible. With this said, they offer a tour of aspects of Revelation and its appropriations that they find most offensive to a queer audience.[6] The authors note, for instance, that the text maintains strict gender boundaries, as it valorizes what they see as a sexless or celibate heteromasculinity (i.e., the 144,000 male virgins), precluding the possibility of a redemptive queer reading (Pippin and Clark 2006, 758–61).[7] A more fundamental criticism of Revelation offered by Pippin and Clark is that the text's vision of the end requires and consequently creates outsiders through dualistic language and the creation of strict boundaries. This need for outsiders or evildoers stems from the conviction that Jesus will come only when there are those who need to be damned (764–65). Furthermore, apocalyptic narratives draw people into an inner circle of elites by allowing them to be voyeurs of the salacious acts of the sinful and of the terrifying violence of the divine (763). This, in fact, is one of the ways that the Whore functions in Revelation, according to Pippin's earlier book, *Death and Desire*, in which she describes the judgment of the Whore as "the ultimate misogynist fantasy" (1992, 67).

Despite Pippin and Clark's unequivocal judgment, for many the question of whether or not Revelation offers anything of value to queer readers remains legitimate. This is true not only for queer individuals situated within confessional contexts who continue to seek ways of making sense of the "texts of terror" that sit alongside stories of liberation within the canon (Guest 2005), but also for many who have felt the punch of apocalyptic rhetoric. The continuing use of resources from the apocalyptic imagination, including images and rhetoric, to create a cultural anxiety about queer bodies and sexualities, urges us, as Catherine Keller argues, to pay "attention *to and through* apocalypse" (2006, 8). As long as apocalyptic ways of thinking and speaking are used to celebrate gay-bashings, to blame queer people for natural disasters, to refuse giving basic human rights to those in LGBTQ communities and the like, there remains a need

---

6. Unfortunately, a full engagement with Pippin and Clark's essay and its critique of Rev is beyond the scope of this presentation.

7. For another reading of the 144,000 male virgins that reads this imagery in relation to Roman discourses about masculinity and that has an eye toward queer issues, see Huber 2008.

for queer readers to explore and reassess apocalyptic traditions. There is, additionally, a need to continue thinking through texts, such as Revelation, that have historically been used against queer individuals and groups (Cobb 2006).[8] By working through apocalyptic narratives and wrestling with the images that have been used to oppress, we begin to disarm the elements of texts that have been used to repress and begin to assign new meanings to others. Avoiding interaction with Revelation and other apocalyptic texts actually creates a sense that they are somehow untouchable or nonnegotiable. This takes power from the queer interpreter and places it in the hands of those who continue to use Revelation and other apocalyptic texts as weapons. Furthermore, Keller notes that the tendency to "purge" one's rhetoric of apocalyptic elements often leads to replicating those very elements.

In light of this, the following reflects an initial attempt at a queer-lesbian reading that pays attention to and through Revelation's image of the Whore. It attends *to* John's image of the Whore by addressing the text of Revelation from a queer perspective that remains in conversation with the text's historical and rhetorical context. This reading pays attention *through* the Whore by approaching issues raised in queer discourses, including places where queer discourse intersects with feminist thought, through the lens of Revelation's Whore imagery.

Gazing at/through the Whore

In Rev 17, John describes being lifted into the wilderness to see the judgment of the Great Whore (τῆς πόρνης τῆς μεγάλης), who is identified as "Babylon."[9] The name Babylon signals for the audience, aware of Jewish prophetic traditions, that the Whore personifies a city, specifically an imperial city. Babylon refers to the quintessential "evil" city in Jewish tradition. This is a city opposed to the people of God, as Babylon destroyed

---

8. Some queer interpreters reject the notion that queer readers can or should "stick it out" with biblical texts such as Rev. They argue that we have simply spent too much valuable time and energy trying to work with texts that have little to yield, that our time would be better spent on creating new and liberating traditions. J. Michael Clark is particularly noted for articulating this view (Guest 2005, 258–60).

9. My reading focuses upon the image of the Whore in ch. 17, although I do keep one eye on ch. 18. While ch.18 provides interesting points for interacting with queer discourses, this limitation allows for a more concise argument.

the first Jerusalem temple in the sixth century B.C.E., something echoed during the Roman siege of Jerusalem in 70 C.E., when the second temple was destroyed (Friesen 2001, 138–40). Given this connection, for John's audience the most natural analogy to Babylon would be Rome. This connection is solidified when the Whore is described as sitting on seven mountains or hills (17:9), a traditional descriptor for Rome, and as "the great city that rules over the kings of the earth" (17:18).

While the Whore refers to a city and not a literal woman, Revelation's imagery conjures up an image of a woman for its audience to envision and to gaze upon (Rossing 1999, 21–25; Frilingos 2004, 58–60). An angel informs John that he will show him the judgment of the Whore. The language of showing prompts the audience to visualize along with John as he is taken to see the Whore. Even though the angel informs John that the Whore will be judged, suggesting her opposition to God, John "wonders with great wonder" when he finally sees her (17:6). She is clothed in purple and scarlet and draped with gold and jewels. John's wonder or amazement when he sees Babylon is emphasized in the Greek text with the use of the related terms θαυμάζω and θαῦμα in v. 6, as well as in v. 7 when the angel asks John, "Why are you amazed?" or "Why are you wondering?" Of all the things that John witnesses on his visionary tour, the Whore is the only thing at which he *shows* amazement, although he does fall at the feet of the risen Christ when he sees him.[10] Some scholars describe John's wondering at the Whore as a negative reaction or as a relatively neutral reaction (e.g. Aune 1998, 3:938). In contrast, Christopher A. Frilingos argues,

> The angel's interrogative is balanced by moments in which θαῦμα is a proper reaction to the book's visions: John reports that "the song of Moses and the song of the Lamb" intoned by the faithful in heaven includes the verse "Great and amazing (θαυμαστὰ) are your deeds, Lord God the Almighty!" (Rev. 15:3). Two verses before John himself describes the scene as "great and amazing (θαυμαστόν): seven angels with seven plagues, which are the last, for with them the wrath of God is ended" (Rev. 15:1). Given these passages, which place θαῦμα in a positive context, is the angelic reproach of John a rejection of wonder *qua* wonder or is it, rather, an intervention? The angel's remark disrupts the moment,

---

10. Interestingly, the verb θαυμάζω also describes the reaction of the people of the earth to the beast in Rev 13:3 and 17:8. Additionally, Rev does describe things within the text as amazing (θαυμαστά), but this is the only time when John enacts a state of wonder.

shifting the focus from John's reaction to the image of Babylon, which gives rise to the seer's response in the first place. (Frilingos 2004, 51)

John's wonder is a response that the angel, who gives voice to the author, apparently deems unacceptable. It is a reaction that requires at least an explanation. This implies that John's amazement at the Great Whore is a sign of his interest in, perhaps even his desire for, her. In fact, θαυμάζω could be used in contexts of desire. For instance, this term appears in the story of Judith. As the beautiful heroine, Judith, walks through the camp of the Assyrian general Holofernes, his troops "wonder" (ἐθαύμαζον) at her beauty (Jdt 10:19).

John's wonder at the Whore sparks my own interest, as a queer woman, in the Whore. As a feminist, I understand the danger in John's use of feminine stereotypes. Revelation's feminine images are far from developed images of actual women; rather, John uses archetypical images of women (e.g., mother, whore, bride), defined primarily in relation to men, as rhetorical tools (Schüssler Fiorenza 1991, 13). Pippin is one of the most outspoken critics of Revelation's use of feminine imagery in this way. She maintains that John uses these images to manipulate the desire of the audience that he assumes to be male (Pippin 1992, 72–74). However, in that brief moment, having been prompted throughout the narrative to "Look!" along with John, *my* eyes gaze at the Whore as John gazes. Like John, I hear that the Whore faces divine judgment and yet I find her fascinating and at least somewhat desirable. Perhaps this desire stems from the fact that she is labeled a "mystery." [11] This language evokes notions of secrecy and even, perhaps, "the closet"—the life of secrecy that shapes so many queer lives, even after they have come out (Sedgwick 2006, 68). Whatever the Whore's mystery happens to be, whether she is in the closet or not,[12] Revelation's apparent

---

11. The Greek in 17:5 is ambiguous, and it is difficult to determine whether "mystery" is part of the Whore's name or a reference to her name as a mystery: "And upon her forehead a name had been written, a mystery [or, Mystery], Babylon." "Mystery" is also used in 17:7 in reference to the Whore and her relationship to the beast that she rides, which has seven heads and ten horns. Since this second use is not a reference to the Whore's name, I opt to read the first use of mystery as a characterization of the woman's name, as mysterious or thought-provoking.

12. The concept of "sexual identity" is widely believed to be anachronistic when talking about the ancient world, even though same-sex practices were acceptable when they fit within the guidelines for active and passive partners (Parker 2001). Moreover, I am not arguing that John shapes the Whore as a queer woman. Instead, I am sug-

attempt at capturing the attention or the gaze of the male audience member has worked to capture the gaze of the lesbian-identified interpreter.

While "the gaze" is discussed typically within critical film studies, it has been appropriated in discussions of textual sources, including biblical texts. Frilingos, for example, appropriates this idea in his analysis of Revelation (2004, 39–42). This appropriation is quite on target. As noted above, Revelation is a text that readily employs the language of vision, coaching the audience to envision along with the text. In light of this, theory on the gaze seems to be a relevant tool for thinking about how a reader of Revelation, including a queer reader, might interact with images that John prompts his audience to see.

That John's use of feminine imagery, supposedly intended to harness the desire of a male audience, captures the gaze of a lesbian interpreter is not surprising. Queer readers throughout history have read against the heteronormative assumptions and codes embedded in texts ranging from classic novels to pop songs to popular films (Guest 2005, 197). The gaze, the visual attention directed toward an object of desire, often presumes a heterosexual male spectator in film, as Laura Mulvey first noted in her 1975 essay, "Visual Pleasure and Narrative Cinema." The invisible male spectator, moreover, stands in a position of power over the female character, since it is for him that the female character is created. Subsequent scholars have argued that while films and texts have traditionally assumed a male gaze, this does not preclude women spectators from appropriating the gaze (e.g. Doty 1995, 77; de Lauretis [1988] 1993, 150–52). And, while they debate over why and how it happens, queer and lesbian critics recognize that lesbians can and do identify with male characters, that they can even take on the role of the invisible male spectator (Straayer 1995). This entails stepping into a role typically understood as masculine and, yet, the lesbian spectator often enacts a different power dynamic within this role. In other words, the lesbian gaze can be quite different from the male gaze, which assumes a power over the one being gazed upon. The lesbian gaze, in contrast, is often shaped by a desire for reciprocity—a glance back (Straayer 1995).[13]

gesting that elements within the narrative can be read as queer by a reader who reads within the queer vernacular.

13. In addition, de Lauretis reminds interpreters that the lesbian gaze, as well as lesbian desire, is not a single and undifferentiated thing. There are different gazes and different desires among lesbians (de Lauretis [1988] 1993, 152).

Interestingly, in LaChapelle's queer visioning of Madonna as the Whore, the Whore appears to gaze back at the viewer. Her eyes meet the viewer with a look that can be read as powerful. As I read Revelation, however, nothing in the text signals to me that the Whore looks back at me. She appears as a character on display. In spite of this, John arguably wants his audience to read the Whore as a character who desires power, even though she might not be a powerful character. In ch. 18, Revelation depicts the Whore's inner monologue: "For in her heart, she says that, 'I rule as a queen and I am not a widow. I will never see grief'" (18:7).[14] Asserting her identity and power as a queen (perhaps *this* is her mystery!) to herself has a different effect than a gaze that communicates her power. Rather, the inner monologue rings of someone powerless trying to convince herself of her greatness. The Whore's assertion that she is "not a widow" and that she will "never see grief," moreover, implies that she refuses to imagine herself in relation to those who are least powerful, often characterized as widows (and orphans) in the Jewish prophetic tradition (e.g., Isa 1:17).

Perhaps the Whore's lack of interest in catching my eye has little to do with me and more to do with the fact that she's busy. Even before the text prompts the audience to wonder along with John at the Whore, John's angel guide announces that she "has committed fornication" (ἐπόρνευσαν) with "the kings of the earth" (17:2). She is also identified as the "mother of whores" (17:5), implying that Babylon has been living this life for some time. That the Whore is sexually engaged with male partners, kings (unless they are drag kings), might cause some queer interpreters to wonder about the Whore's mystery: perhaps she is not in the closet.[15] However, the gender of the Whore's partners does not disrupt her ability to queer heteronormativity. The Whore's actions do challenge modern heterosexual assumptions about what constitutes acceptable sex and work. Eva Pendleton, a sex-radical feminist and queer theorist,

---

14. This is a paraphrase of Isa 47:8, where a personified Babylon says in her heart, "I am, and there is no one besides me; I shall not sit as a widow or know the loss of children" (NRSV).

15. Some queer individuals stereotype bisexuals and lesbians who have sex with men as "fence-sitters" or as "less queer" than lesbians or gays (Shokeid 2001). There are a number of reasons why lesbians, those women who identify themselves primarily through their erotic relationships with women, have sex with men. These range from financial reasons to wanting to participate in a variety of sexual practices, including some with male partners. These do not necessarily make them any less queer (e.g., Califia 2005).

argues that both queer and straight sex workers "queer" heterosexuality in a variety of ways. For example, sex workers challenge the cultural assumption that sex should be something done for love or enjoyment and not for money.[16] In offering sex for money, sex workers shed light on the economic exchange that actually occurs in many sexual relationships, including marriage relationships. In contrast to marriage relationships, Pendleton and other sex-radical feminists argue, in the sex worker's relationship with her or his client the economic power resides in the hands of the sex worker, rather than the other way around. Pendleton further argues that sex workers, especially queer women who sell sex to men, prove the performative nature of gender and sexual identity, as they enact a variety of identities for different clients (1997, 78–79). In this vein, the Whore is by definition a queer character.

The understanding of sex work that imagines the Whore as an image of queer strength is complicated by the fact that prostitution in the first century had a different cultural valence than in modern sex-radical feminism. The Greek word πόρνη can be translated into English with either "prostitute" or the pejorative term "whore." Thomas A. McGinn notes that in the Roman world, prostitution was socially accepted and legal, although being a prostitute meant one was morally suspect (1998, 10). Prostitution safeguarded societal order by providing free males an option for sex outside of marriage other than adultery (17).[17] While adultery for women consisted of any sexual relationship outside of marriage, for men adultery consisted of sexual relationships only with married women (Gardner 1986, 127). Adultery, which could yield a heavy penalty under Augustan law, was perceived as a social threat for a number of reasons (37). It complicated issues of patrimony and it typically involved a violation of another man's honor, serious issues in a culture built around the notion of a *pater-familias*. A woman, for instance, brought shame upon the male head of her

---

16. It should be noted that Eva Pendleton and other sex-radical feminists understand sex workers as those who are able to *choose* prostitution as a form of work and not those individuals who are coerced, physically, mentally, economically, culturally, into prostitution (Pendleton 1997; Queen 1997). Needless to say, this is only a percentage of sex workers living in the world, as many are trafficked against their will, even in the United States.

17. The operating assumption here, obviously, was that males would not be satisfied with a single sexual partner. Stoic discourses on marriage and sex, which argue for moderation, sex without desire, and mutual consent between (married) partners, seem to belie a cultural assumption that men might have sex with multiple partners.

household by having a sexual affair with someone to whom she did not "belong." Within the complex system of Roman honor and shame, a man (married or not) visiting a prostitute was understood as a relatively amoral act, since it did not involve a violation of anyone's honor. According to the cultural understanding of prostitution, visiting a prostitute could even be understood in positive terms. So, Martial encouraged an inexperienced groom to visit a brothel-keeper so she could "make him a man" before his wedding night (Martial 1978–1979, 11:78). Despite the cultural importance of prostitution, for women and men being a prostitute was regarded as one of the most shameful or dishonorable professions possible (along with acting!) (Edwards 1997, 66–95). This was doubly so for female prostitutes, who were marginalized by virtue of their gender as well as profession (Edwards 1997, 82; McGinn 1998, 15).

John's use of πόρνη draws upon the cultural assumption that prostitution was a shameful profession. He uses this terminology pejoratively as he characterizes the "sins" of Babylon or, as noted above, Rome.[18] Belying the fact that most prostitutes in the Roman world would have been of lower social classes, including slaves and ex-slaves, Revelation underscores the Whore's obvious affluence (McGinn 2004, 60).[19] As Hanna Roose notes, John shows little concern for depicting the actual social phenomenon of prostitution in the Roman world (2005, 233). Drawing upon Hebrew Bible traditions about Babylon, as well as the trading center of Tyre, Revelation emphasizes the Whore's access to precious and exotic goods (Royalty 1998, 63–65). She is clothed in purple and scarlet, luxury fabrics in the ancient world, and in precious gems, stones, and gold (17:4). In the next chapter, the luxuries of the Whore are cataloged in a description of her destruction:

> And the merchants of the earth weep and mourn for [Babylon], since no one buys their cargo anymore. Cargo of gold, silver, precious stones, pearls, fine linen, purple, silk, scarlet, and all kinds of scented wood, all articles of ivory … wine, olive oil, choice flour and wheat, cattle and sheep, horses and chariots, slaves—and human lives. "The fruit which satisfied your soul has gone from you, and all the dainties and splendor are lost to you, and they will never be found again!" The merchants of these things, those who became wealthy from her, will stand far off,

---

18. This is my reason for using the term "Whore" rather than "Prostitute."

19. McGinn notes that terms used to describe lower-class businesses, such as inexpensive lodgings (*stabulum*) and taverns (*taberna*), were also used as euphemisms for brothels, reflecting something of the class status of Roman prostitutes (2004, 18–22).

in fear of her torment, weeping and mourning aloud, "Woe, woe, the
great city, clothed in fine linen, in purple and scarlet, adorned with gold,
jewels, and pearls!" (Rev 18:11–16)

The list of Babylon's cargoes describes not only the Whore's wealth, but the
list alludes to the far reach of her empire (Bowditch 2006, 307). The Whore
is an imperial city that has access to the finest luxuries the world has to
offer, since she has control of the places that produce such goods. Elsewhere in Revelation John alludes to the empire's economic exploitation of
Asia Minor, one of Rome's sources for olive oil and wine (6:5–6; Howard-
Brook and Gwyther 1999, 98–99). Likewise, the reference to slaves and
human lives, listed like other forms of cargo, offers a grim reminder that
imperial systems rely upon the commoditization of individuals. While
empires treat humans as material goods, they are ultimately expendable.
Thus, Revelation implicates the Whore in the deaths of those who follow
the Lamb, supposedly innocent victims according to the narrative (17:6).

As the references to slavery and human trafficking imply, Revelation
presents an image of the Whore as someone who wields power over people.
Or, at the least, she is a character who desires power, as suggested above.
Alluding to the Whore's identity as Rome, the city that sits on seven hills,
John describes the Whore as sitting on seven kings, people of power. The
Whore literally rides upon the backs of those who finance and empower her
(17:9–14). Not only does the Whore gain power from her associations with
the kings of the earth, but she exercises power over the people of the earth:
"The inhabitants of the earth have become drunk upon the wine of her fornication" (17:2; cf. 14:8). The Whore's influence upon the people of earth,
according to John, impairs their judgment and makes them as delusional or
as drunk as the Whore who carries her own large, golden cup (17:4).

Revelation's dismay over the people of earth's drunkenness reflects
John's concern over the threat of cultural assimilation. The people of the
earth have become like the Whore (i.e., they have assimilated to imperial
culture) by drinking the wine of her fornication (πορνεία). In the prophetic
traditions, fornication or adultery language often functions as a metaphor
characterizing Israel's supposed apostasy and its inappropriate political
associations (e.g., Ezek 16; Day 2000). As Peggy Day observes, this emotionally charged language describes a breach in the covenant between God
and God's people, as Israel adopts the practices, including cultic practices,
of other nations (2000, 242). Echoing his prophetic predecessors, John uses
the language of fornication in conjunction with other references to assimi-

lation, namely eating "idol meat" (εἰδωλόθυτον; 2:14, 20). Although some early Christians may have understood eating idol meat (e.g., buying and eating meat that had been offered as a sacrifice in Roman temples, participating in meals held at trade guilds where meat may have been dedicated to the gods) as pragmatic, others understood it as an accommodation to the religious and political beliefs of the culture (e.g., 1 Cor 8:7–13; Moore 2006, 116). This accommodation would have likely afforded those in John's audience social and political acceptance (Schüssler Fiorenza 1991, 56). Thus, by pairing references to the eating of idol meat with the imagery of fornication, Revelation's point is clear: assimilation into the empire is seductive (Rossing 1999, 129).

Before reading *through* the Whore's promise of assimilation toward a queer perspective, it is important to turn our attention to the end of Rev 17. In contrast to the beginning of John's vision, which highlights the allure and power of the Whore, in these final verses we, John and his reader, see the Whore stripped and burned by the kings of the earth: "And the ten horns that you saw and the beast, they will hate the Whore and they will make her desolate and naked and they will devour her flesh and they will burn her in fire" (17:16). When we imagine the Whore as a woman, the language and imagery of the text is horrific. The language of making the Whore desolate, which literally suggests making the Whore into a desert (ἠρημωμένην ποιήσουσιν αὐτήν), evokes images of rape according to Pippin (1999, 94). Although Barabara Rossing argues against Pippin's reading of this, noting that ἐρημόω is primarily used to describe when land is deforested or razed (1999, 90), I would argue that the text uses the language metaphorically to describe the "razing" of a woman's body just as a forest might razed. The image of the kings devouring the Whore, furthermore, suggests not just cannibalism but the kings' absolute power over the Whore. Not satisfied with using the Whore, they make her part of themselves (Carpenter 1995, 117). In some sense, the imagery suggests that the powerful eventually feed upon those to whom they give power.

In spite of Revelation's assertion that the Whore is an imperial city and not an actual woman, Pippin explains that John wants his readers, namely male audience members, to take a perverse pleasure in watching the destruction of the female figure they once desired (1992, 67, 86). Revelation does, in fact, encourage its audience to rejoice in the Whore's demise, when the choirs of heaven proclaim, "Hallelujah! Salvation, glory, and power to our God … for he has judged the great whore who corrupted the earth with her fornication and he has avenged the blood of his slaves from her hand" (19:1–2). That the destruction of the Whore is ultimately defined as God's act of judgment underscores that the audience should approve of this turn of events.

As a queer-lesbian reader who initially desires the Whore, I take little pleasure in the depiction of the Whore's demise. I find some reassurance in the image of empire collapsing in upon itself; however, the stark imagery makes it difficult for me to rejoice along with the voices of heaven. In *Death and Desire*, Pippin makes a similar observation, writing, "Having studied the evils of Roman imperial policy in the colonies, I find the violent destruction of Babylon very cathartic. But when I looked into the face of Babylon, I saw a woman" (1992, 80). My resistance to the text at this point stems from my desire for the Whore as well as a certain identification that I have with the Whore. This sense of identification, however, should not be interpreted as my wanting to become the Whore. As described above, the lesbian gaze often desires a glance back that is reciprocal but not necessarily narcissistic. Valerie Traub, for instance, argues against the assumption that the lesbian gaze is either a desire to really become a man (transvestitism) or a desire to make one's self into the other woman (narcissism) (Traub 1995). While I do not necessarily seek to become the Whore, in this moment, when I see the Whore's judgment, I identify with her as a queer woman, especially since the threat of violence looms over the heads of most individuals who identify as queer. I recognize that there are some shared experiences between us and I hope that a violent end will not be among those experiences. Thus, in my viewing there is both an experience of distance that wants closeness with the Whore, the experience of a desiring spectator, and a certain sense of closeness that ultimately wants some distance from the Whore because of a forced recognition of shared vulnerability.

Buying into/with the Whore

As mentioned above, one of the aspects of the Whore's allure is the promise of assimilation. This temptation presents itself not just to "the people of the earth" who have become drunk off of the Whore's fornications (17:2). Rather, Revelation's narrative suggests that this is ultimately the temptation presented to John's audience (Rossing 1999, 129). One of John's primary aims is to convince the churches of Asia Minor to resist the hegemony of the Empire and the allure of accommodation in all of its forms. The temptation to appropriate the patterns and plans of the dominant culture is something that many queer individuals face. As with the Whore, whose vision of assimilation has a clear economic aspect, the attempt to assimilate queers into the dominant culture takes place in the marketplace. As the growing number of "lifestyle" magazines, available at your nearest Borders or Barnes and Noble, demonstrates, gays and lesbians specifically are now niche markets. In *Selling Out: The Gay and Lesbian Movement Goes to Market*, Alexandra Chasin describes this as the "enfranchisement" of gays and lesbians (2001, 46). More than ever, our communities are courted by a host of companies, from credit cards to vodka to online dating services, wanting our allegiances. Just as the Whore appears queer at times, the marketing aimed at LGBTQ communities often has a veneer of queer: a television ad for an online travel agency, for instance, depicts a cool-looking lesbian couple outsmarting a dull-witted, straight couple in a game show competition for last-minute hotel reservations.[20] The ad draws in the queer viewer who would like to believe that lesbians are naturally more edgy or cooler than buttoned-up heterosexuals. It is easy to confuse this flattery with acceptance. Despite this, California Governor Arnold Schwarzenegger revealed the economics behind political and social acceptance when he commented on the state's ruling (since overturned) in favor of marriage equality, "I hope that California's economy is booming because everyone is going to come here and get married!" (Christensen 2008, 27). Although it is always nice to be wanted, Chasin and others point out that acceptance into the dominant culture comes with conditions. One commentator describes these conditions as the "heterosexualization of gay culture" (Daniel Mendelsohn, as quoted in Chasin 2001, 45). Gay culture, moreover, is made monolithic when, for example, marketing to lesbians encourages us to identify with a particular sort of lesbian, a lesbian palatable to the dominant culture of heterosexuality. This lesbian is white, educated, childless, and relatively wealthy (Clark 1995). While a few of us, including myself, may fit this image, endorsing this image and allowing it to become *the* image of lesbianism is an essentialist move that cuts against the very heart of queerness (493).

As Revelation's image of the Whore implies, absorption into the dominant culture means more than risking distinctive and queer identities (as though that was not bad enough). After describing the destruction of the Whore, the angel who narrates the vision reminds both John and the reader of Revelation that the Whore represents "the great city that rules over the

---

20. This commercial for Orbitz can be viewed online at http://www.commercial-closet.org/. Commercial Closet is an organization dedicated to analyzing the portrayal of LGBTQ individuals and issues in advertising around the world.

kings of the earth" (17:18). This may not mitigate the gruesome image of the Whore's destruction, but it does remind the reader that the Whore offers assimilation into an empire and all that it represents. Among these things is a sense of power, albeit a power that is always derivative. The Whore rides upon the backs of kings, until she is no longer useful to the kings. This should prompt us to wonder whether and/ or when queer communities can expect to be devoured in a similar way by those who want us to assimilate.

Assimilation into the world of the Whore entails, moreover, participation in the violence she wields over others. As Alan Sinfield argues in *Cultural Politics—Queer Reading*, while some may see questions of imperialism as tangential to the domain of queer theory, the opposite is quite true. Imperial powers, ancient and modern, maintain their power by imposing hierarchies, sometimes violently, upon others. This includes policing hierarchies of gender and sexual identity, as well as using these hierarchies to shame and oppress. This was made clear, Sinfield observes, in the pictures of torture from Abu Ghraib in which commonly held assumptions about gender, that females are less powerful than males, were used to humiliate detainees (2005, xii-xiii). Likewise, the sexualization of the torture evidenced in the same photos, which depicted male prisoners simulating sex acts with one another, reflects the way that imperialism uses hierarchies of sexuality to maintain power over others. Buying into the system of empire implicates us in the use of such tactics. When I desire the Whore and when I identify with the Whore, I am reminded that even as a queer reader, I risk complicity in the sins of the Whore.

A PARTING GLANCE AND APOCALYPTIC POSSIBILITIES

Paying attention to and through Revelation's image of the Whore reveals a picture even more multivalent than the David LaChapelle image referenced at the beginning of this essay. Attending to Revelation's image, we do see that as a metaphorical representation of an imperial city, such as Rome, the image of the Whore is integral to Revelation's critique of empire. As such it indicts imperial power on a number of fronts, including its conspicuous consumption, its economic exploitation of others, its use of violence and lack of concern for human life, and its ability to delude the people of the earth. Even more importantly, the image of the Whore, as mentioned above, points to the seductive nature of assimilation.

Reading through the image of the Whore, we see a more ambivalent image. Even though the image seems scripted to appeal to a male audience, the image inadvertently sparks the interest of a queer-lesbian reader. I am drawn into the Whore's allure in part because she looks a little queer to me. However, she ultimately resists definition. In this way, the Whore is a true mystery. The allure of this mystery fades as I recognize that John constructs the image by drawing upon the first-century assumption that prostitutes are shameful. The double standard that presents visiting a prostitute as morally acceptable, yet denigrates the prostitute her- or himself, certainly plays into the gender hierarchies of heteronormativity. Furthermore, as I witness the destruction that befalls the Whore, her demise at the hands of the kings of the earth, I am placed in a position of ambivalence. On one hand, I find some satisfaction in the destruction of empire. On the other hand, I am troubled by the image of violence because of my sense of identification with the Whore. It is not always easy to separate the image of the Whore as city from the image of the Whore as woman. Although the image of the Whore's destruction is abhorrent and potentially prohibits one from finding any simple meaning in the text as a woman, it disrupts my gaze enough to force me to consider how I, along with the queer communities in which I participate, have become like the Whore. That is, it forces me to consider whether (or how) I have become drawn into the false promises of empire and its fantasy of power.

Reading Revelation from a queer perspective does not promise easy answers, as we see with the image of the Whore. Aspects of the text offer possible entry points for queer readings of Revelation, including the image of the 144,000 male virgins (Huber, 2008), the ambiguous gender of the Lamb, and the overall rhetorical trope of revealing what is hidden. These possibilities, however, must be negotiated within a text that employs imagery of violence and destruction and that runs the risk of replicating empire, as Stephen D. Moore argues (2006, 118–21). John may need to look at the Whore with a more self-reflective eye: he may have been so amazed by the Whore that he has become dumbstruck, blind to the fact that his narrative replicates the very rhetoric that supports the Whore. Likewise, as we gaze at the Whore or other images within the text, we need to be self-reflective, lest we mimic empire as well.

Further contributing to the difficulties inherent in reading Revelation queerly is the fact that apocalyptic rhetoric has become a central part of the vernacular of those who condemn gays, lesbians, bisexuals, transsexuals and other queers. Disentangling Revelation and its images from this appropriation of apocalyptic rhetoric is a time- consuming task. However, this process will, I hope, yield new ways of thinking about Revelation. At the very least, through this process we can learn how to negotiate difficult texts, finding ourselves addressed by them and even challenged by them. More importantly, by engaging the texts and traditions of Revelation, we are addressed as potential subjects of imperialistic assimilationist projects, an incredibly important critique for an increasingly accepted LGBT community in twenty-first-century America.

Works Consulted

Aune, David E. 1998. *Revelation*. 3 vols. Dallas: Word.

Bowditch, Lowell. 2006. Propertius and the Gendered Rhetoric of Luxury and Empire: A Reading of 2.16. *Comparative Literature Studies* 43:306–25.

Califia, Patrick. 2005. Gay Men, Lesbians, and Sex: Doing It Together. Pages 22–27 in *Queer Theory*. Edited by I. Morland and A. Willox. New York: Palgrave Macmillian.

Carey, Greg. 2008. The Book of Revelation as Counter-Imperial Script. Pages 157–76 in *In the Shadow of Empire: Reclaiming the Bible as a History of Faithful Resistance*. Edited by R. A. Horsley. Louisville: Westminster John Knox.

Carpenter, Mary Wilson. 1995. Representing Apocalypse: Sexual Politics and the Violence of Revelation. Pages 107–35 in *Postmodern Apocalypse: Theory and Cultural Practice at the End*. Edited by Richard Dellamora. Philadelphia: University of Pennsylvania.

Chasin, Alexandra. 2001. *Selling Out: The Gay and Lesbian Movement Goes to Market*. New York: Palgrave Macmillian.

Christensen, Jen. 2008. Love! Valour! Commerce! *The Advocate*, July 1:27.

Clark, Danae. (1991) 1995. Commodity Lesbianism. Pages 484–500 in Creekmur and Doty 1995.

Cobb, Michael. 2006. *God Hates Fags: The Rhetoric of Religious Violence*. New York: New York University Press.

Creekmur, C. K., and A. Doty, eds. 1995. *Out in Culture: Gay, Lesbian, and Queer Essays on Popular Culture*. Durham, N.C.: Duke University Press.

Day, Peggy L. 2000. The Bitch Had It Coming to Her: Rhetoric and Interpretation in Ezekiel 16. *BibInt* 8:231–54.

Doty, Alexander. 1995. There's Something Queer Here. Pages 71–90 in Creekmur and Doty 1995.

Edwards, Catherine. 1997. Unspeakable Professions: Public Performance and Prostitution in Ancient Rome. Pages 66-95 in *Roman Sexualities*. Edited by Judith P. Hallet and Marilyn B. Skinner. Princeton: Princeton University Press.

Friesen, Steven J. 1993. *Twice Neokoros: Ephesus, Asia and the Cult of the Flavian Imperial Family*. Leiden: Brill.

———. 2001. *Imperial Cults and the Apocalypse of John: Reading Revelation in the Ruins*. Oxford: Oxford University Press.

Frilingos, Christopher A. 2004. *Spectacles of Empire: Monsters, Martyrs, and the Book of Revelation, Divinations*. Philadelphia: University of Pennsylvania Press.

Gardner, Jane. 1986. *Women in Roman Law and Society*. London: Croom Helm.

Guest, Deryn. 2005. *When Deborah Met Jael: Lesbian Biblical Hermeneutics*. London: SCM Press.

Howard-Brook, Wes, and Anthony Gwyther. 1999. *Unveiling Empire: Reading Revelation Then and Now*. Maryknoll, N.Y.: Orbis.

Huber, Lynn R. 2008. Sexually Explicit? Re-reading Revelation's 144,000 Virgins as a Response to Roman Discourses. *Journal of Men, Masculinities and Spirituality* 2.1:3–28.

Jack, Alison. 2001. Out of the Wilderness: Feminist Perspectives on the Book of Revelation. Pages 149–62 in *Studies in the Book of Revelation*. Edited by S. Moyise. Edinburgh: T&T Clark.

Keller, Catherine. 2006. Ms. Calculating the Apocalypse. Pages 1–13 in *Gender and Apocalyptic Desire*. Edited by B. E. Brasher and L. Quinby. London: Equinox.

Lauretis, Teresa de. (1988) 1993. Sexual Indifference and Lesbian Representation. Pages 141–58 in *The Lesbian and Gay Studies Reader*. Edited by H. Abelove, M. A. Barale, and D. M. Halperin. New York: Routledge.

Martial. 1978–1979. *Epigrams*. Translated by W. C. A. Ker. Rev. ed. 2 vols. LCL. Cambridge: Harvard University Press.

McGinn, Thomas A. 1998. *Prostitution, Sexuality, and the Law in Ancient Rome*. New York: Oxford University Pres.

———. 2004. *The Economy of Prostitution in the Roman World: A Study of Social History and the Brothel*. Ann Arbor: University of Michigan Press.

Moore, Stephen D. 2006. *Empire and Apocalypse: Postcolonialism and the New Testament*. Sheffield: Sheffield Phoenix Press.

Mulvey, Laura. 1975. Visual Pleasure and Narrative Cinema. *Screen* 16 (3):6–18.

Parker, Holt N. 2001. The Myth of the Heterosexual: Anthropology and Sexuality for Classicists. *Arethusa* 32:313–62.

Pendleton, Eva. 1997. Love for Sale: Queering Heterosexuality. Pages 73–82 in *Whores and Other Feminists*. Edited by J. Nagle. New York: Routledge.

Pippin, Tina. 1992. *Death and Desire: The Rhetoric of Gender in the Apocalypse of John*. Literary Currents in Biblical Interpretation. Louisville: Westminster John Knox.

———. 1999. *Apocalyptic Bodies: The Biblical End of the World in Text and Image*. London: Routledge.

Pippin, Tina, and J. Michael Clark. 2006. Revelation/Apocalypse. Pages 753–68 in *The Queer Bible Commentary*. Edited by Deryn Guest et al. London: SCM.

Queen, Carol. 1997. Sex Radical Politics, Sex-Positive Feminist Thought, and Whore Stigma. Pages 125–35 in *Whores and Other Feminists*. Edited by J. Nagle. New York, NY: Routledge.

Roose, Hanna. 2005. The Fall of the "Great Harlot" and the Fate of the Aging Prostitute: An Iconographic Approach to Revelation 18. Pages 228–52 in *Picturing the New Testament: Studies in Ancient Visual Images*. Edited by A. Weisenrieder, F. Wendt, and P. von Gemünden. Tübingen: Mohr Siebeck.

Rossing, Barbara R. 1999. *The Choice between Two Cities: Whore, Bride, and Empire in the Apocalypse*. Harrisburg, Pa.: Trinity.

Royalty, Robert M. 1998. *The Streets of Heaven: The Ideology of Wealth in the Apocalypse of John*. Macon, Ga.: Mercer University Press.

Schüssler Fiorenza, Elisabeth. 1991. *Revelation: Vision of a Just World*. Proclamation Commentaries. Minneapolis: Fortress.

Sedgwick, Eve Kosofsky. 2006. *The Epistemology of the Closet*. 2nd ed. Berkeley: University of California Press.

Shokeid, Moshe. 2001. You Don't Eat Indian and Chinese Food at the Same Meal: The Bisexual Quandry. *Anthropological Quarterly* 75:63–90.

Sinfield, Alan. 2005. *Cultural Politics—Queer Reading*. 2nd ed. London: Routledge.

Straayer, Chris. 1995. The Hypothetical Lesbian Heroine in Narrative Feature Film. Pages 44–59 in Creekmur and Doty 1995.

Traub, Valerie. 1995. (Dis)articulations of *Black Widow*. Pages 115–36 in Creekmur and Doty 1995.

Queer Theory, Postcolonial Theory, and Biblical Interpretation: A Preliminary Exploration of Some Intersections*

Jeremy Punt

1. Introducing the Issue

Queer theory is generally believed to be inspired by Michael Foucault;[1] is often associated with the theoretical work done by philosophers and sociologists like Judith Butler, Gayle Rubin, Eve Kosofsky Sedgwick, and Jeffrey Weeks;[2] and flows from the experience of a new generation of LGBT (lesbian, gay, bisexual, and transgendered), feminist, and civil-rights activists.[3] Queer theory, in a word, questions and destabilizes sexual identities and countercultural prejudice against sexual minorities such as homosexuals (Donovan 2001, 266 n. 72). Without claiming too much for queer theory, it in the end goes up against the entire paradigmatic system of meaning that produces heterosexuality and homosexuality, and treats

---

* This is the edited version of a paper read at the SBL International Meeting in Singapore, 26 June–1 July 2005.

1. The claims are often stronger; e.g., Schneider (2000a, 3) holds that queer theory emerged after the 1985 translation of Foucault's *History of Sexuality*. Foucault enabled the emergence of queer theory with his critique of power and identity as cultural productions and his focus on "a necessary and mutually defining binary relationship between subjugated and dominant identities" (Schneider 2000b, 209).

2. Foucault's work did not adequately account for gender, an issue Butler investigated from the perspective of the performance of cultural norms rather than the social inevitability of biology and bodies. Sedgwick expanded on Foucault's theories with her insistence on the necessity of homosexuality for heterosexual identity production (Schneider 2000b, 209).

3. Queer theory can be considered as an offshoot of postmodernist feminism (so Donovan 2001, 266 n. 72; cf. Jeffreys 1996, 359–82).

religious ideas as the cultural means of production for that system (Schneider 2000a, 3; 2000b, 208). Operating with a strong notion of the historical and social construction of society's beliefs about human sexual nature, basic premises of queer theory include the denunciation of the idea that sexuality is a universal and eternal drive, *and* the affirmation that sexuality is best viewed from a social-constructionist position. Sexuality and erotic desire in particular only exist within and not above or beyond history and are therefore always interpreted within history (Stuart et al. 1997, 3; cf. Seidman 1996a, 8–9).

Queer theory together with other critical theories such as place theory,[4] relies on postcolonial theory. Place theory connects identity and social location and holds that human identity is located, developed, and sustained in place.[5] Queer theory, which is not (necessarily)[6] primarily about sexual identity, is related to place theory, since queer theory destabilizes the self-evidence of power and marginality, center and periphery,[7] which are important issues in postcolonial theory.

This contribution is a modest attempt to situate and investigate important lines that characterize queer theory as an "umbrella term" given to the variety of critical approaches encapsulated by it.[8] A further goal is to juxtapose the postcolonial and the queer while considering theoretical conver-

---

4. One of the strong advocates of place theory rightly protests the "hegemony of time" in, e.g., Jesus scholarship and insists that questions of place are neglected (Moxnes 2003, 6). But are time and place as heuristic categories to be separated so neatly?

5. Place is not restricted to material place such as homes, imperial places, cities, but extends also to ideological place, for example family, gender, and power as well as social place, including conventions and institutions, and mental place, that is, on the level of thought and imagination.

6. Seidman (1996a, 11), however, sees queer theory as "contesting ... [*sc.* the assumption of a unified homosexual identity] and therefore the very telos of Western homosexual politics."

7. The relationship between place and gender is often assumed, as in the antiquated wisdom expressed by notions such as "a woman's place is in the kitchen" (Moxnes 2003, 16) or "this is a man's world." Gender is about more than social relations and involves also spatial dimensions.

8. However, given the broad spectrum of meanings attributed to and uses of queer theory, generalization is dangerous. The variety in queer theory is at least in part brought about by its scope of investigation: "Because the status of sexual identity itself is part of the question, the scope of queer studies is necessarily diffuse" (Schneider 2000b, 209). Douglas Hall (2003) prefers to speak of queer *theories*.

gence and divergence and to inquire about possible interaction between the two theoretical paradigms. Finally, the possibilities emerging from such comparison for biblical interpretation, for elucidating texts and for providing alternative hermeneutical frameworks, alert to issues of gender and inclusivity, are considered.

2. Queer Theory: Beyond Homosexual Liberation and Feminism?

Queer theory[9] is immersed in a larger debate and is a remaining difficulty for the foreseeable future, namely the (perceived) tension between queer theorists and homosexual liberationists, since the latter's notion of a natural homosexuality[10] that springs from something essential and ineradicable is the exact issue[11] that queer theory challenges.[12] More than just a difference in opinion, queer theory questions the ability of homosexual

---

9. Queer theory is used in a wide-ranging set of perspectives, which include all gay, lesbian, bisexual, and transgendered experiences and, on the other side of the spectrum, "a theoretical sensibility that pivots on transgression or permanent rebellion" (Seidman 1996a, 11).

10. Terminology used to refer to sexual orientation is fraught with difficulty and politically laden. "Homosexual" and its derivatives are seen as inadequate, suggesting an essence as distinct from heterosexual, and are often perceived as too political, a late nineteenth-century, psychologically defined "condition distinct from and parallel to heterosexuality ... an abstract construct superimposed upon the widely diverse reality of human experience" (Holben 1999, 4). Sex reformer Karl Kertbeny coined the term "homosexual" in 1868, and Swiss medical practitioner Karoly Maria Benkert used it in 1869 in opposition to the expansion of antisodomy laws in Prussia (Elliott 2001, 122; cf. Holben 1999, 6; Moore 1998, 258). Interestingly, the invention of a homosexual category made its opposite possible in 1890, rendering "heterosexuality." The terms "gay" or "lesbian"—often seen as white, middle-class labels—are commonly subsumed in "queer," as an empowering and inclusive term regardless of the color of those involved (Holben 1999, 248 n. 5; cf. Seidman 1996a, 10). Cf. below for the different body politics of gay and lesbian and queer thinking.

11. A similar debate is found in feminist circles, where fears are harbored about the dissolution of "essential woman" in favor of "separate, diverse local genders," and its ill effects for the political goals of feminism (Tolbert 2000, 101).

12. Without discounting the severity of the disagreement between these two configurations regarding the basis of homosexual identity, common ground exists in the acceptance of homosexuality as a social reality for people sharing this identity and the real and enduring effects of this identity on social organization and physical bodies (cf. Schneider 2000a, 3–8). For the social context of the rise of queer theory, cf. Seidman 1996a, 9–13.

liberationists to achieve their goals[13] when their program reaffirms the stability of heterosexually defined categories[14] and when their assertion of stable homosexualities reinforces heteronormativity by mirroring heterosexuality oppositionally—which ironically also provides the rationale for its dominance (e.g., Butler 1990, 147; Schneider 2000a, 9; 2000b, 208; Seidman 1996a, 7–11; Weedon 1999, 51–76).

Opponents of queer theory question its perception of an appropriate political agenda beyond sexual politics, arguing for example that queer theory tends to neglect class conflict as simply another, peripheral set of problems, with no critical connection to sexual politics. "The problem with (post-modern) queer theory is that (contrary to its own self-understanding) it works basically not against but in the interest of the (economic) status quo, in the interest of purely cultural reform and not economic revolution" (Morton 1995–1996, 3–4).[15] Another group of vociferous critics of queer theory argues from a position of radical feminism and criticizes queer theory's lack of political action, in that it fails to address the praxis of women's oppression (Jeffreys 1996, 359–62). Blaming queer theory's postmodernist focus on language and binaries, its "anguished introspection" is found to be based on the "postmodern Masters" such as Foucault, and its nonessentialism[16] is seen as nothing else but reinvoked individualism and liberalism covered with some intellectual veneer (359–74, esp. 372).

Partly under influence of postmodern thinking, queer theory focuses its attention on the subjects rather than the object(s) of religious faith, and its broader agenda includes the "workings of cultural formation and compulsory heterosexuality because religion is the locus of that compulsion."

---

13. At the risk over oversimplification, three discursive positions regarding queers and queer sexualities can be marked out: "deviant" as found in homophobic discourse, "normal" as claimed in liberal discourse, and "queer" as found in postmodernist discourse (cf. Kumashiro 2000, 145).

14. "Social constructionist perspectives suggested that 'homosexuality' was not a uniform, identical phenomenon but that its meaning and social role varied historically" (Seidman 1996a, 8).

15. In the wake of postmodernism, "queer theorists set up as the target of their opposition not capitalism but the liberal state," which is in accordance with the rationale that the contemporary is a postcapitalist era in which there is no class struggle (Morton 1995–1996, 4).

16. For Jeffreys (1996, 372), the affirmation of essentialism steers away from biological determinism and focuses on "any similarity amongst a class of people on which political theorising or action can be based."

The compulsory aspect of religion remains even within gay and lesbian theologies where homosexuality is included and affirmed and is therefore "always excluding queers even after homosexuals are admitted" (cf. Schneider 2000a, 10–11). "Because queer theory complicates simple associations of homosexuality with persons, queerness is therefore something more transgressive, more productive of difference, and more disruptive of stable, normative sexual identities than what we think of when we use the terms *gay, lesbian*, or *homosexual*" (Schneider 2000b, 208).

Queer theory occupies a liminal space, since it has "the task of complicating the warring positions without losing sight of the stakes that remain for those they would help" (Schneider 2000a, 11). And therefore queer theory has a double role to play in related contemporary debates: criticism and affirmation.[17] "To the extent that religion produces and legitimates coercive norms, queer theology must critique it and stand outside of it. To the extent that religion transforms fear into life and denial into risk, queer theology should articulate it and support it" (11). But queer theory's own gestation has to be considered against the background of influence such as social constructionism ("queering") and the theoretical and political accommodation of the role of social dynamics and power-play in sex and gender ("querying").

3. Gender, Theory, and Power: Queering and Querying

One of the most important developments in contemporary thinking about bodies in the sense of physical selves and their representation has been the emphasis on the link between bodies and regimes of social and political power or on the relationship between sexual identity and social power. It is the embeddedness of bodies in politics and power, hidden away by moral pretentiousness that was exposed relatively recently by the likes of Foucault, Scarry, and others (LaFleur 1998, 45). And it is the work of theorists such as Butler that has made compelling arguments for the social constructivist nature of gender and sex, as well as the *performativity* of gender[18] that reconceptualized human agency "in a manner that deeply

---

17. Biblical interpretation is also affected if "[t]he Bible is to gays what *Mein Kampf* is to Jews. It is the theory and practice of Homo Holocaust" (Tatchell 2000).

18. "Hence, as a strategy of survival within compulsory systems, gender is a performance with clearly punitive consequences," and "Gender ought not to be construed as a stable identity or locus of agency from which various acts follow; rather, gender

challenged long-held and often intensely defended convictions about the source of 'autonomous' human actions" (Barvosa-Carter 2005, 175; cf. Jeffreys 1996, 362–64).

Gender and its relationship to sex or sexuality is foregrounded since, in the past, sex and gender were traditionally related to biological or anatomical and social categories, respectively, and attributed a sequential order. Gender was seen to reflect the societal patterns established through and for a particular sex, which was understood as a given, as natural, as some essential quality (Boyarin 1998, 117; cf. Butler 1990, 146). A clear and hardly unusual form of gender construction passed off as natural and thus normative, even divinely ordained, and serving the interests of the powerful can be observed in opinions often found in gay reparative-therapy circles.[19] Explaining the design for human sexuality, their point of departure is "polarity in unity," from which is derived or through which is reflected gender differentiation, the latter being the ground of human sexuality.[20] Gender differentiation is therefore neither coincidental nor socially structured but "an eternal, ontological reality existing in the very nature of God."[21] In fact, it is argued, gender differentiation is seen as a "'transcendent reality' having its source in some form of 'polarity in unity' eternally existing in the Godhead" (Holben 1999, 55–56, 88).

Such gender differentiation and similarity extends beyond the biological to include also ontological and epistemological gender polarity. Ontologically, the masculine is believed to be situated in initiation, as elabo-

---

is an identity tenuously constituted in time, instituted in an exterior space through a *stylized repetition of acts*" (Butler 1990, 139–40).

19. The thinking underlying this understanding of homosexuality can be generalized as follows: homosexual *desire* is the result of inadequate relationships with same-sex persons at a young and impressionable age, and can and should be "healed" through reparative counseling. Such healing will disallow "ex-gays" to engage in homosexual *activity*, which in these circles is thought to be avoided also by homosexuals regardless of whether they have been "healed" from homosexuality.

20. "All things, it is argued, in ways we cannot always fully apprehend, are what they are in terms of the balance of opposites. These opposites, moreover, exist in a perpetual tension resulting from the fact that they are also, on some fundamental level, similar, and thus complementary" (Holben 1999, 56).

21. The male-female complementarity is a vital component of Karl Barth's thought on humankind, although the relationship he establishes between this complementarity and the image of God is a "recent theological novelty," unattested in Christian tradition or history and unsupported by biblical texts (cf. Holben 1999, 56, 88).

rated in leadership, authority, and protection of the dependent, as much as the feminine resides in response, including the complementary principles of receptivity, nurturing, and sacrificial love. In such perception, the two genders are characterized by, respectively, discursive reason versus female intuition,[22] and gender differentiation manifests at the level of drives toward power and nurture respectively.[23] The conclusion is the (epistemological) naturalization and thus (political) normalization of gender and sex, where human sexuality is considered proper and appropriate in as far as it constitutes "a living sign of that complementary polarity which is creation's reflection of the nature of the source" (Holben 1999, 57–58).[24]

But reaction to the dominant position of both the male and, more particularly, of heterosexuality did not stay out. As people of homosexual orientation increasingly claimed a place in society, and without relinquishing their sexual orientation in the process, gay, lesbian, and transsexual movements increasingly mobilized themselves and others and became much more vocal in various social locations. "Grouping people together and giving them an identity, teaching them to 'perform' in certain ways, gave them the power to challenge the notion that they were 'sick,' and so the modern lesbian and gay movement was born" (Stuart et al. 1997, 3).

More recently, the dividing lines between sex and gender have become blurred, and the sequential order of the relationship has become all but reversed. In other words, practice or behavior precedes being or identity; it is not the subject that constructs gender but gender that constructs the subject.

From a social-constructionist position it follows that sexual desire cannot be divorced from issues of power and control, "of those who cat-

---

22. A notion found already in Philo, where the image of the divine *logos* led to the creation of the human being in a spiritually unitary form. Gender division arose when the masculine intellect could not rule over but was seduced by the female, affective part of the unitary soul (Ruether 1996, 49).

23. The masculine drive toward power relates the sperm's "attack and penetration" to the "male's aggressive, masterful place in the natural order; conversely the female gender's drive to respond to and receive the male tallies with her receiving, keeping and nourishing, ultimately figures in the creativity of motherhood" (Holben 1999, 57).

24. The practical results of adhering to this supposedly divinely ordained paradigm is well summarized in the words of ex-gay Andy Comiskey, who refers to himself as a "homosexual struggler" when he claims, "Jesus has granted me enough heterosexual desire and personal maturity to love a woman, take her as my wife, and oversee a household and growing family" (quoted in Holben 1999, 73).

egorize and label and of those who are labeled" (Stuart 1997, 3). The history of describing human sexuality is important since it is only during the nineteenth century[25] that the practice appears to describe people in terms of their sexual orientation. Lying at the base of this was the essentialist notion that it was both possible and practical to define people according to sexual orientation (Stuart 1997, 3). Social constructionism as theory is helpful in showing that nothing is "natural" and that heterosexuality is not in some simplistic way the ultimate natural sexual orientation to live by. "Some men and women may be attracted to each other in all times and cultures, but how that attraction is interpreted and the repercussions of it are constructed differently in different times and cultures. The same is equally true of gender" (3). Modern western capitalism made it perfectly clear that it required a certain kind of masculinity and men who would not or could not conform to this requirement were labeled "homosexual."

In response to the debates on sexual identity and social power, queer theory critically analyzes social dynamics and power structures and challenges and deconstructs all claims to normality. It is, therefore, not a return to an essentialist notion of identity, not a definition of an alternative identity, but rather a different stance, a position over and against something[26] (Moxnes 2003, 5–6). Queer theory has also grown beyond the constructionist agenda, although it informs its epistemology. It has moved "from explaining the modern homosexual to questions of the operation of the hetero/homosexual binary, from an exclusive preoccupation with homosexuality to a focus on heterosexuality as a social and political organizing principle, and from a politics of minority interest to a politics of knowledge and difference" (Seidman 1996a, 9). With these shifts in its investigations, queer theory becomes concerned with, and poses the same questions as, postcolonial theory.

---

25. Earlier indications in this regard surface with the medieval notion of "the irredeemable sodomite" (Stuart 1997, 3).

26. In typical postmodern fashion, queer theory also sits with a dilemma regarding the use of "queer" to refer to what lies outside the norm, because as soon as queer is defined, it becomes domesticated, "rendering queer no longer outside of anything, and so no longer queer—in theory at least." In this way, queer theory then also stands to lose its claim to the outsider position in the heteronormative society and its power arrangements, in particular (Schneider 2000b, 206).

4. Intersections: Postcolonial and Queer Theory

Sexuality is inevitably political, particularly so when viewed from a social-constructivist perspective. It exists in so far as and in the forms prescribed by certain systems of power, which reward or punish and encourage or suppress certain practices and identities (Rubin 1993, 34), and elicits comparison with the postcolonial condition. Queer theory, in particular, is not about the study of a minority (the making of gay, lesbian, or bisexual subjects) as such but investigates liminality, marginalization, and exclusion. In contemporary society and certainly in the Two-Thirds World, issues related to sexuality and gender as well as to the lingering effects of colonialism (and neocolonialism) at social, economic, and at times political levels—all of which have great effect on peoples' lives—remain in and also greatly influences communities of faith.

Intersections between queer and postcolonial theories can be investigated in at least six areas (the detail of which will be addressed elsewhere): epistemological and hermeneutical considerations; notions of difference; center and margins, or marginality and exclusion; agency; mimicry, and its avoidance; and prophetic vision for inclusivity or a new world. Do queer and postcolonial theories reveal analogous thinking? The emphasis on liberation through a refocused dynamic between identity and social power is a golden thread running through queer theory and postcolonial theory, but since the theme of liberation or emancipation is for all its importance so broad and encompassing, it may lose its distinctive focus (or foci) in these social programs and is thus a concept that has to be unpacked.

Queer theory critiques the "central pillar" of modern society and contemporary culture—heteronormativity—and is therefore undeniably political (Moore 1998, 259). The increasing involvement of race and class consciousness in queer theory is evident, with queer often seen as an appropriate epithet to white and middle-class, which holds that people from other groups exuding a queer identity are suffering from "white disease" (Kumashiro 2000, 146). "Queer theory loses its cutting edge if it fails to take seriously the depth of significance and the inseparability of race, class, ethnicity, and gender to queer theorizing" (Schneider 2000b, 211).

The strongest connection between queer and postcolonial theories is, I contend, in their concern about the contemporary politics of identity, regarding the categories and institutions, the knowledge(s) and the power plays by means of which social dynamics and people are structured and regulated.

5. Queer Theory and a Politics of Identity?

"Hope for a queer future is not purely hedonistic, it is also political."
(Isherwood and Stuart 1998, 31)

"The deconstruction of identity is not the deconstruction of politics;
rather, it establishes as political the very terms through which identity is
articulated." (Butler 1990, 148)

Queer theory's relationship with the politics of identity is uneasy and vari-
able. "Although I detect a strain of anti-identity politics in some Queer
theory, the aim is not to abandon identity as category of knowledge and
politics but to render it permanently open and contestable as to its meaning and political role" (Seidman 1996a, 12). Queer theory questions fixed
gender identity and associated categories, perceiving identity as multiple,
unstable, and regulatory and as argued above, celebrating difference.

Relating to identity concerns, queering impacts on identity and social
dynamics in many ways. Homosexual identity, for example, is perceived
as a challenge to the patriarchal system, in which the issue of ownership
outranks the importance of romantic love and commitment. Patriarchy
requires monogamous security to safeguard the paternity of children,
while women treasure the perceived security of monogamous relationships beyond their own interests, the very situation, which often fuels
rivalry with other women as possible contenders to their space. In their
personal lives, women are expected to exhibit an ethic of service, dependent on the prioritization of male sexual desire. But also in its public role,
heterosexual monogamy "harnesses women's labor in a way that serves the
system" and keeps the patriarchal hierarchy in place—"homosexuality is
perceived as a threat" (Isherwood and Stuart 1998, 29).

The social constructedness of gender and sex and their multiple meanings renders them fragile and renders the notion of gender identity as well
as its supposed intractable depth and inner substance illusionary (Butler
1990, 146). This is best seen in practices of parody, where the fragility of
gender and sex is underscored by "loss of gender norms" that proliferates
"gender configurations, destabilizing substantive identity, and depriving
the naturalizing narratives of compulsory heterosexuality of their central
protagonists: 'man' and 'woman'" (Butler 1990, 146).[27] Gender parody,

---

27. Celebrity gender benders would include individuals such as Boy George,

gender play, gender bending, or genderfuck is the "mixing of masculine and feminine gender codes in ways that subvert the present bipolar gender system" and is generally perceived as a deliberate attempt to upset gender (Runions 1998, 225; cf. Boer 1998, 168; Butler 1990, 146; Wilkinson and Kitzinger 1996, 377– 78). Gender bending "implies the possibility of doing sex in a way that actively disrupts normative definitions of sex and gender," and "[a]nything that transcends the rigid boundaries of gendered sexuality is to be celebrated" (Isherwood and Stuart 1998, 27).

6. A Queer Optic on Biblical Texts

A queer reading of the New Testament texts therefore goes beyond and even challenges homosexual liberationist readings, which argue for gay and lesbian inclusion from the premise of the naturalness of homosexuality and against claims that sex and sexual desire between men or between women is neither natural nor good. *Gay resistance* challenges Christianity on two levels: justice and relation to the "essence" of God and creation (Isherwood and Stuart 1998, 29). Such liberationist positions hold that homosexuality is a natural variation in human life and provide a strong impetus for a strong rereading of biblical texts, in Leviticus and the Pauline letters in particular, which have traditionally been interpreted to forbid homoeroticism (cf. Nissinen 1998, 123–28). *Queer theory*, on the other hand, challenges the essentialist notions of the former, since it considers sexual identity as a cultural fabrication, and therefore allows for a broader scope of sex and gender possibilities than the homosexual and heterosexual binary. For queer theory, the primary focus is not inversionist readings of biblical prohibitions against homoeroticism but interrogation of the power dynamics that such texts reveal as well as attempts to explain the perceived need for such texts (Schneider 2000b, 208).

But "queer theory" is about more than reading strategy, since it also constitutes the broader canvas for a variety of issues in biblical scholarship and develops and is molded amidst society's broader debates and anxieties. In a way akin to the religious disputes of earlier centuries, "disputes over sexual behavior become the vehicles for displacing social anxieties,

Prince, and Annie Lennox, and Madonna in particular (Wilkinson and Kitzinger 1996, 377).

and discharging their attendant emotional intensity" (Schneider 2000b, 209; referring to Rubin).

BIBLICAL INTERPRETATION: QUEER AND POSTCOLONIAL BEGINNINGS?

Gender theories often still tend to perpetuate the insider/outsider rhetoric so common in patriarchal identity and power,[28] whereas queer theory allows for a critical approach not only to social identity and location but also to social systems and institutions. In the history of the interpretation of the Bible in Western culture, constructs of gender and sexuality were determined by binary opposites, and within the ancient hierarchy of the human being, the soul or mind or spirit always triumphed over the body. With patriarchy firmly entrenched, the female was primarily culturally constructed in a bodily sense, exemplified in privileged hierarchical oppositions of "man-mind-speech" lording it over or dominating "woman-body-writing."

Preconceived and socioculturally formed ideas often prevent Bible readers from noticing the queer instances in the biblical narratives.[29] "Much of the biblical story is of a kind of taunting, and then a wrestling match, between the deity (sometimes in angelic form) and human beings, many of whom wish to match him in developing a perfect body. … The rivalries seem to have been sexuo-religious in all instances and homoerotic at times" (LaFleur 1998, 46).[30] A central notion for eman-

---

28. Manuell Castells, the famed sociologist well-known for his work on the information society, claims there are four reasons why the patriarchal system is being resolved globally. The economy was transformed and the labor market changed as the educational opportunities for women increase; people are now exercising control over childbirth; feminists are playing an increasingly strong role in society; and the influence of globalization and the spread of knowledge impacts on traditional systems and values.

29. E.g., "the maleness of Jahweh or any other preeminent deity is merely the idolatrous projection of their own gender by the human males who controlled the writing of the scriptures," according to feminist theorists (LaFleur 1998, 46).

30. And at a later stage, erotic power and women's relation to the divine emerged. In the Middle Ages, female mysticism was one consequence of exclusion of women brought on by increased clericalism, which again was the result of increased ecclesial activity through the sacraments, relics, and others to deal with the body and suspicions against it. Female mysticism fed off deeply embodied, erotically charged encounters between women and Christ. Women in the Middle Ages "subverted the patriarchal

cipatory theologies is the concern with justice as *the* direction of God, who is unfolding through the bodies of individuals and in the lives of the oppressed in particular.[31]

The focus on the "prophetic outsider ministry of Jesus" is a focal point in gay and lesbian theologies and informs a Christian theology that emphasizes justice and inclusion rather than tradition and commandment, relationality and mercy rather than purity. Whereas "queer theory as intellectual acrobatics of difference and performance cannot encompass this move or even begin to approach it, ... theology that shifts its locus to the Act-Up,[32] dangerously kind Jesus is certainly queer and cannot be fixed" (Schneider 2000a, 11).

In inclusive readings of the New Testament, the focus is on the position and attitude of Jesus toward the marginalized of society, showing his concern for them while reserving his criticism for those who judge the marginalized ones (Nissinen 1998, 127). Not discounting the value of such interpretation, there is a need to move beyond notions such as Jesus' acceptance of the leprous outcasts as depicted in the New Testament Gospels, emerging so frequently as a topic in HIV/AIDS discussions. The notion of "the habilitation and incorporation of lesbians and gays in Christian communion as a rehabilitation of Christianity into a more life-giving and ultimately more Christian religion" (Schneider 2000a, 7; with reference to John McNeill) is important, but calls for appropriate hermeneutical grids for reading the Bible are at least as important.

GENDER, SEXUALITY, AND PAULINE THEOLOGY

The traditional, and often heterosexist argument regarding the ultimate goal of human sexuality being that of completeness, establishing the "wholeness of the sacred order," is found to be evidenced in the Pau-

---

association of fleshiness with femaleness by obtaining bodily knowledge of Christ in their own flesh" (Isherwood and Stuart 1998, 69).

31. When erotic is understood to mean the innate dynamic drive expressed in the deepest desire for union with others, and God as "empowered physicality," then "love-making is justice making as it fuels our indignation at the pain and exploitation of the bodies of others" (Isherwood and Stuart 1998, 48; referring to Heyward). Thus the distinctions between sex, spirituality, and God are blurred (cf. Ellison 1999, 312–22).

32. An acronym for "AIDS coalition to uproot prejudice" (cf. also numerous websites in this regard).

line symbolism used to express the relationship between Christ and the church. The church is described as the body of Christ, "the form in time of that reality outside of time which is the destiny of all creation remade and redeemed in the new heaven and earth" (Holben 1999, 58). However, Paul's advocacy of celibacy as the preferred option for Christians gives the lie to ascribing to him either a strict gender differentiation based on sexuality or otherwise, or an absolute, heterosexist position regarding procreative sex.[33] Furthermore, gender hierarchy as representative of the cosmic order was a given in the first-century world, with the debate being restricted to one between competing ideologies on the status of the cosmic order. Was gender hierarchy equal to divine design for life on earth, to be superseded only when this world passes away, or was it the result of the soul's fall away from God, to be transcended through spiritual transformation (Ruether 1996, 50)?

A queer (que[e]rying) reading of Paul as suggested by Moore (1998, 250–74) focuses attention on the difference in perceiving sex, gender, and sexuality in the first century and today. Discussing Rom 1:26–27, Moore argues that the study of contemporary first-century authors exhibits an understanding of "homosexuality" that differs radically from modern perceptions, not the least because sexuality was not separated by a homosexual-heterosexual dividing line but adhered to a boundary informed by social status and determined by activity and passivity. Free-born males ruled the roost and asserted their masculinity through (sexual) activity, by penetration, in contrast to being soft and being penetrated, which was a role reserved for those lower down the social ladder, regardless of their sex: women, slaves, effeminate males, eunuchs, "barbarians," "captives," and so forth.[34] "The reduction of sexual relations to the act of penetra-

---

33. "Body politics which becomes body theology in a truly radical and transforming way" (Isherwood and Stuart 1998, 31) is obviously the ideal.

34. Others object to this description, e.g., "I must applaud recent studies that have shown unequal-status and active/passive aspects to be a culturally sustained component of an ancient world portrait of homosexuality. But interjecting equal-status or covenant into the equation fails to side-step the problem. The deepest issue for the biblical authors was the breaking of sexual boundaries between male and female" (Webb 2001, 251). Webb's statement betrays his bias through his imposition of context-foreign material onto the biblical authors' frame of reference, claiming it as their theological position in abstraction while in effect discounting their own sociocultural context and the extent to which their context predisposed their theological understanding of human sexuality.

tion enables sex to become a simple yet effective instrument for expressing hierarchical relations" (271). Gender and social status in the first-century Graeco-Roman world were interlinked, rendering "class-infused views of masculinity" (266–67; cf. Vorster 2000, 103–24), and relegating femininity and women along with other nondominant groups to be subsidiaries to free men. Our contemporary binaries fail to address this situation and require the queering of sex, gender, and sexuality.

JESUS IN THE GOSPELS: QUEERING THE HOUSEHOLD AND ITS GENDER ROLES

Halvor Moxnes investigated Jesus' vision of the kingdom of heaven from the perspective of place and queer theory and found it to challenge the first-century household.[35] The household was a place where everyone knew his or her place and had a sense of limits and boundaries; its traditional roles and order were prescribed by the patriarchal social order of the time and inscribed around binaries such as male and female, we and them, inside and outside, central and marginal—with each of the first elements privileged in terms of the societal norms. "The male role is identified with that of the householder as overseer, father, husband, supplier of resources, person responsible for the house and its inhabitants, and so on" (Moxnes 2003, 95–96). The household was an elemental version of the larger community, in the end encompassing everyone (and every social structure and institution) from the village to the nation or people at large.

The focus of Jesus as portrayed in the Gospels is unexpected, singling out young men and encouraging them to leave their households (along with their livelihood, work, and inheritance), which defined their identity and provided them with both a sense of being and social position and function. Jesus further encouraged small children and women,[36] not mar-

---

35. Moreover, Moxnes wants "to challenge the traditional image of men" and "the image of masculinity" among the followers of Jesus (Moxnes 2003, 73).

36. The asceticism of the early Jesus movement was gendered. Young men leaving their household would occupy a *liminal* position in society, in the sense of finding themselves in "a situation in which full members of society are divested of the attributes associated with their previous, structural position." The women associated with the early Jesus movement did not conform to conventional social roles such as "virgin daughter, respectable wife or mother of legitimate children, and were therefore *outsiders*, falling outside the structural arrangements of society (Moxnes 2003, 99–101). On

ried and not childbearing for whatever reasons, toward the kingdom of heaven. "There were structural similarities between the young males who identified with the kingdom of heaven and the women who followed Jesus. They inhabited the same space outside of the household, and thereby outside the village system based on households" (Moxnes 2003, 100–101). And the role that Jesus assumed for himself, claiming to be without a home and not claiming his rightful sonship within his father's household, showed him to be an atypical male in the first century (96).

Queer theory allows for the understanding that while Jesus did not break away from the notion of household altogether, he reenvisioned the composition and function of household and its social place as well as social roles.[37] Jesus refers to his followers in terms of a household, as brother, sister, and mother but not as father or wife and, more importantly, without notions of authority, procreation, or patriarchy—the household is queered in the kingdom.[38] For Moxnes (2003, esp. 72–90) this transformed household with its transgression of roles and order is encapsulated in Jesus' saying about himself and his male followers, who became "eunuchs for the sake of the kingdom of heaven" (Matt 19:12), since to use the eunuch figure was to employ a metaphor that infracted masculine identity.[39] This renders a "queer Jesus," where queer means protest against fixed categories and the affirmation that all categories of identity[40] are historically and socially constructed. "Jesus was an ascetic who transgressed the boundaries of what it meant to be male in first-century Palestine. Moreover, he introduced that transgression as characteristic of the kingdom" (105). Here the

---

the other hand, children and people who lived like angels, i.e., asexually, functioned as the metaphor for the kingdom of heaven (91–93).

37. Traditional interpretations often failed to appreciate the countercultural, radical implications of Jesus' appeal to young men, barren women, and little children to join and thereby redefine the kingdom of heaven contrary to societal conventions.

38. The image is clearly queer from various perspectives, but certainly at the ideological level (Moxnes 2003, 106–7), where a kingdom of eunuchs, barren women, and children clearly presents a queer image constituting a radical break with the social model of the ideal household.

39. Ongoing difficulties of interpretation suggest that this image continues to challenge modern presuppositions about both masculinity and the male identity of Jesus (Moxnes 2003, 89).

40. The motif of renunciation found in the words of Jesus is connected to his notion of a reversal of the male-dominated world, rather than a perpetuation of male ascetic language (Moxnes 2003, 95).

political implications become clear, and postcolonial theory helps to show that when Jesus broke through established social boundaries, he offered an alternative social environment for the household in particular, amidst sociopolitical developments such as Herod Antipas' attempt to establish a new, Greco-Roman style economy that favored cities and the elite.[41]

QUEER AND POSTCOLONIAL THEORETICAL INTERSECTIONS

As was argued above, intersections between queer and postcolonial theories would involve a few areas that are of vital importance from the perspective of both theories: epistemological and hermeneutical considerations; notions of and on difference; center and margins, or marginality and exclusion; agency; mimicry, and its avoidance; and, prophetic vision for inclusivity or a new world (cf. Punt 2008). Again, refocusing the dynamic between identity and social power, and its impact on the way that liberation is conceptualized, seems to be a broad confluence between queer and postcolonial theories.

In terms of biblical hermeneutics, both postcolonial and queer theories are intensely interested in how identities are constructed and disestablished, negotiated and bartered, in the texts, since these theories deal with sexual, racial, colonial, and class domination and seeks to allow the suppressed voices of the subalterns to emerge. Political hegemony and the destabilization of sex and gender, colonial invasion and sexual exploitation often tend to keep close company. While offensives launched against land and body can be investigated from different perspectives, there are connections between humiliation and shame for loss of political and sexual propriety, as Althaus-Reid explains with reference to the invasions of Latin-America by the Spaniards in the fifteenth century: "The story of colonial settlements and imperial control is a story of one basic alliance: the patriarchal one" (2000, 15), and "The nourishment of the European Other did not happen by capital exploitation only, but by sexual agreements" (17). Especially at the geopolitical level, where land and body are

---

41. Challenging Horsley's notion that Jesus wanted to revitalize village life according to traditional values (Moxnes 2003, 151), Moxnes contends that Jesus also broke with local authority and customs, as reflected in his disputes in the villages, which often broached issues about identity. Since Jesus also came into conflict with the elite, his role was ambiguous (154).

reciprocally inscribed by the colonizers, politics and sex are closely related to one another (cf. Punt 2007).

7. Conclusion

> "Queer theory 'queers' taken-for-granted cultural associations concerning all sexual identities (and the social placements that adhere to these identities) by revealing their vulnerability to history and politics, and therefore to change." (Schneider 2000b, 206)

Queer theory does not evade questions about sex, gender, and sexuality but destabilizes the established notions of these identity elements, politicizing them through naturalization, exerting social power through the ascription of people to categories that assign them certain roles and positions and a given status and function. "Queer theology needs both the critical edge that queer theory offers and the prophetic inclusion that liberationists demand" (Schneider 2000a, 11).[42] Queer theory and theology that return to a theological approach to sex and gender find their orientation in the God of the Bible, who has no sex or gender and is beyond sex and gender. "Human beings are images of God as men and women regardless of their gender identity" (Nissinen 1998, 128).

Queer theory requires that new attention be given not only to the interpretation of the biblical material on corporeality and the body, on sex and sexuality, and on gender and gender performativity (= roles), but that the very way in which such issues are addressed be considered. How did authors in the Bible think about the body, gender, and sex? What role did they play in the molding of contemporary frameworks of thought, perceptions, and themes on and about the body, sex, and gender? To what extent did they contribute to perceptions about the body, sex, and gender that remain to this day?

Clearly queer theory cannot be positioned as an idiosyncratic or stand-alone exegetical model of some sort[43] but is a broader hermeneu-

---

42. So Tolbert (2000, 101) also argues that in feminism, both the theoretical insights gained from a postmodern approach as well as the repelling of postmodern arguments to sabotage decisive social action is needed.

43. Cf. also the following statement about queer theory: "It is still new enough, and contested enough on every level, that beyond Foucauldian critiques of naturalized sexuality queer theory has not, and perhaps should not yet, resolve into a 'discipline' with an absolute priority of theoretical considerations" (Schneider 2000b, 211).

tical framework that, like postcolonial theory, provides heuristic episte-
mologies for interpreting biblical texts. If it is true that "[t]he New Testament gauges all moral relations by their success in dislodging power
elites and including 'the poor'" (Cahill 1995, 274), both queer and postcolonial theories can be useful in contributing hermeneutic grids feed-
ing into sociopolitical awareness, providing tools for analyzing patterns of
(enduring) hegemony, criticizing binary and other methods of identifying
and excluding outsiders, and constructively posing alternative (radical?)
visions for thinking about and structuring society in ways characterized
by inclusivity and equality.

Works Consulted

Adam, A. K. M., ed. 2000. *Handbook of Postmodern Biblical Interpretation.*
St. Louis: Chalice Press.

Althaus-Reid, Marcella. 2000. *Indecent Theology: Theological Perversions
in Sex, Gender and Politics.* London: Routledge.

Barvosa-Carter, Edwina. 2005. Strange Tempest: Agency, Poststructur-
alism, and the Shape of Feminist Politics to Come. Pages 175–89 in
Butler Matters: Judith Butler's Impact on Feminist and Queer Studies.
Edited by M. S. Breen and W. J. Blumenfeld. Hampshire: Ashgate.

Bell, Diane, and Renate Klein, eds. 1996. *Radically Speaking: Feminism
Reclaimed.* London: Zed Books.

Boer, Roland. 1998. King Solomon Meets Annie Sprinkle. *Semeia* 82:151–
82.

Boyarin, Daniel. 1998. Gender. Pages 117–35 in Taylor 1998.

Butler, Judith. 1990. *Gender Trouble: Feminism and the Subversion of Identity.* New York: Routledge.

Cahill, Lisa S. 1995. Sex and Gender Ethics as New Testament Social Ethics.
Pages 272–95 in *The Bible in Ethics: The Second Sheffield Colloquium.*
Edited by J. Rogerson, M. Davies, and M. D. Carroll R. JSOTSup 207.
Sheffield: Sheffield Academic Press.

Donovan, Josephine. 2001. *Feminist Theory: The Intellectual Traditions.*
3rd ed. New York: Continuum.

Elliott, Anthony. 2001. *Concepts of the Self.* Cambridge: Polity Press.

Ellison, M. W. 1999. Erotic Justice. Pages 312–22 in *Sexuality: A Reader.*
Edited by K. Lebacqz and D. Sinacore-Guinn. Cleveland: Pilgrim.

Hall, Donald E. 2003. *Queer Theories.* Basingstoke, Hampshire: Palgrave
MacMillan.

Holben, L. R. 1999. *What Christians Think about Homosexuality: Six Representative Viewpoints.* North Richland Hills: BIBAL.

Isherwood, Lisa, and Elizabeth Stuart. 1998. *Introducing Body Theology.* Cleveland: Pilgrim.

Jeffreys, Sheila. 1996. Return to Gender: Post-Modernism and Lesbianandgay Theory. Pages 359–74 in Bell and Klein 1996.

Kumashiro, K. 2000. Review of William F. Pinar, ed., *Queer Theory in Education. Journal of Homosexuality* 39:144–52.

LaFleur, W. R. 1998. Body. Pages 36–54 in Taylor 1998.

Moore, Stephen D. 1998. Que(e)rying Paul: Preliminary Questions. Pages 250–74 in *Auguries: The Jubilee Volume of the Sheffield Department of Biblical Studies.* Edited by David J. A. Clines and Stephen D. Moore. JSOTSup 269. Sheffield: Sheffield Academic Press.

Morton, Donald. 1995–1996. The Class Politics of Queer Theory. *The Alternative Orange* 5 (1):1–8. Online: www.etext.org/Politics/AlternativeOrange/5/v5n1_qt.html. Repr., *College English* 58:471–82.

Moxnes, Halvor. 2003. *Putting Jesus in His Place: A Radical Vision of Household and Kingdom.* Louisville: Westminster John Knox.

Nissinen, Martti. 1998. *Homoeroticism in the Biblical World: A Historical Perspective.* Minneapolis: Augsburg Fortress.

Punt, Jeremy. 2007. Sex and Gender, and Liminality in Biblical Texts: Venturing into Postcolonial, Queer Biblical Interpretation. *Neot* 41:382–98.

———. 2008. Intersections in Queer Theory and Postcolonial Theory, and Hermeneutical Spin-Offs. *Critical Theory and Biblical Interpretation* 4.2:24.1–24.16. doi:10.2104/bc080024.

Rubin, Gayle. S. 1993. Thinking Sex: Notes for a Radical Theory of the Politics of Sexuality. Pages 3–44 in *The Lesbian and Gay Studies Reader.* Edited by H. Abelove, M. A. Barale, and D. M. Halperin. London: Routledge.

Ruether, Rosemary Radford. 1996. Gender Equity and Christianity: Premodern Roots, Modern and Postmodern Perspectives. *USQR* 50:47–61.

Runions, Erin. 1998. Zion is Burning: "Gender Fuck" in Micah. *Semeia* 82:225–46.

Schneider, Laurel C. 2000a. Homosexuality, Queer Theory, and Christian Theology. *RelSRev* 26 (1):3–12.

———. 2000b. Queer Theory. Pages 206–12 in Adam 2000.

Seidman, Steven. 1996a. Introduction. Pages 1–29 in Seidman 1996b.

——, ed. 1996b. *Queer Theory/Sociology*. Oxford: Blackwell.

Stuart, Elizabeth, et al. 1997. *Religion Is a Queer Thing: A Guide to the Christian Faith for Lesbian, Gay, Bisexual and Transgendered People*. Cleveland: Pilgrim.

Tatchell, Peter. 2000. 2000 Years of Church Homophobia. Online: www. petertatchell.net/religion/2000.htm.

Taylor, Mark C., ed. 1998. *Critical Terms for Religious Studies*. Chicago: University of Chicago Press.

Tolbert, Mary Ann. 2000. Gender. Pages 99–105 in Adam 2000.

Vorster, Johannes N. 2000. (E)mpersonating the Bodies of Early Christianity. *Neot* 34.1:103–24.

Webb, William J. 2001. *Slaves, Women, and Homosexuals: Exploring the Hermeneutics of Cultural Analysis*. Downers Grove, Ill.: Intervarsity Press.

Weedon, Chris. 1999. *Feminism, Theory and the Politics of Difference*. Oxford: Blackwell.

Wilkinson, Sue, and Celia Kitzinger. 1996. The Queer Backlash. Pages 375–82 in Bell and Klein 1996.

WHAT HAPPENS WHEN CLOSETS OPEN UP? A RESPONSE

Michael Joseph Brown

The essays in this Semeia Studies volume present an almost dizzying array of expressions of the application of queer theory to biblical studies. One thing that seems to bind them together, however, is the cautionary phrase, "Be careful." Each of the authors, in his or her own way, applauds the growing acceptance of LGBT individuals in the larger society as well as queer theory's advancement in the realm of biblical studies. Nevertheless, each strikes a cautionary note.

I am not sure that a comprehensive understanding of queer theory comes through in these articles, but maybe that is the point. In my understanding, queer theory is a form-critical theory, influenced heavily by the work of Michel Foucault, that emerged in the last part of the twentieth century out of the fields of LGBT and feminist studies. Moving beyond the concern of who is sleeping with whom or what is "natural" or "unnatural" sexual behavior, queer theory focuses on the notion of identity, including sexual identity, especially when such identity is figured as deviant over against what is considered normative. As Michael Ryan says quite poetically in his work *Literary Theory*, "In the late 1960s, closets opened, and gay and lesbian scholars who had up till then remained silent regarding their sexuality or the presence of homosexual themes in literature began to speak" (Ryan 1999, 115).

One of the things these articles make clear is that identity is a political category. By political, I am drawing from the work of Douglas Sturm, who defines the "political" as "the public dimension of our common existence. Politics, in the deepest and broadest sense, is the public side of the adventure in which the entire community of being is involved" (Sturm 1988, 92). In other words, each of these articles, in one way or another, addresses the patterns of behavior that shape and reshape us as a communal entity. What would have been exciting, although it does not come across explicitly in the articles I will discuss, is the repositioning of the political conversation from one of civil rights to one of human rights. Again, Sturm is helpful on this point. He argues that human rights is a more satisfying conceptual category than the traditional American concern for civil rights. Civil rights is a classical liberal notion of the protection of the "individual over against government, a protection against the arbitrary imposition of tyranny, a wall of separation between public and private spheres of life" (Sturm 1998, 18). Nevertheless, this classical notion of civil rights is based on an ontological perspective that often puts individuals in conflict with each other. By contrast, human rights as conceived by Sturm is based on a different ontological orientation. Because he approaches this subject from a process perspective, the notion of the self is not conceived merely as the independent individual over against other independent individuals. It is, rather, thoroughly relational. As he argues,

> The point of the idea of human rights is to designate the kind of context most conducive to the self's agency within the ongoing passage of events. The self as subject is to be cherished, but cherished not as a distinct monad, separate from all other subjects, rather as a sensitive and creative participant in an adventure in which all creatures are engaged and are dependent on each other for sustenance and fulfillment. (Sturm 1998, 26)

I point this out because this collection of articles desires to discuss the political in some fashion or another, but one gets the sense that many of the authors struggle with conceptual categories that do not allow them to move persuasively beyond classical liberal political theory toward one that emphasizes our relationality and interdependency.

The article that attempts to deal most directly with the question of the political character of existence, which I choose to highlight, is Hornsby's "Capitalism, Masochism, and Biblical Interpretation." Looking at the question of queerness from the perspective of the power of global capitalism, Hornsby argues,

> A mode of survival for this type of capitalism is that it must covertly produce those persons 1) whom the mainstream considers "other" and 2) who must accept that their value is no more than what the status quo deems it to be. In other words, perception of otherness must be both external and internal. Not only must the dominant fiction define the one who is not "normal," the "abnormal" or "queer" person must also accept

(and, perhaps, desire) his or her own situation. This is where Christianity comes in. As one of the primary items in the capitalist tool belt, Christianity has, since its origins, (re)produced the false dualisms necessary for power's sustenance and the creation of the other. (139)

As this quotation indicates, Hornsby is committed to the notion of dualisms, although she labels such dualisms as false, an understanding she relates directly to the function of Christianity in Western culture. The power exerted through capitalism, Hornsby argues, has been used to create and perpetuate otherness as a necessary consequence of the commodification of humanity.

As capitalism has changed, so has its interest in othering individuals. Whether conceived as postmodern or postindustrial, Hornsby's article makes the salient point that the nature of capitalistic commodification is changing. This, in turn, allows for greater self-actualization for some who had been othered under the old capitalistic regime. As she says, "My prediction is this: as the need for *definite* sexualities and genders becomes less important to the needs of capitalism, gender fluidity and masochism move to the center" (141). Although one might applaud such a move in social perception, Hornsby is a lot more cautious. She views this simply as a move to create more docile human beings—human beings who would function best under the new capitalistic regime.

The creation of this docile humanity is a move toward masochism, according to Hornsby. This embracing of masochism is the result of a reinvigorated Pauline Christianity, with its emphasis on "idealized suffering, willful self-sacrifice, glorified humiliation, and romanticized slavery" (142). Indeed, Hornsby is correct in her assessment that scholars have revived a once-defunct interest in Paul's use of slave language as a vehicle for understanding himself and discipleship more generally. (To be entirely transparent, I too, have written on this subject; see Brown 2001, 723–37.) Although I would disagree with Hornsby's implicit assertion that all such assessments of Paul's use of slave language amount to a romanticizing of slavery, I do receive her point that such analyses of Paul's language and conceptual categories can promote, even if unintentionally, a theological anthropology that promotes docility in the face of oppression.

The type of masochism that interests Hornsby is something more than that of a sexual nature. Of course, given the nature of the volume, such a masochistic understanding always resides below the surface, and the author seems to play with the notion from time to time. What interests

Hornsby explicitly is "moral masochism," which she defines as "not only an internalized need to be punished but, more importantly, a sense of joy in self-deprivation" (142). To augment her argument, the author points to Mel Gibson's *The Passion of the Christ* as an example. She argues that the gruesome cinematic depiction of Jesus' death contributes to the larger cultural fascination with such moral masochism. Yet, the problem with such depictions of Jesus, according to the author, is that they promote the Freudian feminization of human beings. That is, they seek to mold human beings into compliant and self-sacrificing individuals, docile commodities to be used by the capitalist system.

What it means to be a "good person," according to Hornsby, is decided by the interests of power. Biblical scholars are no less complicit in this enterprise than are any other manufacturers of culture, according to the author. Although she recognizes what might appear to be the advancement of society on the issue of sexuality, Hornsby warns that such acceptance of fluidity in sexuality is not a true advance in the political landscape. It is simply the result of the shift to postmodern capitalism. "Sure, it is a good thing that queer sexualities are becoming more normative," she writes, "but queer sexualities are manufactured and serve power just as much as any sanctioned sexuality" (153).

Although Hornsby's article is quite perceptive and compelling, I am always somewhat suspicious of discourses of power that cast human agency in such a diminished light. Complicity with larger cultural, political, and economic forces is most definitely a part of the human experience, whether recognized or not. Nevertheless, I resist the idea that human beings are simply commodities to be used—shaped and reshaped—by a faceless, omnipotent enterprise such as global capitalism. This is not to say that such suprahuman processes do not exist. They most certainly do. Yet, the issue of agency in these discussions is often anemic, in that they do not appear to take seriously the patterns of behavior, both individual and corporate, that bring about such political juggernauts. Moreover, such discourses often ignore the possibility that there could be a positive "lure"— to use a process term—in the social phenomenon. Even if, as Hornsby argues, the greater acceptance of queer sexualities is partly the result of a change in the configuration of capitalism, this does not exclude the possibility that the introduction of this novelty in the construction of sexuality is not an advancement or potential creative transformation, even if a tentative one, in the relational interdependence that we experience as community.

Arguably, on the other end of the interpretive spectrum is Jione Havea's, "Lazarus Troubles," which draws upon the resources of a community of interpreters to queer John 11:1–44. Havea appropriates the perspective of Stephen Moore and puts the text in the hands of prisoners at Parklea Prison in Australia. Moore's approach, according to Havea, is to use "queer" as a "cipher" to draw out what stands over against the "natural" and to find what inheres in the "natural" that can be used to subvert it. Moore's interpretive strategy is experienced creatively as Havea presents this communal appropriation of the Lazarus narrative.

As the article unfolds, the first thing the prisoners assert is that Lazarus was under a death sentence. Seeing Lazarus' tomb as analogous to a prison cell, many identified with the biblical character's situation. Living as they do in the midst of death, these prisoners see it as an inescapable, ever-present reality. As Havea writes, "The story of Lazarus is simply about death, not because there is hope for resurrection but because death and death sentences are real" (160). In fact, Havea points out that many of the prisoners are more troubled by Lazarus' resurrection than they are by his death. At least death offers the opportunity for escape. Resurrection—a narrative phenomenon that most readers would see as the redemptive move in the story—presents a problem for this set of readers because it just brings Lazarus back to the same set of existential problems that he had prior to his death. Even worse, actually, because now Lazarus has a whole new set of individuals who will now seek to end his life again.

"Love is deadly," writes Havea. In a prison environment such as Parklea, love is demonstrated not through sexual activity. It is demonstrated by "doing a walk." By this the prisoners mean the willingness of an individual to undergo beating, inflict violence, or even lay down one's own life for one's friend. As Havea points out, "It is not such a big deal for the prisoners if Jesus had a sexual relationship with Lazarus ... and/or with his sisters, but it is unacceptable that no one offered to 'do a walk' for Lazarus" (162).

According to Havea and the prisoners, to "do a walk" is no different from the Johannine love command (John 15:13). If the greatest expression of love is laying down one's life for one's friend, then the prisoners maintain that Lazarus experienced no such love. Although many claimed to have loved Lazarus (e.g., Jesus, his sisters), none of them were willing to perform the ultimate loving act—to "do a walk"—for him. In fact, such emotionalism without the concomitant activity of "doing a walk" renders the love command hollow.

The prisoners did not accept the narrative's reasoning for Jesus' delay, and so they developed other rationales for his prolonged absence. Nevertheless, when Jesus does arrive, what he does still did not satisfy the prisoners. As they saw it, Jesus' exercise of power was for his own self-aggrandizement and not for the sake (or love) of Lazarus. As they see it, instead of "doing a walk" for Lazarus, Jesus "does a prayer" for him. This prayer to God is meant to highlight the power of Jesus and to glorify God (11:42). As the prisoners see it, this is really not for the sake of Lazarus and is suspicious, to say the least.

In fact, in some ways Jesus has turned the tables on Lazarus. Instead of "doing a walk" for Lazarus, Lazarus "does a walk" for Jesus. Calling back Lazarus from the dead did not, in the eyes of the readers, provide him with any sort of blessing. In fact, as they saw it, it was something of a curse. Raising Lazarus from the dead was a way in which Jesus could highlight his own power/authority without any real concern for the effect it would have on the life of Lazarus. As Havea points out, "Then, like a ruthless master who would not let a poor slave die, Jesus called Lazarus back as if the hassles of life were preferable over the peace of death" (166).

The final scene of the narrative episode upset the prisoners most. When Lazarus came forth from the tomb, instead of embracing his "beloved" Lazarus, Jesus passes him off to others. As individuals who hope to be free some day, these prisoners look forward to coming from the tomb-like conditions of the prison and they certainly do not expect the response that Jesus gave Lazarus. Instead of leaving them stripped and in the hands of others, these prisoners expect that loved ones will embrace them, clothe them, and take them into their safety. Jesus does none of this. Whether there is a sexual component to Jesus' love for Lazarus or not does not seem to concern the prisoners. If there is more there than simple friendship, then it actually makes the entire scene more unacceptable to the prisoners. As Havea writes, "Jesus called Lazarus to come out and then left him hanging. This did not satisfy the prisoners, who understand the resurrection of Lazarus as a 'coming out' kind of event … Lazarus did come out. But Jesus did not come out fully. Resurrection should not be a wham-bang-get-out-of-here experience" (170).

Havea's article is interesting as an experience of queering a traditional reading of the raising of Lazarus by placing it in the hands of a community of interpreters with a distinct perspective on issues of life and death. One cannot read this article without recognizing how differently these readers understand, appropriate, and experience death than do, arguably, those who are not confined in the prison-industrial structure. After reading their experiences of the text, I, too, began to question Jesus' motives for bringing Lazarus back from the dead, as if life by necessity is always preferable to death.

Unlike the previous article, which looked at the larger social situation from the top down, this article looks at a text (John 11:1–44) and the accompanying social situation from the bottom up. This bottom-up view calls into question some of the existential assumptions that most nonprisoners would take for granted (e.g., the preference for life over death). In some respects, what is queer about this reading is that it comes through individuals whose identities are considered nonnormative. Ideas such as death, life, and love are reconfigured in this reading according to the life experiences of individuals who are (or at least feel) alienated by the larger community. It is difficult to overlook the lingering issue of agency that comes from our examination of the Hornsby article. Unlike that earlier article, which cast individuals as "pawns" in the machinations of a postmodern global capitalism, Havea's article deals with agency in a more intimate, if not equally political, manner. Both analyze patterns of behavior that shape and reshape what it means to be community in a historically rooted time and space. For the prisoners, agency is always an act of self-creation in relation to the environment of death that surrounds and seeks to overwhelm them.

To the prisoners, agency is not only important, but it is also closely connected with a certain construction of integrity. Their criticisms of Jesus in the narrative often center around whether his actions are grounded in a recognizable code of ethics. This is a rather powerful critique. As I understand the prisoners' critique, Jesus' actions are at odds with the identity they expect of an individual whose loved one has become desperately ill and died. This article, although it may not touch on traditional queer themes, does queer the text in that it delves into the identities of the readers and the narrative characters in a way that compelled at least me as a reader to question my normative reading of the passage. In this sense, the multiple intersections that made up the identities of the readers and the biblical characters came together to develop a reading of a familiar passage that challenges heteronormative reading practices.

The issue of multiple intersections arises as well in an interesting article by Sean Burke, "Queering Early Christian Discourse: The Ethiopian Eunuch." Burke sees ambiguity as an interesting place to investigate the process of queering. Since he has a distinctive perspective on queer theory and its relationship to identity construction, I think it is important to highlight this in my discussion of his article. He says, "I think queer theorists are right to insist that identity categories remain arbitrary, totalizing, exclusionary, normative, and regulatory social constructions that function by denying difference and suppressing ambiguity" (176). Thus, Burke seeks to explore the story in Acts regarding the Ethiopian eunuch by looking at the places where his identity intersects with others—creating, in effect, identity instability—enabling a queer reading of the passage.

Burke recognizes and highlights the various questions or ambiguities that have haunted the story of the Ethiopian eunuch. Looking at these ambiguities, he does not see these as problems to be resolved. By contrast, he sees this as an opportunity for conducting a queer analysis of the narrative.

As Burke examines the landscape of masculinity in the Greco-Roman world, he divides humanity between "men" and "unmen" (i.e., women, foreigners, slaves, and children). The ideological keystone to masculinity was the ability to dominate "unmen." In this instance, a eunuch destabilized the category "man" in that he did not have the ability to impregnate women. Burke argues that this was the same for court eunuchs as well as for the *galli*, the devotees of the cult of Cybele.

Having destabilized the dominant understanding of masculinity, the eunuch represented a point of ambiguity and dis-ease for ancient notions of gender construction. As Burke says, "[T]hese eunuchs embodied the troubling proposition that the relatively simple procedure of castration could produce an irreversible loss of masculinity or even a loss of humanity, if recognition as human depends upon a stable gender identity" (181). Although Burke would not anachronistically label such individuals as "transgendered" or "gay," he does maintain that being (or being made) a eunuch queers identity, even in the ancient context.

As he reads the story from Acts, Burke points out all of the ambiguities involved in the text. Instead of attempting to resolve them, as most commentators do, Burke argues that these ambiguities and multiple intersections provide an opportunity to think outside of the narrowly construed constructions of gender identity. Moreover, he argues that Joel 3:1–5 is the programmatic statement of Acts: that the Spirit will be poured out upon all flesh. Thus, the story of the eunuch represents that statement in a powerful way since, unlike Cornelius, the Ethiopian narrative calls into question many of the supposed stable identity categories of the day.

Equally important for Burke, the story in Acts served an important function for the church as it struggled to accept "others" into its ranks. Thus, the story of the Ethiopian eunuch is a double conversion story. As the author points out, "The early Christians themselves had to be converted to the view that baptism and table fellowship in Christ do not depend on a person's identity—Jew or Gentile, male or female, man or unman, penetrator or penetrated, free or slave, citizen/native or foreigner" (186). He goes on to point out that such "conversion" still needs to take place in Christian communities and urges more study on narrative figures that might queer normative understandings of "insiders" and "outsiders."

Something similar can be found in Lynn Huber's essay, "Gazing at the Whore: Reading Revelation Queerly." In it Huber notes that many scholars have concluded that nothing redemptive for LGBT individuals can be found in the Apocalypse. Pushing back against such a determination, Huber attempts a "queer-lesbian" reading of an important figure in the narrative. What makes Huber's reading of Revelation even more interesting is that she places emphasis on the gaze. Over against masculine or heteronormative ways of "gazing," Huber asserts, "[T]he lesbian gaze can be quite different from the male gaze, which assumes a power over the one being gazed upon. The lesbian gaze, in contrast, is often shaped by a desire for reciprocity—a glance back" (308). With this in mind, Huber attempts to overcome the insider/outsider divide that some have erected regarding the text (e.g., insiders being heteronormative readers and their interpretations). As she says, "As long as apocalyptic ways of thinking and speaking are used to celebrate gay-bashings, to blame queer people for natural disasters, to refuse giving basic human rights to those in LGBTQ communities and the like, there remains a need for queer readers to explore and reassess apocalyptic traditions" (304–5).

Much like Burke's essay, Huber engages the text directly and with precision. After reconstructing the sociocultural context of the *pornē* (i.e., the prostitute), she discusses how the prostitute in Revelation is a potential locus of power, although for most persons in antiquity (and even today) the prostitute would not have been considered as such. Yet, the Whore's power in Revelation is in her ability to lure others into engaging with her. Thus, the potential locus of the Whore's power is in her ability to encourage assimilation to her practices and values. As Huber says, "Revelation's dismay over the people of earth's drunkenness reflects John's concern over the threat of cultural assimilation. The people of the earth have become like the Whore (i.e., they have assimilated to imperial culture) by drinking the wine of her fornication (πορνεία)" (312).

The lure toward assimilation is what is to be resisted in Revelation. Such assimilation is at the heart of Huber's analysis as well. She questions whether those who would encourage assimilation, especially for LGBT individuals, would not bring for those individuals the same fate as the Whore in Revelation: they will be destroyed by those who once gave them power. Nevertheless, Huber highlights the almost irresistible lure that accompanies assimilation and perceived acceptance by a dominant culture, as well as the dread that accompanies it. "[I]n my viewing," she writes, "there is both an experience of distance that wants closeness with the Whore, the experience of a desiring spectator, and a certain sense of closeness that ultimately wants some distance from the Whore because of a forced recognition of shared vulnerability" (314). In other words, the cautionary message of the Apocalypse is one that may need to be heeded by queer individuals as well.

As I said at the beginning of this essay, the articles in this volume demonstrate a wide array of ways to queer the Bible. Yet, the ones I chose to highlight all strike a similar cautionary note: Be careful. As LGBT individuals begin to experience wider acceptance by the wider culture, they need to keep in mind that their agency can be at risk. The political community engages in patterns of practice that can either empower or sap the agency of its members. These commentators recognize that potential and warn readers that acceptance into the larger society may not be a laudatory step forward.

Works Consulted

Brown, Michael Joseph. 2001. Paul's Use of *Doulos Christou Iesou* in Romans 1:1. *JBL* 120:723–37.

Ryan, Michael. 1999. *Literary Theory: A Practical Introduction*. Oxford: Blackwell.

Sturm, Douglas. 1988. *Community and Alienation: Essays on Process Thought and Public Life*. Notre Dame, Ind.: University of Notre Dame Press.

———. 1998. *Solidarity and Suffering: Toward a Politics of Relationality*. Albany: State University of New York Press.

Contributors

Ellen T. Armour holds the E. Rhodes and Leona B. Carpenter Chair in Feminist Theology at Vanderbilt Divinity School. She is the author of *Deconstruction, Feminist Theology, and the Problem of Difference: Subverting the Race/Gender Divide* (University of Chicago Press, 1999) and co-editor of *Bodily Citations: Judith Butler and Religion* (Columbia University Press, 2006).

Michael Joseph Brown is Associate Professor of New Testament and Christian Origins at Emory University. He is the author of, among other books, *Blackening of the Bible: The Aims of African American Biblical Scholarship* (Trinity Press International, 2004), as well as numerous other essays on contextualized readings of scripture.

Sean D. Burke is Assistant Professor of Religion at Luther College in Decorah, Iowa. He earned his Ph.D. in Biblical Studies (New Testament) at the Graduate Theological Union, and in his dissertation he applied queer theory to the interpretation of the story of Philip and the Ethiopian eunuch in Acts 8:26–40.

Heidi Epstein is Assistant Professor of Religion and Culture at the University of Saskatchewan and author of *Melting the Venusberg: A Feminist Theology of Music* (Continuum, 2004). In her latest articles on contemporary musical settings of the Song of Songs, she is crafting interdisciplinary conversations between New Musicological and feminist/queer biblical hermeneutics to articulate the Song's role in romantic love as a cultural practice.

Deryn Guest is Senior Lecturer in the Department of Theology and Religion, University of Birmingham. She is the author of *When Deborah Met*

Jael: Lesbian Biblical Hermeneutics (SCM, 2005) and co-editor of *The Queer Bible Commentary* (SCM, 2006). She works principally in the area of contemporary biblical hermeneutics, specifically in the ways gender theory and queer theory are utilized in the interpretation of scriptural texts.

Jione Havea is a native of Tonga (South Pacific) and Senior Lecturer in Hebrew Bible–Old Testament at United Theological College and School of Theology, Charles Sturt University (Australia). Jione's recent publications include "Mothering: Eve, Hagar and Mistress of Joseph," and "David W[e]aves".

Teresa J. Hornsby is an Associate Professor of Religious Studies at Drury University in Springfield, Missouri. She is the author of *Sex Texts from the Bible* (Jewish Lights, 2007) and works extensively in the area of the Bible and sexual ethics. Her most recent publications are "Anointing Traditions," in *The Historical Jesus in Context* (ed. Crossan et al.; Princeton University Press, 2006) and "Putting Abortion on the Curriculum" in the *Chronicle of Higher Education.*

Lynn R. Huber is Associate Professor of Religious Studies at Elon University in North Carolina. She is the author of *"Like a Bride Adorned": Reading Metaphor in John's Apocalypse* (T&T Clark, 2007), along with other pieces on Revelation's gendered imagery.

S. Tamar Kamionkowski is Associate Professor of Bible and Vice President for Academic Affairs at the Reconstructionist Rabbinical College. She is the co-editor of *Bodies, Embodiment and Theology of the Hebrew Scriptures* (T&T Clark, 2010) and the author of *Gender Reversal and Cosmic Chaos: Studies in the Book of Ezekiel* (Sheffield Academic Press, 2003). She has written numerous articles on biblical literature, feminist readings of biblical texts, and the intersection between scholarship and social justice.

Joseph A. Marchal is assistant professor of religious studies at Ball State University, where he teaches feminist, postcolonial, and queer approaches to biblical interpretation. He is the author of *The Politics of Heaven: Women, Gender, and Empire in the Study of Paul* (Fortress, 2008) and is currently preparing a volume on queer approaches to Paul's letters.

Jeremy Punt is associate professor of New Testament in the Faculty of Theology at Stellenbosch University in South Africa. He has published various articles related to hermeneutics and critical theory in New Testament interpretation, including "Power and Liminality, Sex and Gender, and Gal 3:28: A Postcolonial, Queer Reading of an Influential Text."

Erin Runions is Associate Professor in the Department of Religious Studies at Pomona College, with a specialization in Hebrew Bible and cultural studies. Her work brings together politics, culture, and the reading of biblical text, a task that she theorizes most extensively in her books *Changing Subjects: Gender, Nation, Future in Micah* (Sheffield Academic Press, 2001) and *How Hysterical: Identification and Resistance in the Bible and Film* (Palgrave MacMillan, 2003).

Ken Stone is Professor of Bible, Culture and Hermeneutics and Academic Dean at Chicago Theological Seminary. He is the author of *Practicing Safer Texts: Food, Sex and Bible in Queer Perspective* (T&T Clark, 2005) and *Sex, Honor and Power in the Deuteronomistic History* (Sheffield Academic Press, 1996). He is also the editor of *Queer Commentary and the Hebrew Bible* (Sheffield Academic Press, 2002).

Gillian Townsley is a PhD candidate in New Testament studies at the University of Otago, Dunedin, New Zealand.

Jay Twomey teaches courses in the Bible and literature at the University of Cincinnati. He is the author of *The Pastoral Epistles through the Centuries* (Blackwell, 2009) and is currently at work on a book about literary appropriations of Paul.

Manuel Villalobos Mendoza earned his PhD from Garrett Evangelical Theological Seminary. His *Abject Bodies in Mark's Passion Narrative: A Butlerian Interpretation by a Mexicano Del Otro Lado* is being considered for publication. His hermeneutic *del otro lado* seeks to privilege questions and voices of otherness, marginality, gender, masculinity, and borderland.

CPSIA information can be obtained at www.ICGtesting.com
Printed in the USA
268356BV00002B/1/P